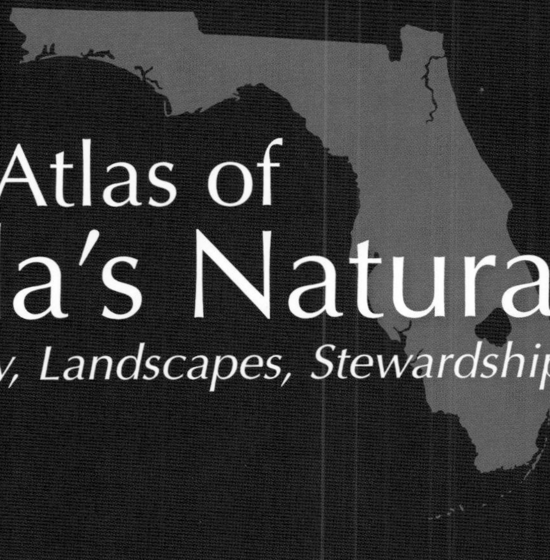

Atlas of Florida's Natural Heritage

Biodiversity, Landscapes, Stewardship, and Opportunities

Florida Natural Areas Inventory

Institute of Science and Public Affairs
Florida State University

COVER PHOTOS

1. Broad-headed skink (*Plestiodon laticeps*), Michael Jenkins
2. Blackwater stream, Suwannee River near White Springs, David Moynahan
3. Wet prairie, Triple N Ranch Wildlife Management Area, Gary Knight
4. Panhandle coast, St. Vincent National Wildlife Refuge, David Moynahan
5. Swamp lake, Bradford Brook Chain of Lakes, Apalachicola National Forest, David Moynahan
6. Dry prairie, Babcock Ranch Preserve, Katy NeSmith
7. Gulf coast lupine (*Lupinus westianus*), Don Herring
8. Prescribed fire in mesic flatwoods, Joe Budd Wildlife Management Area, David Moynahan

Institute of Science and Public Affairs
296 Champions Way, PO Box 3062641
Tallahassee, Florida 32306-2641
(850) 644-2007 www.ispa.fsu.edu

Printed in the United States of America

Library of Congress Control Number: 2011932039
First Edition

ISBN 978-0-9606708-5-7, hardcover
ISBN 978-0-9606708-6-4, softcover

Summary: The Atlas of Florida's Natural Heritage – Biodiversity, Landscapes, Stewardship, and Opportunities *illustrates the natural heritage of Florida, its stewardship, and challenges for policy makers, planners, environmental advocates, residents, and visitors. Includes maps, diagrams, charts, photographs, and text.*

1. Atlases
2. Conservation, Florida
3. Biodiversity, Florida
4. Natural history, Florida
5. Natural communities, Florida

Text printed on acid-free, recycled 80# McCoy matte book FSC stock paper
by B&B Print Source, Tigard, Oregon.

Type set in Optima and Meridien.

SUGGESTED CITATION:

Knight, G.R., J.B. Oetting, and L. Cross. 2011. *Atlas of Florida's Natural Heritage – Biodiversity, Landscapes, Stewardship, and Opportunities.* Tallahassee, FL: Institute of Science and Public Affairs, Florida State University.

Atlas of Florida's Natural Heritage

Biodiversity, Landscapes, Stewardship, and Opportunities

Gary R. Knight
SENIOR EDITOR
DIRECTOR, FLORIDA NATURAL AREAS INVENTORY

Jon Oetting
PROJECT EDITOR

Lou Cross
DESIGN & PRODUCTION EDITOR

Jim Anderson
MANAGING EDITOR

Peter A. Krafft
CARTOGRAPHY

Tanya MA Buckingham
CARTOGRAPHY & DESIGN

David Moynahan
PHOTOGRAPHY EDITOR

Authors

David Almquist, Invertebrate Zoologist, FNAI
Pete Diamond, Field Botanist, FNAI
Caitlin Elam, Field Botanist, FNAI
Kim Gulledge, Community Ecologist, FNAI
Mike Heaney, Field Botanist, FNAI
Brenda Herring, Field Botanist, FNAI
Dan Hipes, Chief Scientist and Senior Zoologist, FNAI
Dale R. Jackson, Zoologist – Herpetology, FNAI
Amy M. Jenkins, Senior Botanist, FNAI
Ann F. Johnson, Senior Ecologist, FNAI
Dean Jue, Research Associate, FREAC
Sally S. Jue, Conservation Lands Biologist, FNAI
Carolyn Kindell, Managed Areas Biologist, FNAI
Amy Knight, GIS Program Specialist, FNAI
Gary Knight, Director, FNAI
Katy NeSmith, Zoologist – Ornithology, FNAI
Jon Oetting, Conservation Planner, FNAI
Frank Price, Data Manager, FNAI
Elizabeth D. Purdum, Research Associate, ISPA
Paul Russo, Field Botanist, FNAI
Gary Schultz, Field Ecologist, FNAI
Glenn Woodsum, Data Manager, FNAI

Illustrators

Diane Pierce
Jean C. Putnam Hancock
Melynda Reid
Additional illustrators credited throughout the book.

Acknowledgments

Scientific knowledge advances by continuously building on the work of others. This atlas, like the body of knowledge upon which it is grounded, is possible only through the contributions of thousands of individuals over the course of many years. We gratefully acknowledge those listed below (in alphabetical order), who provided data, advice, and/or review comments for one or more topics in the atlas.

Brent Anderson, SFWMD
Jason Ayers, USFWS
Mark Bailey, CSE
Eric Baka, LADWF
Wilson Baker
Michael Baranski, FWC
Lee Barnwell, DOF
Gian Basili, SJRWMD
Jim Beever, SWFRPC
John Bente, DEP
Nancy Bissett, The Natives, Inc.
Raoul Boughton, ABS
Robin Boughton, FWC
Pamela Bowen, SJR WMD
Reed Bowman, ABS
Kristen Brengel, TWS
Jim Brenner, DOF
Greg Brock, DEP
Kathy Bronson, USFS
Mike Brooks, FWC
Phillip Brouse, Charlotte County
Jeffrey Buck, Palm Beach County
Dana Bryan, DEP
Joelle Carney, MDFWP
Steven Carpenter, DOF
Linda Chafin, SBGG
Ruark Cleary, FWC
Amy Clifton, ABS
Kathleen Coates, NWFWMD
Matthew Corby, SJRWMD
Jim Cox, Tall Timbers Research Station
Scott Crosby, DOF
James P. Cuda, UF/IFAS
Ken Dancak, USFS
Roy DeLotelle, DeLot. & Guthr., Inc.
David Dorman, USFS
Nancy Douglass, FWC
Jason Drake, USFS
Andrew duMoulin, TPL
John Emery, SWFWMD
Mark Endries, FWC
Curt Flather, USFS
Monica Folk, TNC
Russel Frydenborg, DEP
James Furman, Eglin AFB
Kathy Gault, Eglin AFB
Lauren Gilson, ABS
Doria Gordon, TNC
Peggy Grant, Johnson Engineering
Jim Grubbs, DOF
Asa Haddock, DOF
Bruce Hansen, USF
Dennis Hardin, DOF
Scott Hardin, FWC
Mac Hatcher, Collier County
Chuck Hess, USFS
Richard Hilsenbeck, TNC
Tom Hoctor, UF
Bill Holimon, ARNHC
Brooke Hollander, TEC
Jean Huffman, DEP
Greg Ihle, DOF
Craig Iverson, DOF
Kristina Jackson, FWC
Deborah Jansen, NPS
Michael Jenkins, DOF
Greg Jubinsky, FWC
Walter Judd, UF
Annisa Karim, Collier County
Randy Kautz, BDA, Inc.
Doug Keesecker, Tampa Bay Water
Patricia Kelly, USFWS
Michael Keys, USFWS
Marilyn Knight, USFWS
Paige Koon, SCDNR
Lynn Kutner, NatureServe
Darrell Land, FWC
Patrick Leary
Harry LeGrand, NCDENR
Drew Leslie, FWC
Graham Lewis, NWFWMD
Tim Lewis, FWC
Helen Light, USGS (ret.)
Doug Longshore, DOF
Tricia Martin, TNC
Devon McFall, DOF
Samantha McGee, DEP
Sue McLellan, DOF
Kenneth Meyer, ARCI
Anne Meylan , FWC
Steven R. Miller, SJRWMD
Cheryl Millett, TNC
Gary Mohr, FWC
Paul Moler, FWC
Vincent Morris, DOF
David Morse, DOF
Rosi Mulholland, FPS
Peter Myers, NFF
Stephanie Nagid, City of Gainesville
Reed Noss, UCF
Cathy Olson, Lee County
Jim Ozier, GADNR
Larry Page, FMNH
Maulik Patel, DEP
Dan Pearson, FPS
Charlie Pedersen, DOF
Jennifer Perkins, Camp Blanding JTC
David Printiss, TNC
Erin Rainey, TNC
Jeffrey Reid, USFWS
Bob Repenning, Lee County
Glenn Reynolds, FWC
Rob Riordan, NatureServe
Rob Robbins, FMNH
John Sadler, DOF
Kimberly Sash, FWC
Todd Schneider, GADNR
Brian Scofield, FWC
Ross Scott, FWC
Thomas M. Scott, FGS
Christal Segura, Collier County
Carrie Sekerak, USFS
Steve Shattler, FWC
Parks Small, FPS
Valerie Sparling, FWC
Phil Spivey, GADNR
Gary Sprandel, KDFWR
Stephen Stipkovits, DOF
Libby Stuart, DOF
Beth Stys, FWC
Dan Sullivan, FWC
Kathleen Swanson, FWC
Scott Taylor, DOF
Dennis Teague, Eglin AFB
David Telesco, FWC
Marta VanderStarre, NatureServe
William VanGelder, SWFWMD
Adam Warwick, FWC
Ken Weber, DOF
Nia Wellendorf, DEP
Rick West
Michelle Wilcox, FWC
Brett Williams, Eglin AFB
Wendy Wilsdon, FWC
Morton Winsberg, Professor Emeritus, FSU
Faye Winters, BLM
Bruce Young, NatureServe
David Zierdan, Climate Center, FSU
Scott Zona, FIU
Maria Zondervan, SJRWMD

Acronyms

ABS – Archbold Biological Station

AFB – Air Force Base

ARCI – Avian Research and Conservation Institute

ARNHC – Arkansas Natural Heritage Commission

BLM – U.S. Department of Interior, Bureau of Land Management

CSE – Conservation Southeast

DEP – Florida Department of Environmental Protection

DOF – Florida Department of Agriculture & Consumer Services, Division of Forestry

FIU – Florida International University

FMNH – Florida Museum of Natural History

FNAI – Florida Natural Areas Inventory

FPS – Florida Park Service (DEP)

FSU – Florida State University

FWC – Florida Fish and Wildlife Conservation Commission

FWRI – Florida Wildlife Research Institute

GADNR – Georgia Department of Natural Resources

JTC – Joint Training Center

KDFWR – Kentucky Department of Fish and Wildlife Resources

LADWF – Louisiana Department of Wildlife and Fisheries

MDFWP – Mississippi Department of Wildlife, Fisheries & Parks

NCDENR – North Carolina Department of Environment and Natural Resources

NFF – National Forests in Florida (USFS)

NPS – National Park Service

NWFWMD – Northwest Florida Water Management District

SBGG – State Botanical Garden of Georgia

SCDNR – South Carolina Department of Natural Resouces

SFWMD – South Florida Water Management District

SJRWMD – St. Johns River Water Management District

SWFRPC – Southwest Florida Regional Planning Council

SWFWMD – Southwest Florida Water Management District

TEC – Tropical Environmental Consultants

TNC – The Nature Conservancy

TPL – Trust for Public Land

TWS – The Wilderness Society

UF – University of Florida

USF – University of South Florida

USFS – U.S. Forest Service

USFWS – U.S. Fish & Wildlife Service

USGS – U.S. Geological Survey

Florida State University
Office of the President

I am pleased to present the *Atlas of Florida's Natural Heritage – Biodiversity, Landscapes, Stewardship, and Opportunities* produced by the Florida Natural Areas Inventory program within the Institute of Science and Public Affairs at Florida State University. Florida is an extraordinary state: its geographic location, geological history, and climate have resulted in one of the biologically richest and most diverse places in the United States. No matter where you travel in state—from the longleaf pine forests of the Northwest Florida to the tropical hammocks of South Florida—the natural world invites your exploration.

In this volume, the natural heritage of Florida, its stewardship, and the challenges that lie ahead are skillfully and attractively presented for scientists, policymakers, planners, and environmental advocates as well residents and visitors. I have no doubt this book will be a valuable tool for us all to make informed decisions about the future of our priceless natural environment.

Eric J. Barron, Ph.D.
President

DEDICATION

This atlas is dedicated to the land managers of Florida's public and private conservation lands. Regularly facing and overcoming difficult challenges, these devoted men and women serve us all as effective stewards of Florida's precious natural heritage.

A Simplified Tree of the Diversity of Life

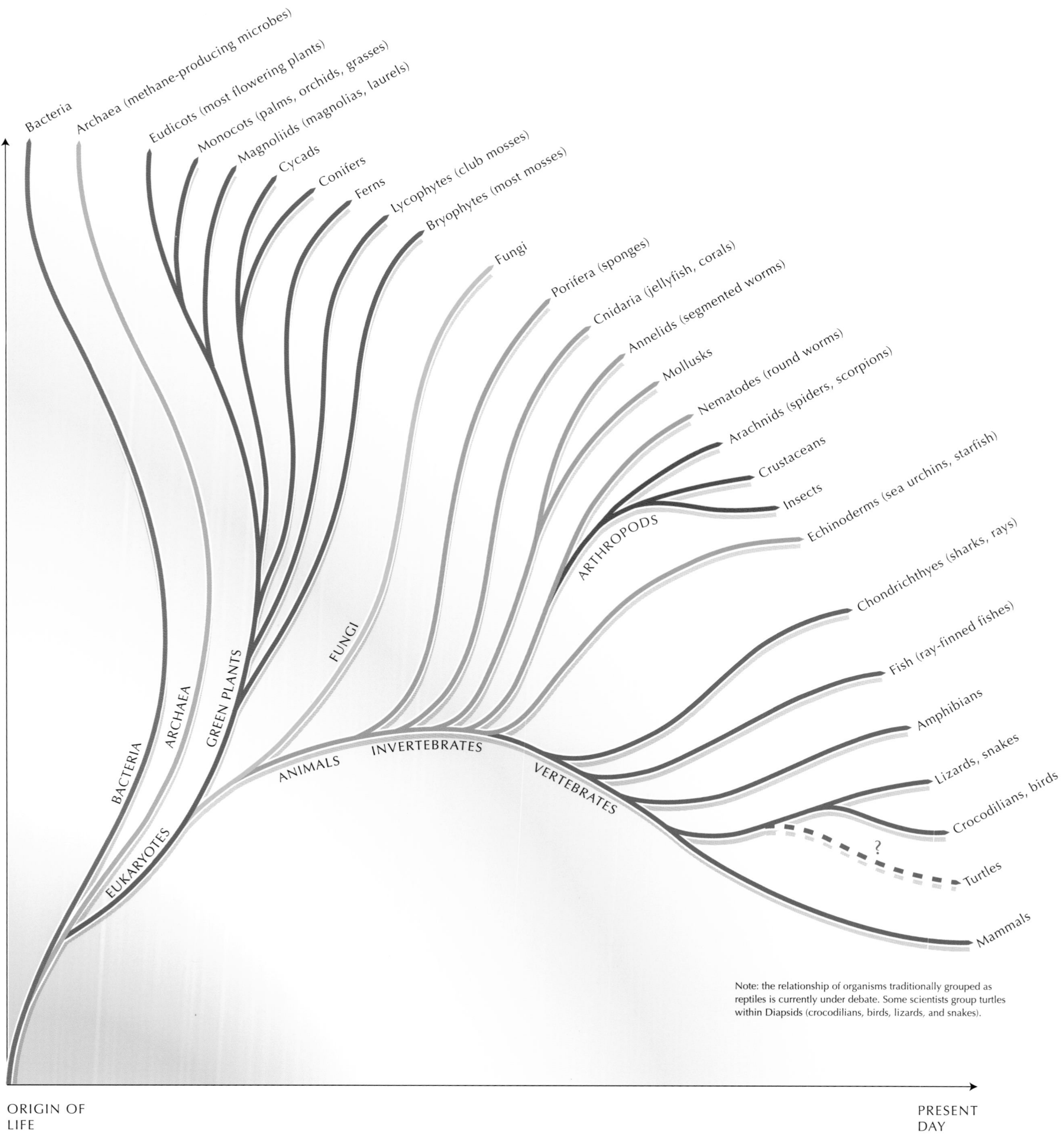

Note: the relationship of organisms traditionally grouped as reptiles is currently under debate. Some scientists group turtles within Diapsids (crocodilians, birds, lizards, and snakes).

Derived from Tree of Life Web Project, www.tolweb.org

Contents

"The nation behaves well if it treats the natural resources as assets which it must turn over to the next generation increased, and not impaired, in value." – Theodore Roosevelt

I INTRODUCTION

Florida is a land of extremes and contradictions. Resorts and amusement parks crowded with international tourists are found merely a few miles from a world of airboats, row crops, and southern drawls. The state's cultural geography can be summed up by the common knowledge among Floridians that the farther north you go, the more southern it gets. Contrasts and extremes predominate Florida's natural heritage as well. At its southern extent Florida is almost tropical, with distinct wet and dry seasons, rare frosts, and plants more common to the Caribbean than the continent, while the temperate north offers chilly winters, deciduous forests, and flora with coastal plain and Appalachian affinities. This section introduces the concept of natural heritage as well as the geophysical setting that gives rise to Florida's unique assemblage of plants, animals, and natural communities.

Marl prairie, Everglades National Park
David Moynahan

About this Atlas

On June 7, 1999, three biologists conducting a survey for rare plant species in the Florida panhandle happened upon a bulldozer operator clearing a 3-acre parcel of scrubby pine flatwoods that supported populations of two critically imperilled species. Chapman's rhododendron (*Rhododendron chapmanii*) and telephus spurge (*Euphorbia telephioides*) are also listed as endangered and threatened, respectively, under the federal Endangered Species Act. Closer inspection confirmed that both populations had been partially or completely destroyed. The biologists' frustration was compounded by the fact that the site was actually being cleared for a public facility. Here were two populations of federally listed species that were well documented by the Florida Natural Areas Inventory, whose mission is to "collect, interpret, and disseminate ecological information critical to the conservation of Florida's biological diversity." Yet people making decisions that most directly affect biodiversity – in this case county officials – were lacking the critical information they needed to avoid harm to these two rare species. While perhaps more compelling in its particulars, this is not an isolated incident. Every day decisions are made across the state of Florida that have significant impact on biodiversity, and all too often these decisions are made without adequate awareness of their impacts. *The Atlas of Florida's Natural Heritage* is intended to address these concerns by raising awareness of the diversity and significance of Florida's ecological resources, and the patterns of their distribution across the state.

Species Richness, Weighted by Rarity

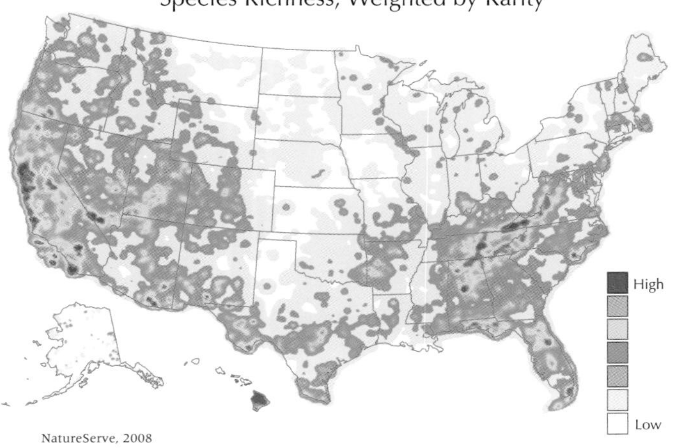

NatureServe, 2008

What do we mean by *natural heritage*? We typically think of heritage in the cultural sense of shared history and traditions. But the term *heritage* can refer to anything inherited or transmitted from the past. When applied to natural resources, *heritage* emphasizes that species, natural communities, air, water, and other elements of the natural world have a past, long before us, and suggests that we as a society have a responsibility for stewardship of those resources – maintaining them in the present and passing them on to the future. In this *Atlas* we offer four themes related to Florida's natural heritage: biodiversity, landscapes, stewardship, and opportunities.

Florida's biodiversity is rich and its landscapes fascinating. From a national perspective, Florida stands out as home to several hotspots of rare and imperiled species (see map). From the world renowned Everglades to an orchid flora that is the most diverse in North America; from one-ton marine turtles that crawl from the sea and nest on Florida beaches to the densest concentration of carnivorous plant species in all of North America; Florida encompasses an extraordinary diversity of plants, animals, and landscapes. The "Elements of Biodiversity" section characterizes the diversity and distribution of species and communities across the state. While not comprehensive, this section attempts to summarize the common, characteristic species and habitats as well as the unique and rare.

Florida's natural resources contribute immensely to the state's economy and quality of life. People flock to Florida to enjoy its miles of sandy beaches, to fish in the state's bountiful lakes and marine waters, and to watch and marvel at its remarkable birdlife or the awe-inspiring spectacle of manatees in a crystal clear spring. Florida's natural areas provide many valuable services such as mitigating the effects of storms and flooding, filtering and storing drinking water, and serving as nursery grounds for commercially valuable fish and shellfish. These "ecosystem services" often go unnoticed, until the natural area is gone and the services are notably lacking. The "Biodiversity Conservation" section outlines major challenges threatening Florida's natural resources, some notable efforts to prioritize places for conservation, and Florida's landmark conservation strategy – the acquisition and management of conservation lands. Finally, "Notable Natural Areas" shifts the emphasis to *place*, and ties together the individual elements of natural heritage to highlight several outstanding natural places in Florida.

The atlas format should also convey that not all species, communities, and places in Florida are equal in ecological significance and conservation priority. Some species are more rare or threatened than others, certain natural communities are of critical ecological importance, and some landscapes stand out in terms of the rarity or sheer diversity of species or communities found there. Indeed, we do not need to fence off the vast majority of the state from economic development in order to maintain the vitality and ecological function of our natural resources. This *Atlas* will show that focused efforts in strategic places could achieve far-reaching results.

This book is ideally intended for all of Florida's citizens. We want the *Atlas* to inspire, educate, and raise awareness of and interest in biodiversity and conservation issues. We specifically want to address those who are informed, interested, or influential in environmental issues, but lack specific information and expertise: planners, policymakers, and environmental advocates, from local to state and federal levels of government as well as non-governmental organizations. We want the *Atlas* to raise their awareness and inform their decision-making. The *Atlas* is also intended to serve as a useful reference for natural resource experts.

Florida owes its rich natural heritage not only to a fortuitous combination of geology, climate, and biology, but also to a history of purposeful conservation and wise stewardship. Today Florida is faced with many challenges: climate change, invasive exotic species, rapid development, and budget shortfalls. It is only through an awareness and appreciation of the diversity and complexity of Florida's natural heritage, and an understanding and knowledge of the ecology of the myriad plants, animals, and natural communities that comprise it, that we will be able to pass this wealth on to future generations.

The Future of Biodiversity in Florida

In the summer of 2010, we asked several leaders in Florida conservation issues to share their thoughts on the future of biodiversity in Florida. They represent a diverse range of backgrounds, including the public and private sectors, politics, and science. Here are their visions for the future.

Addressing Scale and Change in Future Conservation

Jeff Danter, Ph.D.
Florida State Director, 2007-2011
The Nature Conservancy

As conservationists, it is time to change how we think about protecting biological communities and biodiversity in Florida. By eastern U.S. standards, Florida has a strong history of conservation programs. In 2010, more than 10 million acres or 28% of the land area of Florida is in conservation ownership. Florida Forever and Preservation 2000 contributed nearly 1.8 million acres to this total in the past 20 years. In addition, 4 million acres of Florida's marine ecosystems have been protected in federal marine sanctuaries and state aquatic preserves.

Despite these remarkable conservation successes, few would argue that the unique biodiversity of Florida is adequately protected, even in those places already in "conservation protection." The threats facing natural Florida—from land conversion for development and resource extraction, such as water withdrawals, to climate change and sea-level rise—can be overwhelming in scale. These processes threaten not just the unprotected biological assets of Florida, but also the existing conservation estate.

As we move forward in the 21st Century, conservationists must embrace strategies that consider scale and change as primary factors. We know that large, healthy ecosystems are better able to adapt and respond to threats than are small, unhealthy ecosystems. By focusing on ecosystem health, function, and scale of existing conservation assets, conservationists can build the ecosystem resilience needed to protect Florida's biodiversity.

This suggests several changes in approach for the Florida conservation community. First, the criteria by which we prioritize conservation protection projects must evolve. Currently, priority is given to the intrinsic ecological factors of a site. By contrast, higher priority should be given to the contributory value of a project to overall ecosystem health. For example, a land acquisition site contiguous and uphill from an existing coastal protected area might be more important than a "higher quality" unconnected coastal site because the upslope site, when restored, would allow the biological community to migrate in response to sea level rise. Protection of smokesheds, groundwater resources, and agricultural buffers builds the resilience of existing conservation lands in the face of large-scale change. Acquisition of buffer lands, inholdings, and connectors will often contribute more than protection of disjunct tracts of higher biodiversity.

Second, a greater proportion of conservation funding must be dedicated to restoration and management. Ecosystem health and functionality are critical to resilience in the face of both off-site and on-site threats. For example, restoration of coral reefs can build resilience to climate change. Likewise, fire-dependent ecosystems maintained within appropriate fire-return intervals maintain higher biodiversity and can adjust to conservation threats. Funding of proactive restoration strategies and long-term commitment to maintaining ecosystem health through effective management practices are necessary components of a new conservation practice. Indeed, there is anecdotal evidence that Florida's biodiversity is more at risk from management shortfalls of existing conservation areas than from lack of protected status.

We cannot insulate conservation landscapes and waterscapes from large-scale changes. By focusing on resilience, we give ecosystems the ability to adapt—but we will need to change our management and restoration strategies in response to the changing community. This will require a greater commitment to, and investment in, monitoring as a basis for adaptive management.

It is not too soon to begin to envision conservation success for many parts of Florida. Appropriate scale, functionality, and ecosystem health will be the driving variables by which we build enduring conservation assets for the future.

The Future of Biodiversity in Florida

Hillary Swain, Ph.D.
Executive Director and Senior Research Biologist
Archbold Biological Station

Florida is a peninsula of stunning biological serendipity; our little bit of Africa that remained rafted onto North America, located fortuitously for a brilliant bio-fusion of Carolinian temperate with Caribbean subtropical. We shared early landscapes with the desert southwest, avoided the extinction ravages of glaciation, with intermittent isolation to favor the evolution of distinct races and species. Forbidding enough to thwart early European settlement, we harbored many rare species until they were protected legally. An amalgam of biological immigrants, vagabonds, refugees, hermits, relicts, and novelties inhabiting a rich flat tapestry of coastal, upland, and wetland landscapes, our biodiversity has exhibited remarkable resilience in the face of drought and flood, fire and freeze, hurricane, and changes in sea level. For people with a beating ecological heart Florida's biodiversity is intoxicating.

Florida 's conservation trajectory, although positive, always lags inexorably behind losses. After the turn of the century, we laid the groundwork to deal with earlier impacts of overexploitation. Post the first Earth Day we regulated coastal waterways and freshwater wetlands. For the last 25 years we focused a massive conservation effort on purchasing land, an astoundingly successful 2 million acres saved. We will always be appalled at what we lost, but we will be amazed at what we managed to save. Although we know it is not enough.

While we were busy protecting Florida's special areas we hardly envisioned, never mind articulated, the extent to which the looming threats of invasive species and global climate change might undo much of what has been achieved. Public and private land managers now struggle against a guerilla army of invasive plants, animals, and emerging diseases. Nile monitor lizards stalk our land, climbing fern drapes over forested wetlands, and lakes are choked with invasive plants. Our native biodiversity, overwhelmed, needs us to mount its continual defense. Common sense dictates that negative impacts on agriculture, conservation, and public safety should trump desires for an exotic pet, agricultural crop, or garden plant; invasive species are an ecological and economic scourge.

Adding to the onslaught of newcomers, the predictions for sea level rise in Florida raise the hackles of all conservationists and should alarm anyone planning to be here in the latter half of this century. If conservative estimates of up to three feet rise by 2100 are realized, we face considerable challenges throughout the coastal zone. Any higher and the map of Florida will be redrawn over a human generation, prompting almost unfathomable responses in human and wild populations. Florida is not an island, entire of itself, and curtailing sea level rise demands global and not state solutions; we will submerge helplessly if the world does not resolve this threat. But if any state should take a decisive leadership role on sea level rise, it is Florida. Conveniently this isn't just a conservation problem, sea level rise threatens our economic and social fabric… *Therefore, send not to know for whom the bell tolls; it tolls for thee* Florida.

Like earlier essays peering into the future of Florida's biodiversity, I conclude that it will never be as bright as its past. John Muir's sometime delirious Thousand-Mile Walk to the Gulf, John Kunkel Small's impassioned pleas, or Archie Carr's insightful *Dubious Future* all catalogue a foreboding sense of past and future losses. Floridians have accepted environmental protection as beneficial, but the green veneer is fickle, easily undermined by the need for more oil, water, or land. Harry Greene, Cornell University, has written persuasively that "people will care more about, pay more for, and even sacrifice on behalf of things that they understand, so we need to establish biological diversity, ecology, behavior and conservation as among the core components of our scientific literacy." We all know the ultimate key to the future of biodiversity conservation in Florida—that we embrace the wisdom of nature.

Increasing Biodiversity in Florida—Connections and Corridors Strategy

Ernie Cox
President
Family Lands Remembered, LLC

Florida has done a remarkable job in conserving large tracts of important environmental resources. Through the Conservation and Recreational Lands program, Save Our Rivers, P2000, Florida Forever, and other state programs, critical parcels have been acquired and the framework for Florida's "green infrastructure" has been established. Coupled with federal and local efforts, almost 11 million acres of this great state have been permanently placed into conservation uses.

At the same time, Florida has grown significantly in population. The most recent estimates show that almost 19 million people call Florida home and despite a slight decline in population growth during the depths of the recession in 2009, it appears that more people are continuing to move here. Some estimate that another 17 million people will move to Florida over the next 50 years.

More important from a biodiversity perspective is the amount of land that will be used to accommodate these people. Analysis conducted for 1000 Friends of Florida project that an additional 7 million acres of agricultural and natural lands would be converted to development over the next 50 years if historical growth patterns are to continue.

It is clear that we face real challenges in protecting and enhancing the unique biodiversity of this peninsular state. Beyond population growth, we have the challenge of habitat fragmentation, which affects the ability of species to move from place to place with the risk of isolation and impaired genetic diversity.

One part of the solution is the creation of an ambitious strategy to connect important natural resources such as the almost 11 million acres in public conservation ownership. Looking at a statewide map of these existing public lands, one sees the beginnings of a connected system of corridors of natural lands. Connecting the Ocala National Forest to the Okefenokee Swamp, the Florida Panther Wildlife Refuge to the Corkscrew Regional Watershed area, the Babcock Ranch Preserve to the Myakka River State Park, or the many other connections that could be made between existing conservation lands is absolutely critical to the movement of species and improved biodiversity.

Efforts are under way, piece by piece, to create such a connected system. The new Florida Forever ranking system provides additional credit for important corridors. The Florida Fish and Wildlife Conservation Commission, through its Cooperative Conservation Blueprint, is working on three pilot projects to connect such corridors through a coordinated citizens process and active engagement of private landowners. Similarly, the U.S. Fish & Wildlife Service is beginning work on its Peninsular Florida Landscape Conservation Cooperative with the same goal, and to create and then implement a long-term, next step, conservation strategy for the state of Florida.

Integral to both of these strategies is work with private landowners on compatible conservation strategies, so that the land can stay on the tax rolls, the owner can continue certain agricultural operations and maintenance of the property, and create value through conservation strategies. If we are able to make it more profitable to conserve large areas of connected landscapes, more people will pursue conservation. We need more strategies to use the economic engine fueled by the new people moving to Florida, whether we want them here or not, to protect millions of acres of habitat, working agricultural landscapes, and corridor linkages.

If we can engage Florida's landowners in this grand new strategy of conservation, compatible with agriculture and sustainable development in the right locations, we can continue piecing together this statewide patchwork of connected environmental lands. Our children and grandchildren will thank us for our vision and commitment to a better Florida.

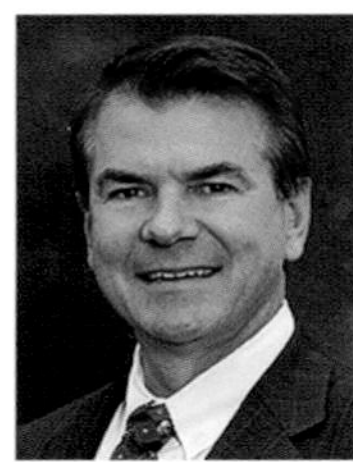

Building Awareness of Biodiversity in Florida

Thad Altman
Florida State Senate, District 24

What is our biggest environmental challenge today? I believe it is people. It is not how many, what they do for a living, political party, or religious affiliation. It is what is in their hearts and minds. Our challenge is building the awareness that we are about to lose something very special to all of us. If we don't do something significant in the near future, the biodiversity of our state is lost, and with it the quality of life that makes Florida special will be gone forever.

We can do this. We have the ability, resources, and the will. The public wants preservation. We are not prevented from protecting our environment from technological, scientific, or economic restrictions. Our technology and scientific knowledge have given us the tools and ability to preserve and restore our natural systems. We can afford it, because the economic benefits of conservation far outweigh the ultimate cost of destruction to our natural systems. What we face is the challenge of moving policy makers toward the political action that is necessary to preserve our environment.

So how do we do it? Here are some political lessons from history.

Big is better than small:

Whether it's going to the moon or building the Panama Canal, people like the bold. They like to know if they are going to invest in a cause that it will be worthwhile and will solve the problem at hand. The simple act of stating and pursuing the bold enables people to realize that it is possible to achieve. We need a large and bold initiative to protect the biodiversity of our state.

Keep it simple:

Einstein said "simplicity is genius." We need straightforward actions to address the serious environmental problems we have today. In the political world if your message is not straightforward and understandable, you have already lost the battle.

Now is the time:

For environmental preservation the adage "later means never" has special meaning. Delay is one of the main tactics for opposition to any cause, but when conservation is delayed, in most cases, valuable habitat is lost forever.

Investing in Florida's Future

Gary R. Knight
Director, Florida Natural Areas Inventory

This book is filled with facts—carefully studied and documented information that we hope will inspire interest in Florida biodiversity and serve as a foundation for informed planning and decision making. When we consider the *future* of biodiversity, however, we must also be concerned with some issues that we do not know today with certainty.

What we do know is that the strength of Florida's economy is tied to tourism, and that people come to Florida not only for the sunshine and warm weather but also to visit our beautiful beaches, to swim and canoe in exquisite springs and streams, and to marvel at the unique ecosystem that is the Florida Everglades. People come to Florida to hunt and fish, to birdwatch or see alligators, manatees, and native orchids. It is clear that a major attraction for Florida tourists is our natural areas and the diversity of wildlife these places support.

We know also that Florida natural areas provide benefits of incalculable worth to Florida through ecosystem services: natural areas filter and store our drinking water, mitigate the damaging effects of storms, help clean the air we breathe, and provide a reservoir of genetic diversity that helps advance agriculture and medicine. And while it is difficult to put a dollar value on beauty, anyone who has ever been to Florida understands the importance of the state's natural landscape for attracting people. Even though all of these benefits are real and have significant financial worth, they typically are not considered when assessing the economic value of natural areas. Such incomplete accounting undervalues Florida's natural areas and misinforms decisions we make planning for the state's future.

Florida's natural areas unquestionably contribute to a higher quality of life for the people who reside or visit here. These special places will not persist, however, without deliberate efforts. It follows, then, that protecting our natural areas should be a strategic investment in Florida's future.

We know how to achieve conservation success. We have the knowledge and tools to guide conservation actions, ensuring that the most important places receive consideration first, that our conservation efforts are both effective and efficient. Florida is a national leader in conservation planning, employing technically advanced analyses grounded on rigorous, well-tested data. The state is also a leader in land management, providing ecologically sound and cost-effective stewardship of lands held in trust for its citizens. And until recently, Florida has been the leader in the U.S. investing in land conservation, through acquisition, conservation easements, and incentive programs.

Although we know much about many of the issues that will influence the future of biodiversity in Florida, that future is still uncertain. The future of biodiversity in Florida critically depends on decisions we make now: planning for smart growth and development that includes conservation, protecting the ecological integrity of existing conservation lands, and continuing our investment in strategic land acquisitions. The future of biodiversity in Florida is in all of our hands; decisions we make today will determine Florida's future forever.

Natural Heritage Methodology

Natural heritage methodology grew out of an increasing need to establish a sound, scientific basis for prioritizing places for conservation. As described in the comprehensive work *Precious Heritage*, "Before the creation of the Natural Heritage Network, the prevailing approach for identifying natural areas in need of protection was to draw up a list of seemingly appropriate sites and then amass information about them" (Stein and Davis, 2000: 24). Natural heritage methodology is based on a coarse filter/fine filter approach that focuses on the locations and status of natural communities and species most in need of conservation attention. Prioritization is fundamental to the entire methodology, with rarity ranks for communities and species as well as quality/viability ranks for individual community or species occurrences.

The natural heritage methodology described here is common to a network that now spans most of the western hemisphere. The methodology recognizes that some places are more important for conservation than others and is designed to help scientists, conservationists, and decision makers efficiently identify the most important places based on the rarity and quality of the species and communities in any location. It is due to this methodology that we can comprehensively describe the geography of Florida's natural heritage throughout this book.

Natural Heritage Network

The natural heritage network was originally founded by The Nature Conservancy in the early 1970s, with the first program established in South Carolina in 1974. The concept was to create a federation of programs in all 50 U.S. states using a common database and data management methodology to document the extent of biodiversity throughout the country, with an emphasis on rare and threatened species and natural communities. Many programs were established within state environmental protection or natural resource agencies, while some are housed within universities (including FNAI, at Florida State University), and one remains under TNC administration.

Over time the heritage network has expanded throughout Canada and 12 Latin American countries. In 1994, the Association for Biodiversity Information (ABI) was formed to more closely coordinate activities of the network, and ABI transformed into NatureServe in 2001 as The Nature Conservancy transferred administration of the network to NatureServe.

All programs in the heritage network use a common data management system outlined on these pages, based on the original concepts of elements, element occurrences, and rarity ranks. Today, the NatureServe network stands as the most comprehensive source of information on the locations and status of biodiversity and natural communities throughout the western hemisphere.

NatureServe Heritage Network

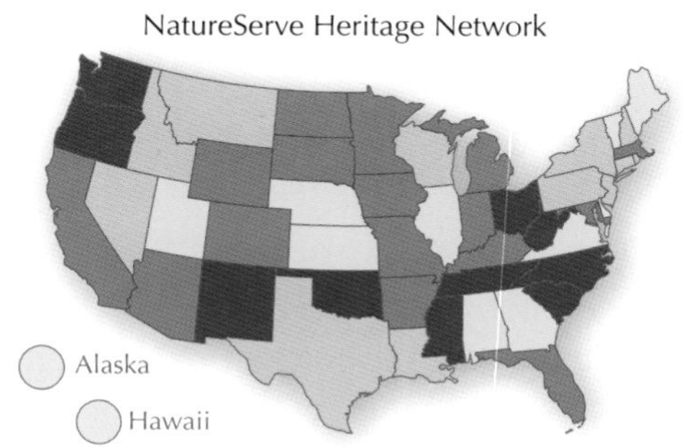

Dates when Program Started

- 1974–1977
- 1978–1981
- 1982–1985
- 1986–1989

Element Occurrences

The fundamental unit of data tracked by FNAI and other heritage programs is the element occurrence, or EO. An "element" is a species, subspecies, natural community, or other important natural feature (such as a geological feature or bird rookery). An element occurrence is a single spatially distinct occurrence of an element. An element can have multiple EOs. For species, an EO generally represents an ecologically distinct population, although multiple populations may sometimes be grouped into a single EO. Natural community EOs usually represent a single patch or stand of the community type, but multiple nearby patches may sometimes be grouped as well. Most importantly, an element occurrence is intended to be an ecologically viable occurrence, which is more than a mere observation or random sighting. A population/community is expected to be present and persisting over time in order to meet the standard for an element occurrence.

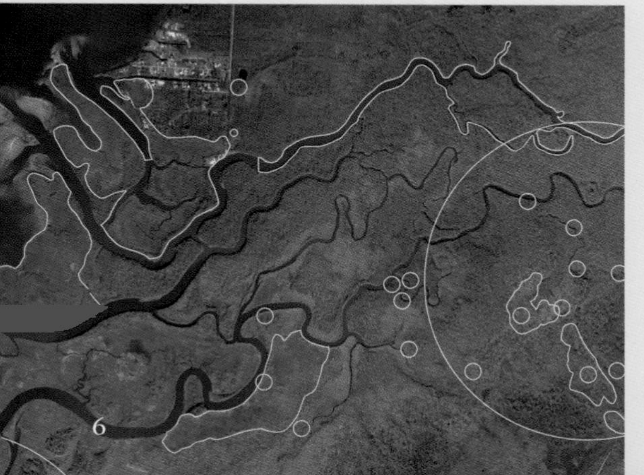

Element occurrences are mapped as polygons in a Geographic Information Systems (GIS) database. These polygons may take a variety of forms and sizes based on the biology of the element and the spatial precision of the source data. Populations occupying a very small area (such as for many rare plant species) may be mapped as a single point with a buffer added to represent locational uncertainty (the small circles in the example at left are examples of EOs with low uncertainty, while the large circles are EOs with higher uncertainty). Occurrences that span a larger area may be mapped as complex polygons indicating the extent of area known to be occupied. The aerial photo (left) shows a winding linear polygon representing a species that occupies that portion of the river.

The vast majority of element occurrences are based on original field surveys. About one-third of those surveys have been conducted by FNAI field staff.

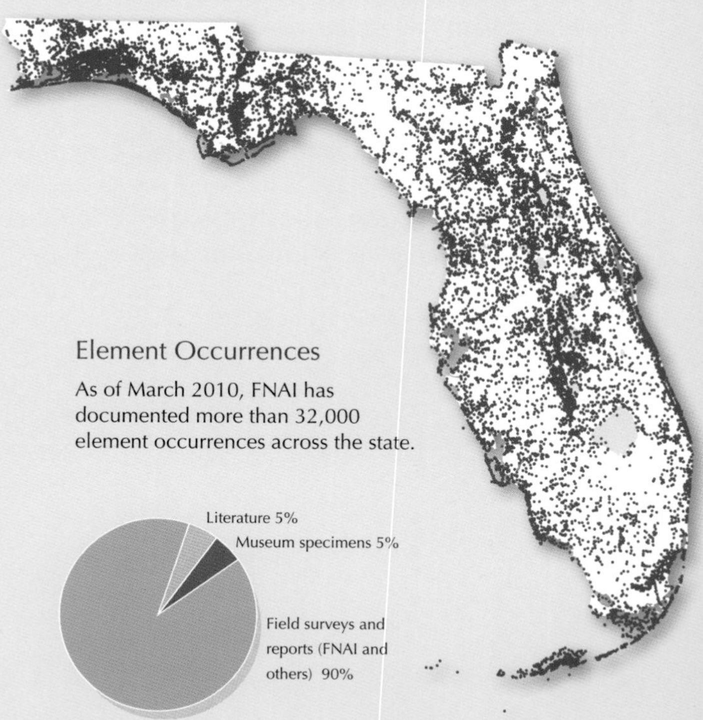

Element Occurrences

As of March 2010, FNAI has documented more than 32,000 element occurrences across the state.

Heritage Data Requests

Like most heritage programs, FNAI responds to hundreds of requests every year for data and other information on rare species locations, ecology, and conservation issues. These requests come from a variety of sources, including government agencies, private consulting firms, schools, and local citizens. Requests may be as large as a federal agency reviewing potential environmental impacts of a proposed multistate pipeline or as small as a local resident concerned about development activities adjacent to their property. FNAI's standard data report includes a detailed map of the requested site with information on rare species, habitat, and natural communities in the vicinity. Increasingly, FNAI provides data in the form of Geographic Information Systems (GIS) files or on the web with online mapservers (www.fnai.org).

Heritage programs are not environmental advocacy groups; information is provided to all sides of an environmental issue, including private developers, regulatory agencies, and grass-roots environmental groups. The goal is to get sound, scientific information on species and natural communities in the hands of all those involved in important decisions that impact biodiversity.

FNAI Data Requests by Client

2005–2010

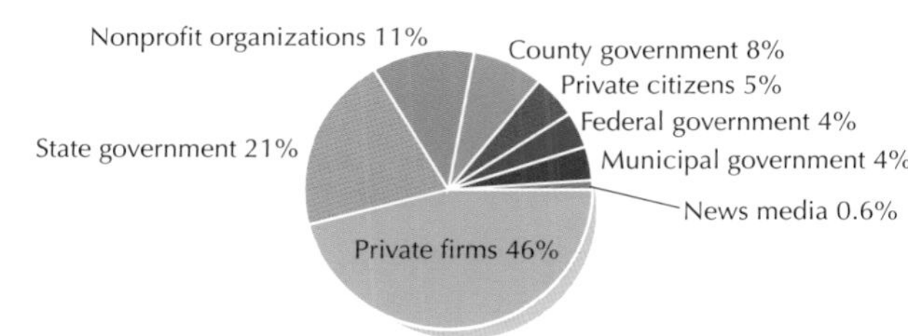

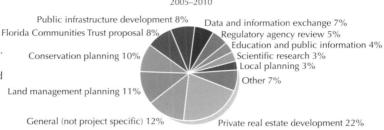

FNAI Data Requests by Project Type

2005–2010

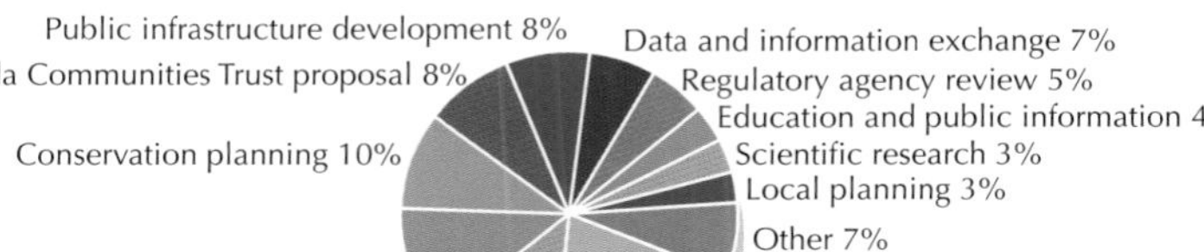

American alligator
(*Alligator mississippiensis*)

Ranking and Tracking

A key component of NatureServe heritage methodology is the ranking of species and natural communities by rarity and threat. NatureServe and FNAI maintain global and subnational (state) rarity ranks for each element in the database. These numeric rankings range from 1 (critically imperiled) to 5 (demonstrably secure). Elements may be ranked as common globally, but rare in Florida (such as the green violet (*Hybanthus concolor*), highlighted in the table at right). Subspecies (or varieties for plants) are given separate ranks from their parent species, denoted by a T (such as the Florida grasshopper sparrow, *Ammodramus savannarum floridanus*, noted in the table). These ranks are relied upon by state and federal agencies to inform conservation planning and in some cases guide regulatory requirements. A full explanation of the ranks assigned by NatureServe and FNAI (and used throughout this atlas) may be found in the appendix.

FNAI typically tracks all species ranked S1-S3 in Florida, as well as all federally listed species occurring in the state. Some less-rare species are also tracked if they are thought to be of conservation interest, while many species that are likely in the S1-S3 range are not yet tracked due to lack of scientific information (particularly for invertebrates).

Examples of Global and State Ranks

Rank	Species	Comments
G1/S1	Four-petal pawpaw (*Asimina tetramera*)	Very rare species–endemic in two counties in southeastern Florida.
G5/S1	Green violet (*Hybanthus concolor*)	Found throughout eastern U.S., but only one Florida population, in the panhandle.
G5T1/S1	Florida grasshopper sparrow (*Ammodramus savannarum floridanus*)	Grasshopper sparrows are found throughout the U.S., but the Florida subspecies is restricted to dry prairie in South Florida.
G3/S2	Arogos skipper (*Atrytone arogos arogos*)	Generally considered rare but locally abundant in some states.
G5/S4	American alligator (*Alligator mississippiensis*)	Once considered rare and threatened, population has recovered since federal listing.

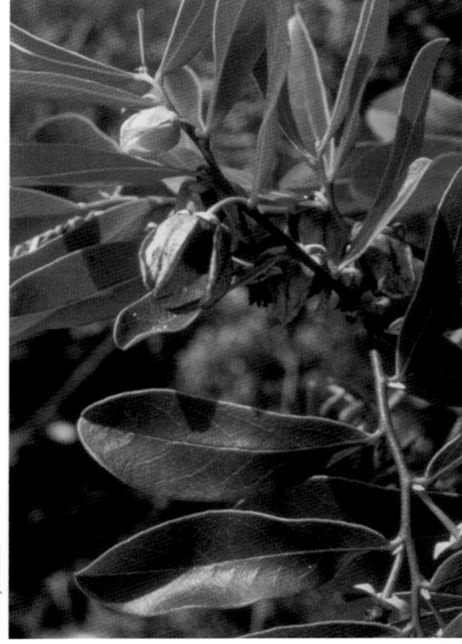

Four-petal pawpaw
(*Asimina tetramera*)

Tracking Florida's Biodiversity

Documenting element occurrences in a natural heritage database is a rigorous effort. The process begins with reliable information from a variety of sources, often field surveys by FNAI's own staff. Source information is then entered into Biotics, NatureServe's data management system that combines a relational database with Geographic Information Systems (GIS).

An FNAI scientist maps locations in Biotics mapper while occurrence and element-level information are recorded in Biotics tracker. Every occurrence in the database is subject to a quality control review by a different scientist. Once entered, data are available for analysis and reporting for a range of purposes from site-specific environmental reviews to statewide conservation planning.

Species Tracked by FNAI

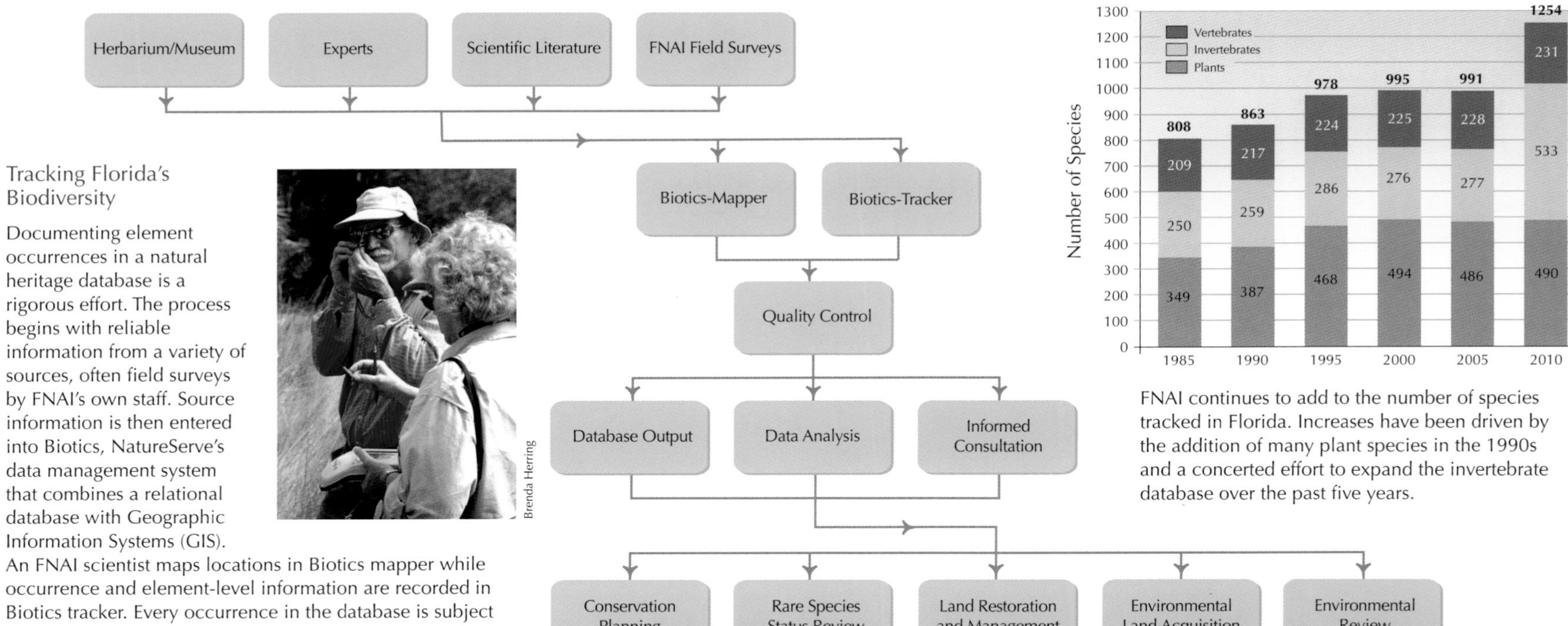

FNAI continues to add to the number of species tracked in Florida. Increases have been driven by the addition of many plant species in the 1990s and a concerted effort to expand the invertebrate database over the past five years.

Geology and Soils

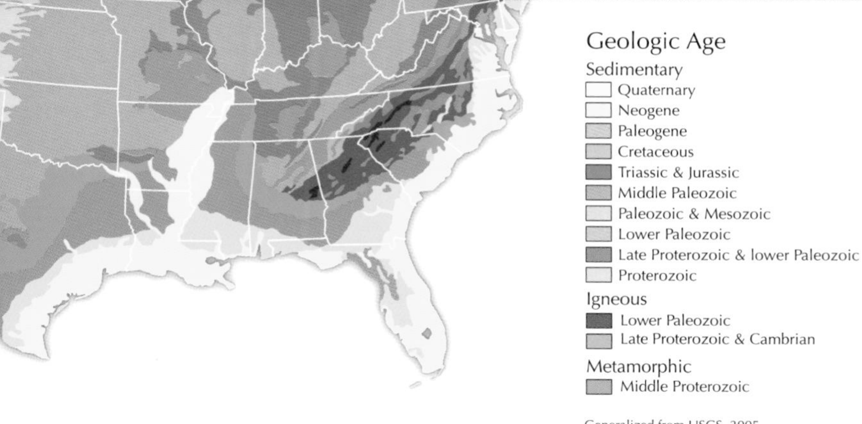

Generalized from USGS, 2005

An area's geologic structure has a major influence on surface water and groundwater conditions as well as physiography. In Florida, steephead ravines and sinkholes are examples of the interplay between geology, climate, and natural communities.

All surface exposures in Florida are sedimentary rocks of Cenozoic age (65 million years ago to present). Much of Florida, however, is blanketed with relatively young sediments (less than 2 million years old). The older sediments are frequently exposed along rivers and streams and in sinkholes in parts of the west central peninsula and the north central panhandle. The oldest outcrops in Florida are part of the Avon Park Formation and were deposited over 40 million years ago during the Middle Eocene.

Carbonate sediments (limestone and dolostone) were deposited over a large portion of the Florida Platform during much of the Cenozoic. Siliciclastic sediments (sand, silt, and clay) did not reach the platform in any significant quantity until the Miocene. Currents flowing in the Gulf Trough isolated the platform. In response to sea level variations and increased sediment supply from the north, the trough was filled, and the siliciclastics spread over the platform covering it entirely during the Pliocene. The siliciclastic sediment supply decreased in the Pleistocene and limestone was once more deposited on the southern portion of the platform. The area of the modern Everglades was a shallow lagoon where calcareous and bryozoan reefs eventually formed the limestone that underlies the Everglades today.

Soils and the underlying geological substrate on which they develop contribute greatly to the myriad of habitats that can be exploited by organisms with various environmental tolerances. For instance, siliciclastic dune deposits that have been weathered and leached by long exposure to rainfall give rise to desert-like, acidic, nutrient-poor sands on which endemic scrub plants and associated animals have persisted along the ancient central ridges of the peninsula. In contrast, outcrops of near-surface limestone in the big bend area produce neutral or basic soil conditions ideal for development of tall, lush hammocks populated by palms or hardwoods. Thus, the environments structured by geologic history are the foundation upon which a remarkable array of life forms creates the natural communities of Florida.

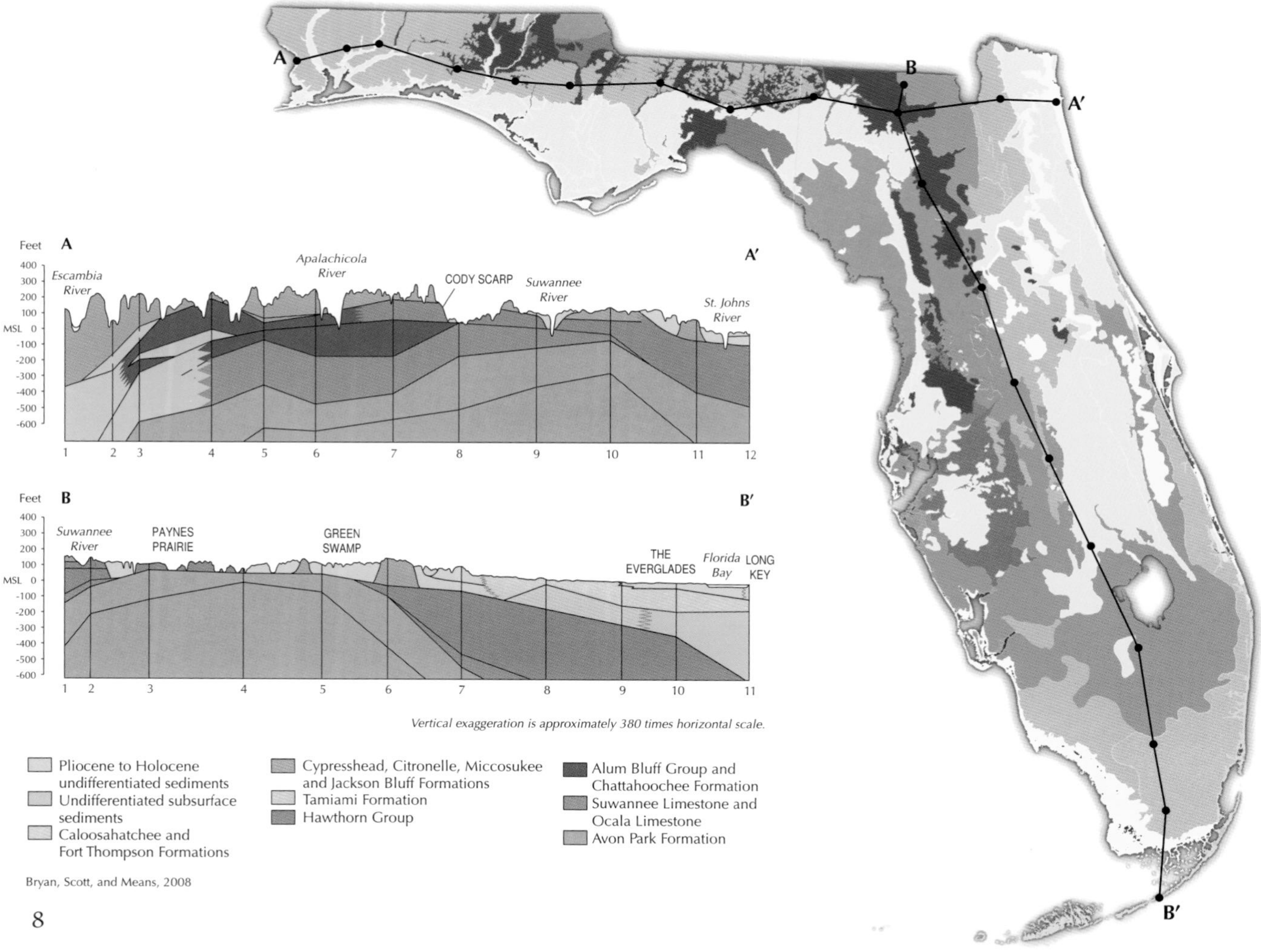

A A' B B'

Feet A A'
400 300 200 100 MSL 0 -100 -200 -300 -400 -500 -600
Escambia River
Apalachicola River
CODY SCARP
Suwannee River
St. Johns River
1 2 3 4 5 6 7 8 9 10 11 12

Feet B B'
400 300 200 100 MSL 0 -100 -200 -300 -400 -500 -600
Suwannee River
PAYNES PRAIRIE
GREEN SWAMP
THE EVERGLADES
Florida Bay
LONG KEY
1 2 3 4 5 6 7 8 9 10 11

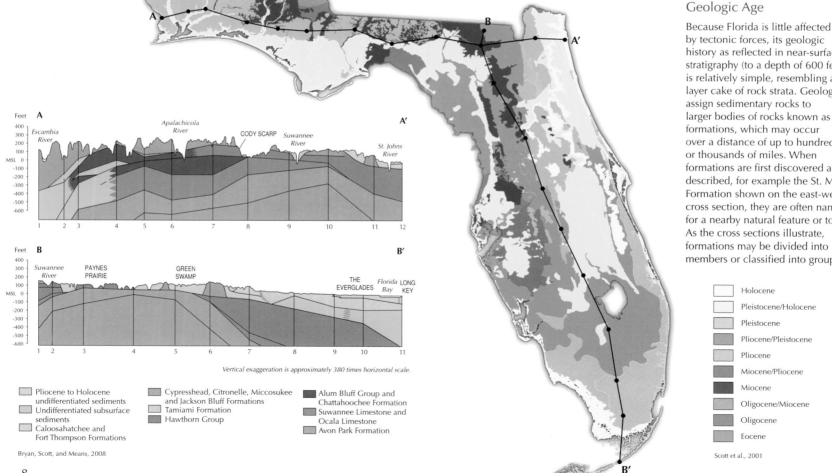

Vertical exaggeration is approximately 380 times horizontal scale.

- Pliocene to Holocene undifferentiated sediments
- Undifferentiated subsurface sediments
- Caloosahatchee and Fort Thompson Formations
- Cypresshead, Citronelle, Miccosukee and Jackson Bluff Formations
- Tamiami Formation
- Hawthorn Group
- Alum Bluff Group and Chattahoochee Formation
- Suwannee Limestone and Ocala Limestone
- Avon Park Formation

Bryan, Scott, and Means, 2008

Geologic Age

Because Florida is little affected by tectonic forces, its geologic history as reflected in near-surface stratigraphy (to a depth of 600 feet) is relatively simple, resembling a layer cake of rock strata. Geologists assign sedimentary rocks to larger bodies of rocks known as formations, which may occur over a distance of up to hundreds or thousands of miles. When formations are first discovered and described, for example the St. Marks Formation shown on the east-west cross section, they are often named for a nearby natural feature or town. As the cross sections illustrate, formations may be divided into members or classified into groups.

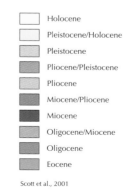

- Holocene
- Pleistocene/Holocene
- Pleistocene
- Pliocene/Pleistocene
- Pliocene
- Miocene/Pliocene
- Miocene
- Oligocene/Miocene
- Oligocene
- Eocene

Scott et al., 2001

Limestone
Limestone/dolomite
Dolomite
Clayey sand
Medium fine sand & silt
Sandy clay and clay
Gravel & coarse sand
Shelly sand & clay
Shell beds
Peat
Florida Department of Natural Resources, map series 1975-81
Thomas A. Scott, FGS
Rich Green, FGS
A
B
Soils of the Western Highlands
Mostly Entisols. Dominated by nearly level to sloping, excessively drained thick sands. Primarily used for field crops, tobacco, watermelons, and forest products and for citrus in the south.
A Mostly Alfisols and Ultisols. Dominated by gently sloping, well-drained sandy soils with loamy subsoils underlain with phosphatic limestone. Primarily used for field crops, tobacco, vegetables, and pastures and for citrus in the south.
Soils of the Central Ridge
B Mostly Entisols. Dominated by nearly level to sloping, excessively drained thick sands. Primarily used for field crops, tobacco, watermelons, and forest products.
Mostly Ultisols. Dominated by level to sloping, well-drained loamy soils and sandy soils with loamy subsoils. Primarily used for field crops, pastures, and forest products.
Soils of the Flatwoods
Mostly Spodosols. Dominated by nearly level, somewhat poorly to poorly drained sandy soils with dark, sandy subsoil layers. Primarily used for pastures, vegetables, flowers, and forest products and for citrus in the south.
Soils of Organic Origin
Mostly Histosols. Dominated by level, poorly drained organic soils underlain by marl and/or limestone. Primarily used for sugarcane, vegetables, pastures, and sod.
Soils of Recent Limestone Origin
Mostly Entisols. Dominated by level, very poorly drained marly and very thin sandy soils underlain by limestone. Used for winter vegetables in localized areas.
Miscellaneous Coastal Land Types
Mostly beaches, dunes, tidal marshes, and tidal swamps. Dominated by nearly level to sloping sandy beaches and adjacent sand dunes; also level, very poorly drained coastal marshes and swamps of variable-textured mineral and organic soils subject to frequent tidal flooding. Primarily used for recreation and wildlife.
— — Soils north of this boundary are considered in the thermic temperature regime. The thermic temperature regime is where the mean annual temperature 20 inches below the soil surface is 59°F (17.5°C) to 72°F (22°C) with 9°F (5°C) or more variability between mean summer and winter temperatures. Soils occurring south of this boundary are considered to be in the hyperthermic temperature regime. The hyperthemic temperature regime is where the mean annual temperature 20 inches below the soil surface is higher than 72°F with 9°F or more variability between mean summer and winter temperatures.
U.S. Department of Agriculture, Soil Conservation Service, 1982

Dolostone

Limestone quarry near Marianna in the panhandle

Vulcan Quarry, Hernando County, limestone with clay-filled cavities

Grandin Sand Pit, Putnam County

Peat mine, Orange County

Shells, Rucks Pit, Ft. Drum, Florida

Environmental Geology

The environmental geology map shows a simplified scheme of rock and sediment types regardless of age and nomenclature. The westernmost portion of the panhandle is the only place in Florida where sandy clay, clay, gravel, and coarse sand are found at the surface. Clayey sands cover most of the areas of highest relief in Florida. Areas of fine sand, shelly sand, silt, and clay represent recent geological deposits and occur mostly inland from the East Coast and extend to the West Coast in the south central portion of the state. Peat, common in the Everglades, began forming about 6,000 years ago from the decay of sawgrass.

Soil Characteristics

The character of soil depends on the mineralogy of underlying rock as well as climate and plant cover. Spodosols, somewhat poorly to poorly drained sandy soils with a dark sandy subsoil layer, are the most common soils in the state. Soils in Florida vary from place to place but are generally sandy and low in fertility. Florida's most fertile soils are in upland regions of northern Florida, once part of a thriving cotton belt, and south of Lake Okeechobee, where sugarcane and winter vegetables are grown.

Physiography

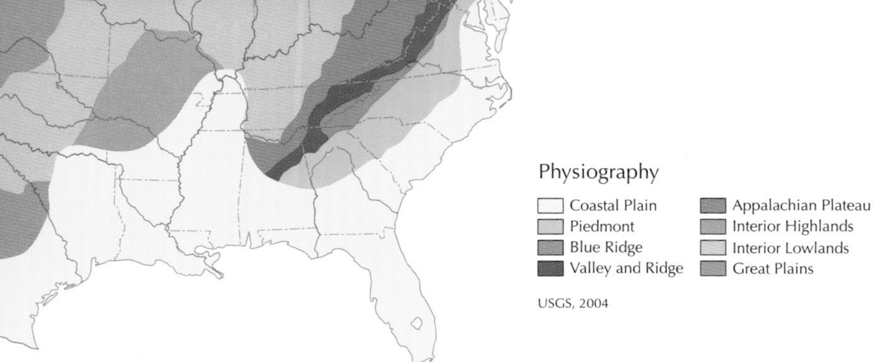

Physiography

- Coastal Plain
- Piedmont
- Blue Ridge
- Valley and Ridge
- Appalachian Plateau
- Interior Highlands
- Interior Lowlands
- Great Plains

USGS, 2004

Terraces and Shorelines

- 170–320 feet
  Includes Hazlehurst terrace (Cooke, 1939), Coastwise delta plain (Vernon, 1942), part of the high Pliocene terrace (MacNeil, 1949) Coharie terrace
- 70–170 feet
  Includes Sunderland terrace (Cooke, 1939), Okefenokee terrace (MacNeil, 1949) Wicomico terrace
- 25–70 feet
  Penholoway terrace, Talbot terrace
- 0–25 feet
  Pamlico terrace, Silver Bluff terrace

Schmidt, 1997

The earth's surface is dynamic, a continuously changing expression of underlying geologic structures and erosion and deposition by wind and water. Physiography, also referred to as geomorphology, is the study and division of the landscape based on terrain, rock type, and geologic structure and history. In the broadest physiographic sense, Florida is part of the Coastal Plain and is the only state whose area straddles both Gulf and Atlantic sections of the plain.

Physiographic Regions

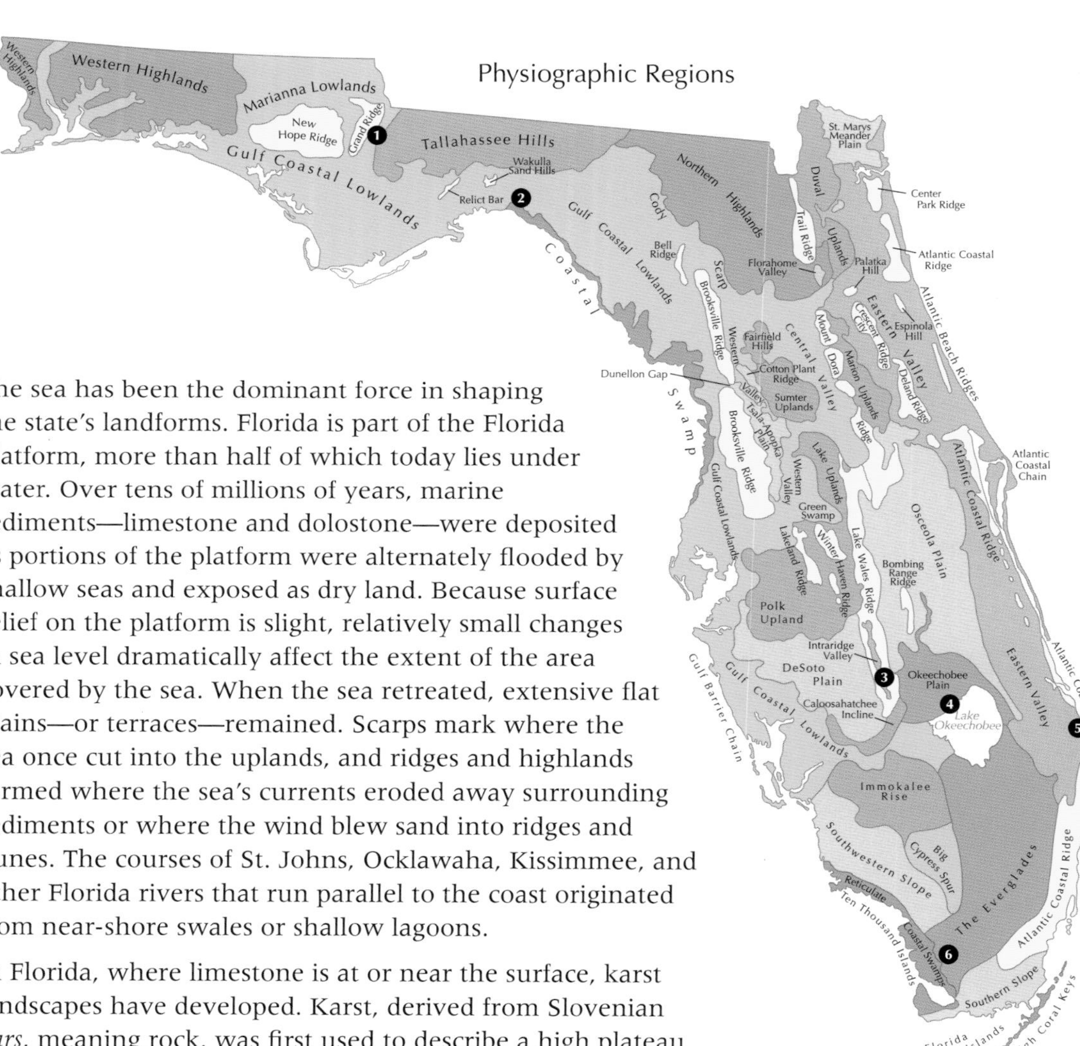

Schmidt, 1997

The sea has been the dominant force in shaping the state's landforms. Florida is part of the Florida Platform, more than half of which today lies under water. Over tens of millions of years, marine sediments—limestone and dolostone—were deposited as portions of the platform were alternately flooded by shallow seas and exposed as dry land. Because surface relief on the platform is slight, relatively small changes in sea level dramatically affect the extent of the area covered by the sea. When the sea retreated, extensive flat plains—or terraces—remained. Scarps mark where the sea once cut into the uplands, and ridges and highlands formed where the sea's currents eroded away surrounding sediments or where the wind blew sand into ridges and dunes. The courses of St. Johns, Ocklawaha, Kissimmee, and other Florida rivers that run parallel to the coast originated from near-shore swales or shallow lagoons.

In Florida, where limestone is at or near the surface, karst landscapes have developed. Karst, derived from Slovenian *kars*, meaning rock, was first used to describe a high plateau in Slovenia. The limestone that underlies Florida and other karst regions of the world, including the Yucatán peninsula, parts of Cuba, and southern China, is easily dissolved by water charged with carbon dioxide from the air and from decaying plants, dotting the landscape with sinkholes, depression ponds, caves, and disappearing streams.

1 Alum Bluff

Thomas M. Scott

2 Woodville Karst Plain

Elizabeth Purdum

3 Sand Dunes, Highlands County

Thomas M. Scott

4 Lake Okeechobee

Thomas M. Scott

5 Anastasia Formation

Thomas M. Scott

6 Western Everglades

Thomas M. Scott

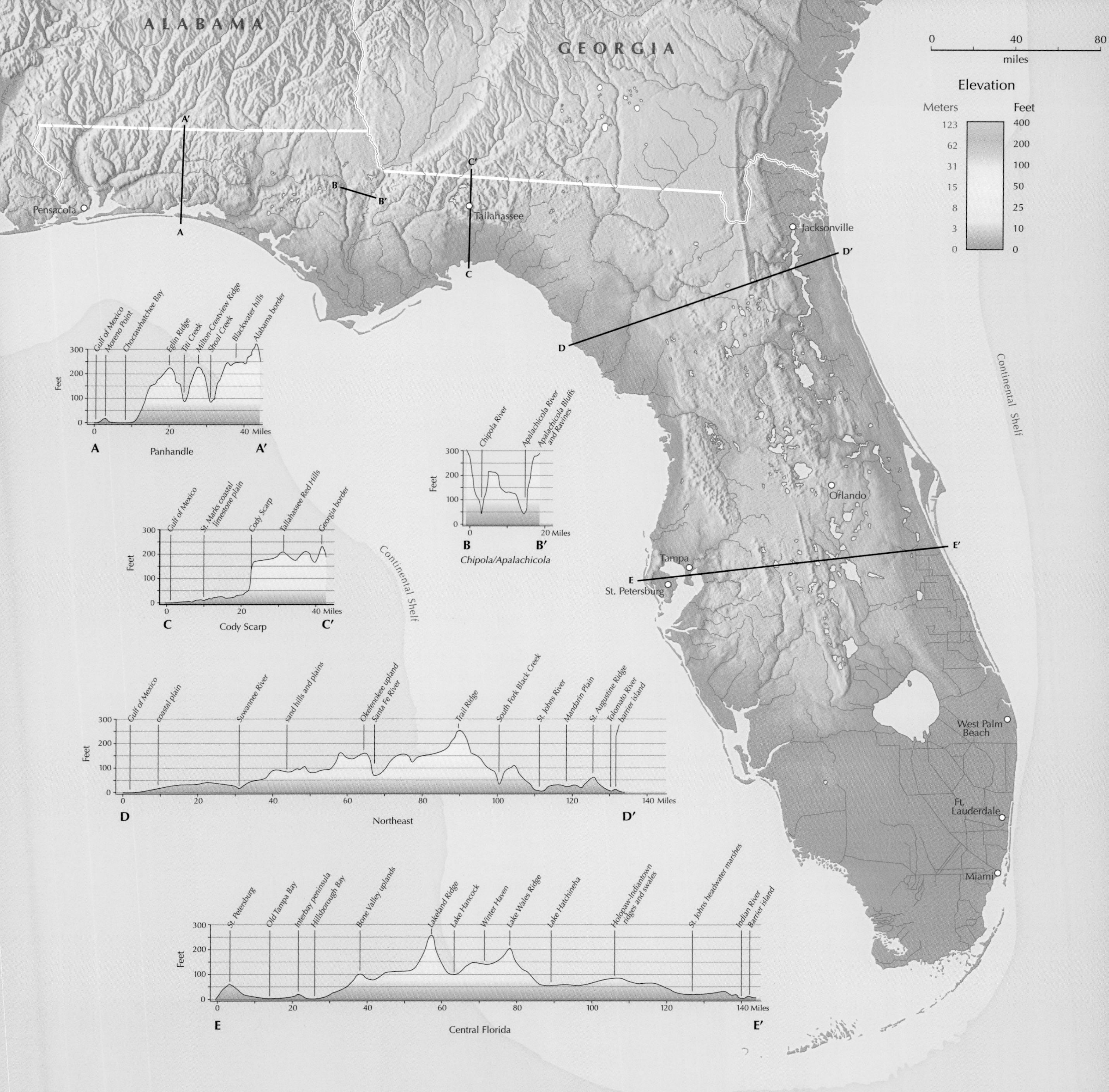

Elevation and Natural Community Types

Elevation along with landforms, substrate, soils, hydrology, climate, and fire influence natural community types. With a range in elevation of less than 350 feet, Florida exhibits more subtle changes than mountainous regions where vegetation zones correspond to decreases in temperature as elevation increases. In Florida, because of variation in soil, substrate, and rainfall and complex interactions between surface water and groundwater, a few inches in elevation may result in dramatic changes in natural community types within a small area.

The cross sections on the map illustrate some of the places in Florida where changes in elevation most clearly contribute to changes in natural communities. Along the eastern tributaries of the Apalachicola River, steephead ravines 50 to 100 feet deep have formed from the lateral seepage of groundwater rather than from erosion by surface water. Here, sandhills are found along the tops of the ridges, slope forest along the more mesic upper and mid slopes, and bottomland forest, floodplain forest, or baygall on the lower more hydric slopes.

The ridges in Central Florida, some as high as 300 feet, were formed 1 to 3 million years ago by ancient islands and sand dunes that remained elevated above the surrounding landscape long after the ocean receded. Here, islands of rare scrub no wider than a few miles are found on white sand in a matrix of sandhill communities.

Water Resources

Water is the thread connecting all ecosystems on earth, as well as the sculptor of ancient and modern landforms. In Florida, water flows from upland ecosystems through rivers, swamps, and freshwater marshes, and eventually to salt marshes, mangroves, seagrass beds, and coral reefs along the coast. Much of southern Florida is so flat that rainwater has nowhere to go and may remain on the land for days or weeks. Water and fire account for much of the subtlety we see in Florida's natural communities.

In 2007, FNAI, with funding from the Florida Department of Environmental Protection, began updating its categorization of natural communities first published in 1990. FNAI has identified 23 terrestrial communities (uplands dominated by plants not adapted to inundation during 10% or more of the growing season), 20 palustrine communities (freshwater wetlands; plants adapted to inundation during 10% or more of the growing season), and 2 marine communities (tidal marsh and tidal swamp). Twenty-two aquatic communities are to be updated at a later date.

Florida has abundant surface water in springs, rivers, lakes, bays, and wetlands. Of the 84 first-magnitude springs (those that discharge water at a rate of 100 cubic feet per second or more) in the United States, 33 are in Florida, more than in any other state. Within Florida's boundaries are approximately 10,000 miles of rivers and streams and 7,800 lakes. Although more than half of Florida's wetlands have been drained, vast and diverse wetlands still remain. The Everglades and Big Cypress Swamp cover much of southern Florida, and some Florida wetlands, for example, mangrove swamps and hydric hammocks, rarely occur in other states.

The state's largest rivers, the Apalachicola, Suwannee, and St. Johns, have only a fraction of the flow of the continent's and the world's largest rivers. Two of these—the Apalachicola and the Suwannee—originate outside the boundaries of the state. The Apalachicola-Chattahoochee-Flint River basin is located in Georgia, Alabama, and Florida with its headwaters in Georgia above Sidney Lanier Reservoir. The Suwannee River basin begins in the Okefenokee Swamp and two of its tributaries, the Withlacoochee (distinct from the southern Withlacoochee) and the Alapaha, also originate in Georgia. The St. Johns River originates in the broad marshes of Indian River and Brevard counties and flows 310 miles north to the Atlantic.

Florida Drainage Area

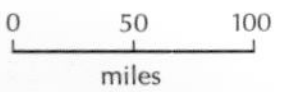

Lakes are especially numerous in the high sandy uplands of the central peninsula and the St. Johns region. Lake Okeechobee is by far the largest lake in the state and the second largest lake in the continental United States.

In Florida, surface water and groundwater are connected, often in complicated and changing ways that are largely invisible at the land's surface. Springs are the expression of groundwater at the land surface and the source of many rivers in the state including the Wakulla and the Ichetucknee. Groundwater is also visible in sinkhole lakes, breaches in the land surface into the underlying aquifer. Where limestone is near the surface or overlain by thick layers of sand, stream beds are permeable and surface water and groundwater are constantly exchanged. Some streams flow underground for miles and surface in springs while others flow below ground to the coast and then emerge offshore in the ocean floor.

Protecting water resources is critical to the health of both Florida's natural and human communities. Areas of high aquifer recharge and springsheds are especially vulnerable to the effects of development. Recognizing this, the Florida Forever Act includes high recharge areas and springsheds in its land acquisition criteria as well as surface waters and many other natural resources.

David Moynahan

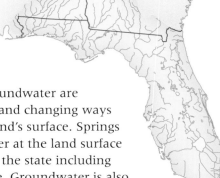

Saltmarsh, St. Marks National Wildlife Refuge

David Moynahan

Spring, Chipola River

David Moynahan

Cypress, Fisheating Creek

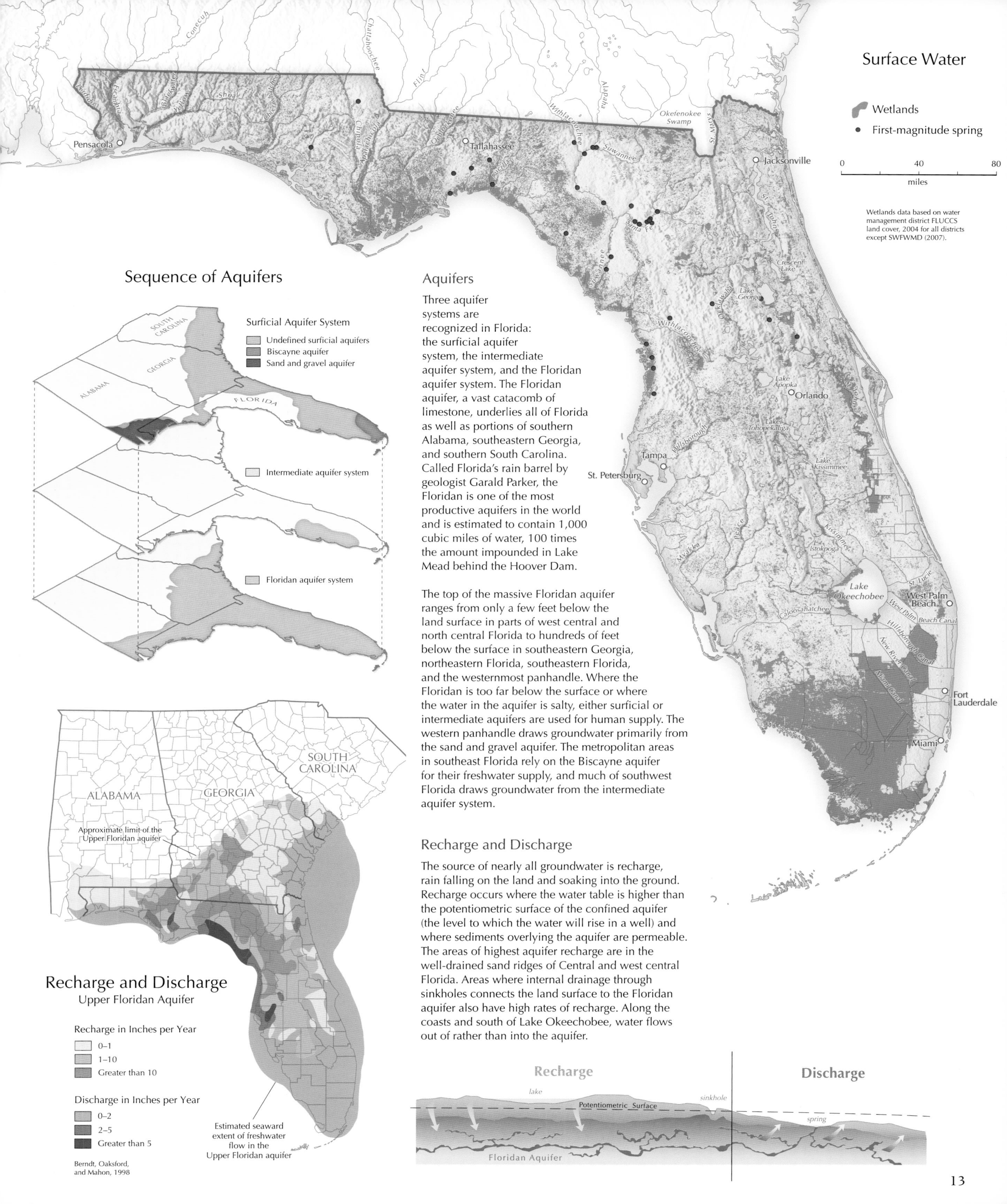

Aquifers

Three aquifer systems are recognized in Florida: the surficial aquifer system, the intermediate aquifer system, and the Floridan aquifer system. The Floridan aquifer, a vast catacomb of limestone, underlies all of Florida as well as portions of southern Alabama, southeastern Georgia, and southern South Carolina. Called Florida's rain barrel by geologist Garald Parker, the Floridan is one of the most productive aquifers in the world and is estimated to contain 1,000 cubic miles of water, 100 times the amount impounded in Lake Mead behind the Hoover Dam.

The top of the massive Floridan aquifer ranges from only a few feet below the land surface in parts of west central and north central Florida to hundreds of feet below the surface in southeastern Georgia, northeastern Florida, southeastern Florida, and the westernmost panhandle. Where the Floridan is too far below the surface or where the water in the aquifer is salty, either surficial or intermediate aquifers are used for human supply. The western panhandle draws groundwater primarily from the sand and gravel aquifer. The metropolitan areas in southeast Florida rely on the Biscayne aquifer for their freshwater supply, and much of southwest Florida draws groundwater from the intermediate aquifer system.

Recharge and Discharge

The source of nearly all groundwater is recharge, rain falling on the land and soaking into the ground. Recharge occurs where the water table is higher than the potentiometric surface of the confined aquifer (the level to which the water will rise in a well) and where sediments overlying the aquifer are permeable. The areas of highest aquifer recharge are in the well-drained sand ridges of Central and west central Florida. Areas where internal drainage through sinkholes connects the land surface to the Floridan aquifer also have high rates of recharge. Along the coasts and south of Lake Okeechobee, water flows out of rather than into the aquifer.

Climate

Florida's warm climate and abundant rainfall contribute to its biodiversity. The northern two-thirds of the state have a humid subtropical climate; the southern third, a tropical savanna climate with distinct wet and dry seasons.

Rainfall throughout Florida varies considerably from season to season and from year to year as well as from place to place. Stations within the same city often record large differences in the amount of rainfall. Many of Florida's counties have distinct rainfall zones based on subtle geographic features, vegetation, and water bodies.

The wettest places in Florida are in the panhandle and the southeastern portions of the state. In the panhandle, rain falls throughout the year with the greatest amounts falling during the summer and during the winter months as cold fronts sweep across the northern portions of the state. In southeast Florida, the Gulf Stream contributes both moisture and instability to the air. There, especially just inland from the coast, thunderstorms are very frequent from May through October. Many of Florida's natural communities evolved in concert with fires ignited by lightning. The lowest amounts of rainfall occur in the Keys and the central portion of the peninsula.

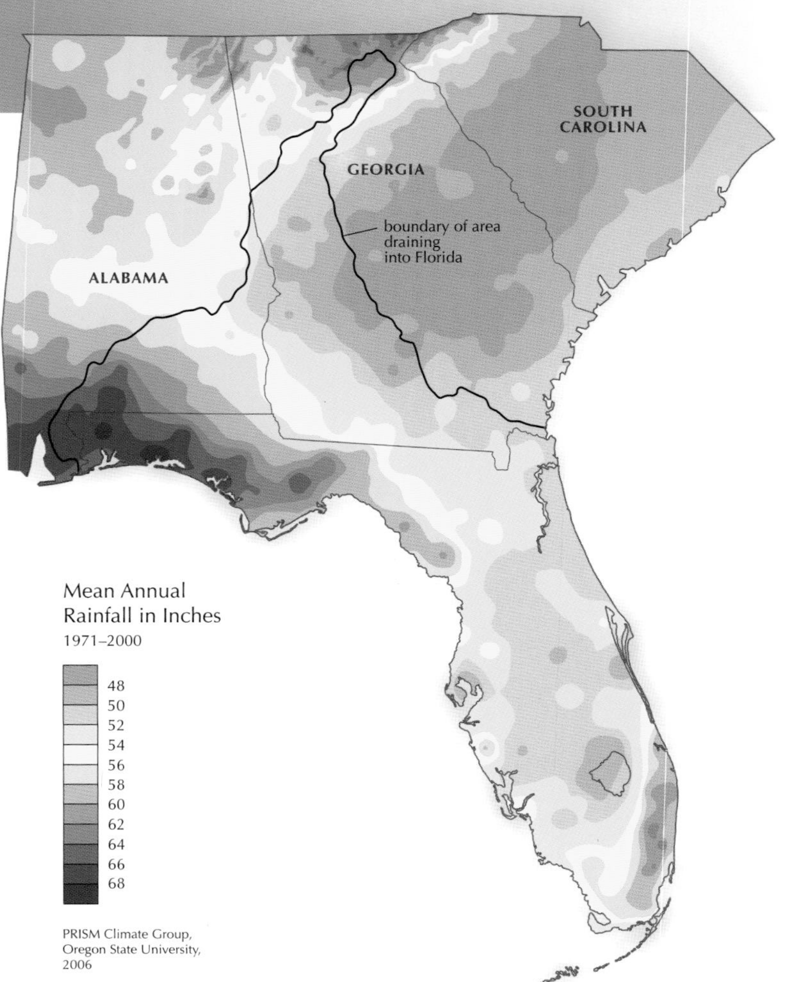

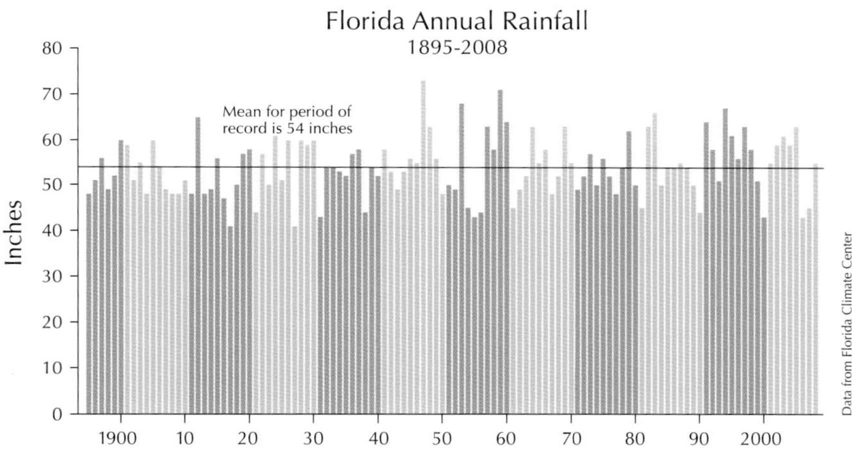

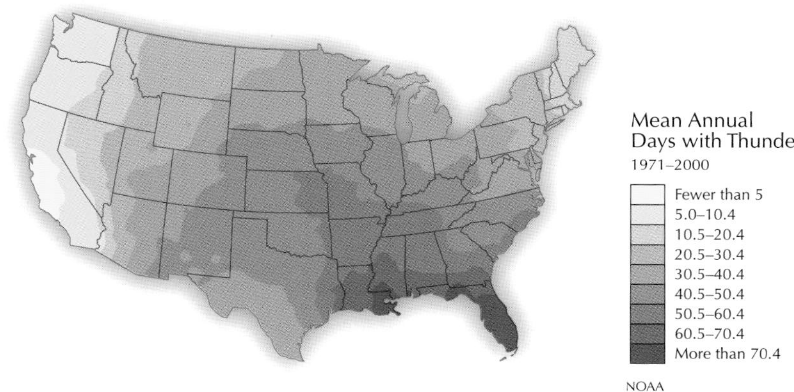

Temperature

Temperatures are high throughout Florida in the summer, with the highest temperatures occurring in inland northeast and north central Florida and inland southwest Florida. The least differences between the coldest and warmest periods of the year are found from Miami Beach to Key West, where barely 25° F separates the average maximum temperature of the warmest day of the year and the average minimum temperature of the coldest night of the year. The greatest differences (over 55° F) are found in the interior of North Florida.

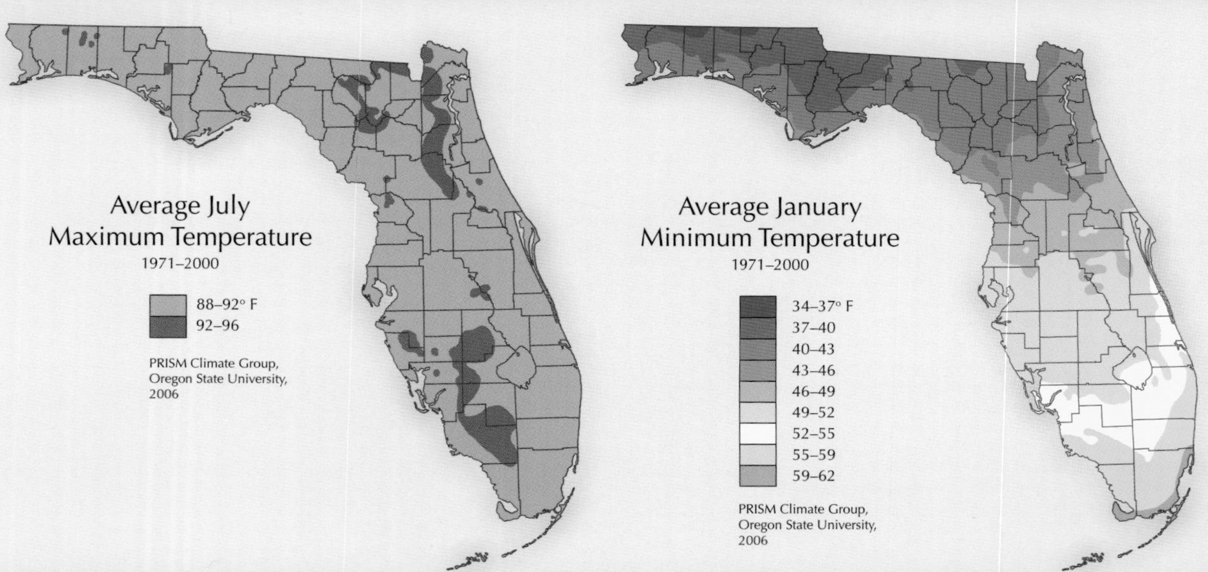

January

February

March

April

May

June

July

August

September

October

November

December

Rainfall

Mean Monthly Rainfall in Inches
1971–2000

0.8–1.2
1.2–1.6
1.6–2.0
2.0–2.4
2.4–2.8
2.8–3.2
3.2–4.0
4.0–5.0
5.0–6.0
6.0–8.0
8.0–12
12–16

Data from Florida Climate Center

Storms in North Atlantic, August 26, 1999

Haven for Hurricanes

Florida's peninsular shape and long coastline place it in the direct path of Atlantic hurricanes. Hurricanes commonly develop from weak troughs of low pressure that form in the lower latitudes over the Atlantic Ocean and then drift toward the west. Several low-pressure systems may be evident on satellite imagery on any given summer day in the Atlantic and the Caribbean.

Nearly half of all hurricanes that have reached the United States since 1886 have made landfall in Florida. The southeast coast and the panhandle are most susceptible to hurricanes. The northeast coast and the peninsular Gulf coast are least likely to be affected by tropical storms. If a storm enters the gulf, it will commonly continue toward the northwest resulting in a high incidence of landfalls along the Louisiana and Texas coast as well as Alabama and the western panhandle.

South Florida ecosystems have been shaped by and are adapted to hurricanes. Many of Florida's tropical plants originating in the West Indies are thought to have been spread by hurricanes. Within 20 days of Hurricane Andrew in 1992, surviving trees and shrubs were sprouting new growth and grasslands looked essentially the same as they had before the storm (Alper, 1992).

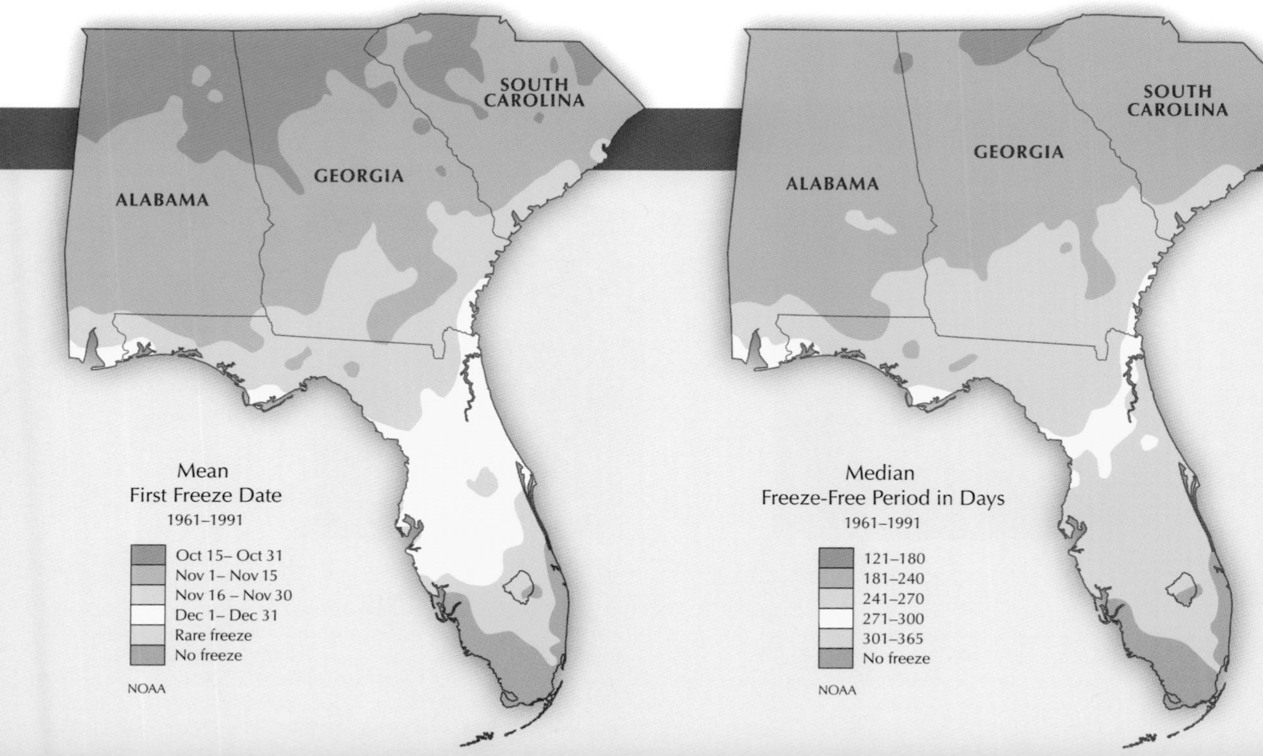

During the winter, no part of Florida—not even Key West—escapes periodic blasts of cold air from the north. In North Florida, freezing temperatures arrive earlier, last longer, and are lower than farther south. The frequency of freezes decreases rapidly south of a line running roughly between St. Augustine and Cedar Key. The last freeze of the winter is normally considerably later in the interior of the peninsula than along the coasts.

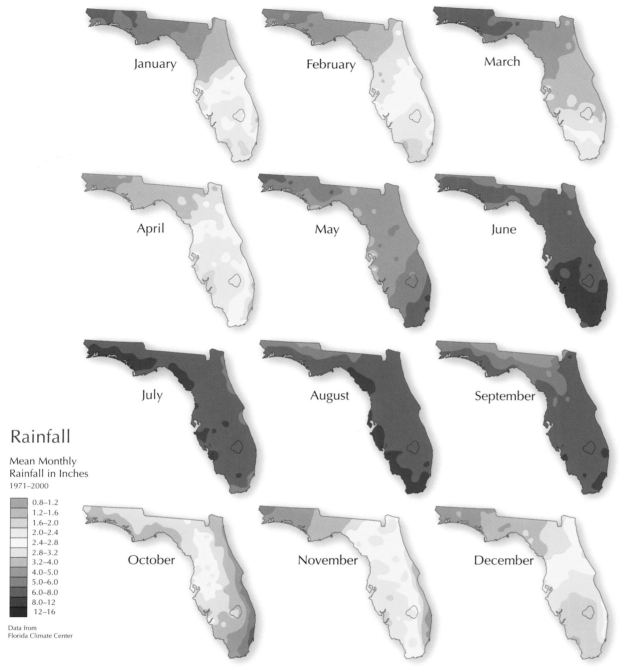

Land Cover

Florida's land cover maps describe the landscape in terms of vegetation and/or land use classes. The maps are typically derived from remotely sensed data such as satellite imagery or aerial photography. Areas are classified according to the signatures, or similarity of characteristics, that can be detected with these methods. Depending on the classification scheme, scale, and intended purpose of the data, land cover has a variety of applications, from landscape-scale biodiversity analyses to site-specific habitat management.

Land cover helps paint the broad picture of land uses in Florida. About one-sixth of Florida's land has been developed, with much of this development concentrated along our coasts. Approximately one-third of the state has been converted to agricultural land uses, with extensive pine plantations in the northern half and pasture, citrus groves, and sugarcane more common in the southern half. Approximately half of the state is still covered by forests, grasslands, swamps, and other natural vegetation; much of these remaining natural areas are preserved within Florida's conservation lands, which represent about one-third of the state.

The vegetation classes of an ecologically based land cover help explain patterns of biodiversity and provide information about the distribution of species. Species habitat maps, including occurrence-based habitat, potential habitat, and predictive range models, are all commonly derived from land cover. Land cover is the foundation of many statewide conservation planning datasets including rare species habitat conservation priorities, strategic habitat conservation areas, ecological greenways, and underrepresented natural communities. Land cover/vegetation maps are also essential tools for land managers who must plan for prescribed fire, invasive species control, and other natural-community-based management activities.

A View of the Past

Historical vegetation maps, such as the 1967 Davis Map, estimate the extent of vegetative communities prior to European settlement. A comparison of the historical versus current distribution of natural communities gives us a picture of what has been lost and can help to prioritize future protection. For example, the once extensive longleaf pine-wiregrass ecosystem known as sandhill has been largely converted to agriculture, pine plantations, and residential areas. Because sandhill now occupies a fraction of its former extent, it is a priority for state protection efforts.

Presettlement Vegetation

- Mesic pinelands
- Scrub and sandhill
- Upland hardwood
- Non-forested uplands
- Forested wetlands
- Non-forested wetlands
- Open water

Davis, 1967

Green Swamp

Aerial photography from the 1930s through the 1950s exists for much of Florida, enabling the creation of detailed historical natural community maps. In this example, a historical natural community map was created for Green Swamp in southwest Florida based on 1941 aerial photography. Maps like this can help guide the restoration efforts of land managers. FNAI has created historical natural community maps for about 2 million acres of conservation lands in Florida.

Detail of Green Swamp, 1941

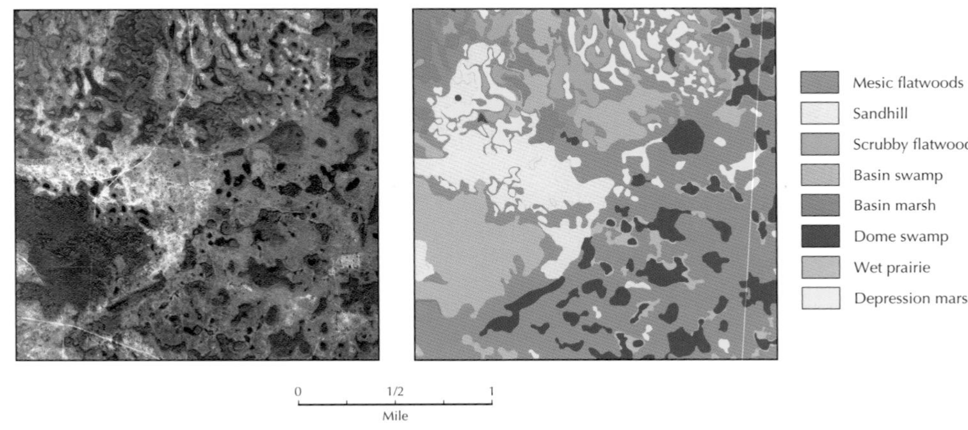

0 1/2 1
Mile

Land Cover Data Comparison

Florida has a wealth of land cover data from statewide to regional to site-specific datasets. The appropriate use of any land cover will depend on factors such as scale, resolution, accuracy, time-frame, classification system, and purpose for which it was created. In the examples at right, three distinct landcovers are compared: 1) the 2003 Florida Vegetation and Landcover (FLVEG) developed by the Florida Fish and Wildlife Conservation Commission; 2) Land Use/Land cover data developed for each of Florida's five water management districts based on the Florida Land Use, Cover and Forms Classification System (FLUCCS); and 3) Natural Community Mapping data developed by Florida Natural Areas Inventory (FNAI) for many of Florida's state conservation lands. Note in the examples that the center area is identified as a combination of wetland types by FLVEG and FLUCCS, and as wetland surrounded by upland by FNAI.

Aerial Photograph

0 1/4 1/2
Miles

This is a view of 1-foot resolution 2008 Digital Orthophotography zoomed at 1:15000 scale. The photo and land cover examples that follow are from the Guana River Wildlife Management Area and adjacent residential lands in St. Johns County.

FLVEG

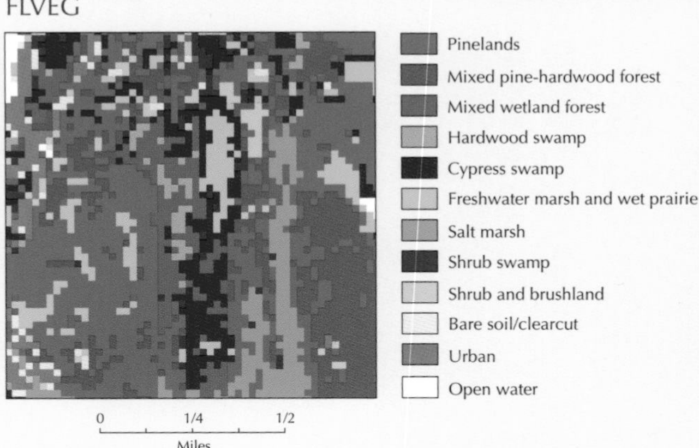

0 1/4 1/2
Miles

FLVEG is a statewide land cover that includes 43 vegetation and land use classes for Florida: 26 natural and semi-natural vegetation types, 16 types of disturbed lands (e.g., agriculture, urban, mining), and 1 water class. It is derived from 2003 Landsat Enhanced Thematic Mapper plus imagery with a pixel size of 30m. FLVEG provides a relatively detailed ecological classification with other land uses lumped into broad categories (e.g., urban).

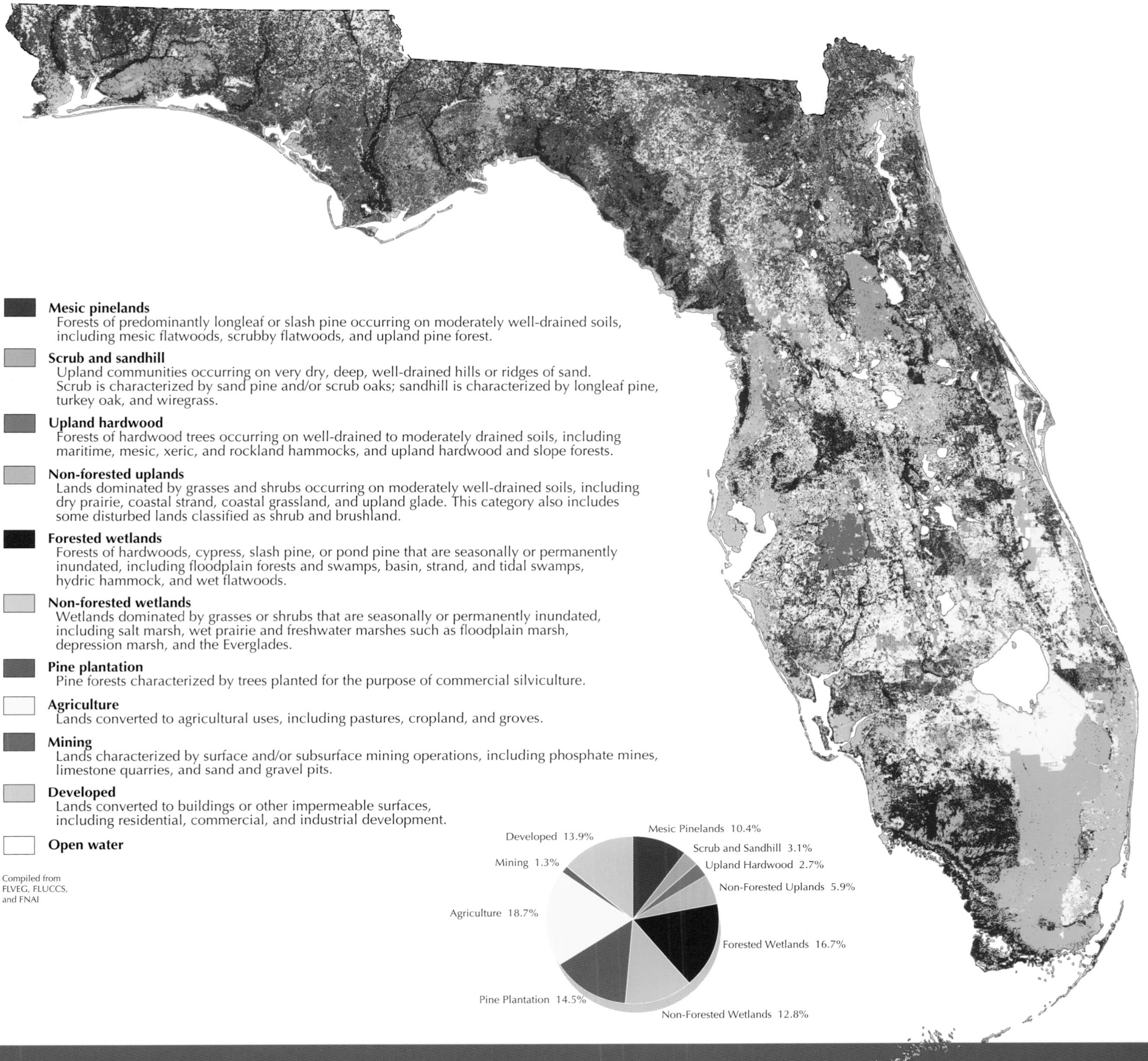

Mesic pinelands
Forests of predominantly longleaf or slash pine occurring on moderately well-drained soils, including mesic flatwoods, scrubby flatwoods, and upland pine forest.

Scrub and sandhill
Upland communities occurring on very dry, deep, well-drained hills or ridges of sand. Scrub is characterized by sand pine and/or scrub oaks; sandhill is characterized by longleaf pine, turkey oak, and wiregrass.

Upland hardwood
Forests of hardwood trees occurring on well-drained to moderately drained soils, including maritime, mesic, xeric, and rockland hammocks, and upland hardwood and slope forests.

Non-forested uplands
Lands dominated by grasses and shrubs occurring on moderately well-drained soils, including dry prairie, coastal strand, coastal grassland, and upland glade. This category also includes some disturbed lands classified as shrub and brushland.

Forested wetlands
Forests of hardwoods, cypress, slash pine, or pond pine that are seasonally or permanently inundated, including floodplain forests and swamps, basin, strand, and tidal swamps, hydric hammock, and wet flatwoods.

Non-forested wetlands
Wetlands dominated by grasses or shrubs that are seasonally or permanently inundated, including salt marsh, wet prairie and freshwater marshes such as floodplain marsh, depression marsh, and the Everglades.

Pine plantation
Pine forests characterized by trees planted for the purpose of commercial silviculture.

Agriculture
Lands converted to agricultural uses, including pastures, cropland, and groves.

Mining
Lands characterized by surface and/or subsurface mining operations, including phosphate mines, limestone quarries, and sand and gravel pits.

Developed
Lands converted to buildings or other impermeable surfaces, including residential, commercial, and industrial development.

Open water

Compiled from FLVEG, FLUCCS, and FNAI

Developed 13.9%
Mesic Pinelands 10.4%
Scrub and Sandhill 3.1%
Upland Hardwood 2.7%
Non-Forested Uplands 5.9%
Forested Wetlands 16.7%
Non-Forested Wetlands 12.8%
Pine Plantation 14.5%
Agriculture 18.7%
Mining 1.3%

FLUCCS

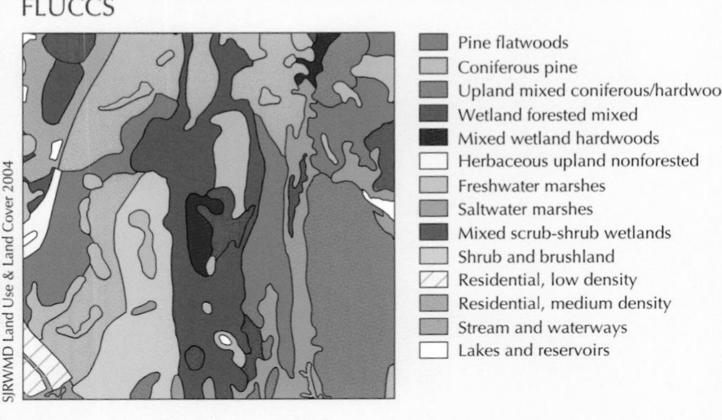

The FLUCCS is a hierarchical scheme that is classified at four levels with increasing specificity. Polygons are delineated based on aerial photography. Although the FLUCCS classification has fairly detailed categories for natural vegetation, the traditional emphasis has been on land use. Note the classification of medium-density residential versus low-density residential.

FNAI

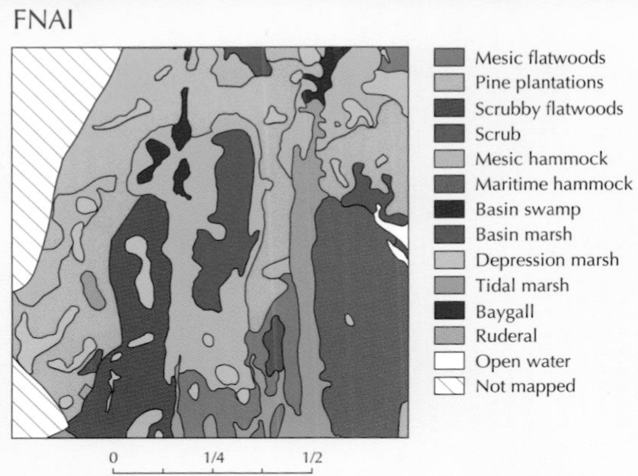

FNAI has developed natural community maps for about 2.5 million acres of state and federal conservation lands. Polygons are ground-truthed then delineated from aerial photography with a half-acre minimum mapping unit. Maps are based on the FNAI natural community classification, which identifies about 60 distinct terrestrial and freshwater types statewide.

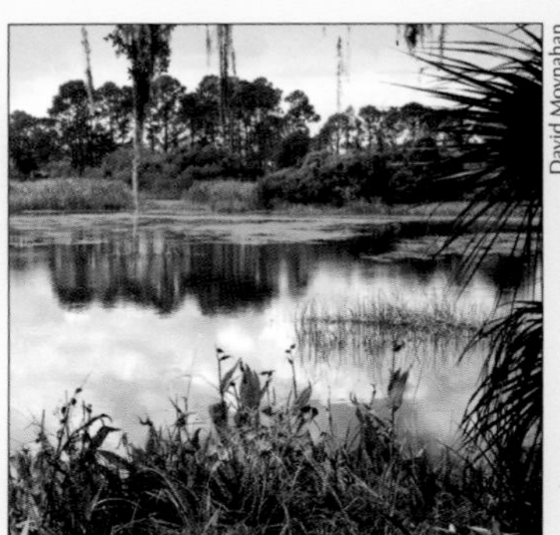

Basin marsh, Guana River WMA

Ground-truthing requires on-site visitation to verify the vegetation, land use, or natural community type at a given location. The payoff for this intensive effort is increased data accuracy.

Biogeography

Plant and animal species are unevenly distributed geographically, both on a worldwide scale and in Florida. Some places naturally support more species than others. The reasons why living things are distributed the way they are involve a complex, interrelated combination of factors, both past and present, including geological history, climate, topography, soils, oceanic currents, and the ways the species themselves have evolved to adapt to their changing surroundings. The science concerning the geographic distribution of plants and animals is called "biogeography."

Contemporary biogeography evaluates the habitat preferences of species using current climatic, geological, geographic, and cultural factors to explain plant and animal distributions. Historical biogeography relates species distributions to past geologic and climatic events. In many instances, both past and present environmental factors dictate species distributions. These factors help explain why Florida is a biodiversity hotspot in the United States, and why some regions within Florida naturally support more species than others.

Museum of Florida History

An extensive fossil record that includes American mastodons (*Mammut americanum*) offers corroborating evidence of a cooler Florida in millenia past. These tusked browsers once inhabited cold, spruce woodlands, a forest community that today exists in northern temperate and boreal areas of North America.

Panhandle disjuncts

NE FL disjuncts

Apalachicola Embayment and Arcto-Tertiary Relicts

Lake Wales Ridge endemics

South Florida and Keys endemics and West Indies affinities

Biogeography in Florida: Case Studies

Disjunct Populations

In North Florida several species, including the bluenose shiner (*Pteronotropis welaka*), frosted flatwoods salamander (*Ambystoma cingulatum*), and ciliate-leaf tickseed (*Coreopsis integrifolia*), are each present in the western Florida panhandle, absent in the middle panhandle even though suitable habitat exists, and then present in northeast Florida. Geological events such as fluctuating sea levels are thought to have influenced the species' current distributions.

Apalachicola

The plant genus *Torreya*, once widespread across the northern hemisphere, is now found only in isolated pockets in California, China, Japan, and the ravine forests of the upper Apalachicola. Florida torreya (*Torreya taxifolia*) is an ancient relict species that found refuge in the ravines of the Apalachicola basin millions of years ago and has persisted there ever since. More recently (21,000-18,000 years ago) plants and animals migrated south ahead of continental glaciers. Many species with northern affinities, such as baneberry (*Actaea pachypoda*) and copperhead (*Agkistrodon contortrix*), are found today at their southernmost extent in the Apalachicola ravines. Flatwoods, wet prairies, and cypress wetlands of the lower Apalachicola River support a high concentration of endemic species. Florida skullcap (*Scutellaria floridana*) and white birds-in-a-nest (*Macbridea alba*) are among the many species associated with the Apalachicola Embayment, an area flooded by shallow marine seas some 125,000 years ago.

Lake Wales Ridge Endemics

The Lake Wales Ridge region is renowned for harboring a high number of endemic species. Over the past 5 million years this region was periodically isolated from continental North America when much of Florida was submerged during long interglacial periods. The long geographical and habitat isolation of these islands led to the development of new species, such as the recently discovered Auburndale scrub scarab (*Polyphylla starkae*), that were no longer able to interbreed with their continental counterparts.

South Florida

South Florida harbors a unique flora and fauna primarily due to contemporary ecological factors, rather than past geological events. Its subtropical latitude, unique soil/rock substrates, and proximity to the West Indies, with which it shares many species, has created a suite of species that are unique to this area of North America. The area has only been exposed since the Pleistocene Epoch (1.8 million to 10,000 years ago) and is therefore only relatively recently available for colonization.

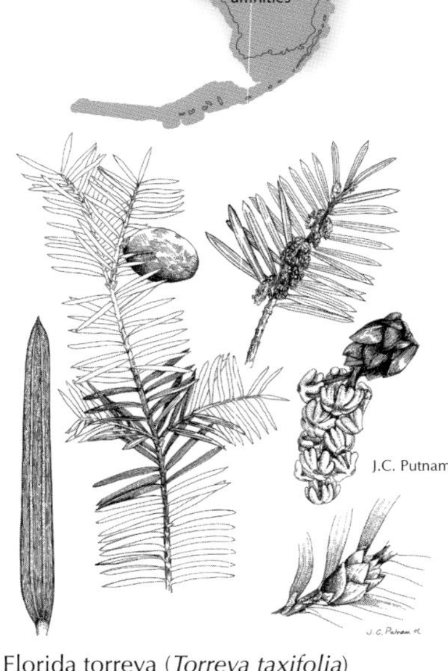
J.C. Putnam

Florida torreya (*Torreya taxifolia*)

Dave Almquist

Auburndale scrub scarab (*Polyphylla starkae*)

The Drifting Continents

The continents were not always in their current positions. Over the past 450 million years the large plates on which these enormous land masses rest have been reconfigured numerous times. Approximately 237 mya there was a single continent called "Pangaea" surrounded by a vast ocean, Panthalassa. This land mass separated and collided multiple times along plate boundaries forming mountains and volcanoes and moving through the ocean until the continents reached their current positions. Life on the continents was also affected by these drastic relocations, and these geological events can explain some species distributions today such as that of the Florida torreya (*Torreya taxifolia*), a species with close relatives in California and China. Geological evidence has shown that Florida was, in fact, once connected to what is now Africa. The continents are still shifting very slowly and are expected to once again become a single land mass in the next 250 million years.

↓ Approximate location of Florida

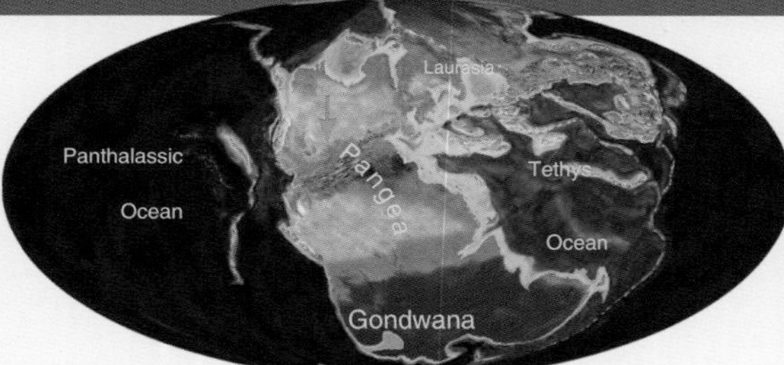

Early Triassic Period, 237 mya

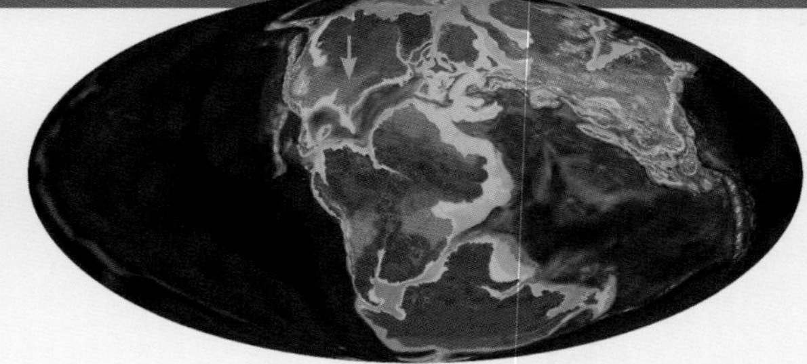

Early Jurassic Period, 195 mya – dinosaurs and early mammals present

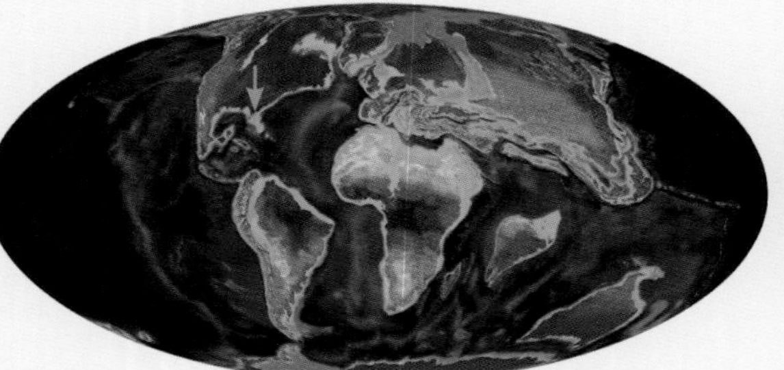

Late Cretaceous Period, 94 mya

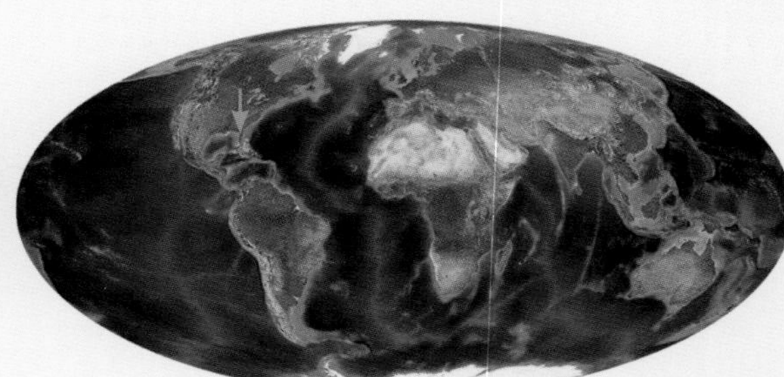

Present Day

Illustrations: Ronald C. Blakey, Professor Emeritus of Geology, Northern Arizona University

Florida's Changing Coastline

Sea level changes caused by fluctuating glaciers in the north have alternately submerged and exposed large areas of land in Florida, including portions of the continental shelf. Deep sandy soils, remnant ancient shorelines, geological deposits, fossils, and current species distributions are all the evidence that remains. During the coldest period, when the ice sheets extended the farthest south, the continental shelf was exposed to a depth of 120 meters (394 feet) below the present sea level. During the warmest period, when the glaciers had receded to their minimum level, any land in Florida below 35 meters (115 feet) above the current sea level would have been submerged by the sea. The remaining elevated portions of the Florida peninsula became small islands during this period and provided refuge for plants and animals. The isolation of these islands facilitated the development of new species. As the climate continues to change, these faraway glaciers are still influencing sea level and, inevitably, the coastline of Florida today and in the future.

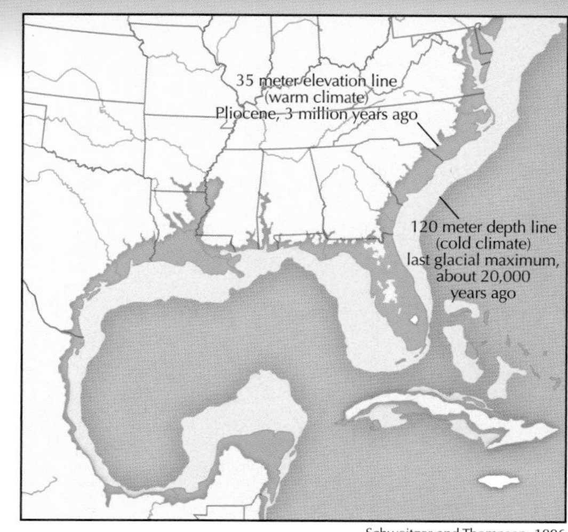

Schweitzer and Thompson, 1996

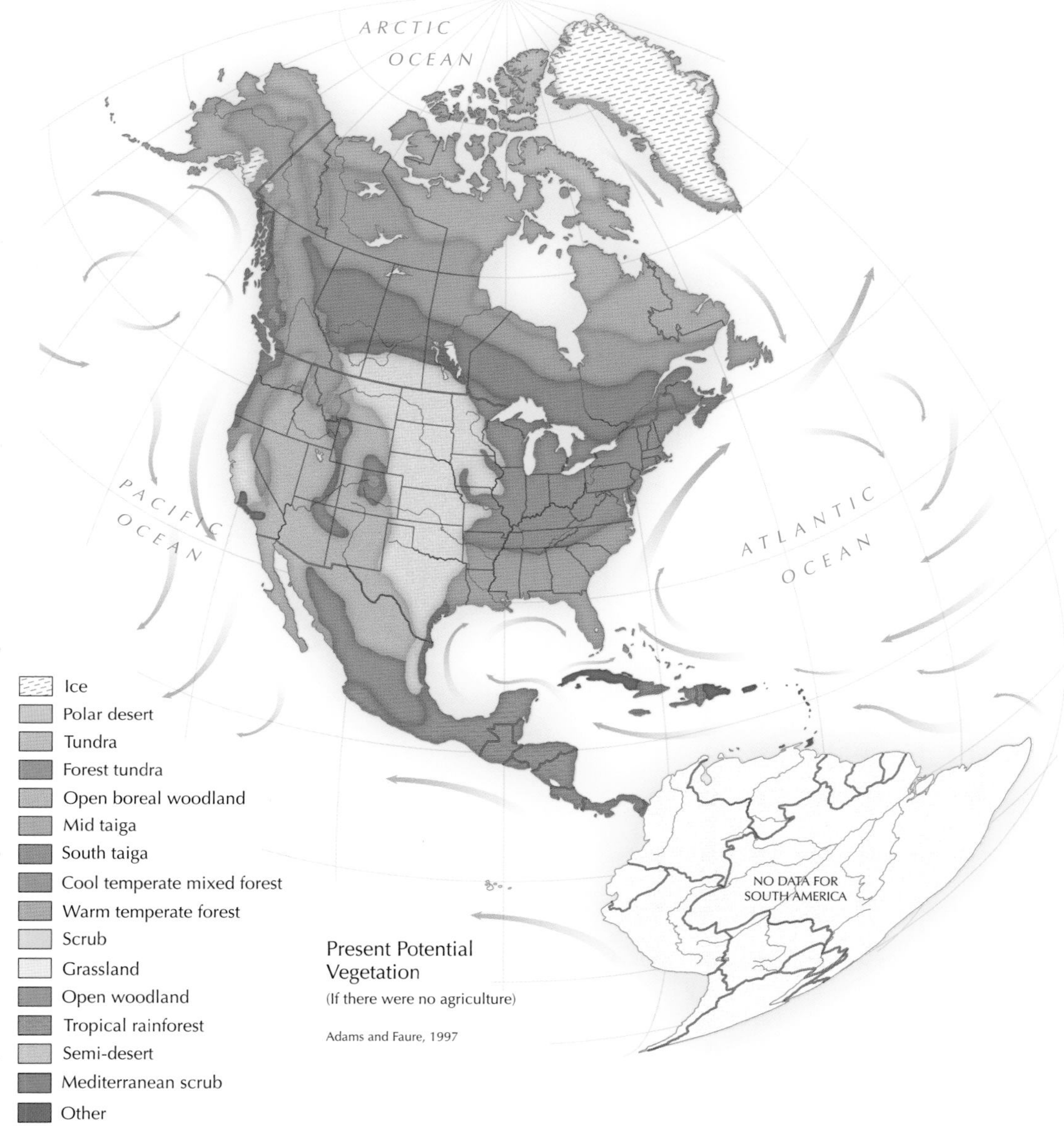

Present Potential Vegetation
(If there were no agriculture)

Adams and Faure, 1997

Florida's Vegetation and the Last Glacial Maximum—Past to Present

As glaciers advanced and receded over the past three million years, vegetation patterns throughout North America have also changed. Until approximately 4,500 years ago, environmental conditions such as climate, carbon dioxide levels, sea level, and sea surface temperatures were very different from today. During the Last Glacial Maximum (18,000 years ago) a sheet of ice several hundred meters thick covered most of Canada and extended as far south as the Missouri and Ohio rivers.

Remnants of the vegetation patterns from this period of glaciation have persisted. Some species now have more limited, or more expanded, ranges while other species have disappeared completely. As the northern glaciers advanced, Florida's climate became much cooler and drier. Scientific evidence indicates that when the glaciers were at their peak the Florida peninsula was dominated by a desert of shifting dunes or sparse scrub vegetation and northern Florida was forested with open woodland.

The panhandle was a mixture of xeric pine forests and, along fire-protected river valleys, mesic mixed conifer and deciduous tree forests that are similar to the Appalachian region today. As glaciers receded over the next 13,000 years, the climate became warmer and more humid, facilitating the expansion of warm temperate forests into the Florida peninsula and the expansion of subtropical species into South Florida. The warm Gulf Stream ocean current contributes to South Florida's subtropical climate.

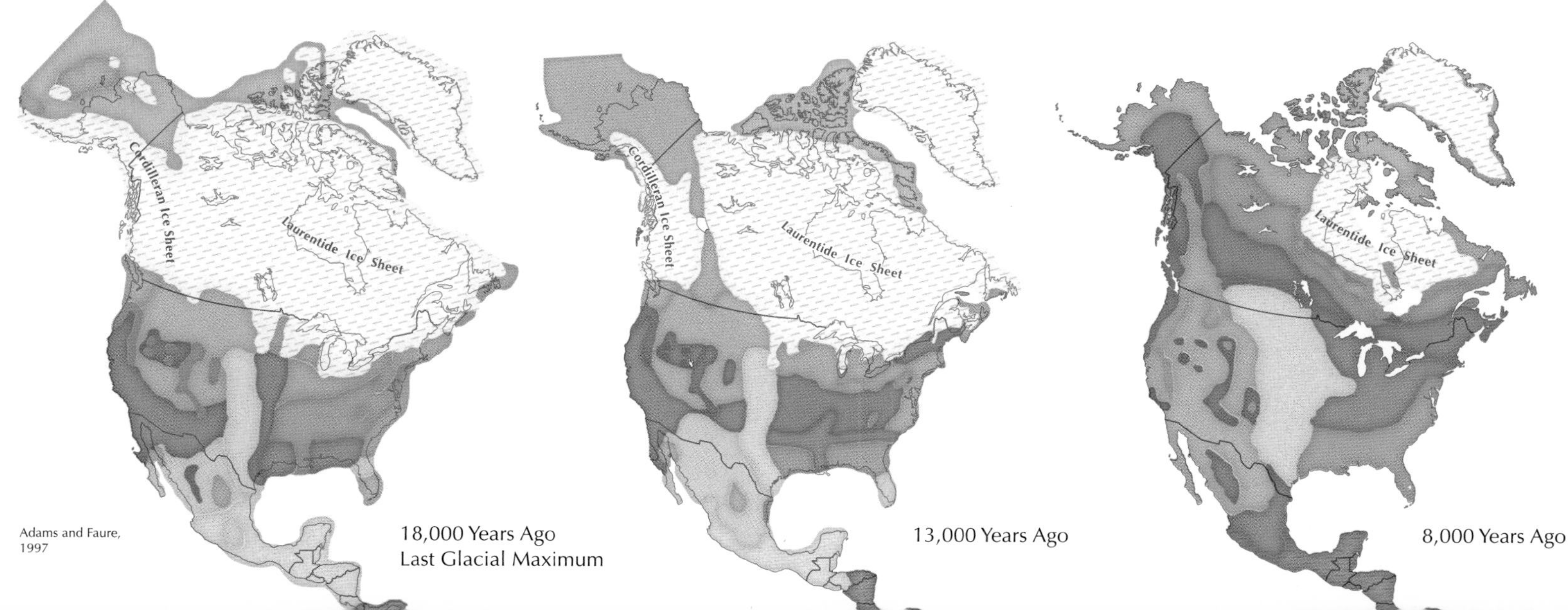

Adams and Faure, 1997

18,000 Years Ago
Last Glacial Maximum

13,000 Years Ago

8,000 Years Ago

"When you have seen one ant, one bird,
one tree, you have not seen them all."
– E. O. Wilson

II ELEMENTS OF BIODIVERSITY

Biodiversity is all living things. The fundamental elements of biodiversity are the myriad plants, animals, fungi, and microorganisms that share this world with us. Because individual species do not exist in isolation, but coexist with and are dependent on each other, the concept of biodiversity also incorporates natural communities—distinct and recurring assemblages of plants and animals that are naturally associated with each other and their physical environment. This section summarizes the species and communities that are common and characteristic of Florida, as well as many rare, unique, and ecologically significant elements of Florida's biodiversity.

Horseshoe crab (*Limulus polyphemus*), salt marsh, Mashes Sands Park
David Moynahan

Natural Communities: Overview

A natural community is a distinct, recurring assemblage of plants, animals, fungi, and microorganisms generally associated with certain physical conditions on the landscape. Ordinary English words for describing portions of a natural landscape—"forest," "woods," "meadow," "marsh," "thicket," and "swamp"—differentiate plant groupings by easily observed differences in their structure (for example, trees, shrubs, or grasses and other herbs) and by whether the soil is wet or dry. Some common terms, such as "piney woods" or "oak hammock" are derived from the most prominent plant species.

In developing comprehensive or formal classifications of natural communities, biologists focus on the same features: structure (tree, shrub, and herb layers), occurrence in wet or dry areas, and species composition. Classifications of Florida communities share many of the same categories but vary in detail because of different purposes for which they were developed. "Land use" or "land cover" classifications are designed primarily for statewide mapping and include broad categories that can be distinguished by eye on aerial photography or by different colors on infrared satellite imagery. Examples of land use or land cover classifications include Florida Department of Transportation's Florida Land Use, Cover, and Forms Classification System (FLUCCS) and Florida Fish and Wildlife Conservation Commission's statewide Vegetation and Land Cover map.

Classification systems designed for conservation strive to encompass all natural communities regardless of whether they can be distinguished on aerial photography or satellite imagery. The 2010 FNAI classification, published in conjunction with the Florida Department of Environmental Protection as the *Guide to the Natural Communities of Florida* and used in this atlas, delineates 81 natural communities. Both physical features (upland or wetland and substrate type) and biological features (tree/shrub/herb structure and species composition) are used to distinguish the 81 communities. The level of detail in the FNAI system is useful for fine-scale mapping (with ground-truthing) and for developing management plans.

At its highest level the FNAI classification groups natural communities based on hydrology, landscape position, and dominant species into twelve categories: five upland, three wetland, three aquatic, and one subterranean. Upland categories are hardwood forested uplands, high pine and scrub, pine flatwoods and dry prairie, coastal uplands, and sinkholes and outcrops. Wetland categories include freshwater non-forested wetlands, freshwater forested wetlands, and marine (intertidal) vegetated wetlands. Aquatic categories are ponds and lakes (lacustrine), rivers and streams (riverine), and marine/estuarine. The subterranean category includes two natural communities (aquatic and terrestrial caves).

A natural community in the FNAI system, for instance, "salt marsh," can include a number of zones dominated by different plant species, such as black needlerush (*Juncus roemerianus*), saltmarsh cordgrass (*Spartina alterniflora*), and perennial glasswort (*Sarcocornia perennis*), in different parts of the overall landscape under tidal influence. These finer-scale units, or plant communities, based on dominant plant species, are treated in the U.S. National Vegetation Classification (USNVC), developed by The Nature Conservancy and now maintained and updated by NatureServe. This classification system currently recognizes over 350 plant communities (termed "associations") in Florida.

Indicator Species

Nonbotanists can most easily identify natural communities if there is a clear structural difference between them or if there is a difference in principal species. Where the structure and principal species are similar, a few key indicator species may be useful for distinguishing communities. For example, both scrub and coastal strand may occur close to the coast and both may be dominated by dense stands of evergreen shrubs. Myrtle oak (*Quercus myrtifolia*), however, is an indicator species found in scrub but not in coastal strand, whereas tough buckthorn (*Sideroxylon tenax*) is an indicator species found in coastal strand but not in scrub. Indicator species are also used in the field to delineate the legal boundaries of wetlands.

Gary Schultz

Coastal scrub

Ann F. Johnson

Myrtle oak (*Quercus myrtifolia*)

Kim Gulledge

Coastal strand

Kim Gulledge

Tough buckthorn (*Sideroxylon tenax*)

Five basic factors account for differences in natural communities: climate, topography, parent material, flora and fauna, and time available for the community to develop. At any given site, climate and available flora and fauna are generally the same, so the most likely factor affecting natural community distribution is topography and its effects on drainage. If two different communities occupy the same elevation on a site, then either parent material or time for development may account for the difference.

Independent Variable	Example of Factors Affecting Plant Communities	Examples of Ecological Responses	Resulting Community
Topography	Slight rise in elevation →	Rainwater runs off or through substrate more quickly →	Pine flatwoods
	Slight drop in elevation →	Rainwater collects in closed basins →	Depression marsh
Climate	Subtropical →	Plant species intolerant of freezing weather thrive →	Mangrove swamp and salt marsh
	Temperate →	Plant species tolerant of cold survive →	Salt marsh only
Parent material (soils & geology)	Calcareous Miocene loamy soils →	Soils hold relatively greater moisture, are more fertile →	Slope forest
	Acidic Quaternary sandy soils →	Soils are relatively well drained, are less fertile →	Sandhill
Organisms	Invasive Australian pine seeds present →	Australian pine out-competes native species →	Australian pine monoculture
	Invasive Australian pine seeds absent →	Native species thrive with no competition →	Diverse maritime hammock
Time	Few years since last fire →	Woody shrubs with open sandy areas →	Oak scrub
	Decades since last fire →	Woody species form closed canopy →	Xeric hammock

Major, 1951

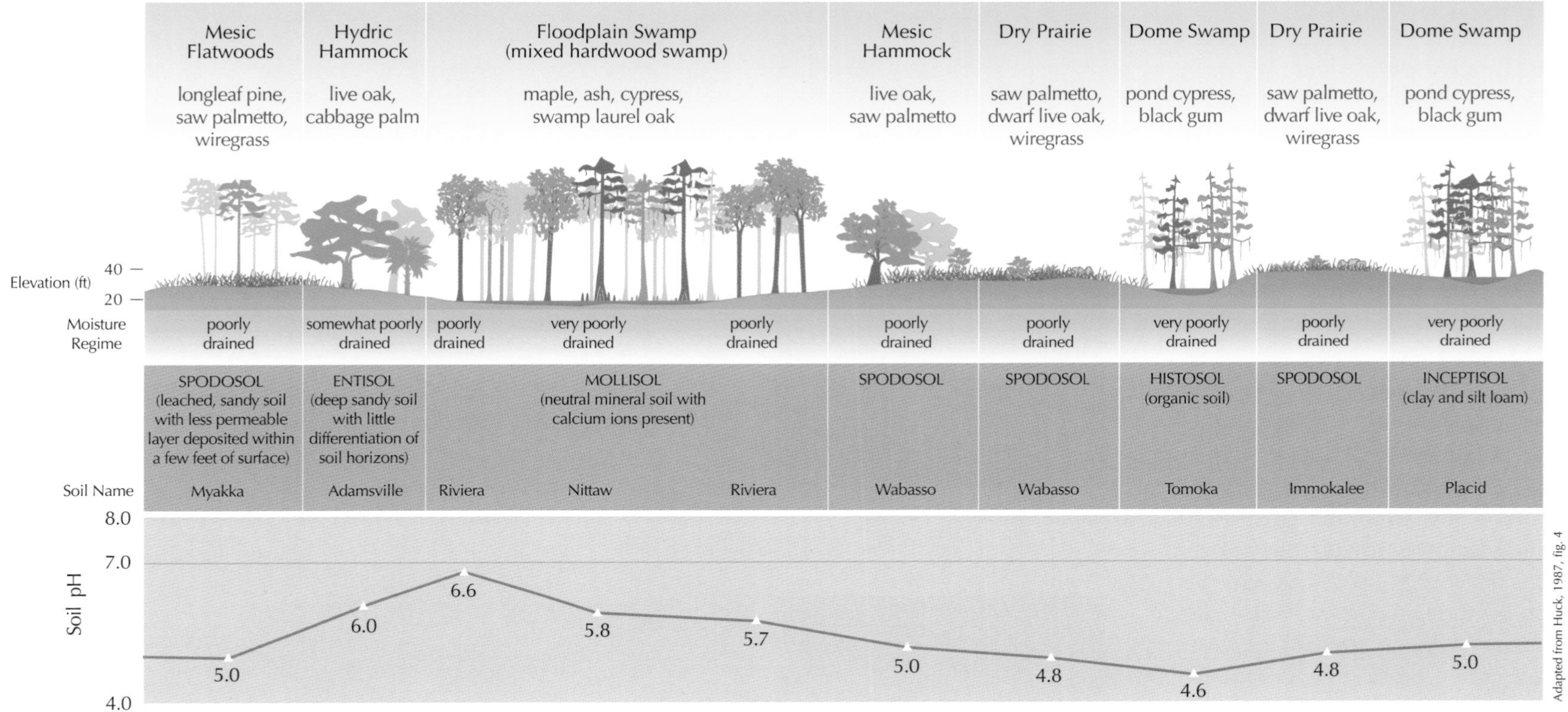

Profiles illustrate natural community distribution in relation to physical factors of the environment. In this example, elevation, soil type, and soil acidity (pH) are shown in relation to the distribution of communities along a transect across Bull Creek in eastern Osceola County. In this low, flat landscape, dry prairie and mesic flatwoods occupy the slightly higher areas. At the lowest elevations, two dramatically different swamp communities are found: an 80-foot-tall mixed hardwood-cypress-cabbage palm floodplain forest along Bull Creek and 30-foot-tall cypress dome swamps in isolated dry prairie depressions.

The Important Role of Fire

The importance of fire in maintaining natural communities became apparent after fire exclusion became widespread in the 1950s. These two photos from Archbold Biological Station in Highlands County were taken at the same location, one in 1929, the other in 1984 (same tree on right is marked with an arrow in both photos). In 55 years without fire, this site changed from an open sandhill community of scattered pines and small oaks with a wiregrass ground cover to a dense woody scrub community with a thick understory of tall evergreen oaks. Reintroducing fire in a controlled way to restore and to maintain natural communities is a central concern for land managers in Florida today.

Alexander Blair

1929

R.L. Myers

1984

Landscapes

Florida ecosystems encompass a complex network of intergrading natural communities, recurring groups of plants and animals that are associated with particular physical factors, such as soil type, rainfall, and climate. Understanding how these communities fit together within the broader landscape is often as important as understanding the individual communities themselves. For example, types and arrangement of natural communities in a given area can often be predicted by the local physical geography, or physiography. In spite of its limited range of elevation, Florida's physiography produces unique mosaics of natural communities in different areas of the state.

Where natural communities meet, ecotones are formed. The term "ecotone" describes the transition from one type of vegetation to another and reflects a physical transition in the environment. Ecotones may exist as a sharp, easily distinguished line where species composition changes radically across a short distance but are more often a broad area where species from the two interfacing communities find suitable habitat. Some plants exploit the specific conditions found on certain ecotones. The rare Panhandle lily (*Lilium iridollae*) typically grows in seepage area ecotones where woody vegetation starts to gain dominance but where sunlight from the open herbaceous seepage slope is still plentiful. Ecotones are also important for many animals, allowing them to utilize two communities within a short distance.

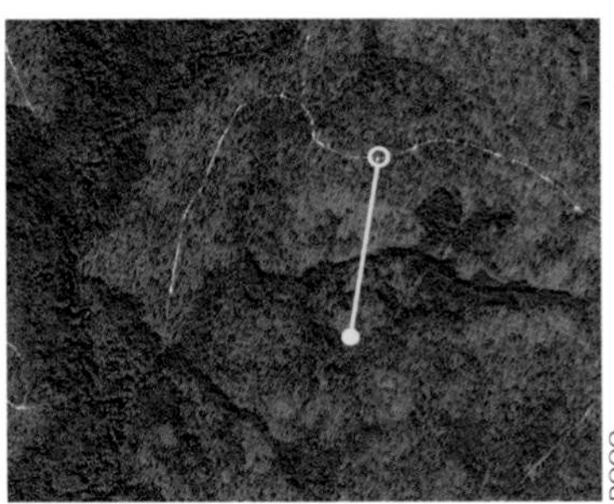

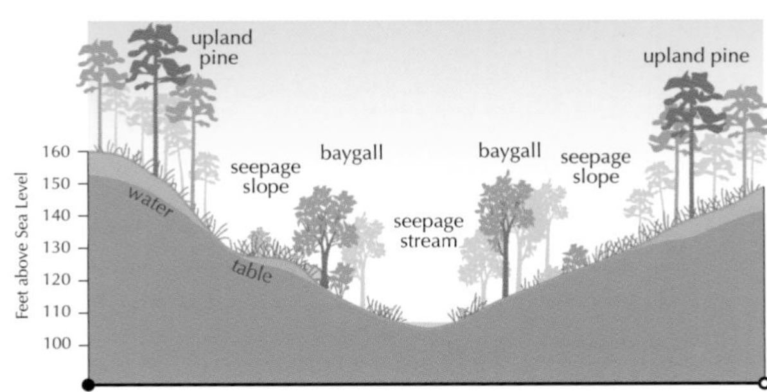

Blackwater River State Forest – Numerous small streams dissect rolling hills in Florida's western highlands, creating a pattern of high upland pine or sandhill communities that grade downhill into seepage communities as the soil surface intersects the water table. These waters form the base flow in seepage streams that drain towards larger rivers.

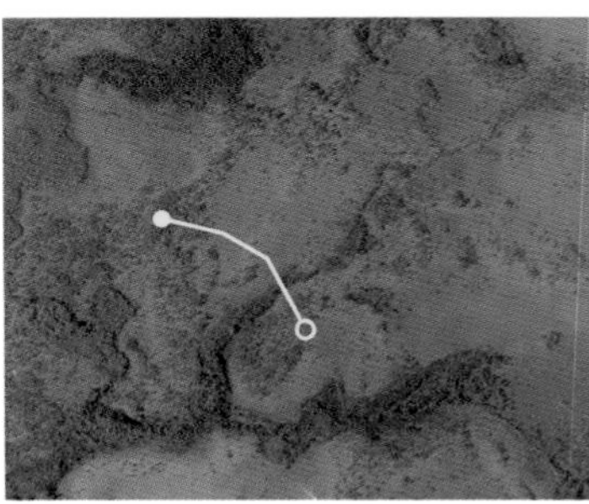

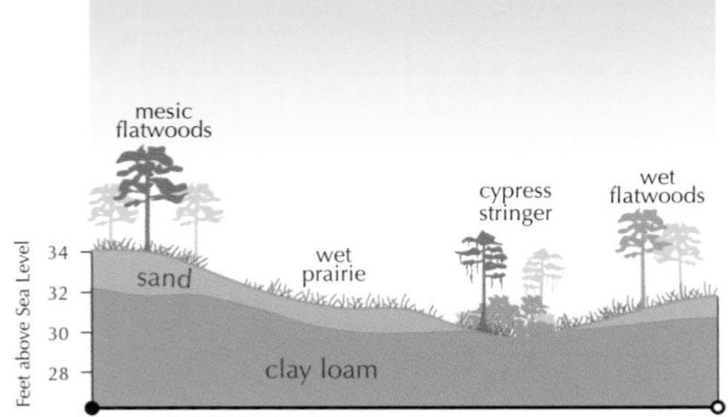

Apalachicola National Forest – The Gulf Coastal Lowlands is an area of relatively flat land dominated by pine flatwoods. Clayey subsoils in the region of the Apalachicola embayment trap water and create flat wet prairies that slowly drain via narrow cypress stringers.

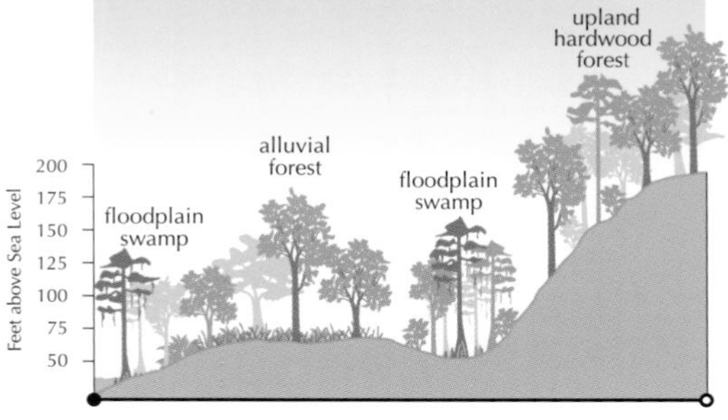

Torreya State Park – The upper reaches of the Apalachicola River—the largest in Florida in terms of flow—cuts sharply into the clay hills along its eastern bank and forms steep slope forests. The river's floodplain, more than one mile wide, alternates between alluvial forests on slightly higher ground and floodplain swamps on the most frequently flooded portions.

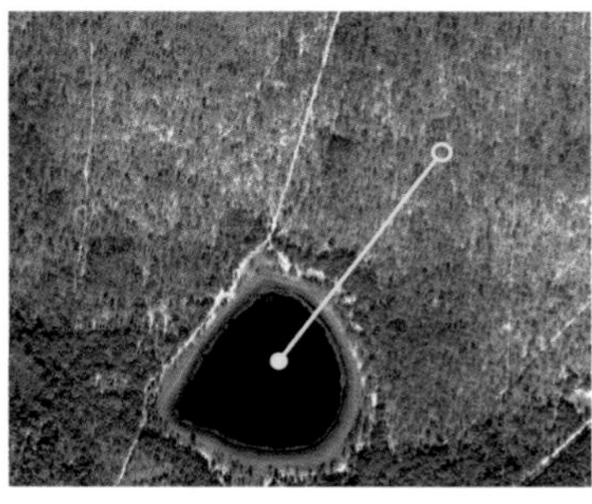

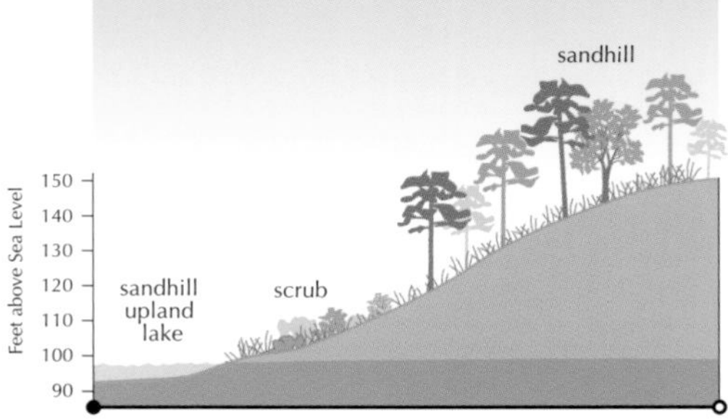

Ordway-Swisher Preserve – Xeric sandhills of the Central Lake District are riddled with ephemeral ponds called sandhill upland lakes. Although frequent, low-intensity fires are natural in this region, the lower slopes surrounding lakes and marshes are in natural fire shadows that do not burn as often, leading to the development of scrub communities around these lakes.

FWC

Elevation Makes a Difference

Despite the variation in physiography across the state, certain general patterns of vegetation continually repeat themselves, particularly in relation to elevation. Upland ridges and flats are usually dominated by pines in fire-maintained natural communities such as mesic flatwoods or upland pine. Slopes often form natural fire shadows that protect fire-intolerant hardwood trees, allowing the formation of mesic hammocks, upland hardwood forests, or similar communities. Wetlands—marshes or swamps—form in the lowest areas and are often associated with streams, rivers, or lakes.

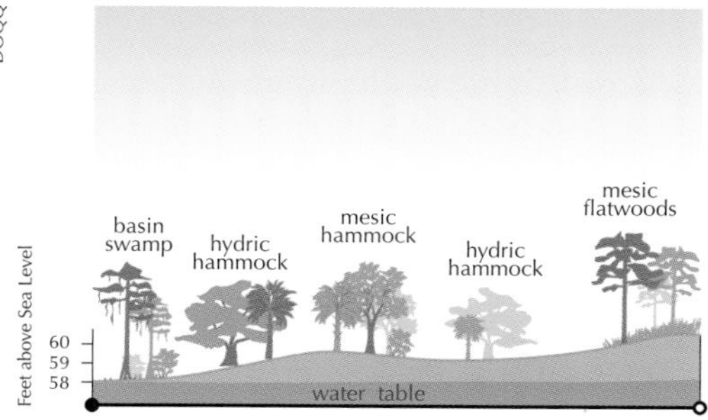

Cypress Creek Flood Detention Area – Calcareous soils within parts of the Gulf Coastal Lowlands create conditions that are conducive to the formation of hydric hammocks. These cabbage palm and oak dominated hammocks are interspersed with fire-protected mesic hammocks that occupy slight rises.

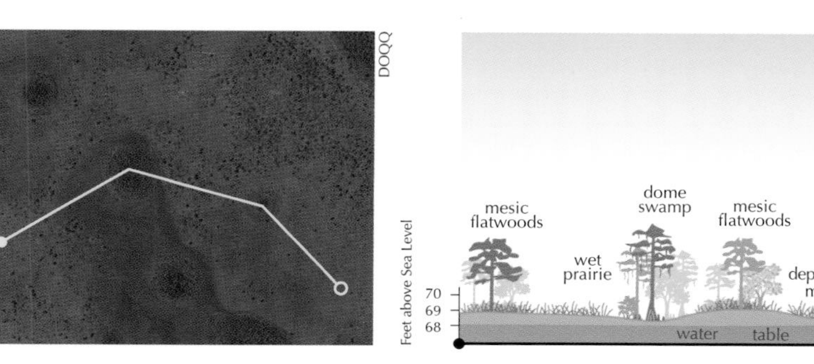
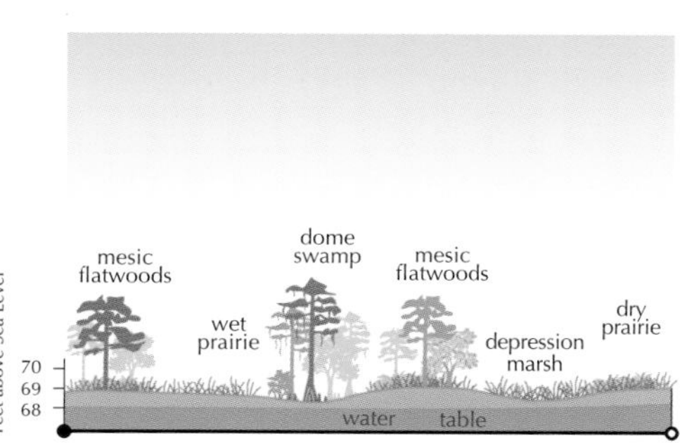

Three Lakes Wildlife Management Area – During periods of heavy rainfall, water flows in sheets across the flat DeSoto and Osceola plains and low-relief, broad, marshy drainage ways. These conditions produce a pattern of dry prairies and mesic flatwoods that intergrade almost imperceptibly with swaths of slightly lower wet prairie. Depression marshes and dome swamps occupy isolated bowl-shaped depressions where water stands for much of the year.

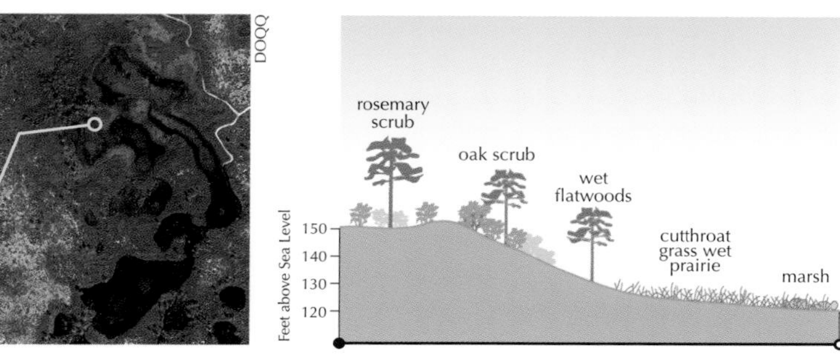

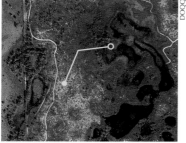

Archbold Biological Station – High ancient sand dunes form the Lake Wales Ridge, a four- to ten-mile-wide band that stretches for 100 miles down the middle of the central peninsula. Sandhill and scrub communities occupy the deep, xeric sands, while marshes are common in isolated, often linear depressions. Groundwater seepage from the surrounding high pine and scrub is conducive for the formation of rare cutthroat grass (*Panicum abscissum*) seeps.

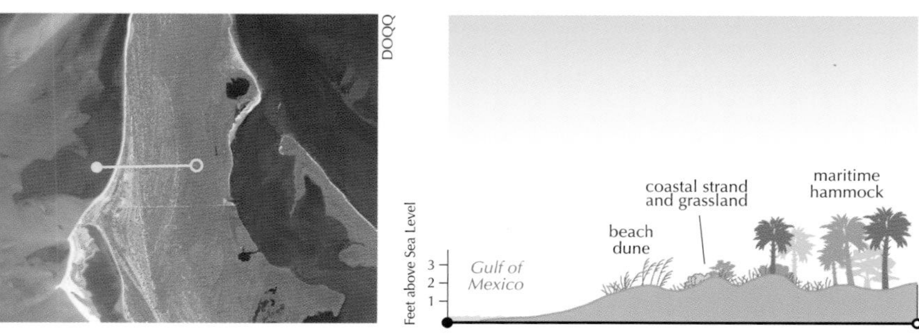

Cayo Costa Island – Barrier islands are young, dynamic systems that are rapidly formed and eroded by coastal processes. These plant communities often follow a predictable pattern of pioneer vegetation on the foredune nearest the sea, followed by more stable grasslands that grade to progressively woodier vegetation. This buffer of evergreen shrubs and small trees helps to shield inland areas from damaging salt spray.

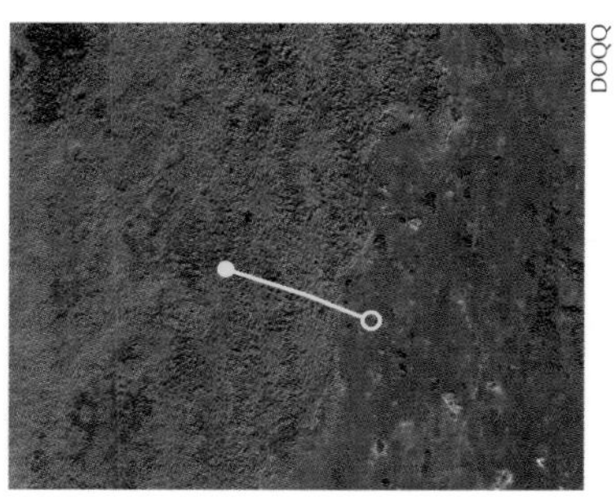

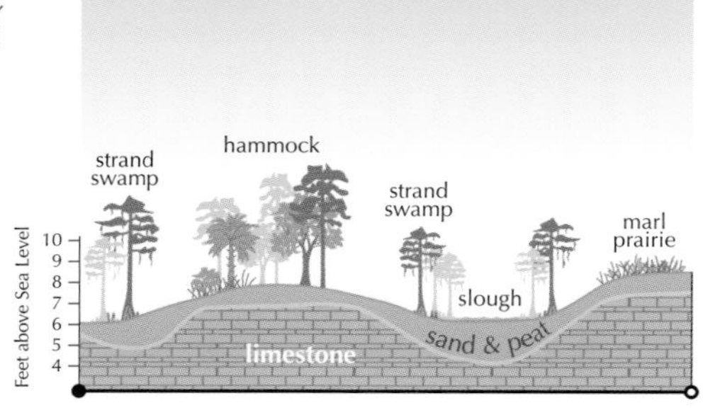

Big Cypress National Preserve – In South Florida, marl soil, or calcitic mud, is constantly being deposited in wetlands where surface water is high in calcium carbonate from the dissolution of shallow underlying limestone. In the Big Cypress, strand swamps and sloughs within linear limestone troughs are situated in a northeast to southwest pattern through marl prairies with stunted cypress trees.

Everglades National Park – Pine rocklands form on exposed limestone of the southern Atlantic Coastal Ridge and are interspersed with rockland hammocks, shaded forests with an accumulated soil layer of partially decomposed leaves that may build the community up to a slightly higher elevation.

Large Extent Uplands

Five natural communities, mesic pine flatwoods, dry prairie, upland pine forest, sandhill, and upland hardwood forest, constitute the most common upland vegetation types found in presettlement Florida, as well as the most frequent and familiar natural upland landscapes on remaining conservation lands today. The term "upland" generally describes land where the soil is dry and flooding is rare. In much of the panhandle and along central peninsular ridges, uplands are on rolling hills where rainwater drains quickly. The flatlands of much of the peninsula also contain uplands, although these are areas where only a few feet of elevation can mean the difference between a flooded wetland and a normally dry upland. Predictably, these uplands vary considerably in regards to specific hydrology, soil conditions, and fire frequency, factors which, in turn, influence vegetation structure and species composition.

It is often useful to consider the spatial scale and pattern of a natural community. Large extent uplands normally occupied vast unbroken tracts of land prior to human settlement. Upland hardwood forests created mainly linear or large patches in areas of rich soil or in landscape positions that were naturally fire protected, often lining the ecotone between pine-dominated systems and frequently flooded bottomlands. Fire-maintained upland communities, mainly mesic flatwoods, dry prairie, upland pine, and sandhill, once formed huge expanses of vegetation, creating a matrix in which smaller patches of marsh, swamp, and scrub were embedded.

Mesic pine flatwoods, sandhill, and upland pine are all savanna-like woodlands with an open canopy of mainly longleaf pine (*Pinus palustris*), although other species, particularly slash (*Pinus elliottii*) and loblolly (*Pinus taeda*) pines, are far more common today than in the historical landscape. Virtually all original stands of longleaf pine were removed by logging operations in the early 20th century and subsequent planting of slash pine has greatly increased this species in most upland communities. Longleaf pine, and slash pine to a lesser extent, is resistant to frequent low-intensity fires that naturally occur every few years or even annually. Repeated burning keeps the understory vegetation low and prevents hardwood trees from becoming overgrown.

A Mosaic of Habitats

Most of Osceola County is in the Eastern Flatwoods District, a physiographic region where level topography creates a landscape of open pine woodlands and treeless prairies dotted with small cypress swamps classified as dome swamps. The image is a 2004 true color aerial photograph of land within Three Lakes Wildlife Management Area. The green and light tan areas seen mostly on the right and left sides of the photo are uplands—either mesic flatwoods with tall pines clearly visible or dry prairie with virtually no trees.

These two upland communities form the matrix in which other communities, mainly wetlands, are embedded. Saw palmetto and evergreen runner oaks typical of the uplands remain green even during the winter months when this photograph was taken. In contrast, the grasses and cypress trees of the wetter areas are dormant during the coldest part of the year and appear grey on the image. This allows us to distinguish a network of slightly lower wet prairie that runs through the flatwoods and dry prairie. Not only is the color different, but the apparent texture is much smoother due to the lack of shrubs in wet prairie.

Within this network, small depressions allow the formation of dome swamps, isolated wetland forests of cypress that are typically round. In the absence of artificial firebreaks, such as the small roads seen in this photograph, lightning strikes would have been able to ignite and burn vast areas of this flat land unimpeded, since there are few streams or large forested wetlands to slow the spread of fire. Plants and animals of the uplands and grassy wetlands alike are adapted to these frequent fires that may have occurred yearly in some areas. The slightest topographic variation provides wildlife with a mosaic of habitats in which to breed, forage, roost, and shelter.

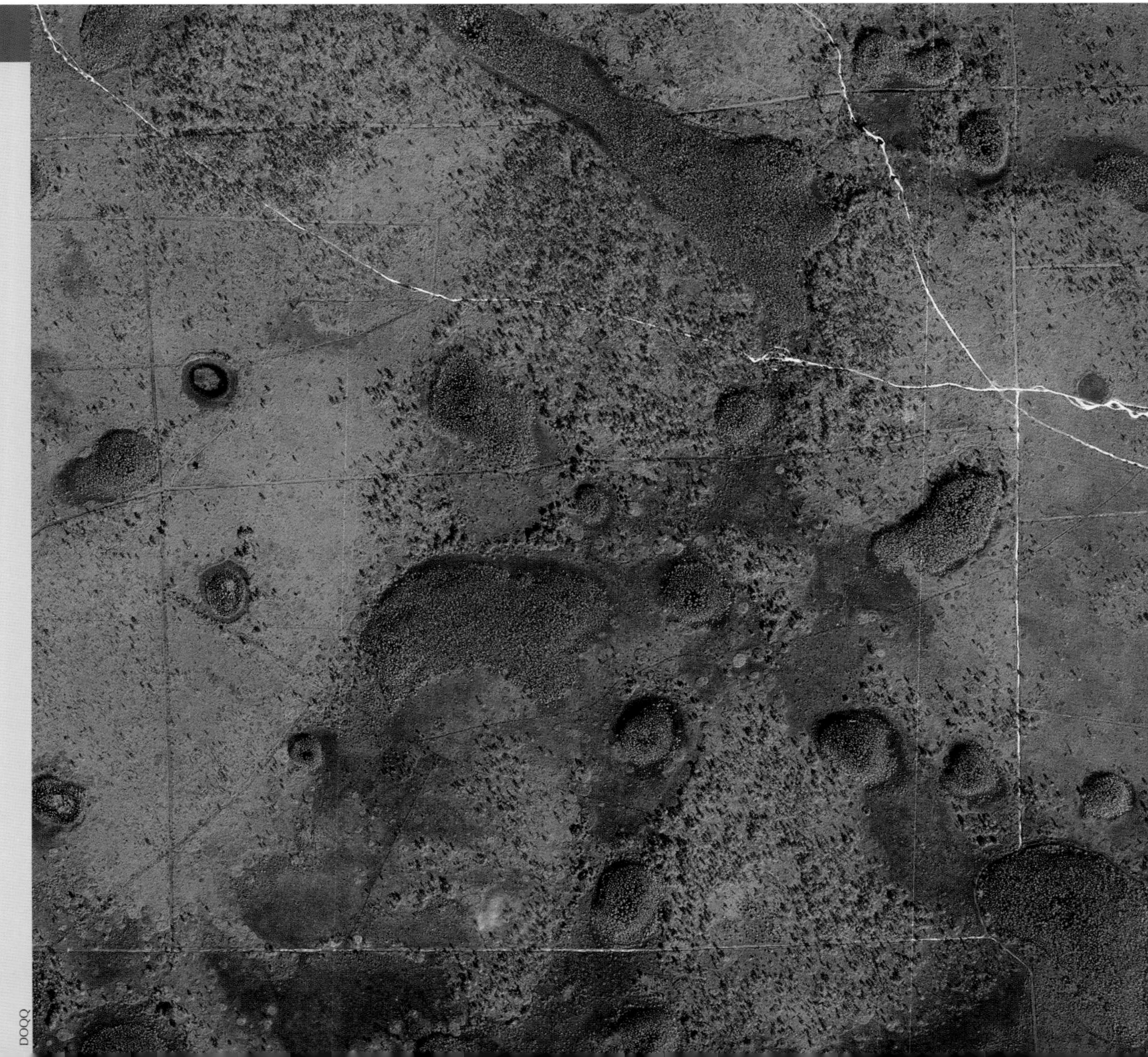
DOQQ

Amy M. Jenkins

Upland Pine Forest

Part of the historical high pine system that once stretched in a vast grassy sea across much of the southeastern United States, upland pine is a community of tall longleaf pines in a carpet of wiregrass and other grasses and herbs. Deciduous oaks are occasionally scattered in the understory, but are rarely dense, creating an inviting park-like landscape on rolling hills of clay and loamy soils in the panhandle and northern peninsula. As with other pinelands, upland pine depends on frequent low-intensity fires to maintain pine dominance and limit hardwood growth. Although soils are often sandy, high clay and loam content creates mesic conditions which support a richer understory than is generally found in sandhill communities. One square meter of land can support as many as 40-50 different species of herbs.

Gary Knight

Upland Hardwood Forest

Mesic forests of oak, hickory, magnolia, beech, and a diversity of other hardwood species were historically far less common in Florida than open pinelands. Yet these hardwood forests, often referred to collectively as hammocks, are important features of the environment, developing naturally where soils are richer and/or in areas protected from burning by topographic position. Fires burn more easily upslope than downslope, so areas that are intermediate in elevation between infrequently burned floodplains and frequently burned high pine communities will naturally receive fewer fires, allowing the establishment of hardwoods that are intolerant of burning. These species, in turn, affect the local conditions by increasing shade and humidity, thereby reducing the chance of fire spreading into the community. The result is a rich, cool, shady forest with a diverse canopy. Trees and herbs typical of Appalachian forests find refuge in these conditions, particularly in the steep slope forests of the upper Apalachicola River. In the peninsula, northern species gradually decrease, hardwood forests become more evergreen, and tropical species increase in the understory and canopy.

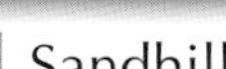

Gary Knight

Sandhill

The ancient dunes that form ridges and hills of deep sand in the peninsula and parts of the panhandle support a xeric high pine system dominated by longleaf pine and wiregrass. Turkey oak, a deciduous hardwood adapted to the dry soil conditions of sandhills, is a frequent understory component. However, its growth is restricted by frequent low-intensity ground fires that naturally occur every one to three years, maintaining the sandhill as an open grassy community. While similar to the upland pine community, sandhill is more prone to invasion by scrub oaks when fire has been removed from the system.

Ann F. Johnson

Dry Prairie

A unique habitat in the U.S., dry prairie landscapes form large flat expanses in the central to southwestern peninsula. Like pine flatwoods, these have a solid low-growing cover of wiregrass, saw palmetto, runner oak, and other shrubs and herbs, but the ubiquitous pines that dot most of Florida's uplands are conspicuously absent. Visitors to these prairies are greeted by a smooth, unbroken expanse of knee-high shrubs and grasses, glimpses of crested caracaras, and the buzzing insect-like songs of Florida grasshopper sparrows. Ecologists hypothesize that the treeless condition results from a combination of environmental factors that exist in areas of the central peninsula. The exceptionally flat topography, soils that impede drainage, and frequent fires, sometimes even occurring annually, create an environment in which pine seedlings are unable to establish.

Gary Knight

Pine Flatwoods

Throughout much of Florida, the scenery was historically dominated by flatlands with an open canopy of towering longleaf pine trees and a relatively short understory of saw palmetto and wiregrass, along with a wide diversity of other shrubs and sun-loving herbaceous plants. Soil moisture in pine flatwoods ranges from relatively wet to dry but most soils fall within the mesic range. The land may flood for short periods of time, only to be parched during the dry season. Flatwoods form the matrix community in much of Florida, the upland environment in which small basin wetlands and larger stream and floodplain systems are embedded. Together, these communities provide habitat for a myriad of plants and animals that depend on this environmental mosaic.

Large Extent Lowlands

Florida has a richly deserved reputation as a state full of grassy marshes and tall cypress swamps festooned with epiphytes. Freshwater wetlands cover between one-quarter to one-third of Florida, compared with only around 5% in the continental United States. These lands occupy low areas, usually where the water table is at or just below the surface. The frequently saturated or flooded conditions create special soil characteristics and promote the growth of plants that are specifically adapted to wet environments.

By the Acre

Natural communities occupying wetlands in Florida fall into several categories based on type of vegetation, flooding regime, soil characteristics, and other factors. Some communities, such as the various types of cypress swamps, are forested. Others, such as marshes and wet prairies, are dominated entirely by shrubs or herbs.

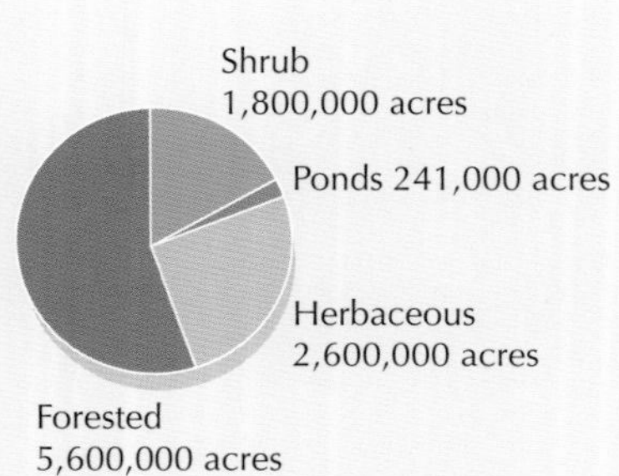

Frequency and type of flooding is highly variable across different types of wetlands. Many wetlands act as collection basins for local rainfall through surface-water runoff or seepage from adjacent uplands. An impermeable clay layer underlying many basins slows or prevents further downward movement of water into the soil, and these depressions are usually underwater during the rainy season. Floodplain wetlands are inundated as rivers overflow their banks on a yearly basis, but in near-coastal situations, tidal action creates a daily flooding pattern even in freshwater environments.

Development and modifications of wetlands are a serious threat in Florida, where total losses are estimated at around 50% since the 18th century. Further threats to wetlands quality include logging and pollution from agricultural runoff. Recent efforts to halt wetland destruction and restore these critical habitats are resulting in a slower rate of loss.

Healthy freshwater systems provide important habitat for fish and wildlife and create vibrant estuarine habitats downstream. Moreover, Floridians directly benefit from wetlands through increased water quality, flood protection, and recreational opportunities such as canoeing, bird watching, fishing, and hunting.

A Shifting Landscape

Alluvial rivers such as the Choctawhatchee are high-energy streams that carry large sediment loads of clay, sand, and silt, and exhibit strong seasonal flooding that supplies the floodplain with pulses of oxygenated water, delivering nutrients and sediments to the ecosystem. In terms of flow, the Choctawhatchee is the third largest river in the state. Like other high-energy rivers, its course is continually changing as it meanders within the active floodplain that is evident in this color infrared aerial photography.

These photographs are useful for easily distinguishing types of vegetation that show up as various shades of red, pink, and grayish-blue. The river is a bright blue, a color indicating high sediment loads in infrared photography (in contrast to the black appearance of the nearby clear-water upland lakes). Dark red areas on the left and right sides of the image indicate pine-dominated uplands or planted pine plantations, while the smooth light pink areas indicate agricultural fields. In the floodplain, the action of the river over many years has created a pattern of higher ridges and lower swales.

Although the landscape may appear to be flat, a topographic map created from LiDAR (Light Detection And Ranging) data reveals subtle elevation changes that allow a diversity of plant species to thrive, each adapted to specific conditions. The lower, more frequently flooded backswamps have mainly cypress and tupelos and appear gray or dark blue in the infrared photograph. Open water streams flow in the lowest channels, invisible underneath the tree canopy, distributing water across the floodplain. Higher ridges and riverside levees support hardwoods and some pines that are adapted for short seasonal flooding. Abandoned river channels called oxbows are clearly visible, and the river has recently cut a channel across a meander loop (indicated by an arrow).

Changes in the river and floodplain are even more apparent when compared with the same view of the floodplain in this 1949 photograph.

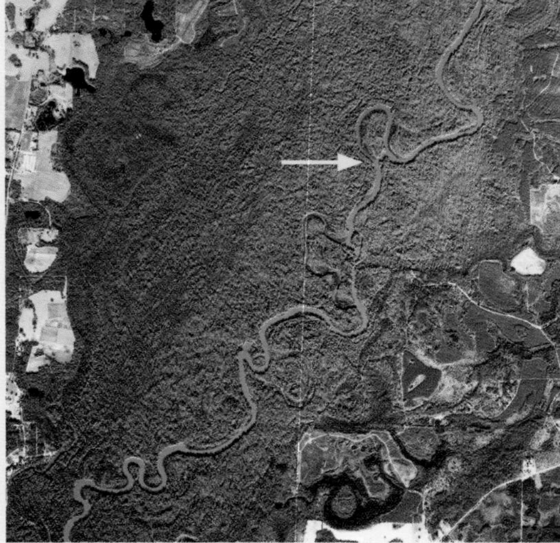

1999 color infrared

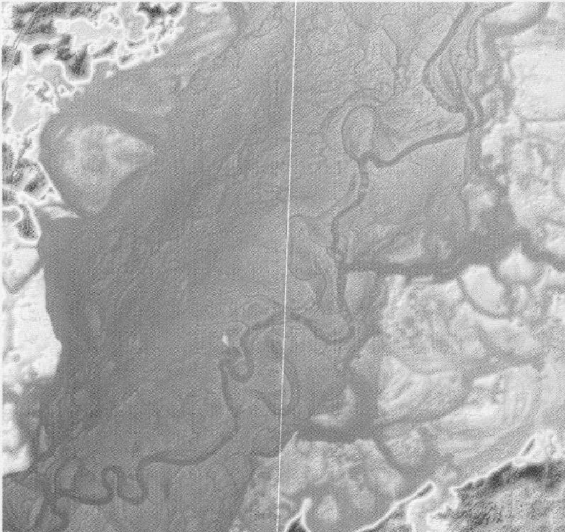

LiDAR elevation

1949

Bill Stinson

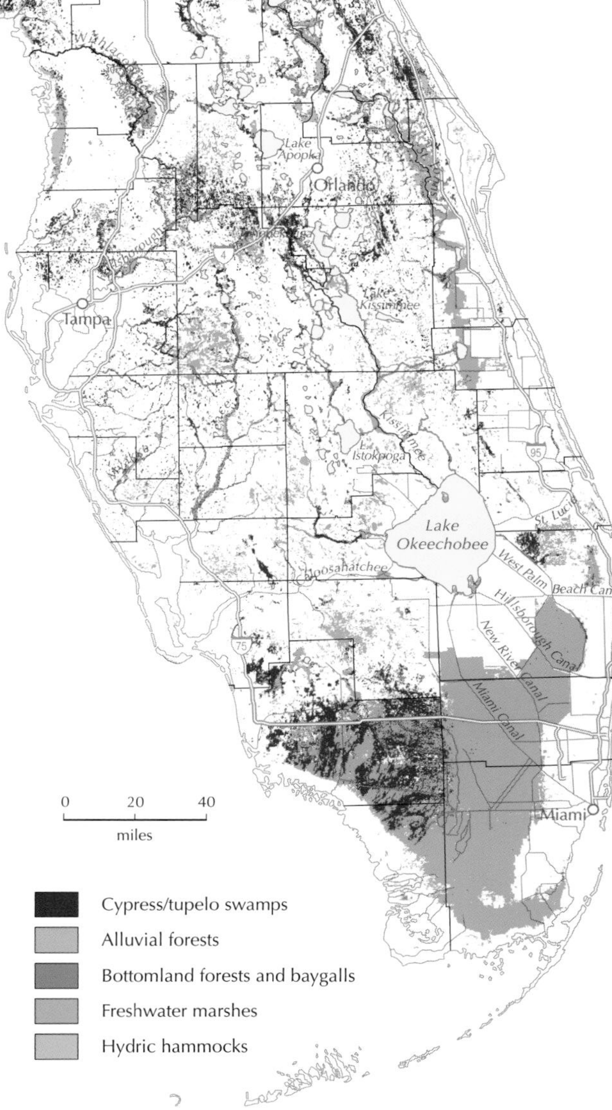

Gary Knight

Cypress/Tupelo Swamps

Stately cypress trees draped with gray Spanish moss are an iconic image of Florida's natural beauty and the dominant canopy species of swamps in the state. Swamps are the most frequently flooded wetland forests, and they can be categorized by a combination of landscape position, size, flooding pattern, fire frequency, and substrate. Swamps along rivers and streams are called floodplain swamps, while more isolated depressions are dome swamps or basin swamps, depending on size and fire frequency. In South Florida, strand swamps with cypress and hardwoods covered in epiphytic bromeliads and orchids occupy shallow channels in the underlying limestone. Fire is a natural event in most swamps that helps to limit hardwood growth and preserve a cypress canopy. Almost all swamps have been impacted by cypress logging, and large old-growth trees are now quite rare.

Dan Hipes

Freshwater Marshes and Prairies

From tiny depressions that dot pine flatwoods communities to endless vistas of sawgrass in the Everglades, marshes are a common feature of the Florida landscape. Although these herbaceous or shrubby wetlands are normally flooded, dry seasons offer the opportunity to explore marshes when only the deepest portions remain underwater. Patterns of vegetation reflect differing water depths, from grasses and sedges along the dry and intermediate zones to broadleaf emergents and cattails in deeper areas to floating plants in permanently flooded portions. Marshes are often referred to as "prairies." For example, Paynes Prairie in Alachua County is an enormous marsh in a former lake bed. The Florida Natural Areas Inventory, however, reserves the term "wet prairie" for wetlands with a shorter period of inundation that promotes dense growth of wiregrass, wiry beaksedges, and pitcherplants. Regular burning controls the overgrowth of shrubs in marshes and wet prairies. Varying hydrology, fire frequency, and soil types together create a diverse landscape that is critical for maintaining healthy populations of wading birds, game fish, and other wildlife.

Amy M. Jenkins

Alluvial Forests

Bottomland Forests and Baygalls

In river basins and along streams, shady forests of mainly deciduous trees grow on land of intermediate elevation between uplands and cypress swamps. Species in these habitats can withstand occasional floods—the water table is never far below the soil surface—but the ground underfoot is often dry enough to walk without difficulty. Bottomland forests are especially common along blackwater rivers. Larger alluvial rivers, like the Apalachicola, experience regular flooding during the early growing season, and trees must be able to withstand having submerged roots just as their leaves are emerging from winter dormancy. These communities are distinguished as alluvial forests, and they are prone to yearly disturbance from active floodplain dynamics as the fluctuating river deposits sediment, builds out point bars, and leaves behind old channels called "oxbows." Bottomland and alluvial forests are often found in a complex wetland mosaic with swamps, baygalls, and open water rivers and floodplain lakes.

Gary Knight

Hydric Hammocks

Evergreen forests of oaks, cabbage palms, and southern red cedar are encountered primarily in the Florida peninsula where the combination of a warmer climate and neutral soil conditions create a unique environment known as hydric hammock. The less acidic conditions are attributable to the presence of limestone near the surface or abundant shell content in the soil. Species that thrive in neutral to slightly alkaline soils, such as rattan vine, are often found in these hammocks. This community ranges from tiny pods of cabbage palms and oaks on shelly sand in the upper St. Johns river floodplain marshes to extensive forests in the Gulf Hammock region on the west coast of the peninsula where Eocene-aged limestone is frequently found exposed at the soil surface.

Kim Gulledge

White twinevine
Sarcostemma clausum

Scrub

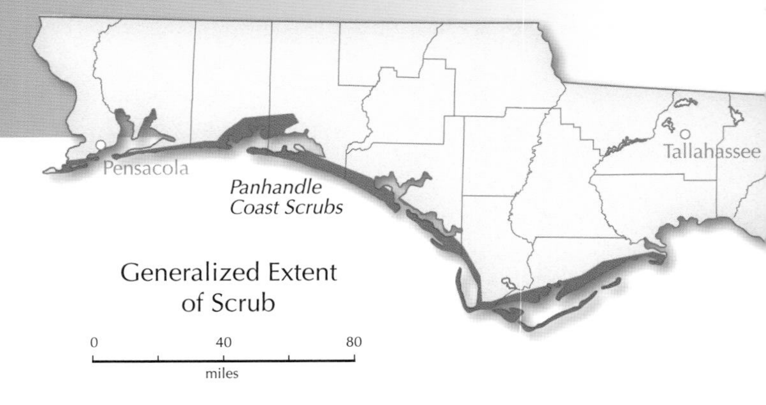

Scrub is a natural community consisting of a fairly dense, low stand of evergreen shrubs, with or without a pine canopy, and is found only in Florida and adjacent coastal Alabama and Mississippi. It occurs on dry, infertile, sandy ridges that were deposited as dunes or offshore bars, either at the current coast or inland when sea level was higher in Plio-Pleistocene time. The five signature scrub species found in scrubs throughout the state are: three species of shrubby oaks, myrtle oak (*Quercus myrtifolia*), sand live oak (*Quercus geminata*), and Chapman's oak (*Quercus chapmanii*); Florida rosemary (*Ceratiola ericoides*); and sand pine (*Pinus clausa*). The most common form of scrub is oak scrub, dominated by the three shrubby oaks, with scattered rosemary and sand pine. Florida rosemary may predominate in scrubs on recent dunes along the panhandle coast and on dry ridge-crests inland. Sand pine may form a canopy over either rosemary or the shrubby oaks in infrequently burned scrubs.

Ann F. Johnson
Chapman's oak (*Quercus chapmanii*)

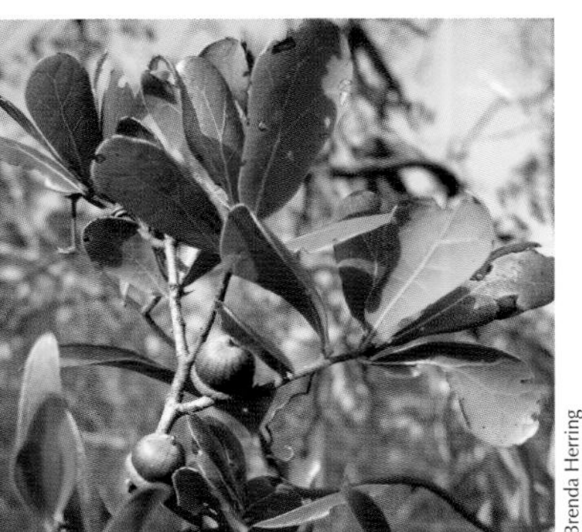
Brenda Herring
Myrtle oak (*Quercus myrtifolia*)

Scrub develops over long periods of time often in isolated patches, such as a dry ridge separated from other uplands by water or wetlands. This long isolation explains the many endemic species found on scrub, including 36 plant species, 1 lichen, 4 vertebrates, and more than 54 arthropods, with new species continuing to be found. Natural fires probably burned into scrubs from the more easily ignited surrounding dry prairies and flatwoods, perhaps once every 5 to 10 years in the denser oak scrub and less frequently in the more open stands of rosemary. A sand pine canopy develops in less frequently burned areas, where the chance of fire is lessened, either by a water barrier or by distance from more easily ignited habitats.

Florida Scrub	
Acres of scrub in Florida, current	ca. 430,000
Acres of scrub in Florida, predevelopment	ca. 979,000
FNAI Global Rarity Rank	G2
FNAI State Rarity Rank	S2

Sand live oak (*Quercus geminata*)

Brenda Herring

Florida rosemary (*Ceratiola ericoides*)
Ann F. Johnson

Scrub Variants in Florida

Gary Knight

Rosemary Scrub

Rosemary scrub is dominated by Florida rosemary (*Ceratiola ericoides*), a needle-leaved shrub in the heath family (Ericaceae). Rosemary produces many small fleshy fruits and grows rapidly from seed, colonizing new sites much faster than the slower-growing shrubby oaks. It occupies the crests of inland ridges in both the panhandle and peninsula, as shown here at Carter Creek Preserve on the Lake Wales Ridge, and is also one of the first shrubs to colonize coastal dunes in the panhandle. The open spaces between the shrubs are the favored habitat of many of the rare endemic plants on the Lake Wales Ridge.

Brenda Herring

Sand Pine Scrub

Sand pine scrub, shown here in the Ocala area, is distinguished by a canopy of sand pine (*Pinus clausa*), a short-needled pine that readily seeds into dry infertile sites and may form a closed canopy over either the shrubby oaks or rosemary. Sand pine is killed by fire and re-colonizes from seed. Repeated fires at intervals shorter than 10 years can eliminate sand pine from a site, since it does not mature rapidly enough to re-seed in less than 10 years. Sand pine may also invade scrubs (and other dry natural communities) where fire has been artificially excluded, both by active suppression and by roads and houses providing barriers to its spread.

Gary Schultz

Oak Scrub

Oak scrub is the most common type of scrub community in Florida, shown here at Cape Canaveral. It is composed of the three shrubby oaks, all of which re-sprout rapidly after fires, unlike rosemary which is killed by fire and must re-colonize from seed. The three oaks have similar growth habits, but can be distinguished by their leaves. Myrtle oak leaves are shiny, hairless, and green on both sides; sand live oak leaves are dark green on top, paler beneath, and usually curved under; Chapman's oak leaves are flat, with irregular wavy edges, and are yellowish or grayish beneath.

Gary Schultz

Oak Scrub (Lake Wales Ridge)

Oak scrub on lower elevations on the Lake Wales Ridge in Central Florida has a fourth species of shrubby oak, known as scrub oak (*Quercus inopina*). Scrub oak is closely related to myrtle oak which it replaces in these lower scrubs on the ridge. It differs from myrtle oak in having oblong, inrolled, vertically oriented leaves. Scrubs on the Lake Wales Ridge tend to have more openings between the patches of shrubs than scrubs elsewhere, a condition favorable for the Florida scrub-jay, as well as many endemic herbs found on this ridge, the geologically oldest in Florida.

Scrub oak (*Quercus inopina*)

FWC

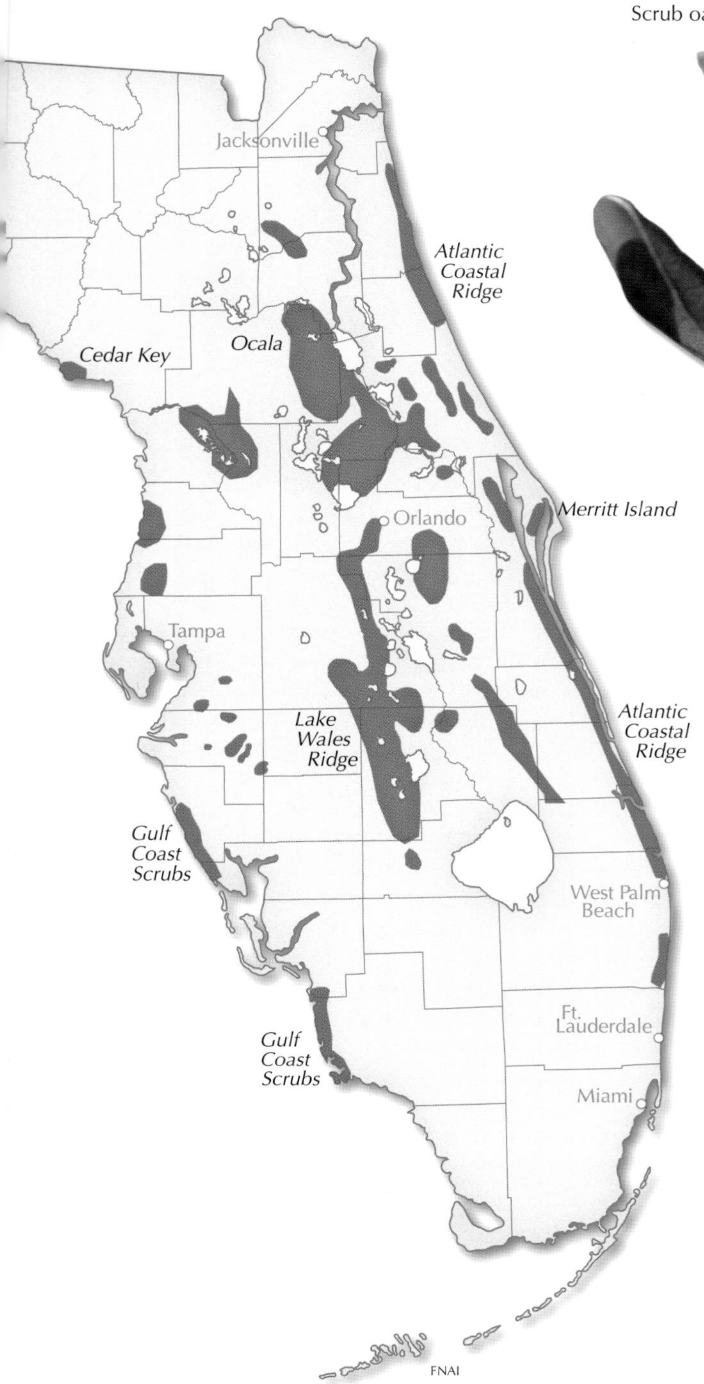

FNAI

Scrub on the Ridge

Realizing in the late 1980s that the only scrub left in the long run may be what is in parks and preserves, federal, state, and local governments, along with nonprofit conservation groups, have made a concerted and cooperative effort to acquire scrub lands, especially on the endemic-rich Lake Wales Ridge. Within the last two decades, 21,500 acres of scrub and sandhill have been acquired for conservation on the Lake Wales Ridge, with almost as many acres identified as still in need of preservation. As of 2003, 60% of remaining scrub and sandhill on the ridge (dark green on map) was either acquired or targeted for acquisition, representing 8% of the presettlement extent of these communities (light green).

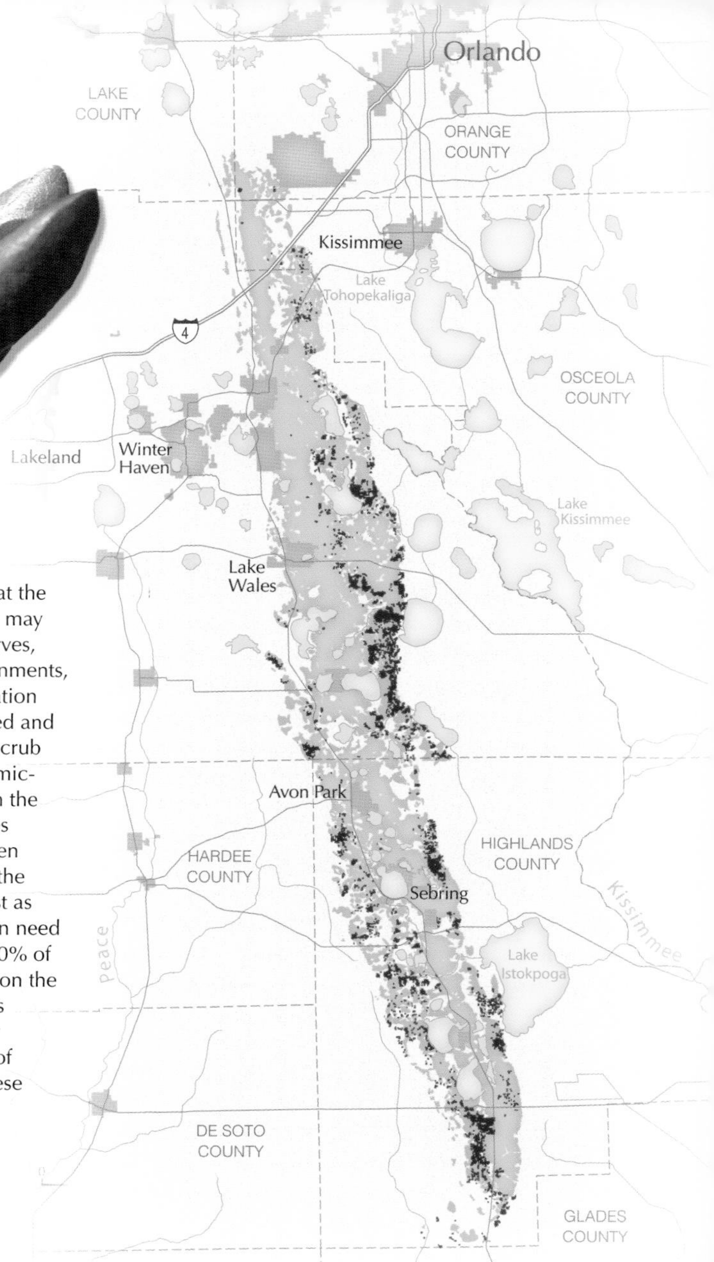

Presettlement

2003

Adapted from Turner, Wilcove, and Swain, 2006

Lost Habitat

Since it is located on the highest land, scrub occupies some of the most desirable building sites in the state and consequently has suffered disproportionately large losses in area compared with other natural communities as Florida's population has grown. An example is the scrub in the vicinity of Destin in Walton County in the Florida panhandle. In 1995, the boundaries of Henderson Beach State Park (outlined in black) enclosed a small area of scrub (dark red vegetation) within a much larger mosaic of scrub and wetlands on the outskirts of the city. Nine years later, the park encloses what remains of scrub in the vicinity, the rest having been developed. (Preserved areas are wetlands.)

LABINS, DEP

Henderson Beach, 1995

LABINS, DEP

Henderson Beach, 2004

Coastal Communities

At over 3,000 miles (exclusive of the Keys), Florida's coastline is longer than that of any other state except Alaska. About two-thirds of it is sandy, high-wave-energy coastline, occupied by dunes and beaches. The low-wave-energy coast, occupied by salt marshes and mangroves, is concentrated in the big bend region where the peninsula curves around to join the panhandle, and at the southern tip of the state. Florida's long coastline stretches across two climate zones, warm temperate and subtropical, which are reflected in the transition from salt marsh to mangrove vegetation in the vicinity of Tampa and Cape Canaveral. On sandy coasts, the same pioneer grasses on beach dunes range throughout the state; however, more inland dune vegetation also shows a transition to tropical species in about the same area as the mangrove/salt marsh transition. In addition to climate, stable dune vegetation also reflects differences in substrate. Stable dunes on the acid sands of the panhandle support scrub and mesic flatwoods, whereas stable dunes on less acid, shell-plus-quartz sands of the peninsula support coastal strand and maritime hammock.

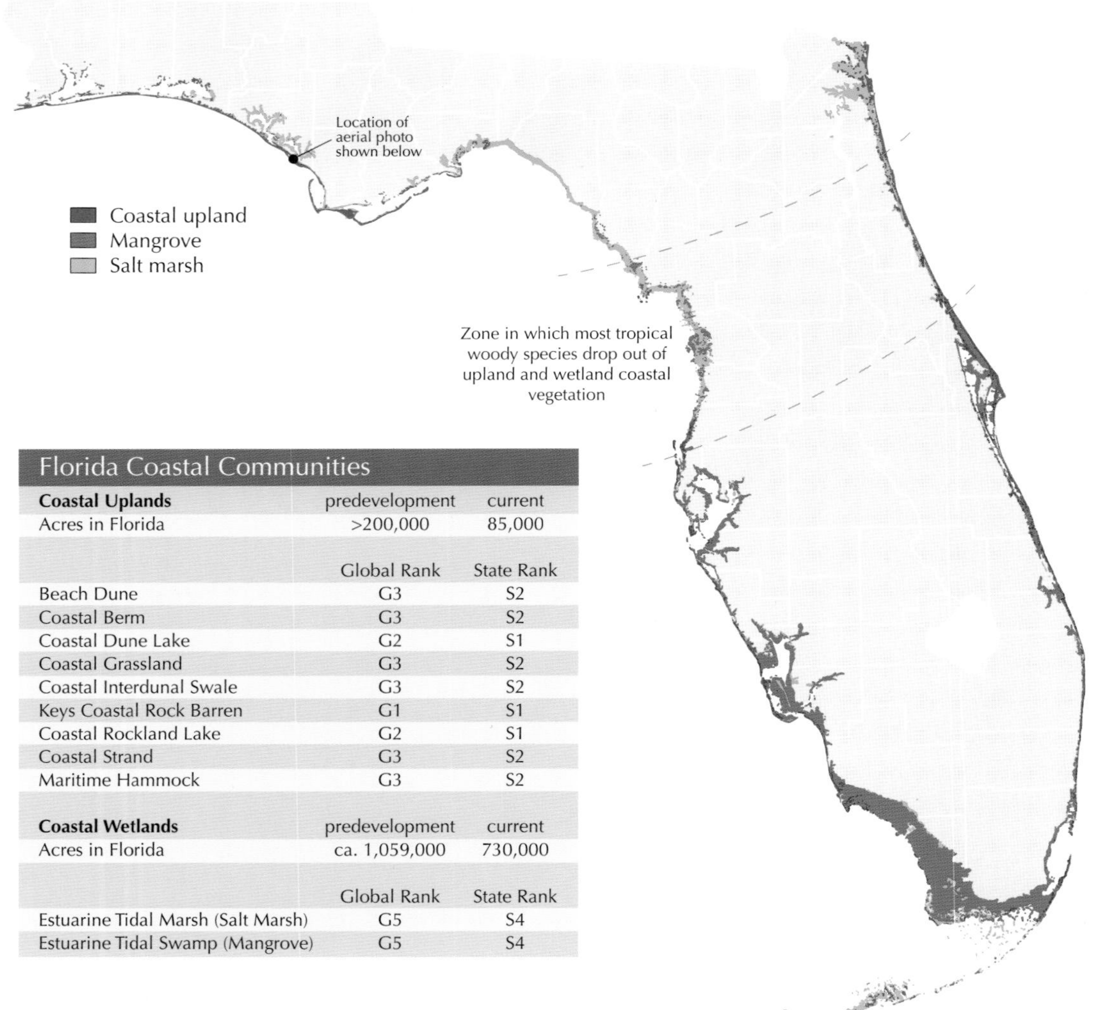

Florida Coastal Communities

Coastal Uplands	predevelopment	current
Acres in Florida	>200,000	85,000
	Global Rank	State Rank
Beach Dune	G3	S2
Coastal Berm	G3	S2
Coastal Dune Lake	G2	S1
Coastal Grassland	G3	S2
Coastal Interdunal Swale	G3	S2
Keys Coastal Rock Barren	G1	S1
Coastal Rockland Lake	G2	S1
Coastal Strand	G3	S2
Maritime Hammock	G3	S2
Coastal Wetlands	predevelopment	current
Acres in Florida	ca. 1,059,000	730,000
	Global Rank	State Rank
Estuarine Tidal Marsh (Salt Marsh)	G5	S4
Estuarine Tidal Swamp (Mangrove)	G5	S4

Changing Coastal Vegetation: Crooked Island West

Zonation is characteristic of coastal vegetation. Successive dune ridges inland from the beach often show a change from pioneering coastal grasses nearest the beach to other types of vegetation, culminating in woody vegetation resembling that found on the mainland. A coastline that has been building seaward allows us to follow how such coastal zonation develops. At Crooked Island West on Tyndall Air Force Base east of Panama City in Bay County, aerial photographs from1980, 1983, and 1986 record a rapidly prograding shoreline that built seaward over 0.2 miles in seven years. At each successive shoreline, a dune ridge was built up above the beach as pioneering dune grasses, such a sea oats (*Uniola paniculata*) or, in this case, bitter panicgrass (*Panicum amarum*), trapped sand blown off the beach and grew upward under burial. As a new dune ridge formed in front of the earlier ridge, it protected the earlier ridge from windborne sand and salt spray off the beach, permitting different plants to colonize it and to replace the pioneering species.

By comparing the positions of these ridges (magenta lines) on a current aerial with shorelines on earlier aerials, the dates when each of four ridges on the most recent aerial stood at the shoreline can be identified. In 1987, vegetation on each of the ridges was sampled across transect A–A′ from what was then the shoreline ridge inland. (The coast has since continued to build seaward as shown on this 2004 aerial.) The first two ridges (1987 and 1986) are covered by the pioneer bitter panicgrass, whereas the inner two (1983 and 1980) are dominated by Gulf bluestem (*Schizachyrium maritimum*), still a coastal specialist, but a finer grass than bitter panicgrass and one that tolerates only a moderate rate of sand burial. Thus, in our example, bitter panicgrass that presumably formed the 1983 ridge when it was at the shoreline was replaced by bluestem within one to three years of its being protected by a more seaward ridge. Likewise, since the second ridge (1986) has been protected for less than a year by the current shoreline ridge and still has bitter panicgrass, we know that under a year is too short a time for Gulf bluestem to replace bitter panicgrass. And since the 1980 ridge still has Gulf bluestem and has been protected by the third ridge for between three and seven years, we know that that is insufficient time for other vegetation to replace Gulf bluestem.

By piecing together many similar examples along the coast, we can begin to predict how dune vegetation will change and how rapidly these changes will occur once a dune ridge is protected from the coastal stresses of wave erosion, sand burial, and salt spray found at the shoreline.

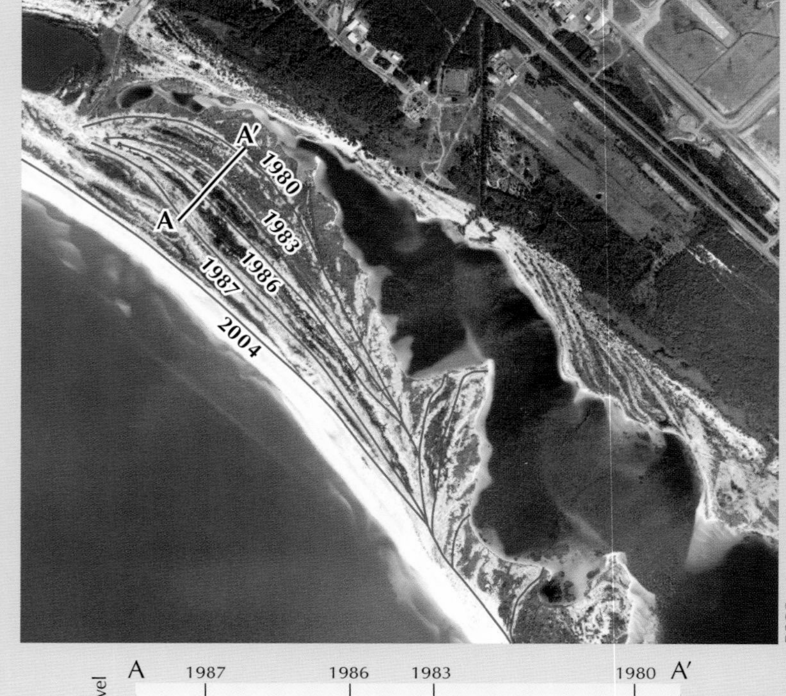

Panhandle Sandy Coast

Carolyn Kindell

Ann F. Johnson

Beach Dune

On sandy coasts, the beach dune community that occupies the upper beach and first dune is composed of specialized pioneer grasses and forbs, most of which range throughout the state. Sea oats (*Uniola paniculata*) and bitter panicgrass (*Panicum amarum*) are the primary dune-building grasses. The upper beach is colonized by the seacoast marshelder (*Iva imbricata*) and shoreline sea purslane (*Sesuvium portulacastrum*), often accompanied by the wide ranging runners of railroad vine (*Ipomoea pes-caprae* ssp. *brasiliensis*) and beach morning glory (*Ipomoea imperati*).

Coastal Grassland

The coastal grassland community develops when the first dune above the beach is protected from salt spray and sand burial by a new dune ridge. As the beach builds seaward, the pioneer grasses of the beach dune community are replaced by other grasses and forbs of the coastal grassland community. These species do not range along the entire coast but change as one goes southward. The acid sugar sands of the panhandle coastal grasslands are dominated by Gulf bluestem (*Schizachyrium maritimum*), a grass endemic to the northeast Gulf coast from Florida to Mississippi, whereas a variety of forbs and grasses comprise the coastal grasslands of the peninsula.

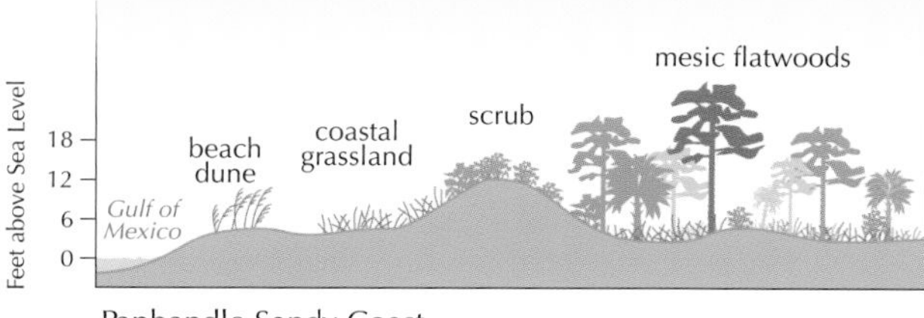

Panhandle Sandy Coast

Peninsular Sandy Coast

Gary Schultz

Ann F. Johnson

Coastal Strand and Maritime Hammock

Coastal strand is a dense shrubby community found in the transition zone to maritime hammock on quartz sands mixed with shell along both coasts of the peninsula. The shrubs are kept low by salt spray blowing off the water, and they gradually increase in height with distance from the coast until they merge into tree-sized species forming the canopy of maritime hammock. Nearest the coast saw palmetto (*Serenoa repens*) forms a nearly pure stand with occasional stunted cabbage palms (*Sabal palmetto*). Further inland shrubs become prominent, including tough buckthorn (*Sideroxylon tenax*) and Hercules' club (*Zanthoxylum clava-herculis*) mixed with dwarfed live oak (*Quercus virginiana*), red bay (*Persea borbonia*), and cabbage palms, which gradually increase in height inland until they form the canopy of maritime hammock. In the tropical portion of the coast, sea grape (*Coccoloba uvifera*) is found closest to the coast and like live oak may increase in height to form a canopy of maritime hammock with increasing distance from the coast or with protection from a tall dune. Joining it in the canopy are other tropical tree species, often including gumbo limbo (*Bursera simaruba*) and white stopper (*Eugenia axillaris*), among others.

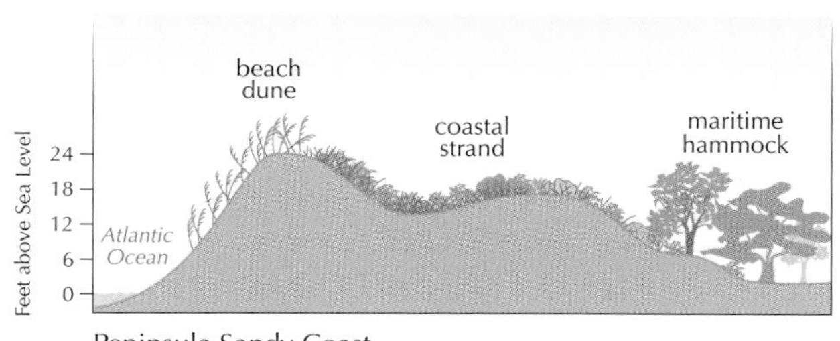

Peninsula Sandy Coast

North Florida Salt Marsh

David Moynahan

Salt Marsh

Salt marsh consists of vast expanses of either salt marsh cordgrass (*Spartina alterniflora*) or black needlerush (*Juncus roemerianus*). Which species predominates depends on the amplitude of the tides. Where the tidal amplitude is greater, as along the extreme northeast coast of Florida, salt marsh cordgrass predominates, since it thrives under longer flooding; where tidal amplitude is lower, as in most of Florida, black needlerush covers most of the marsh. On higher salinity salt flats, which are seldom flooded, both species are replaced by either the low grasses, saltgrass (*Distichlis spicata*) and shoregrass (*Monanthochloe littoralis*), or the succulents, saltwort (*Batis maritima*) and perennial glasswort (*Sarcocornia perennis*).

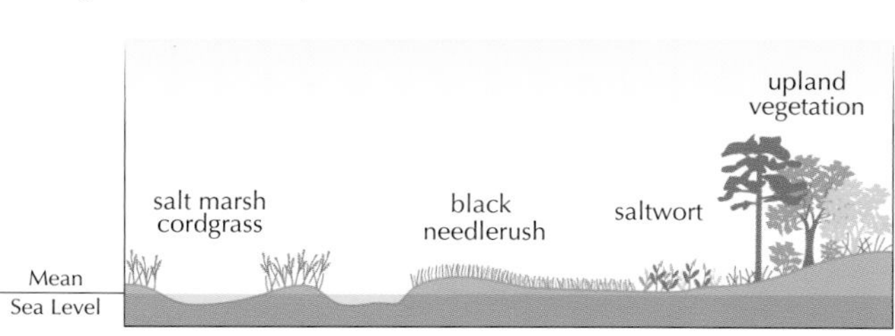

North Florida Salt Marsh

South Florida Mangrove Swamp

David Moynahan

Mangrove Swamp

Mangrove swamps are formed by three species of mangrove: red mangrove (*Rhizophora mangle*) nearest the open water and black mangrove (*Avicennia germinans*) and white mangrove (*Laguncularia racemosa*) further inland. Buttonwood (*Conocarpus erectus*) occurs on the inland edges; it tolerates brackish groundwater but not regular inundation. Salt flats are also found in mangrove swamps and are colonized by the same species as they are in salt marsh, along with stunted mangroves. Salt marsh and mangrove swamp form some of the most productive habitats in Florida and are important nurseries for fish and other marine life.

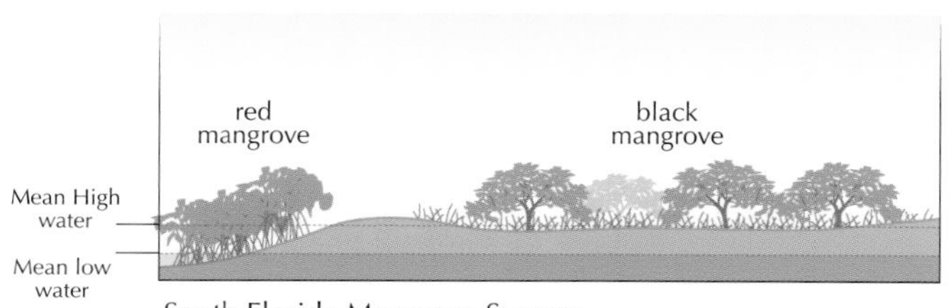

South Florida Mangrove Swamp

Everglades

The Everglades is a large grassy marsh that originally formed a broad curving band stretching 100 miles from the south end of Lake Okeechobee to Florida Bay, between higher land in the Big Cypress to the west and the coastal ridges along the Atlantic Ocean on the east. It comprises most of the interior portions of Palm Beach, Broward, and Miami-Dade counties. This landscape is not drained by the usual system of rivers and streams because its extremely gentle relief near sea level precludes the down-cutting of deep channels. The north end of the original Everglades is less than 25 feet above sea level, sloping seaward at the scarcely perceptible gradient of less than 3 inches per mile. Rainwater, plus overflow from Lake Okeechobee, flowed slowly through it as sheet flow in the summer wet season, contracting into a series of broad sloughs in the winter dry season. Today only the southern third of this marsh remains in relatively undisturbed condition as part of Everglades National Park.

Everglades Drainage Basin

The Impact of Development

Shown in this 2004 aerial photograph are Parkland and Coral Springs northwest of Fort Lauderdale in Broward County, examples of communities built on former glades marsh that would be unsustainable without the canal and levee system that now controls water flow through the Everglades (location shown by the red box on the map at bottom right of facing page).

DOQQ

Alteration of Natural Communities of the Everglades

Donald T. Jones

Glades Marsh

Sawgrass (*Cladium jamaicense*) is the predominant species in glades marsh, forming tall, dense stands on deep peat and short, sparse stands mixed with other marsh plants in wetter areas. Wetter marsh alternates with open water sloughs marked by floating-leaved plants, such as white waterlily (*Nymphaea odorata*). Dotted through the marsh are tree islands, teardrop-shaped higher areas with tropical hardwoods on their higher and broader upstream ends and swampy bay tree forests on their lower narrower downstream portions. Today the continuous tall sawgrass plains that dominated the northern portion of the Everglades have been largely converted to agriculture; water flow through the wetter ridge and slough marsh in the central portion has been interrupted by levees forming the three water conservation areas. This has led to replacement of sawgrass by cattails (*Typha* spp.) on upstream (ponded) side of levees and by weedy species on the water-starved downstream side.

Gary Knight

Mesic Flatwoods

Mesic flatwoods is an upland, pine-dominated community on sandy soil that borders the east and west sides of the northern portion of the Everglades marsh. Drainage of the Everglades opened the wetter portions of this community to invasion by melaleuca (*Melaleuca quinquenervia*).

Gary Knight

Marl Prairie

Marl prairie is an herbaceous wetland community on marl, a calcareous mud, that is inundated for 1-2 months a year (in contrast to 6 or more months for the glades marsh). It is characterized by muhly grass (*Muhlenbergia capillaris*), along with a great diversity of other plants, and is an important feeding area for wading birds, as well as the endangered Cape Sable seaside sparrow (*Ammodramus maritimus mirabilis*), which is dependent on this community for nest sites.

Jim Snyder

Marl Prairie with Pond Cypress

Marl prairies in Big Cypress National Preserve on the western side of the Everglades marsh feature scattered pond cypress (*Taxodium ascendens*; "big" referring to extent of area covered rather than size of the cypress). Aerial views of this community appear as undulating waves of cypress due to the alternation of dwarf cypress on the prairies and taller cypress in the strand swamps.

Paul Russo

Strand Swamp

Strand swamps are forested wetland communities dominated by tall cypress. They occupy long narrow channels in the limestone substrate. Strand swamps are common in the marl prairies of Big Cypress Preserve and formerly occurred along the northeastern border of the Everglades marsh. Pond apple (*Annona glabra*) swamps that once formed the southern border of Lake Okeechobee have been entirely lost.

David Moynahan

Baygall and Rockland Hammock—Tree Island

Tree islands form on higher areas within the Everglades marsh. The number of tree islands in the Everglades marshes has been greatly reduced. Initial drainage of the Everglades eliminated tree islands due to fire burning into the peat soils. Later, water held in the water conservation areas raised water tables above what the trees could tolerate, thereby also eliminating many tree islands.

Gary Knight

Rockland Hammock

Rockland hammock is a diverse tropical hardwood forest found in scattered areas on the elevated limestone of the Everglades Keys and Atlantic Coastal Ridge, which border the eastern side of the Everglades marsh. It develops where there is natural protection from the fires that are common in the surrounding pine rocklands.

Jimi Sadle, ENP

Pine Rockland

Pine rockland is an open pine forest with a diverse tropical understory of shrubs and herbs found on elevated limestone that covers most of the Everglades Keys and formerly a portion of the Atlantic Coastal Ridge. Most pine rockland as well as rockland hammock outside of Everglades National Park has been developed as the urban portions of Broward and Miami-Dade counties.

Drainage Changes to the Everglades

When Florida became a state in 1845, the Everglades was viewed as a major obstacle to settlement. In 1850, Congress granted the state 20 million acres of swamps and "overflowed lands" (over half the area of the state) to sell and raise money for drainage projects. By 1926, five major canals had been built carrying water from Lake Okeechobee to the Atlantic Ocean, and in 1938, a 34-foot levee was constructed around the south shore of Lake Okeechobee for flood control. However, there were problems with overdrainage in dry periods, resulting in peat fires and soil loss in the Everglades and saltwater intrusion along the east coast, as well as major flooding following heavy rains in 1947. The U.S. Army Corps of Engineers solved these problems by dividing the Everglades into drained and undrained portions using a system of canals and levees. Water could be stored in the undrained areas (known as "water conservation areas") to be released to the drained areas (farmland south of Lake Okeechobee and urban and agricultural land east of the eastern levee) for irrigation and groundwater recharge as needed. The northern third of the Everglades marsh south of Lake Okeechobee became the drained Everglades Agricultural Area; the central third became the three water conservation areas where water was impounded by levees to be released as needed; and the southern third was donated back to the federal government for Everglades National Park in 1947.

Historical Flow

SFWMD

The South Florida Water Management District (originally the Central and South Florida Flood Control District) was the state agency created to administer this system of canals and levees, which was completed by the Corps of Engineers in 1963. For the purposes of flood control and water supply this plan worked well: the population of Palm Beach, Broward, and Miami-Dade counties increased from 225,000 in 1950 to over 5 million in 2000, most of it concentrated along the east coast where over half the acreage in agricultural and residential development is built on formerly "overflowed" land. However, alteration of patterns of water flow and increased nutrient content of the water had adverse effects on natural systems. While freshwater flow to the Atlantic more than doubled, water flow through Everglades National Park and into Florida Bay was reduced to 70% of its original volume and this, combined with misdirected and poorly timed water releases to the park, led to changes in the vegetation and declines in wildlife, particularly the breeding bird populations.

Current Flow

SFWMD

Since1994, federal and state governments have been altering water release schedules and buying back both natural land to add to parks and farmland to use for water filtration and storage in an attempt to solve these problems. In 2000, Congress approved funding for an ambitious $7.8 billion plan known as CERP (Comprehensive Everglades Restoration Plan), with costs to be shared with the state, to restore as far as possible, over the course of several decades, the natural functioning of the entire Everglades drainage system from the headwaters of the Kissimmee River that flows into Lake Okeechobee in the north to Everglades National Park and Florida Bay in the south.

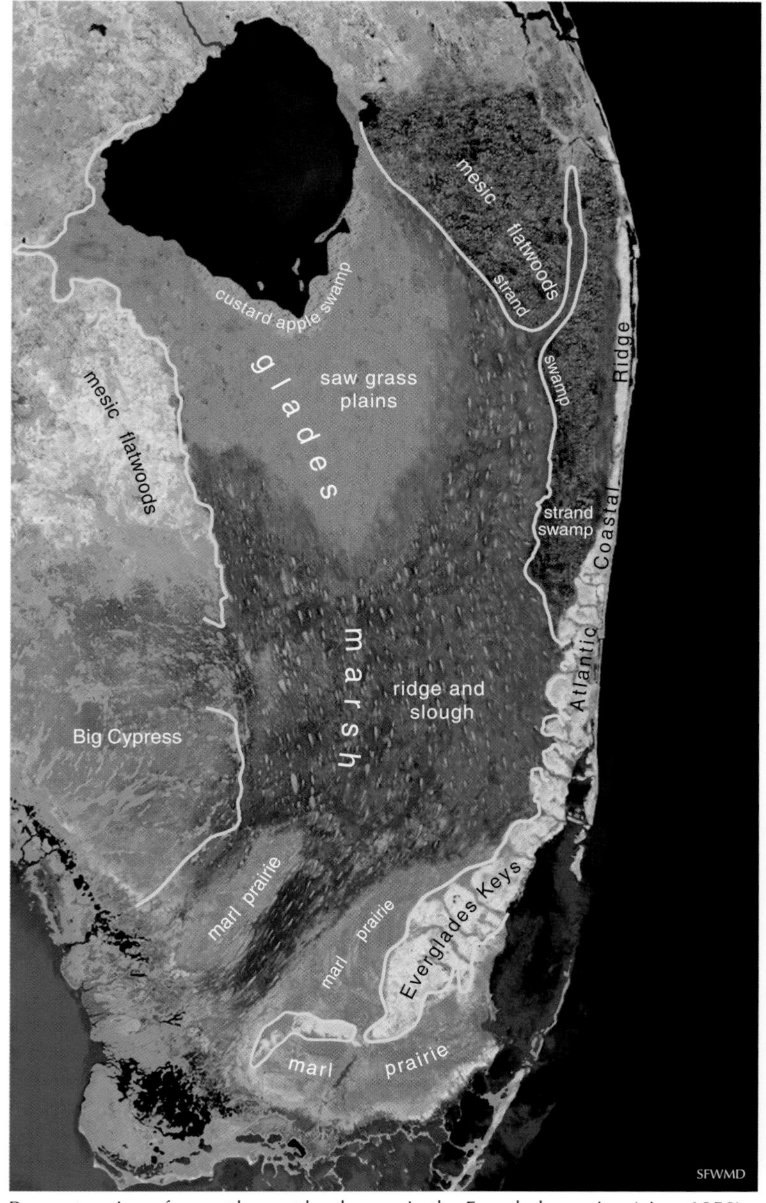

Reconstruction of presettlement land cover in the Everglades region (circa 1850). Yellow line delineates glades marsh and marl prairie.

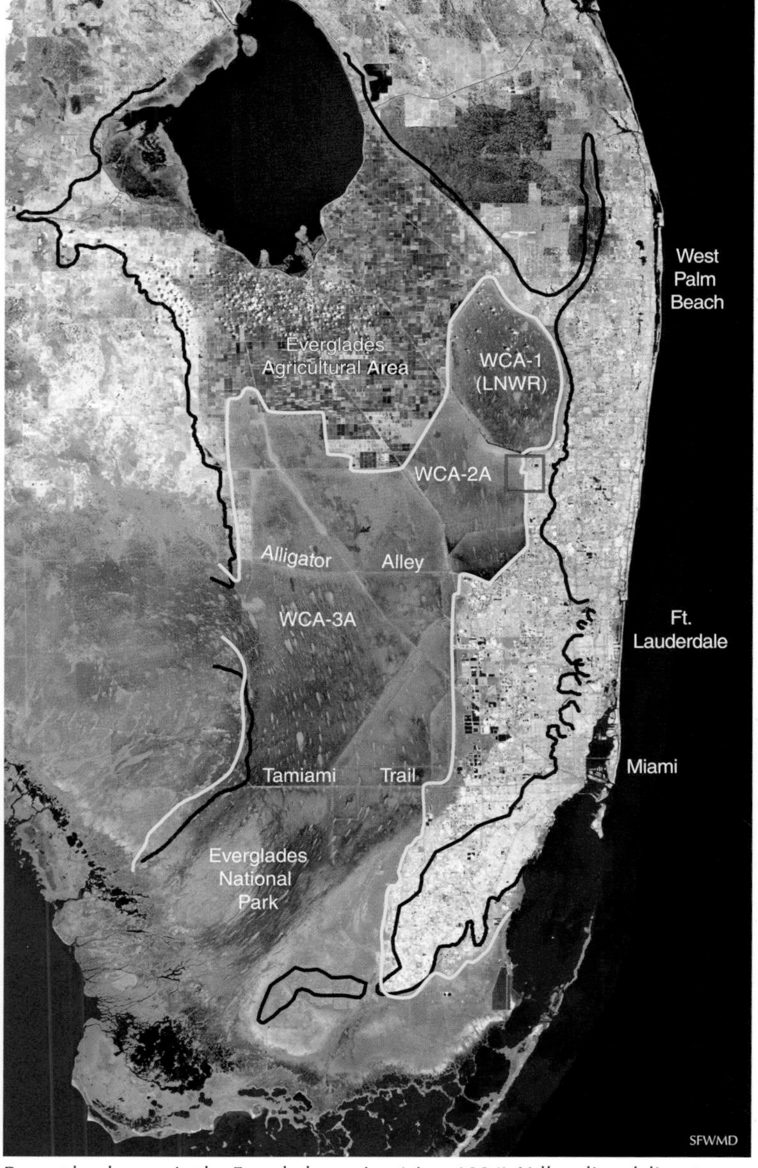

Recent land cover in the Everglades region (circa 1994). Yellow line delineates current extent of glades marsh and marl prairie; black line shows the presettlement extent of these features; red box indicates location of aerial photo on facing page.

Marine and Estuarine Communities

The length of Florida's coastline, coupled with its geologic diversity and the relative protection offered by the Gulf of Mexico, have resulted in the formation of a diverse array of natural communities in the state's coastal waters. The tidal shoreline, which stretches for over 2,000 miles and spans six degrees of latitude, is the second longest of the United States, exceeded only by Alaska. North Florida's oyster reefs and mud flats resemble those of the temperate Carolinas, while South Florida's coral reefs are similar to those in the Caribbean. Other communities such as worm reefs along the southeastern beaches or the vast seagrass beds of the big bend are uniquely Floridian.

Our classification system for the coastal communities of Florida is based in part on the dominant feature found at the interface between the water column and the bottom substrate. Faunal-based communities are dominated by animal species, as in a coral reef, mollusk reef, or sponge bed. Floral-based communities are dominated by plant species, as in a seagrass bed. Mineral-based communities are dominated by the substrate itself, such as a sand bar or limestone outcrop.

Marine and estuarine natural community classification is also based on the salt content (salinity) of the water. In general, estuarine communities have salinity levels between 0.5 and 30 ppt (parts per thousand), and marine communities have salinity levels between 30 and 37 ppt. Estuarine areas may temporarily exhibit freshwater conditions during periods of heavy rainfall or upland runoff, or marine conditions when rainfall and runoff are low. Marine communities receive little influence from freshwater. Because species differ widely in their ability to tolerate salinity, coastal communities may exhibit wide differences in species composition even though they appear physically similar.

Faunal-based Communities

Gary Knight

Mollusk Reef
Submerged and intertidal oyster bars are probably the most well-known example of this type of community in Florida.

Stephen Frink, Stephen Frink Studios

Coral Reef
Coral reefs off the Florida Keys comprise the only barrier reef system on the North American continent and the third largest such system in the world. Reefs are noted for being among the most biologically diverse habitats on earth.

Rodney Bertelsen, FWC

Sponge Bed
Although extensive sponge beds once supported a thriving industry in Florida, the sponge fishery has only barely survived overfishing in the 1890s, sponge blight disease in 1939, and the advent of artificial sponges in the 1950s.

© Scripps Treasure Coast Newspapers

Worm Reef
In Florida, worm reefs may be found in selected locations near shore from Cape Canaveral to Key Biscayne near Miami. Annelid worms use sand grains to construct somewhat fragile shelters that are susceptible to mechanical destruction.

Rodney Bertelsen, FWC

Octocoral Bed
Octocoral polyps all have eight tentacles, and they do not produce the stony coral heads associated with reefs. The soft structure of sea fans and sea feathers allows them to sway with the motion of water currents.

Floral-based Communities

Heather Dine, FL Keys Natl. Sanctuary

Seagrass Bed
Associations of these true flowering plants feature high primary production and remarkably high biodiversity. The vast grass beds of Florida's big bend region, Florida Bay, and the Florida Keys comprise the largest expanse of this valuable resource in the world.

Rodney Bertelsen, FWC

Algal Bed
Algal forms are found in many other types of marine communities, but occasionally they may dominate an area where other community types have not or cannot fully develop.

Mineral-based Communities

Rodney Bertelsen, FWC

Consolidated Substrate
Limestone outcrops and crevasses offer refuge for many organisms, such as the spiny lobster shown here.

Rodney Bertelsen, FWC

Unconsolidated Substrate
The dissociated sediments of this type of community do not offer much in the way of attachment sites, but an abundance of burrowing animals and microscopic plants have found ways to live on or between the grains.

Composite Communities

Rodney Bertelsen, FWC

Composite Substrate
Composite substrates may often exhibit extremely high species diversity because elements of more than one community type occur in close proximity.

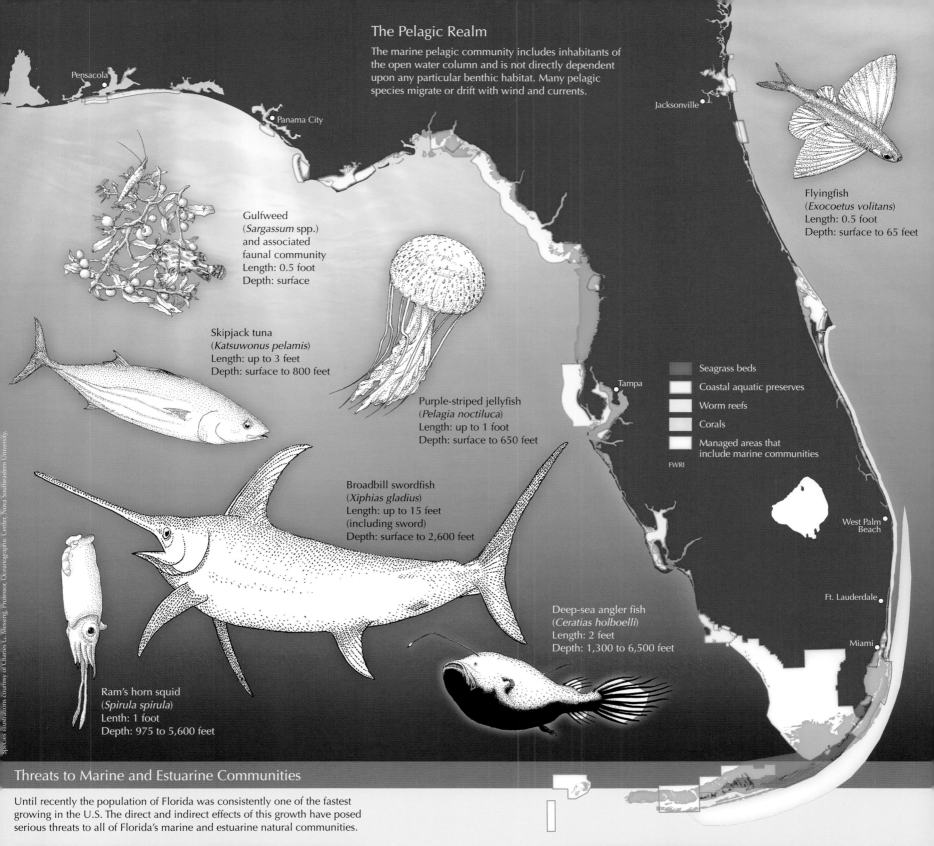

The Pelagic Realm

The marine pelagic community includes inhabitants of the open water column and is not directly dependent upon any particular benthic habitat. Many pelagic species migrate or drift with wind and currents.

Pensacola

Panama City

Jacksonville

Tampa

West Palm Beach

Ft. Lauderdale

Miami

Seagrass beds

Coastal aquatic preserves

Worm reefs

Corals

Managed areas that include marine communities

FWRI

Flyingfish
(*Exocoetus volitans*)
Length: 0.5 foot
Depth: surface to 65 feet

Gulfweed
(*Sargassum* spp.)
and associated
faunal community
Length: 0.5 foot
Depth: surface

Skipjack tuna
(*Katsuwonus pelamis*)
Length: up to 3 feet
Depth: surface to 800 feet

Purple-striped jellyfish
(*Pelagia noctiluca*)
Length: up to 1 foot
Depth: surface to 650 feet

Broadbill swordfish
(*Xiphias gladius*)
Length: up to 15 feet
(including sword)
Depth: surface to 2,600 feet

Deep-sea angler fish
(*Ceratias holboelli*)
Length: 2 feet
Depth: 1,300 to 6,500 feet

Ram's horn squid
(*Spirula spirula*)
Lenth: 1 foot
Depth: 975 to 5,600 feet

Species illustrations courtesy of Charles G. Messing, Professor, Oceanographic Center, Nova Southeastern University.

Threats to Marine and Estuarine Communities

Until recently the population of Florida was consistently one of the fastest growing in the U.S. The direct and indirect effects of this growth have posed serious threats to all of Florida's marine and estuarine natural communities.

DOQQ

Development

While some development such as channel dredging has directly affected these communities, the more lasting threat is posed by the indirect effects of development. Examples include permanent changes in runoff patterns or altered near-shore wave energy produced by coastal armoring or increased boat traffic.

NOAA

Climate Change

Current rates of climate change have the potential to produce shifts in temperature and weather patterns that happen too rapidly for Florida's natural communities to adapt. There is also some evidence that climate change is at least partly responsible for the bleaching and resulting decline of Florida's coral reefs.

David Moynahan

Fishing

Overfishing has been implicated as the cause of reduced populations of popular reef fish including snapper and grouper. Shrimp trawl catches include as much as ten pounds of by-catch fish for every pound of shrimp, and trawling methods have been blamed for the alteration of large swaths of sponge and octocoral beds.

NOAA

Invasive Species

A number of exotic species, including Indo-Pacific swimming crabs, lion fish, and green mussels have been introduced into Florida's marine and estuarine areas. These species have the potential to displace the state's native species.

P. Schmidt, Charlotte (FL) Sun

Non-point source pollution

Increased levels of nutrients and bacteria in stormwater runoff have resulted in fish-killing algae blooms and closure of shellfish harvesting areas statewide.

Important Small Extent Communities

Some of Florida's rarest and most fascinating natural communities cover very small areas of land. These small but vital community types harbor a delight of rare species, both plant and animal, contributing greatly to Florida's biodiversity. The rocklands of South Florida offer a glimpse of communities and species more common in the Caribbean, while the upland glades in the northern panhandle represent a unique limestone outcrop community reminiscent of cedar glades in Georgia, Alabama, and Tennessee. While only a small fraction of Florida's area, springs are more common in Florida than most other places. Seepage slopes are herbaceous communities occurring primarily in the western panhandle, while cutthroat seeps are found on the Lake Wales Ridge. Both can be incredibly diverse with herbaceous species.

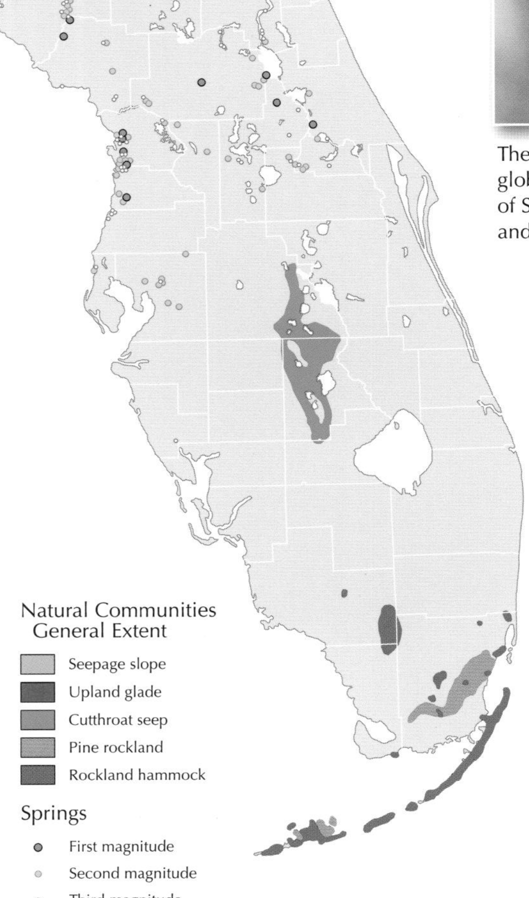

Dave Irving

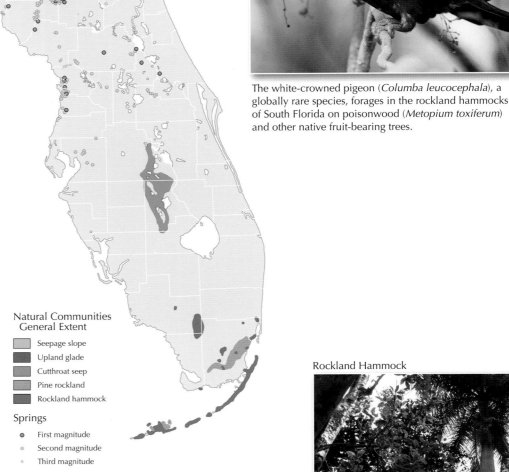

The white-crowned pigeon (*Columba leucocephala*), a globally rare species, forages in the rockland hammocks of South Florida on poisonwood (*Metopium toxiferum*) and other native fruit-bearing trees.

Pine Rockland

Gary Knight

Gary Knight

Locustberry (*Byrsonima lucida*)

Rocklands

Pine Rocklands and Rockland Hammocks

Pine rockland and rockland hammock are unique natural communities found only in extreme southern Florida where limestone is at or very near the soil surface. These distinct community types co-occur in limited areas of Miami-Dade and Monroe counties on the Miami Rockridge, as well as in the Florida Keys and in parts of Everglades National Park and Big Cypress National Preserve.

Pine rockland is a fire-adapted community composed of an open canopy of south Florida slash pine (*Pinus elliottii* var. *densa*) and a diverse array of understory shrubs and herbs, including many tropical species. Rockland hammock occurs within pine rocklands in areas protected from fire, or embedded within several wetland community types. The rockland hammock is a closed canopy hardwood forest dominated by a diverse suite of subtropical trees and shrubs.

Pine rocklands and rockland hammocks support a high diversity of rare plant species, as well as an array of endemic, tropical, and subtropical plants and animals, species that occur nowhere else in the world. Both rockland community types are severely threatened by development pressures in South Florida. The current extent of these communities represents only a fraction—about 2%—of their historical range. Other threats include invasion by exotic plants and animals, sea-level rise associated with global climate change, habitat fragmentation, and, in the case of pine rockland, fire suppression.

Rockland Hammock

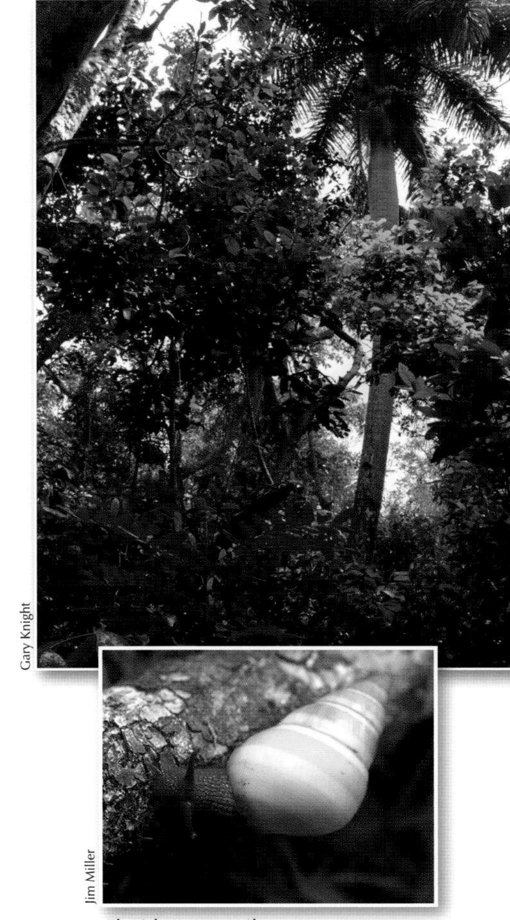

Gary Knight

Jim Miller

Florida tree snail (*Liguus fasciatus*)

Springs

Among Florida's many natural wonders are its more than 700 springs, one of the largest concentrations on earth. Underground water from karst springs exits from tunnels and holes dissolved from a limestone aquifer. Water from a second type of spring, known as a seep, oozes forth from a surficial sand aquifer.

Most of Florida's springs are in the north central part of the state where underground aquifers are closest to the ground surface. Springs are classified by their outflow or water discharge rate. First-magnitude springs are the largest, producing more than 65 million gallons of water per day. Florida has more first-magnitude springs than any other state.

The output from some springs contributes to the flow of larger rivers, while water emanating from other springs gives rise to rivers themselves, known as spring-run streams. A few springs even emerge in the near-shore waters of the Gulf coast.

Springs have been a popular part of Florida's natural heritage since 16th century Spanish explorers first visited famous springs for their healing properties. The popularity of springs for recreation, agriculture and residential uses is also impacting the health of this natural resource. Population growth, urban sprawl, agriculture and a growing demand for water are drawing down aquifer levels and adding higher dissolved nutrient levels, often many miles upstream in spring recharge areas.

Spring

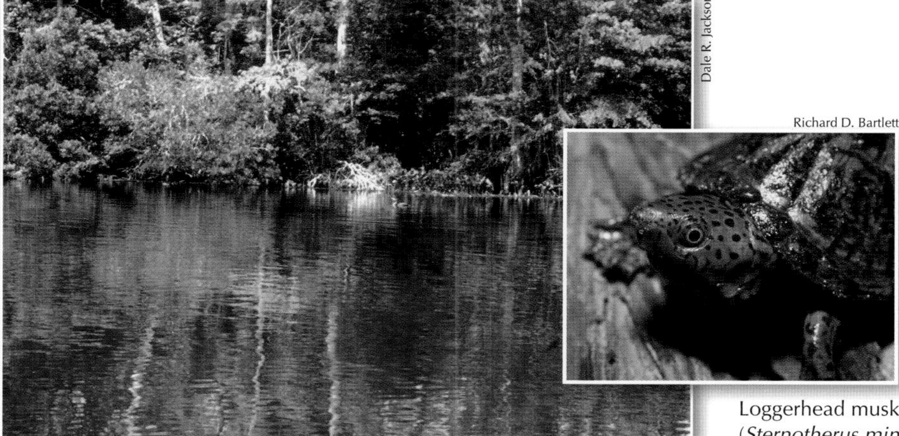

Dale R. Jackson

Richard D. Bartlett

Loggerhead musk turtle (*Sternotherus minor*)

Barrens silky aster (*Symphyotrichum pratense*)

Ann F. Johnson

Upland Glade

Ann F. Johnson

Ann F. Johnson

Pinnate prairie coneflower (*Ratibida pinnata*)

Upland Glades

Upland glade is a largely herbaceous community that occurs on thin soils over limestone outcrops in Jackson and Gadsden counties in the Florida panhandle. It is found in small openings less than two acres in size within an otherwise forested landscape. Upland glade in Florida shares many species with other areas to the north and west where limestone is at or near the surface. These include the cedar glades on limestone outcrops in Tennessee and northern Alabama and Georgia, remnant limestone openings in the Oaky Woods Wildlife Mangement Area in central Georgia, the shallow-soil Black Belt prairies in Alabama and Mississippi, the Kieffer Prairies in Louisiana, and various outcrop and prairie communities in southeastern Texas. Shallow soil depth prevents woody colonization on the rockier portions of the glades. On Florida glades with deeper soils occasional fire may be necessary to prevent the open habitat from succeeding to forest.

Physical disturbance of the ground cover and thin soil substrate poses the primary threat to upland glades, since to nonexperts they appear indistinguishable from an artificial clearing in the forest. Only 3 of the 22 known glades in Florida are protected on public lands. Known glades have been lost to road widening, plowing for game food plots, and limestone mining. In the past, others were probably used for parking logging equipment and as staging areas for timber operations. When the soil is disturbed, glades are vulnerable to critical alterations to the site's hydrology and to invasion by exotic species.

Upland glades are home to many rare plant species, including ten northern species that are rare in Florida, but range widely outside the state. These include Carolina larkspur (*Delphinium carolinianum*), shootingstar (*Dodecatheon meadia*), eastern purple coneflower (*Echinacea purpurea*), barrens silky aster (*Symphyotrichum pratense*), and little-people (*Lepuropetalon spathulatum*).

Cutthroat Seeps and Seepage Slopes

Seepage slopes and cutthroat seeps are herbaceous communities found on continuously wet, but not inundated, soils and subject to frequent fires. They are usually dominated by dense grasses, sedges, and herbs and are found on hillside seeps or in bowl-shaped streamhead areas. Clay lenses in the sandy substrate intersect the slope, impeding groundwater drainage and keeping the upper soil layers saturated most of the year.

Cutthroat seeps (a variant of wet prairie), dominated by the endemic cutthroat grass (*Panicum abscissum*), occur along the eastern and western edges of the Lake Wales Ridge in Central Florida and are characterized by many wildflowers in common with other acidic wet prairie areas. Seepage slopes, known for their gorgeous displays of diverse flowering herbs such as the rare white-top pitcherplant (*Sarracenia leucophylla*), occur in the western Panhandle and northeast Florida.

Seepage slopes and cutthroat seeps are sensitive to relatively slight physical alterations to the soil surface, which can permanently alter the hydrology. Such disturbances include soil rutting caused by trampling, vehicles, plowed fire lanes, or other heavy equipment damage, or placing roads and ditches near the prairies. These disturbances can cause major changes in species composition that require expensive restoration to repair.

Cutthroat Seep

Gary Knight

Seepage Slope

Gary Knight

Michael Jenkins

Crested fringed orchid (*Platanthera cristata*)

Plants: Overview

Florida is home to a unique and diverse assemblage of plant species. Florida has the highest number of plant families and the sixth highest native species richness in the United States, with 243 plant families and approximately 2,600 species. Nearly half of these species belong to 10 large plant families, including the grass, aster, pea, and the sedge families. Florida also stands out among U.S. states for certain groups of species including carnivorous plants, ferns, and orchids. Florida supports one of the largest number of carnivorous plant species, nearly one-half of the orchid species found in North America, and the highest number of fern species in the continental United States. Florida's temperate to subtropical climate also supports a variety of non-native plants from South America and the Old World tropics. Today, an estimated 40% of plant species in Florida (approximately 3,900 species) are naturalized exotic species, and 3% are considered invasive and threaten the biodiversity of natural areas within the state.

In addition to climatic forces, the diversity and distribution of plants in Florida is influenced by variations in topography, soils, geology, rainfall amounts and seasonality, and fire regimes and frequency. These factors, in turn, shape Florida's diverse natural communities, from upland hardwood forests and wet prairies in the panhandle, to pine rocklands and scrub in the peninsula, and their unique suite of species.

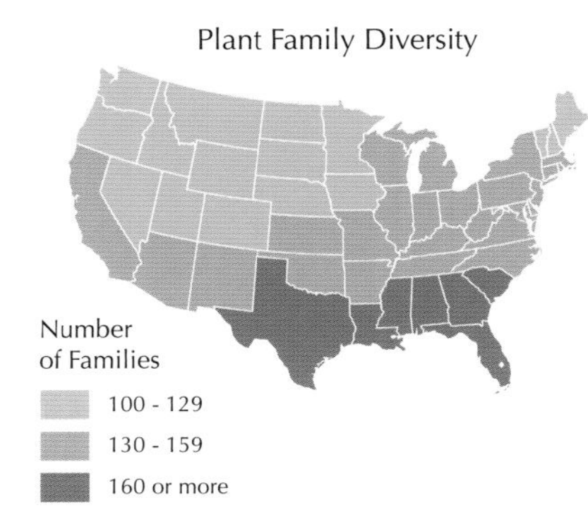

These natural communities are populated by many species common to the Atlantic and Gulf coastal plains. Numerous disjunct, relict, and endemic plant species also contribute to Florida's overall plant diversity. Examples of disjunct species include camphor daisy (*Rayjacksonia phyllocephala*) from Texas, Miccosukee gooseberry (*Ribes echinellum*) from South Carolina, and threadleaf sundew (*Drosera filiformis*) from North Carolina. The topography and moist microclimates of ravines in the Florida panhandle provide refuge for several relict plant species that occur nowhere else in the world, notably the Florida torreya (*Torreya taxifolia*). Many localized areas of Florida have high concentrations of endemic plant species. The central ridge of Florida is rich with endemic plants, such as scrub oak (*Quercus inopina*), due to its unique geological history and semi-arid scrub habitat. Many of Florida's natural communities, both wetlands and uplands, are pyrogenic. The plants that populate these fire-prone communities have adapted to natural fires for thousands of years. Some species are even dependent upon periodic fires for their survival. The cones of sand pine (*Pinus clausa*) only release their seeds when exposed to fire. Another of the state's most fire-adapted—and fire-dependent—species is wiregrass (*Aristida stricta*).

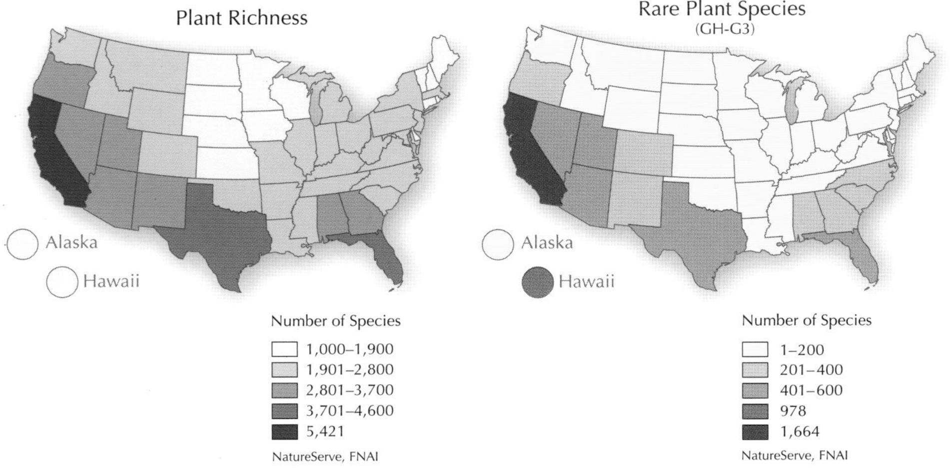

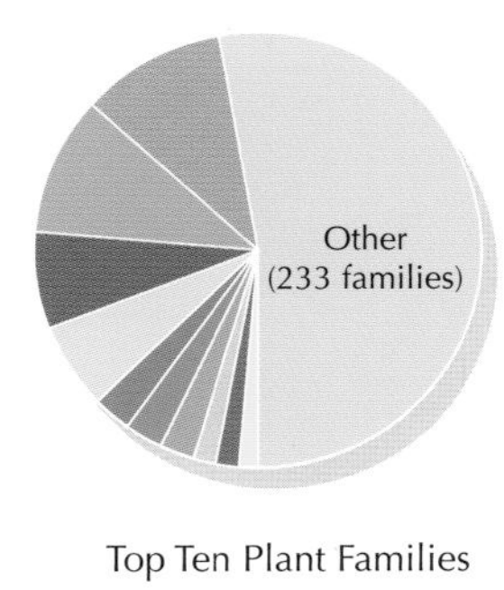

Top Ten Plant Families

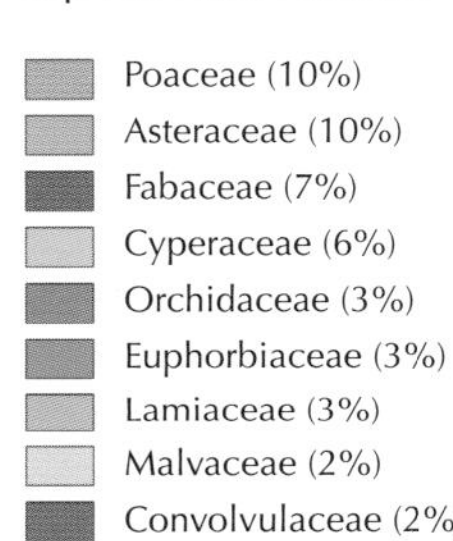

Wunderlin, NatureServe, FNAI

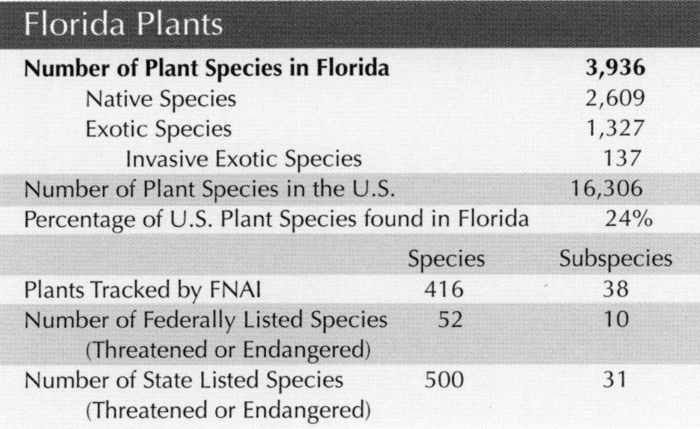

Florida Plants		
Number of Plant Species in Florida		**3,936**
Native Species		2,609
Exotic Species		1,327
Invasive Exotic Species		137
Number of Plant Species in the U.S.		16,306
Percentage of U.S. Plant Species found in Florida		24%
	Species	Subspecies
Plants Tracked by FNAI	416	38
Number of Federally Listed Species (Threatened or Endangered)	52	10
Number of State Listed Species (Threatened or Endangered)	500	31

Wunderlin, NatureServe, FNAI

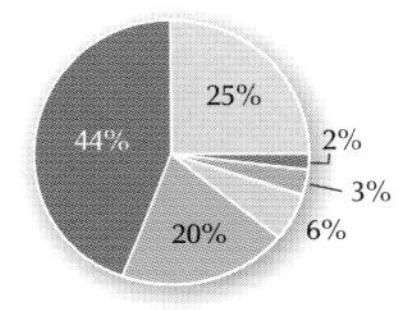

Florida Plants by Global Rarity Rank

About 10% of Florida's plant species are considered rare (GH-G3).

(full species only; see page 142 for rank explanations)

Ethnobotany

Florida's diverse flora also includes numerous plants with ethnobotanical value. These are species for which humans (typically indigenous people) have developed practical uses in their everyday lives. Among these are edible or food crops, plants with medicinal or curative properties, plants used for creating clothing, textiles, and textile dyes, as well as plants that have been important in rituals, ceremonies, and social life. Estimates are that more than one-third of Florida's native plants had some ethnobotanical value to its Native American inhabitants. Seminole Indians traditionally used the root starch from coontie (*Zamia pumila*) to make a flour for "Seminole bread." Saw palmetto (*Serenoa repens*) is considered one of the most useful plants in Florida, providing food, fiber, medicine, roofing thatch, oil, and wax. Doctors today use an extract from the fruit in treating prostate cancer.

Coontie (*Zamia pumila*) root bisected to show texture

Saw Palmetto (*Serenoa repens*) frond (top), berries (bottom)

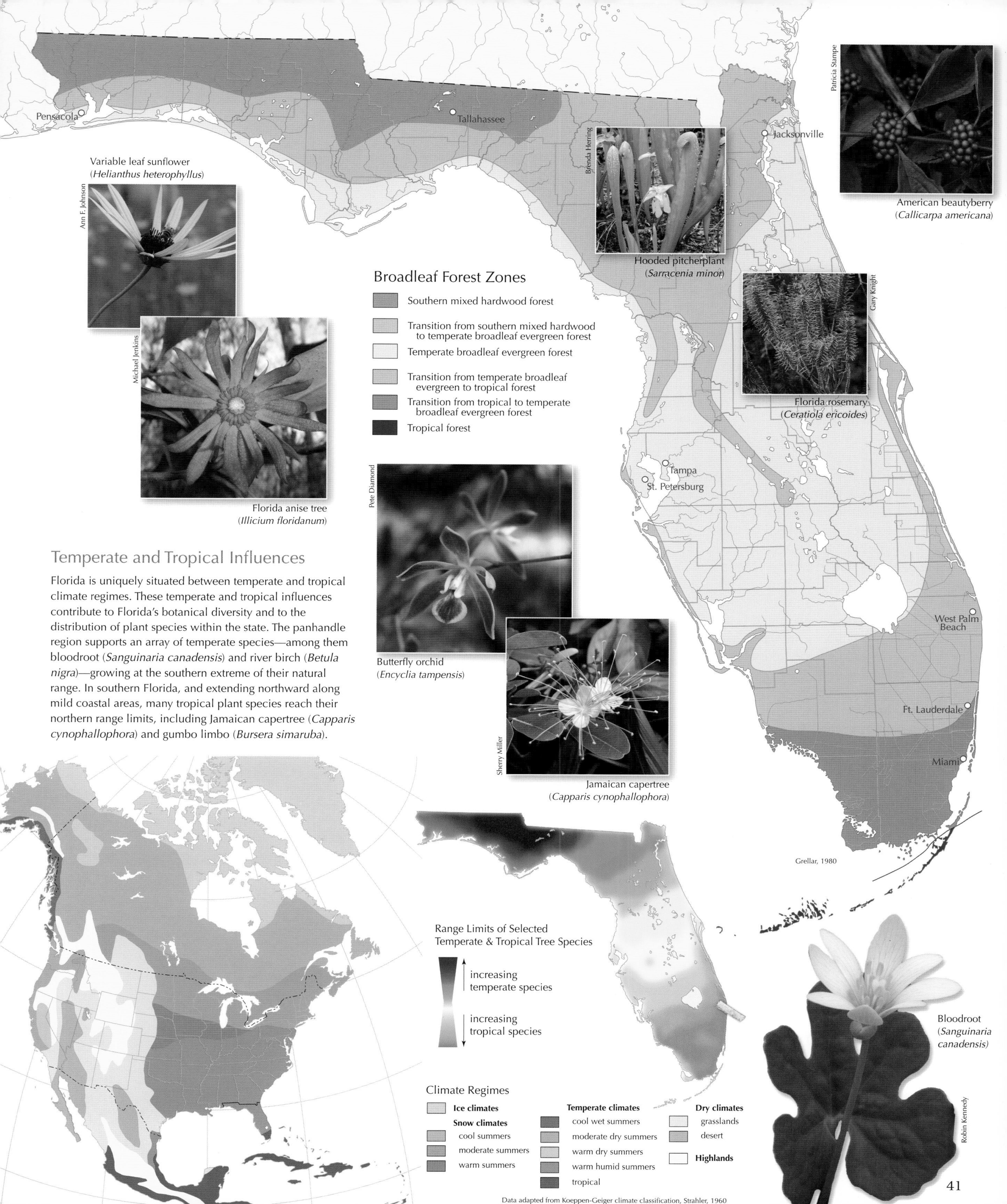

Variable leaf sunflower (*Helianthus heterophyllus*)

Florida anise tree (*Illicium floridanum*)

Hooded pitcherplant (*Sarracenia minor*)

American beautyberry (*Callicarpa americana*)

Florida rosemary (*Ceratiola ericoides*)

Butterfly orchid (*Encyclia tampensis*)

Jamaican capertree (*Capparis cynophallophora*)

Bloodroot (*Sanguinaria canadensis*)

Temperate and Tropical Influences

Florida is uniquely situated between temperate and tropical climate regimes. These temperate and tropical influences contribute to Florida's botanical diversity and to the distribution of plant species within the state. The panhandle region supports an array of temperate species—among them bloodroot (*Sanguinaria canadensis*) and river birch (*Betula nigra*)—growing at the southern extreme of their natural range. In southern Florida, and extending northward along mild coastal areas, many tropical plant species reach their northern range limits, including Jamaican capertree (*Capparis cynophallophora*) and gumbo limbo (*Bursera simaruba*).

Rare Plants

Most plants in Florida occur frequently over a wide area or have stable populations and face few threats to their long-term survival. Yet a subset of Florida's native plants is facing serious pressures that are pushing these species ever closer to extinction. Rare plants now account for nearly 14% of the state's 2,840 native species. This distinction places Florida first among eastern U.S. states and sixth nationally in the percentage of rare plants.

Several factors have contributed to the rarity of these plants. Some species are naturally rare due to biological constraints, such as narrow distribution, poor fertility, or restricted habitat requirements, while others have declined due to a long history of negative human impacts. Some plants are Florida endemics—they occur only in Florida and nowhere else in the world. The very rarest species, those with the fewest populations, are ranked as endangered. These plants are in the greatest danger of extinction throughout all, or a significant portion, of their range. Rare plants with slightly larger populations and that are likely to become endangered within the foreseeable future are deemed threatened.The effects of human activities on native plant populations are felt across Florida. Loss of habitat—the primary threat—includes habitat destruction, logging, conversion to agriculture, urban sprawl, draining of wetlands (hydrological modifications), and fire suppression. Poaching of horticulturally desirable plants such as orchids, bromeliads, and cacti puts additional pressure on already stressed populations. Non-native species—plants, animals and disease vectors—also pose serious concerns. Many introduced plants have escaped cultivation and are out-competing and displacing common and rare native species. A non-native moth is destroying the already rare Florida semaphore cactus *(Opuntia corallicola)*, while tiny Mexican weevils are killing rare bromeliads. Bacterial and fungal diseases are also to blame for declines of certain species, including Florida torreya *(Torreya taxifolia)*.

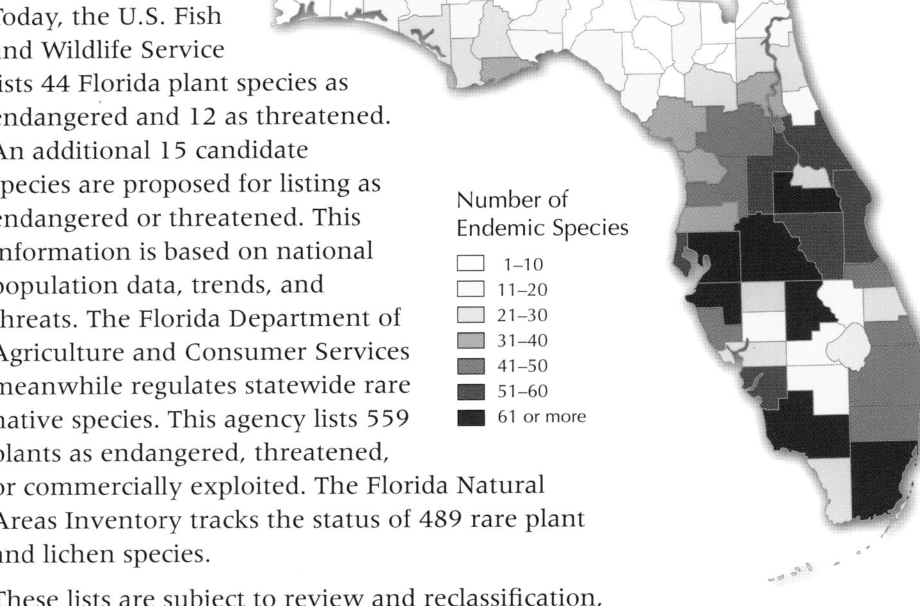

Today, the U.S. Fish and Wildlife Service lists 44 Florida plant species as endangered and 12 as threatened. An additional 15 candidate species are proposed for listing as endangered or threatened. This information is based on national population data, trends, and threats. The Florida Department of Agriculture and Consumer Services meanwhile regulates statewide rare native species. This agency lists 559 plants as endangered, threatened, or commercially exploited. The Florida Natural Areas Inventory tracks the status of 489 rare plant and lichen species.

These lists are subject to review and reclassification, particularly as new plant population field data are evaluated against ongoing threats, habitat restoration, and species recovery efforts. Occasionally, targeted survey efforts may uncover previously unrecorded populations of rare plants. Recent examples include populations of critically imperiled gentian pinkroot *(Spigelia gentianoides)*, perforate reindeer lichen *(Cladonia perforata)*, and scrub ziziphus *(Ziziphus celata)*, each of which helps secure the genetic diversity and the protection of these species.

Most rare plant species in Florida find refuge on one or more of the state's many protected conservation lands that stretched across more than 9.3 million acres as of March 2010. Chalky Indian-plantain *(Arnoglossum album)* and small-toothed sedge *(Carex microdonta)* are among at least 19 FNAI-tracked plant species that are currently not protected on any managed areas in Florida.

Florida's Ten Rarest Plant Species	
Brooksville bellflower	*Campanula robinsiae*
Etonia rosemary	*Conradina etonia*
Okeechobee gourd	*Cucurbita okeechobeensis*
Garrett's scrub balm	*Dicerandra christmanii*
Godfrey's sandwort	*Minuartia godfreyi*
Florida semaphore cactus	*Opuntia corallicola*
Miccosukee gooseberry	*Ribes echinellum*
silky bluestem	*Schizachyrium sericatum*
Craighead's nodding-caps	*Triphora craigheadii*
scrub ziziphus	*Ziziphus celata*

These ten species are all ranked G1/S1.

Brenda Herring

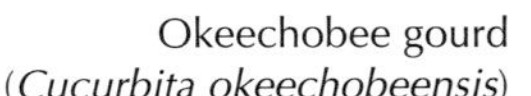

Okeechobee gourd
(*Cucurbita okeechobeensis*)

Rare Plant Hotspots

Florida owes much of its plant diversity to a diverse geography, a complex geology, and temperate and tropical climatic influences. This diversity is expressed most notably in seven distinct areas of Florida that are recognized as globally significant biodiversity hotspots—the West Florida Panhandle, the Apalachicola Prairies and Flatwoods, the Apalachicola Temperate Hardwood Forest, the Lake Wales Ridge, the Miami Rock Ridge, the Florida Keys, and the Atlantic Coastal Ridge. Rare species, however, occur throughout the state.

Ann F. Johnson

Panhandle lily (*Lilium iridollae*)

West Florida Panhandle

The West Florida Panhandle offers a distinct combination of rare plant-rich habitats. Several natural communities, from coastal scrub to the inland sandhill, upland pine, steephead, and seepage wetland systems, contribute many rare species to this significant area.

Amy M. Jenkins

Fringed campion (*Silene polypetala*)

Apalachicola Temperate Hardwood Forest

A landscape of highly dissected uplands on the eastern banks of the upper Apalachicola River forms bluffs and ravines that are rich with rare plants, species at the southern limits of their ranges, and many relicts taking refuge in the moist and steep microclimate.

Anne Cox

Four-petal pawpaw (*Asimina tetramera*)

Atlantic Coastal Ridge

The Atlantic Coastal Ridge is an ancient dune ridge paralleling the southeastern Atlantic shoreline. It is dominated by scrub and shares many scrub endemics with the Lake Wales Ridge. Several rare species are also endemic to this ridge.

Amy M. Jenkins

Florida skullcap (*Scutellaria floridana*)

Apalachicola Prairies and Flatwoods

The expansive lower Apalachicola Prairies and Flatwoods are home to a unique suite of rare and endemic species specifically adapted to a frequent fire regime, including Florida's only two endemic genera: *Harperocallis* and *Stachydeoma*.

Amy M. Jenkins

Ashe's savory (*Calamintha ashei*)

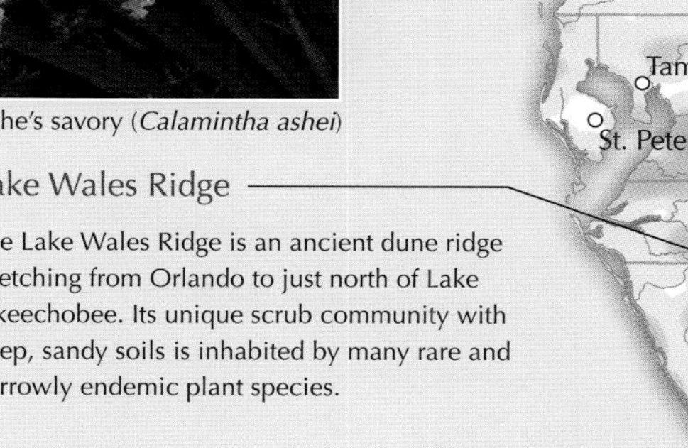

Lake Wales Ridge

The Lake Wales Ridge is an ancient dune ridge stretching from Orlando to just north of Lake Okeechobee. Its unique scrub community with deep, sandy soils is inhabited by many rare and narrowly endemic plant species.

Amy M. Jenkins

Christmas berry (*Crossopetalum ilicifolium*)

Miami Rock Ridge

The Miami Rock Ridge is characterized by its pinelands and tropical hardwood hammocks on very thin soils over limestone. This highly fragmented landscape is noted for its pockets of remaining natural areas with high diversity of rare plants. Pine rocklands alone are critical to at least 51 species of rare plants.

Gary Knight

Small-flowered lily thorn (*Catesbaea parviflora*)

Harper's beauty (*Harperocallis flava*)

Amy M. Jenkins

Florida Keys

The Florida Keys are a subtropical archipelago dividing the Atlantic Ocean from the Gulf of Mexico at the southernmost latitudes of the continental U.S. They are characterized by tropical hardwood hammocks and pine rocklands with many rare plant species and tropical species more typical of the Bahamas and West Indies.

Rarity-Weighted Richness

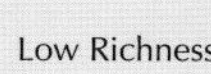

Pines

Florida may be well known for its sandy beaches and expansive swamps, but anyone who has lived or travelled here has marveled at the majestic pine-dominated forests that define Florida landscapes and culture. The diverse and expansive pine forests of Florida are quintessential to local literature and song and have been an economic mainstay for hundreds of years.

Seven species of pine are native to Florida, and each species can be characterized by its appearance and its environment. Pine trees may look similar, but each species has unique physical features and serves particular ecosystem functions. Pine habitats span a wide ecological spectrum, occurring in almost all of Florida's natural plant communities. Many pines are notable for an inherent ability to resist fire. Longleaf pines (*Pinus palustris*) have a fire-resistant sapling stage making them resistant to frequent fires, and pond pines (*Pinus serotina*) have serotinous cones—cones that only open and drop their seeds when the resin holding the scales together is heated by a hot fire. Plants found in regularly burned pine-dominated ecosystems depend on regular fires for survival. Other pines such as loblolly (*Pinus taeda*) and some slash pines (*Pinus elliottii*) cannot withstand fire when they are saplings and are not able to survive in regularly burned habitats.

Aside from being ecologically important, pines are also economically and socially important. Pines, especially slash pine, loblolly pine, and longleaf pine, have been heavily utilized for timber, pulp, tar, and turpentine. Pre-20th-century wooden ships were waterproofed using the tar or pitch that was created here. Rosin, turpentine, and many household products are still produced using pine resin. The timber industry is a large source of jobs and revenue for Floridians. However, large-scale land conversion of native pine woodlands to plantations and developments has reduced the extent of native pinelands and modified their structure. Some forestry practices can be detrimental to the integrity of these natural communities by heavily disturbing the soil and removing the native groundcover. Other, less drastic practices can promote and maintain the function of these forests while satisfying the needs of society.

Pine forests in Florida are a cultural treasure, an important source of jobs and revenue and an invaluable ecological and scientific resource.

State Archives of Florida

Sorting at a logging mill

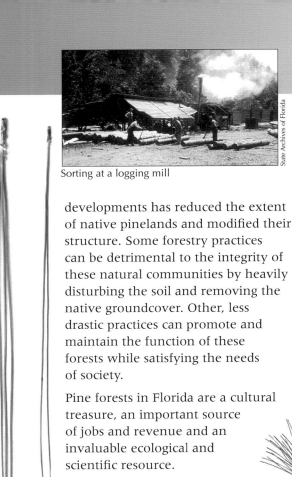

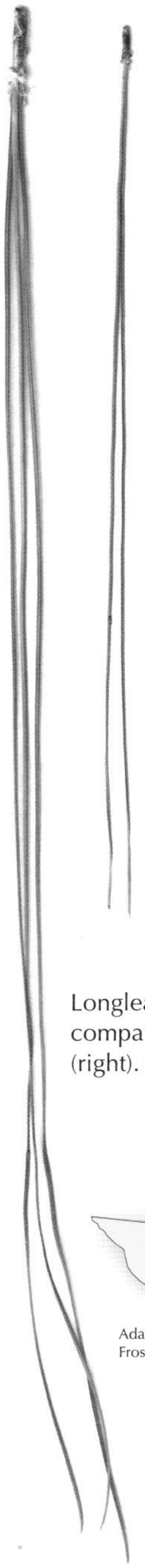

Longleaf pine needles (left) as compared to slash pine needles (right). Scale is 40% of actual size.

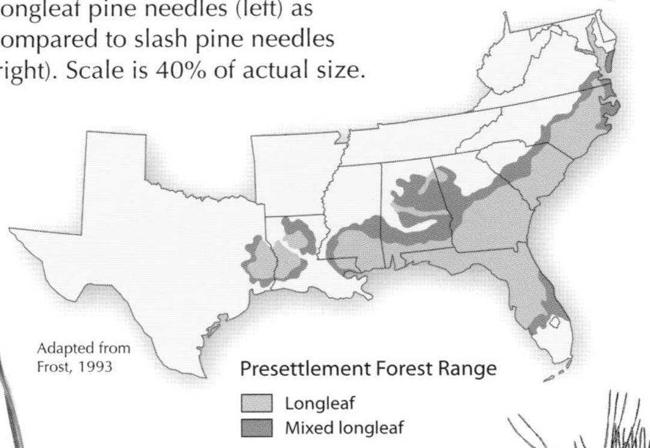

Adapted from Frost, 1993

Presettlement Forest Range

Longleaf

Mixed longleaf

Only 3% of longleaf pine forests, the preferred habitat of many rare species, remain throughout longleaf's natural range. This dramatic decrease is the result of massive land conversion throughout the Coastal Plain for development, agriculture, and timber production.

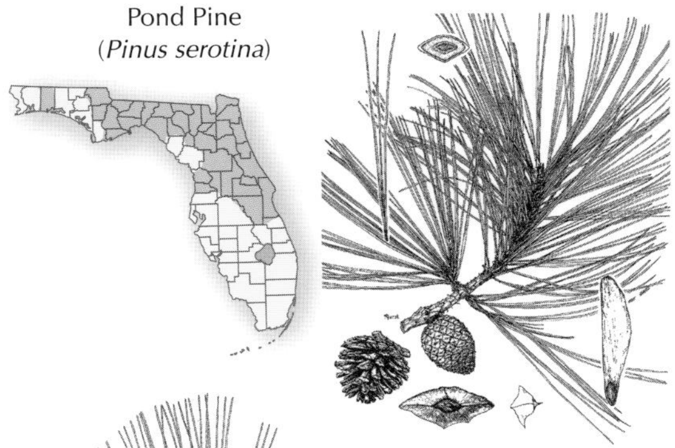

Pond Pine (*Pinus serotina*)

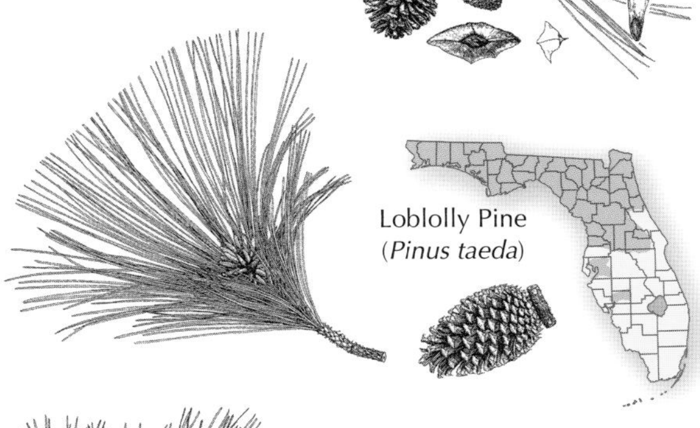

Loblolly Pine (*Pinus taeda*)

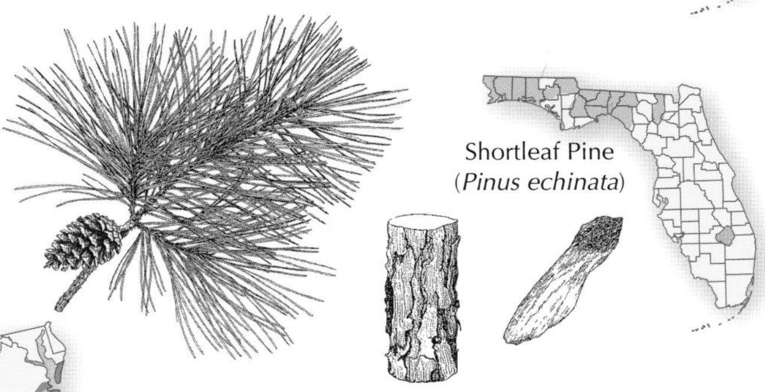

Shortleaf Pine (*Pinus echinata*)

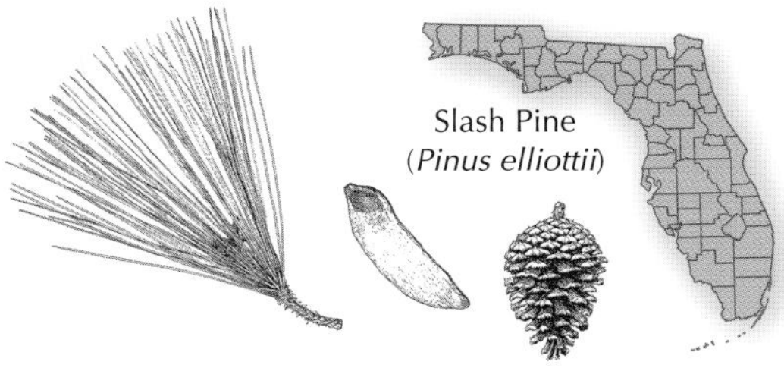

Slash Pine (*Pinus elliottii*)

Spruce Pine (*Pinus glabra*)

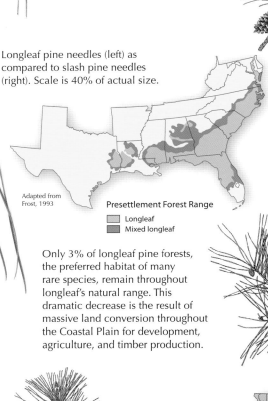

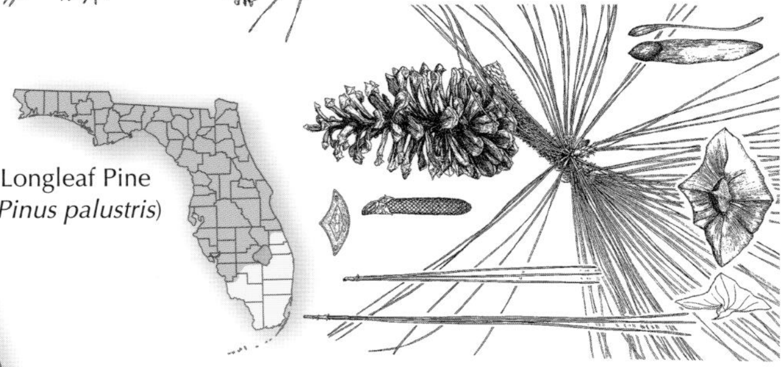

Longleaf Pine (*Pinus palustris*)

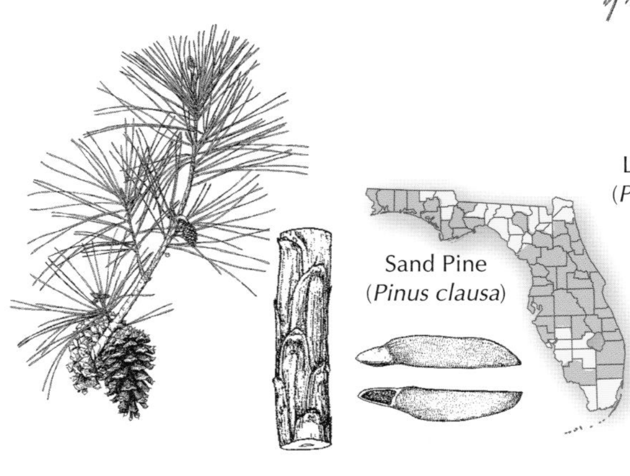

Sand Pine (*Pinus clausa*)

Drawings by Melanie Darst, reprinted by permission from Robert K. Godfrey, *Trees, Shrubs, and Woody Vines of Northern Florida and Adjacent Georgia and Alabama*, figures 3-9. © 1989 by the University of Georgia Press. Range maps drawn from county distributions from Wunderlin and Hansen, 2008.

The genus *Pinus* has evergreen, needle-like leaves held together in fascicles (groups of two or three leaves). Another key feature of these trees is the pine cone, female reproductive structures consisting of spirally arranged woody bracts that enclose and protect the seeds. Distinctive characters, such as bud size and color, needle length and number, and female cone size, shape, and luster are used to differentiate among pine species.

Gary Knight

Pine-dominated communities provide important wildlife habitat and are recognized as some of Florida's most characteristic and aesthetically pleasing landscapes.

Oaks

The live oak (*Quercus virginiana*) can often obtain very large stature in both forested and open landscapes. This stately tree can possess a crown covering up to one-third of an acre and obtain a 9-foot-diameter trunk.

Many oaks are specialized and have adapted to Florida's often harsh environments. Dwarf live oak (*Quercus minima*) occurs as a groundcover species common in many of the pyrogenic communities of the state and is generally less than 3 feet in height. It never reaches tree status, but can produce acorns at 3 years of age in order to successfully reproduce between frequent fire events.

Often overlooked for the dramatic tropical palms of the coast or the stately pines of Florida's interior, the oaks (genus *Quercus*) of Florida are also one of the main building blocks of the state's ecological diversity. In their maturity, these plants can occur as trees, shrubs, and even low-growing groundcovers and flourish in a wide range of environmental conditions from inundated floodplains to xeric uplands to fire-purified prairies. Many northern species of oaks find their southern range limits within Florida's boundaries. These northern species combined with the oaks of the southeastern coastal plain, many of which are endemic or nearly endemic to Florida, account for the 27 total species of oaks that occur within the state.

Oaks often form the principal framework of many habitats and are integral to the ecology of Florida's natural communities. Scrub, a xeric community primarily composed of four specialized species of oaks, including Chapman's oak (*Quercus chapmanii*), sand live oak (*Quercus geminata*), scrub oak (*Quercus inopina*), and myrtle oak (*Quercus myrtifolia*), is an excellent example of this. Oaks and their leaf litter are relatively fire resistant, which helps create various habitats that either exclude fire or reduce fire frequencies. Left unchecked by fire, oaks can convert open pyrogenic lands to unnatural successional forests, thus reducing species diversity and overall community integrity. Also, many epiphytic plants and lichens are strongly associated with oaks, particularly live oaks, due to the stable microclimate their evergreen canopies supply.

Natural communities containing oaks provide critical food supplies for numerous birds, mammals, and invertebrate species. Approximately 400 Florida butterfly and moth species are known to use oaks. The rare and aptly named Florida scrub-jay is reliant on oak-dominated scrub habitats in peninsular Florida. This species also feeds on acorns during the winter season when insects are scarce. The oaks of Florida are an integral component of the state's biodiversity for the wildlife food source they provide, natural community structure they create, and the aesthetics they contribute to the state's varied landscapes.

Scrub oak (*Quercus inopina*) is the only oak species that is endemic to the state. This species occurs in sandhill and scrub communities in Central Florida and is commonly associated with the Lake Wales Ridge.

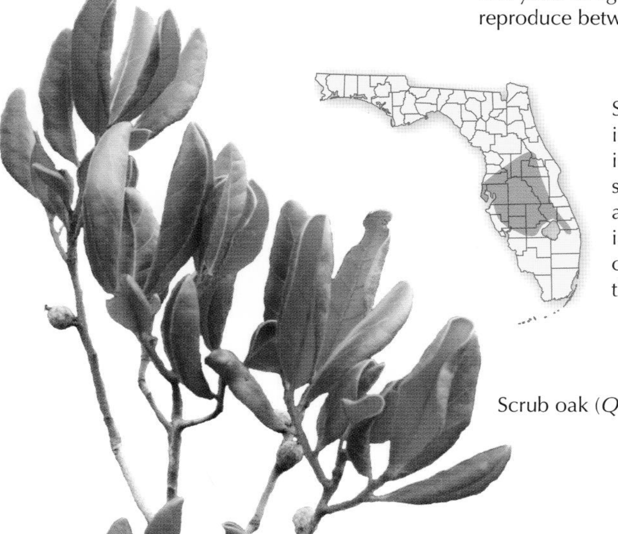

Scrub oak (*Quercus inopina*)

Oak Regions

1 2 3 4 5 6

Oaks

Photo Key	Scientific Name	Common Name	Habitat Hydric	Habitat Mesic	Habitat Xeric	Region
	Quercus alba	white oak		•		1,2
	Quercus arkansana	Arkansas oak		•	•	1
	Quercus austrina	bastard white oak	•	•		1-4
	Quercus chapmanii	Chapman's oak			•	1-5
	Quercus pumila	runner oak		•	•	1-5
A.	*Quercus falcata*	southern red oak		•	•	1-3
	Quercus geminata	sand live oak			•	1-5
	Quercus hemisphaerica	laurel oak		•	•	1-5
E.	*Quercus incana*	bluejack oak			•	1-4
	*Quercus inopina**	scrub oak			•	4
I.	*Quercus laevis*	turkey oak			•	1-4
D.	*Quercus laurifolia*	swamp laurel oak	•	•	•	1-5
	Quercus lyrata	overcup oak		•	•	1-3
C.	*Quercus margaretta*	sand post oak		•	•	1-4
J.	*Quercus marilandica*	blackjack oak		•	•	1,2
	Quercus michauxii	swamp chestnut oak	•	•		1-3
B.	*Quercus minima*	dwarf live oak		•	•	1-5
	Quercus muehlenbergii	chinquapin oak	•	•		1,2
	Quercus myrtifolia	myrtle oak			•	1-5
K.	*Quercus nigra*	water oak	•	•	•	1-5
	Quercus pagoda	cherrybark oak	•	•		1,2
	Quercus phellos	willow oak	•			1-3
H.	*Quercus shumardii*	Shumard's oak		•		1-3
	Quercus stellata	post oak		•		1-3
F.	*Quercus velutina*	black oak		•		1-3
G.	*Quercus virginiana*	live oak	•	•	•	1-6

*denotes an endemic species in Florida

A total of 27 species of oaks, in addition to numerous hybrids, are found within the geographic boundaries of Florida. Oaks are ubiquitous members of the state's flora and occur in both evergreen and deciduous forms with a wide gamut of growth forms and leaf shapes.

Grasses, Sedges, and Rushes

Plants in the Grass Family (Poaceae), Sedge Family (Cyperaceae), and Rush Family (Juncaceae) are found in most of the world's ecosystems and are the dominant vegetation in many natural communities. These three plant families are collectively referred to as graminoids. In Florida, they make up a significant portion of the total flora and dominate many of Florida's natural communities. The Poaceae is the largest plant family in Florida, and the Cyperaceae is the fourth largest.

Graminoids serve important ecological functions in Florida's natural communities. Grass-, sedge- and rush-dominated marshes protect shorelines from erosion, provide floodwater storage, filter excess nitrogen from runoff, and provide habitat for scores of native and economically important species. Wiregrass and other graminoid species with fine, wire-like leaves carry frequent low-intensity fires quickly across the landscape, promoting species richness and the overall health of many fire-maintained plant communities. Graminoids and the expansive communities where they are dominant also serve an important biogeochemical function as a carbon sink, utilizing and storing excess carbon, thereby mitigating the effects of carbon emissions on global climate. Many graminoid species are also rare, some growing nowhere else but Florida; this along with the important ecological and economic roles graminoids play makes their protection a priority to the conservation of global biodiversity.

Despite their lack of showy flowers and sometimes inconspicuous appearance, the contributions of grasses, sedges, and rushes to the health and maintenance of Florida's treasured natural communities are immeasurable.

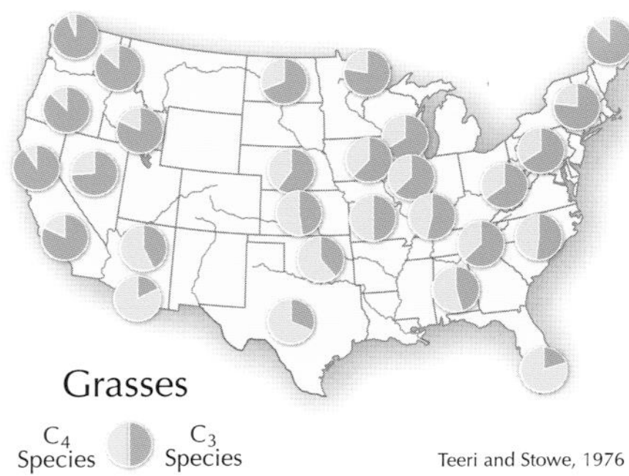

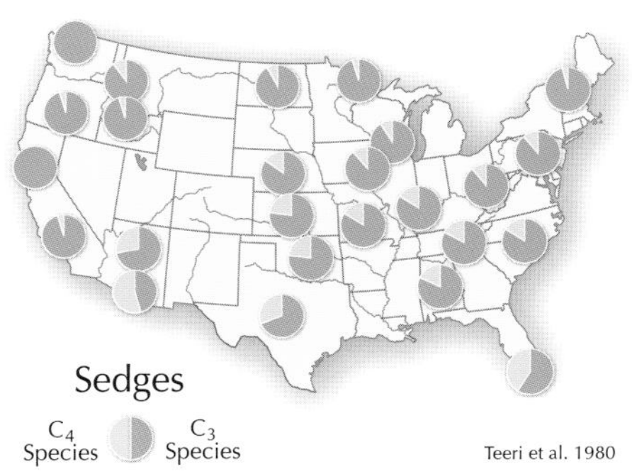

Most cool weather graminoids use a method of turning light and carbon dioxide into energy termed "C3 photosynthesis." Many of Florida's graminoids use a specialized method termed "C4 photosynthesis" that allows them to thrive in the state's high-light and high-temperature environments.

Grass, Sedge, and Rush Families in Florida

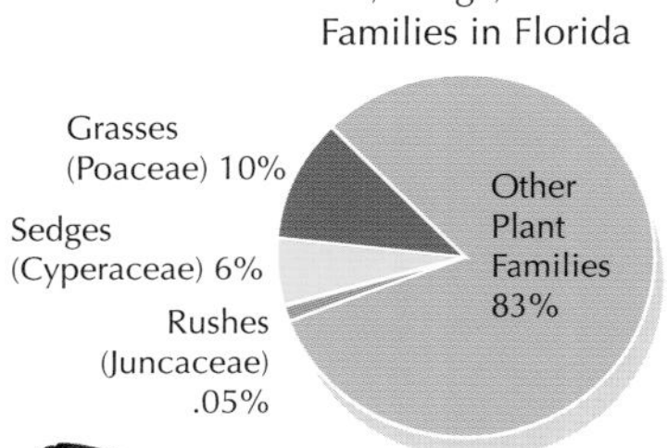

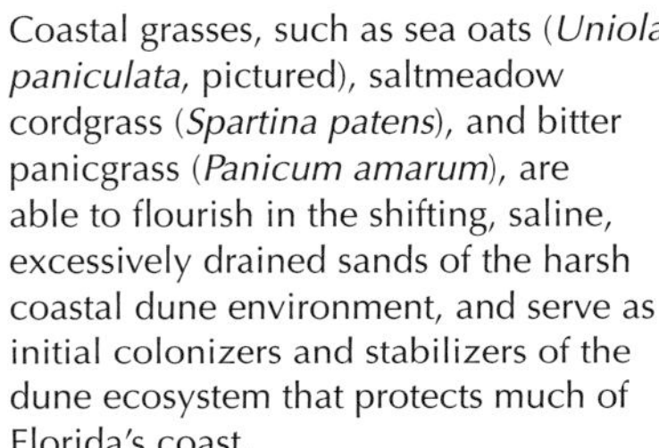

Grasses, Sedges, & Rushes	Poaceae	Cyperaceae	Juncaceae
Plant taxa in Florida	440	268	24
Native taxa	263 (60%)	236 (88%)	24 (100%)
Endemic taxa	15 (3%)	3 (1%)	1 (1%)
FNAI tracked taxa	15 (3%)	13 (5%)	1 (4%)
Exotic Invasive taxa	15 (3%)	3 (1%)	0 (0%)

Dean Jue

Caitlin Elam

In addition to providing wildlife forage and habitat, graminoids can be important host plants for insects. Millet beaksedge (*Rhynchospora miliacea*) is the host plant for the Calhoun's skipper (*Euphyes dukesi calhouni*), a rare butterfly that is only known from Florida.

Caitlin Elam

Gary Knight

Wiregrass (*Aristida stricta*) is the dominant groundcover in Florida's flatwoods and other natural communities, facilitating the spread of habitat-maintaining fires.

Natural Systems Characterized by Grasses, Sedges, and Rushes

Caitlin Elam

Throughout Florida, graminoids, such as the relatively salt-intolerant sawgrass (*Cladium jamaicense*), dominate freshwater marshes and riverine communities, providing habitat and ecosystem services such as water filtration and carbon storage. Sawgrass marshes are especially notable as the primary component of the northern Everglades.

Brenda Herring

Coastal grasses, such as sea oats (*Uniola paniculata*, pictured), saltmeadow cordgrass (*Spartina patens*), and bitter panicgrass (*Panicum amarum*), are able to flourish in the shifting, saline, excessively drained sands of the harsh coastal dune environment, and serve as initial colonizers and stabilizers of the dune ecosystem that protects much of Florida's coast.

Gary Knight

Coastal and South Florida marshlands are dominated by salt-tolerant species, such as saltmarsh cordgrass (*Spartina alterniflora*, pictured), black needlerush (*Juncus roemerianus*), and saltmeadow cordgrass (*Spartina patens*), that form large monotypic stands and provide habitat for many of Florida's coastal animal species.

Gary Knight

Grass species are the dominant understory cover in many of Florida's characteristic flatwoods. One of these dominant species, the state-listed endangered cutthroat grass (*Panicum abscissum*), grows nowhere else but Florida.

Brenda Herring

Some of the worst invasive exotic species in Florida are grasses and sedges. Cogon grass (*Imperata cylindrica*) is one example that, once established, is very time consuming and expensive to eradicate.

Wetland & Aquatic Plants

Wetlands

Wetland Plants	
Acres of wetlands in Florida	10.6 million
Percentage of total land area	31%
Obligate wetland plant species in Florida	525
Percentage of native flora	18%
Facultative wetland plant species in Florida	565
Percentage of native flora	20%
All wetland plant species endemic to Florida	61
All wetland plant species on Florida threatened and endangered plant list	145
All wetland plant species on federal threatened and endangered plant list	7
EPPC Category I Invasive exotic plant species found primarily in wetland habitats	21

Wetlands data based on water management district FLUCCS land cover, 2004 for all districts except SWFWMD (2007).

Key: W = Wetland plants, Aquatic Plants: E = Emergent, F = Floating leaves, S = Submerged

David Moynahan

Scarlet rosemallow W
Hibiscus coccineus

© Bill Boothe

Blue waterhyssop W
Bacopa caroliniana

Paul Russo

Swamp lily W
Crinum americanum

David Moynahan

Yellow-eyed grass W
Xyris sp.

David Moynahan

Blue flag iris W
Iris virginica

Nia Wellendorf

Frog's bit E
Limnobium spongia

Nia Wellendorf

Bullrush E
Scirpus sp.

David Moynahan

Pickerelweed E
Pontederia cordata

Robin Kennedy

Goldenclub F
Orontium aquaticum

© Bill Boothe

Spatterdock F
Nuphar advena

Max Feken

White waterlily F
Nymphaea odorata

John Tobe

Springtape S
Sagittaria kurziana

Mike Wisenbaker

Springtape S
Sagittaria kurziana

Mike Wisenbaker

Waterweed and springtape S
Egeria densa and Sagittaria kurziana

Wetland plants are those whose roots can withstand inundated or saturated soil for relatively long periods without harm. Upland plants are eventually killed by standing water or saturated soil because of low oxygen levels in their roots. Wetland plants survive either by tolerating low oxygen levels around their roots for a certain period, or by having specialized vessels that allow oxygen to diffuse to the roots when they are under water.

Herbaceous wetland plants vary widely in the amount of inundation they can tolerate. Aquatic species with submerged or floating leaves, such as springtape (*Sagittaria kurziana*) or white waterlily (*Nymphaea odorata*) depend on permanent inundation to float their leaves up to the sunlight. Emergent species, such as wild rice (*Zizania aquatica*) or pickerelweed (*Pontederia cordata*) are rooted in the deeper to shallower parts of the fluctuating edges of water bodies and have stiff stems that hold their upper leaves above the normal water level. Least tolerant are opportunistic, seed-banking species, such as lemon bacopa (*Bacopa caroliniana*), that carpet the dried bottoms of lakes and rivers, only to be killed when the water rises again. Trees, such as bald cypress, rooted in the unstable, wet, mucky ground of swamps and bottomlands, may have flared bases which help brace them against toppling over.

As important sources of plant and animal diversity, wetlands are protected by both state and federal statutes. Lists of facultative (found primarily in wet areas but also occurring in uplands) and obligate (found only in wet areas) wetland plant species are published to help delineate the boundaries of legally protected wetlands. The state lists almost 40% of the total flora of Florida as either obligate or facultative wetland species, reflecting the region's low relief and ample rainfall. Sixty-one of these wetland species are found only in Florida. Many wetland plants are dependent on a specific regime of fluctuating water levels; if water is either drained or permanently impounded, the high diversity of species originally present is often replaced by only one or two that can tolerate such non-fluctuating conditions. In addition, most Florida wetland species are adapted to the low nutrient levels in Florida waters; when the nutrient levels are raised by pollution, exotic wetland species, such as water hyacinth (*Eichhornia crassipes*) or hydrilla (*Hydrilla verticillata*) proliferate, displacing the native species and choking waterways used by boaters.

Palms

Kim Gulledge

Amid Florida's diversity of habitats and plants, palms are probably the most prominent and iconic image of the state's natural heritage. Often referred to as "palm trees," these plants are actually more closely related to grasses than to typical tree species such as oaks. Palms are monocots and lack the "true wood" that other trees produce through secondary growth. The thick fibrous stems of palms are created through a specialized type of primary growth. Once produced, a palm trunk remains the same diameter throughout the plant's life, although the actual plant may reach a substantial height.

Florida boasts more native palm species than any other state in the contiguous U.S. due to its warm climate and proximity to the West Indies, a region rich in palm diversity. Four shrubby palm species found in the southeastern U.S. and seven tree palms distributed in the Caribbean are all native to Florida. These palms grow in a variety of natural communities, from swampy floodplains to dry sandy scrub and salt-sprayed coastal strands.

Palms, like other vascular plants, have clusters of specialized cells known as xylem and phloem that are necessary for water and food transport. In palms (above), these cells are produced as the trunk gains height and are scattered throughout the stem. Trees such as oaks and pines (above) produce these cells continually with secondary growth, resulting in a pattern of annual growth rings.

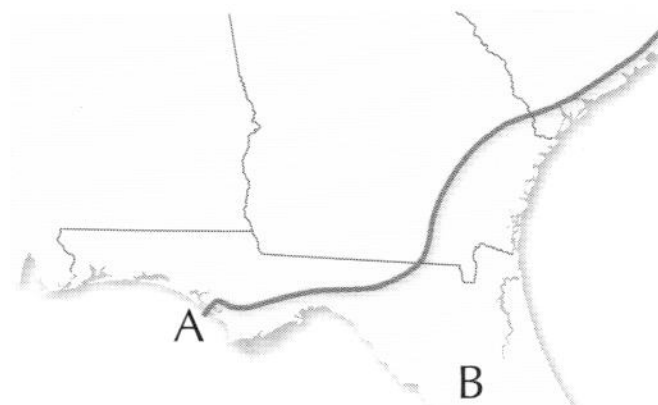
A
B
C
A – northern extent of cabbage palm
B – dwarf palmetto and needle palm reach their southern limits in this region
C – six of the Caribbean tree palm species are restricted to South Florida

Shoestring fern (*Vittaria lineata*)
Paul Russo

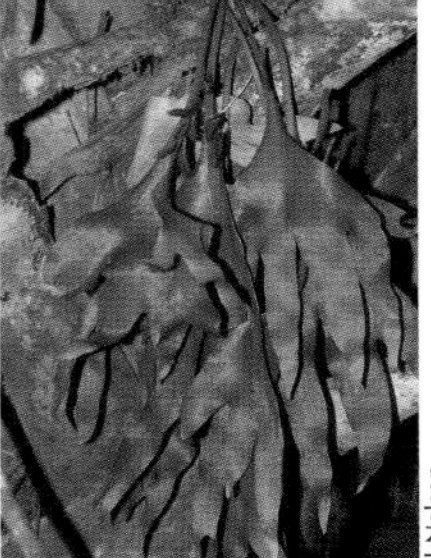

Hand fern (*Ophioglossum palmatum*)
State listed endangered
Gil Nelson

Epiphytes

In shady hammocks and swamps, cabbage palm trunks provide specialized habitat conditions for several epiphytic ferns.

Leaf Shape

Palms have large leaves with plications (folds). The leaf is divided into segments in one of three basic patterns: pinnate, palmate, or costapalmate. Recognition of leaf type is important in palm identification.

Palmate—fan-shaped with the segments radiating from a central point of attachment, much like fingers from the palm of your hand.

Pinnate—feather-like with the segments disposed evenly along a long stalk.

Costapalmate—intermediate between pinnate and palmate with segments that arise from an elongated leaf stalk.

Palmate
Pinnate
Costapalmate

Southeastern U.S. Distribution

Four Florida palm species do not have tropical affinities, but are instead native to the Southeastern Coastal Plain. These are all shrubs and grow in a variety of habitats ranging from floodplains to scrub.

Ronald Lange

Saw palmetto *(Serenoa repens)*
Forming a dominant groundcover in mesic flatwoods.

Kim Gulledge

Scrub palmetto *(Sabal etonia)*
Florida endemic, grows in dry scrub and sandhill communities.

Kim Gulledge

Bluestem palmetto *(Sabal minor)*

Kim Gulledge

Needle palm
(Rhapidophyllum hystrix)

Kim Gulledge

Florida's state tree, cabbage palm
(Sabal palmetto)
Found throughout most of Florida and along the coast to North Carolina.

Caribbean Distribution

Seven Florida palm species are distributed primarily in the West Indies. With the exception of cabbage palm, these species are restricted in the continental U.S. to South Florida and are listed as either threatened or endangered in Florida. All of these species produce aerial stems.

STATE LISTED ENDANGERED

Scott Zona

Florida cherry-palm
(Pseudophoenix sargentii)

Scott Zona

Florida thatch palm
(Thrinax radiata)

Scott Zona

Florida royal palm
(Roystonea elata)

STATE LISTED THREATENED

Scott Zona

Brittle thatch palm
(Thrinax morrisii)

Pete Diamond

Everglades palm
(Acoelorraphe wrightii)

Pete Diamond

Silver Palm
(Coccothrinax argentata)

Non-native Palms

The warm climate of South Florida allows gardeners to enjoy the outdoor cultivation of a large variety of non-native palms. A visit to Fairchild Tropical Botanic Garden demonstrates the assortment of palm species from around the world that can be grown in the Miami area. Most of these palms are unable to reproduce outside of cultivation, but some may escape to become naturalized in the wild and may even become nuisance invasive species in natural habitats. Fifteen non-native palms are naturalized in Florida, and six of these are considered Category II invasive plants due to their potential to displace native plants.

Invasive Palms

- *Chamaedorea seifrizii*
- *Livistona chinensis*
- *Phoenix reclinata*
- *Ptychosperma elegans*
- *Syagrus romanzoffiana*
- *Washingtonia robusta*

Wildflowers

1 Alfred Schotz

Cruise's goldenaster
(*Chrysopsis gossypina* ssp. *cruiseana*)
Gulf Islands National Seashore
Habitat: Beach dune

J F M A M J J A S O N D

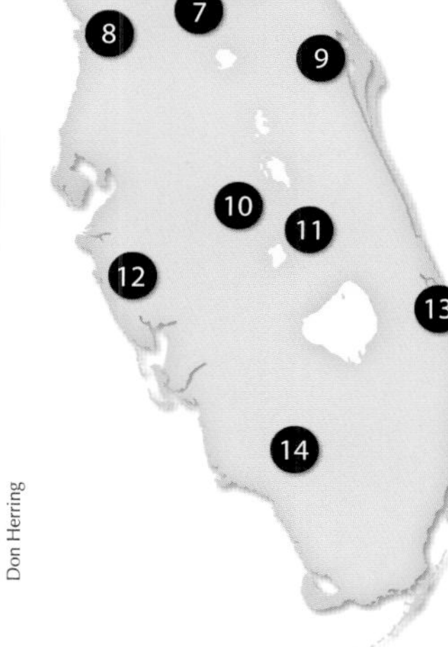

Exemplary sites where each wildflower species can be observed. Site names are listed under each species photo.

Wildflower is not a precise or technically defined term. What gets counted as a wildflower is therefore in the eyes of the beholder. For the purposes of this atlas, any native or naturalized plant with conspicuous, colorful flowers or flower-like bracts qualifies; and by that definition, almost 70% of Florida's native plants, nearly 2,000 species, can justly be called wildflowers. Three plant families in particular—the sunflower, pea, and orchid families—together provide more than 850 colorful types of wildflowers, representatives of which are found throughout the state.

Opportunities abound to see natural wildflower displays in Florida: pitcherplant prairies in the panhandle; pond apple sloughs in South Florida; deciduous hardwood forests of North Florida in early spring; and flatwoods throughout the state, especially in autumn when members of the sunflower family are abundantly flowering. Florida truly is *La Florida*—a flowering land—the name given this region by its first European explorer Juan Ponce de León. Wildflowers can be found throughout Florida, but there are some places at certain times of the year presented here that deserve special attention because of the beauty and richness of their wildflower displays.

J F M A M J J A S O N D

The green bar indicates the best time to observe selected species.

HIGHLIGHTED SPECIES

2 Amy Jenkins

Wild columbine
(*Aquilegia canadensis*)
Florida Caverns State Park
Habitat: Upland hardwood forest

J F M A M J J A S O N D

3 Gary Knight

Trout lily
(*Erythronium umbilicatum*)
Angus Gholson Nature Park
Habitat: Upland hardwood forest

J F M A M J J A S O N D

4 Don Herring

Bartram's rosegentian
(*Sabatia bartramii*)
Apalachicola National Forest
Habitat: Wet prairie

J F M A M J J A S O N D

5 Amy M. Jenkins

Florida balm
(*Dicerandra densiflora*)
O'Leno State Park
Habitat: Sandhills

J F M A M J J A S O N D

6 Don Herring

Large-leaved grass-of-parnassus
(*Parnassia grandifolia*)
Cross Florida Greenway
Habitat: Stream-run; stream margins

J F M A M J J A S O N D

7 J.B. Miller, SJRWMD

Treat's zephyrlily
(*Zephyranthes atamasca* var. *treatiae*)
Emeralda Marsh Conservation Area
Habitat: Wet prairie

J F M A M J J A S O N D

8 Kim Gulledge

Florida alicia
(*Chapmannia floridana*)
Withlacoochee State Forest
Habitat: Sandhills

J F M A M J J A S O N D

9 Alfred Schotz

Celestial lily
(*Nemastylis floridana*)
Salt Lake Wildlife Management Area
Habitat: Wet flatwoods

J F M A M J J A S O N D

10 Michael Jenkins

Florida bonamia
(*Bonamia grandiflora*)
Hickory Lake Scrub
Habitat: Scrub

J F M A M J J A S O N D

11 Ann F. Johnson

Many-flowered grass-pink
(*Calopogon multiflorus*)
Kissimmee Prairie
Habitat: Dry prairie

J F M A M J J A S O N D

12 Brenda Herring

Pine lily
(*Lilium catesbaei*)
Myakka River State Park
Habitat: Wet prairie

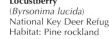

J F M A M J J A S O N D

13 Gary Knight

Yellow milkwort
(*Polygala rugelii*)
Jonathan Dickinson State Park
Habitat: Wet flatwoods

J F M A M J J A S O N D

14 Paul Russo

Stringlily
(*Crinum americanum*)
Big Cypress National Preserve
Habitat: Wet prairie

J F M A M J J A S O N D

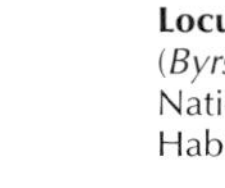

15 Gary Knight

Locustberry
(*Byrsonima lucida*)
National Key Deer Refuge
Habitat: Pine rockland

J F M A M J J A S O N D

Epiphytes

A postcard image of Florida and the Old South is one of gray curtains of Spanish moss (*Tillandsia usneoides*) swaying from the broad, spreading branches of a live oak (*Quercus virginiana*) tree. Spanish moss and other airplants (*Tillandsia* spp.) are part of a fascinating group of Florida plants called epiphytes.

Epiphytes lead a completely aerial existence, perched on the trunks and loftier branches of trees where there is less competition for sunlight and other resources. Epiphytes depend largely on rainfall to deliver water and nutrients, unlike parasites that take life-giving resources directly from their host.

Florida has the most diverse epiphytic flora of any U.S. mainland state. Epiphytes occur in every corner of the state although the diversity increases significantly from cooler, drier northern Florida to warmer and more humid habitats in the central and southern peninsula.

Airplant leaves have tiny, water-absorbing hairs that help capture raindrops and dew, allowing some species to thrive in dry and often exposed situations in sandhill and scrub. Shady hammocks and swamps provide ideal conditions for such epiphytes as ferns, orchids, peperomia, other airplant species, and funnel-shaped, water-holding "tank" bromeliads such as West Indian tufted airplant (*Guzmania monostachia*) and strap airplant (*Catopsis* spp.).

Epiphytes shelter and provide food for a range of insects, birds, amphibians, and mammals. The distribution of Spanish moss across the southeastern U.S. overlaps the ranges of the Seminole bat (*Lasiurus seminolus*) and the northern yellow bat (*L. intermedius*), two species that often roost and bear their young among the plants' leafy tangles.

Many epiphytes in Florida face an uncertain future. Tree felling, loss of habitat, and plant poaching are constant threats. Water-holding bromeliads and some airplants are falling victim to the ravages of the accidentally introduced Mexican bromeliad weevil (*Metamasius callizona*), shown at left. The developing weevil larvae destroy plants by eating (and tunneling) their way through the stem tissue. Researchers are currently assessing the efficacy of a biocontrol program pitting a parasitic fly against the bromeliad weevil.

FNAI

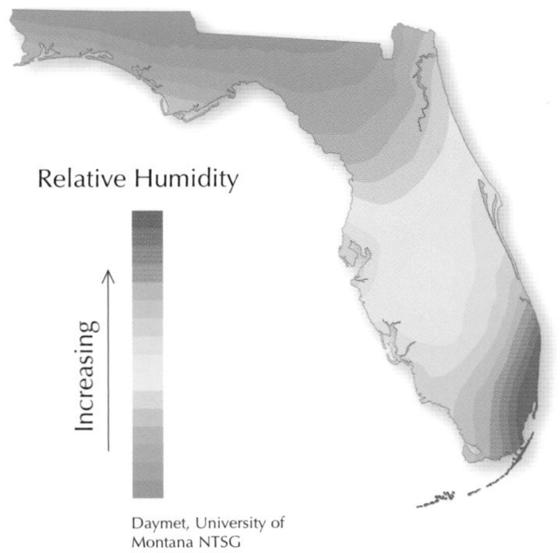

Epiphytes occur throughout Florida but the greatest diversity and concentration of species are found in warmer and more humid habitats of the central and southern peninsula.

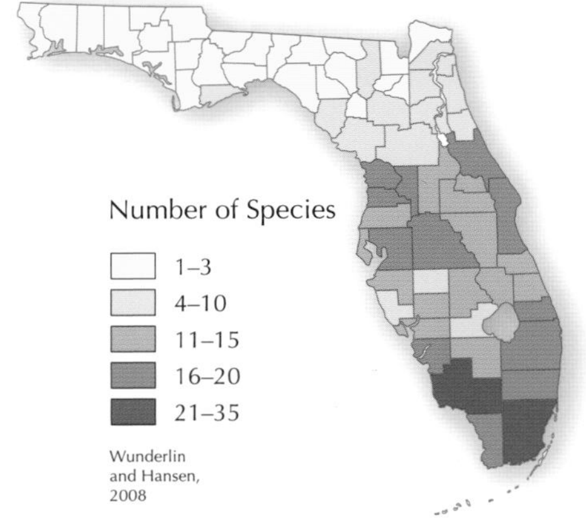

Gary Knight

Pete Diamond

Plume polypody (*Pecluma plumula*) is a graceful fern that adorns mossy tree trunks in wet hammocks and swamps in the Florida peninsula.

Katy NeSmith

The flashy red bracts of common wild-pine (*Tillandsia fasciculata*), an aptly named epiphyte that perches on the trunks of cypress trees (*Taxodium* spp.).

Keith Bradley

Water stored in the fleshy leaves and stems of blunt-leaved peperomia (*Peperomia obtusifolia*) help this epiphyte cope with periods of drier weather.

Pete Diamond

Spanish moss (*Tillandsia usneoides*) and resurrection fern (*Pleopeltis polypodioides* var. *michauxiana*) are the most common epiphytes across northern Florida.

Orchids

HIGHLIGHTED SPECIES

Orchids represent the largest family of flowering plants in the world. These fascinating and enchanting plants are arguably the jewels of Florida's landscape. The 100 or so orchid species that occur naturally within the state represent nearly half of all known orchids in the United States and Canada.

The diversity of habitats in Florida allows for a unique co-mingling of orchid species, many of which exist on the edge of their natural northern or southern range. Orchids are found in each of Florida's 67 counties but few are common and most are slow to colonize. These factors, compounded by widespread habitat loss and poaching, are threatening the very existence of these Florida jewels. Today, three-fourths of the state's resident orchids are listed as threatened or endangered.

Most Florida orchids are terrestrial (ground-dwelling) species. These plants often prefer damp open places such as pine flatwoods, wet prairies, seepage areas, and bogs and marshes associated with basins and rivers. Periodic fire helps maintain these herb-dominated habitats by burning back woody plants and reducing competition for sunlight. The many-flowered grass-pink (*Calopogon multiflorus*) responds in the weeks following a fire by bursting forth in bloom.

A few terrestrial orchids survive in drier habitats. The state-threatened giant orchid (*Pteroglossaspis ecristata*) frequently occurs in flatwoods and occasionally in sandhills. The endangered dancing-lady orchid (*Tolumnia bahamensis*) is endemic to scrub habitat along the Atlantic coast. Rockland orchid (*Basiphyllaea corallicola*), another endangered species, grows in pine rocklands and rockland hammocks.

Florida is unique among U.S. states in that nearly half of all its orchids are epiphytes. These plants are found clinging to the branches of trees or shrubs in high-humidity environments, such as cypress and mangrove swamps, floodplain forests, and hammocks. The diminutive green fly orchid (*Epidendrum conopseum*), which ranges across much of the panhandle and northern peninsula, tolerates sub-freezing winter temperatures. Indicative of their Caribbean ancestry, most epiphytes prefer frost-free habitats in southern Florida. Among the more unusual epiphyte forms in Florida are the vining vanilla orchid (*Vanilla* spp.) and the needleroot airplant orchid (*Harrisella porrecta*), a leafless, gray-green mass of photosynthetic roots.

Prem Subrahmanyam

Pollinators

Some of Florida orchids are self-pollinating, while others require nectar-hungry insects such as bees, wasps, flies, butterflies, and moths to transfer pollen from one orchid flower to another. Above, one of two Florida species of thick-headed fly (*Stylogaster biannulata*) visits the diminutive, half-inch-long flower of threebirds orchid (*Triphora trianthophoros*).

Number of Orchid Species

- 3–13
- 14–19
- 20–25
- 26–39
- 40–56

Wunderlin and Hansen, 2008

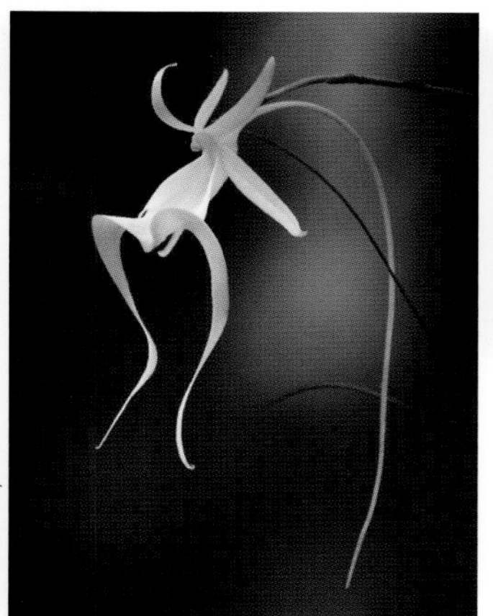

Prem Subrahmanyam

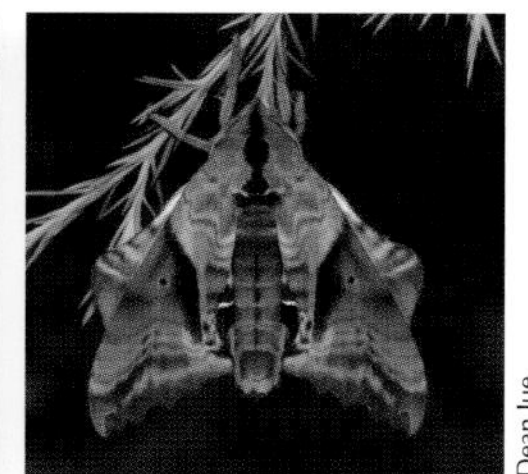

Dean Jue

The giant sphinx moth (*Cocytus antaeus*), with its six-inch, nectar-sucking proboscis, has evolved as the sole pollinator of the leafless ghost orchid (*Dendrophylax lindenii*) shown at left, a rare epiphytic species.

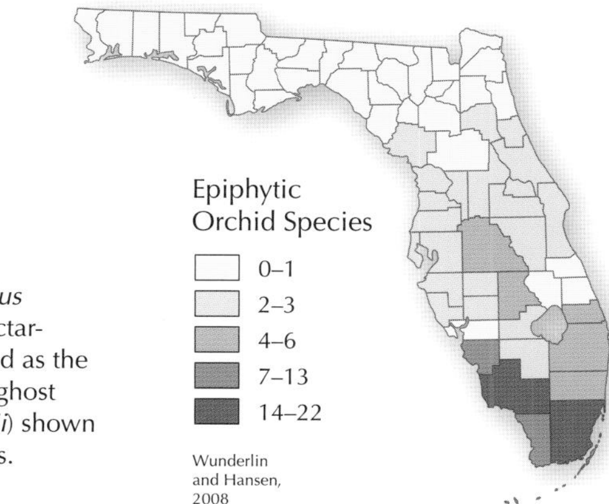

Mike Heaney

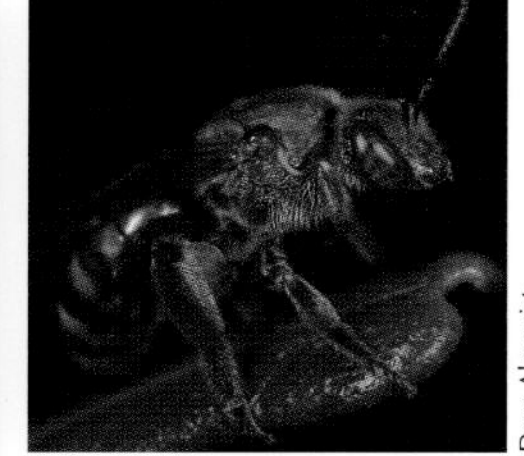

Dave Almquist

The grass-pink orchid (*Calopogon* spp.), shown at left, deceives would-be pollinators with a false promise of sugary nectar. During the ensuing but futile struggle to gather nectar, bees unwittingly carry concealed pollen sacs on their back from one flower to another. Among observed pollinators are some species in the sweat bee family (*Halictidae*), such as this small green bee (*Agapostemon splendens*).

Jim Surdick

Ann F. Johnson

The Southern carpenter bee (*Xylocopa micans*) is one of two known pollinators of the endangered cowhorn orchid (*Cyrtopodium punclatum*). This small native bee is a generalist who gathers nectar from many different flowers, including roundleaf ragwort (*Pakera obovata*).

The low-growing southern twayblade (*Listera australis*), shown at left, recruits tiny fungus gnats and small wasps to pollinate its flowers.

Pete Diamond

Fungal Associates

Orchids are relatively slow-growing compared to most other flowering plants. Many orchids have exacting habitat requirements and require close associations with beneficial mycorrhizal fungi for seed germination and nutrient and mineral absorption. The loss or death of these fungi is an essential reason why wild-collected orchids often perish when removed from their natural habitat. Some terrestrial orchids, with the aid of saprophytic fungi, derive their energy from dead and decaying plant material. One example is the spiked crested coralroot (*Hexalectris spicata*), above, which favors the undisturbed, litter-covered soils of hardwood forests in Northern and Central Florida.

Carnivorous Plants

Among Florida's most unusual plants are those with modified leaf structures designed for trapping and digesting insects. Included within this diverse group of carnivorous, or insect-eating, plants are tube-like pitcherplants, sticky-leaved butterworts and sundews, and vacuum-equipped bladderworts.

The Southeastern Coastal Plain of North America lays claim to the largest diversity of carnivorous plant forms in the world and the highest concentration of species. In Florida, carnivorous plants grow in acidic, nutrient-deficient bogs, swamps, and seepage zones, as well as in freshwater marshes, pine flatwoods, and along the edges of clear, swift-flowing streams. Plants growing in these conditions generally have greater difficulty obtaining and retaining nutrients. Carnivorous plants compensate for nutrient deficiencies by absorbing minerals released from their digested insect prey.

Number of Species

1
2–7
8–12
13–17
18–23
24

Wunderlin and Hanson 2008

Carnivorous Plants

Insects lured to the brightly colored, tubular leaves of pitcherplants (*Sarracenia* spp.) with the promise of a sweet nectar treat sometimes lose their footing on the slickened top edge of the tube. Once inside, downward-pointing hairs further complicate efforts to escape. Exhausted insects ultimately succumb to a soupy brew of digestive enzymes.

Sundews (*Drosera* spp.) and butterworts (*Pinguicula* spp.) ensnare their prey by means of sticky, glandular fluids produced on the upper leaf surface. Trapped insects are digested by means of powerful enzymes contained within the viscous secretions.

Bladderworts (*Utricularia* spp.) bear hundreds of tiny, sac-like traps along their stems. Hapless micro-organisms—aquatic insects, protozoans, tiny crustaceans, rotifers, mosquito larvae—that stimulate the bladderwort's sensitive trigger hairs are quickly sucked inside the bladder with the aid of vacuum pressure. A flap-like door closes behind the prey, sealing it within the trap.

Butterworts

The slick and slippery leaves of Chapman's butterwort (*Pinguicula planifolia*), top, and yellow-flowered butterwort (*P. lutea*), below.

Brenda Herring

Pete Diamond

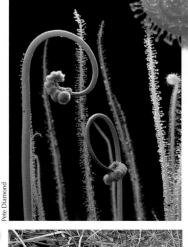

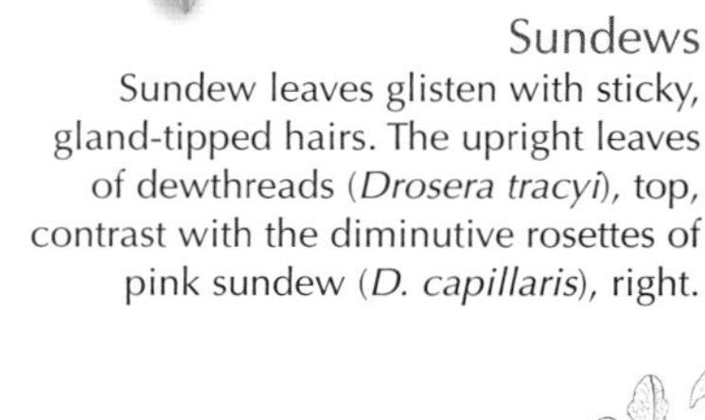

Pete Diamond

Caitlin Elam

Keith Clanton

Sundews

Sundew leaves glisten with sticky, gland-tipped hairs. The upright leaves of dewthreads (*Drosera tracyi*), top, contrast with the diminutive rosettes of pink sundew (*D. capillaris*), right.

Caitlin Elam

Pitcherplants

The tube-like leaves of pitcherplants (below) vary in size, color, and position from the small, prostrate leaves of parrot pitcherplant (*S. psittacina*) to the tall, upright leaves of yellow pitcherplant (*S. flava*).

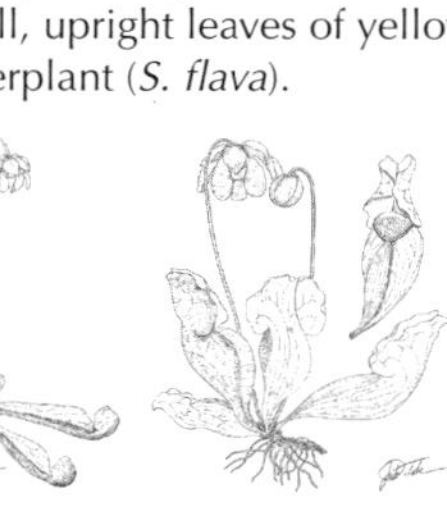

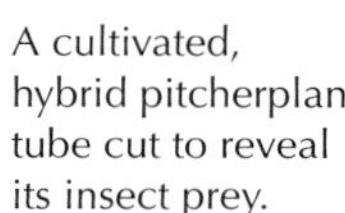

Pitcherplant bog, Blackwater River State Forest

Gary Knight

White-top pitcherplant (*Sarracenia leucophylla*)

Caitlin Elam

Yellow pitcherplant (*Sarracenia flava*)

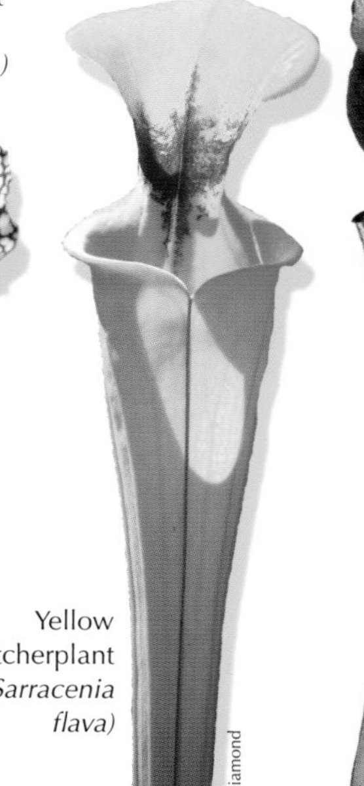

Pete Diamond

A cultivated, hybrid pitcherplant tube cut to reveal its insect prey.

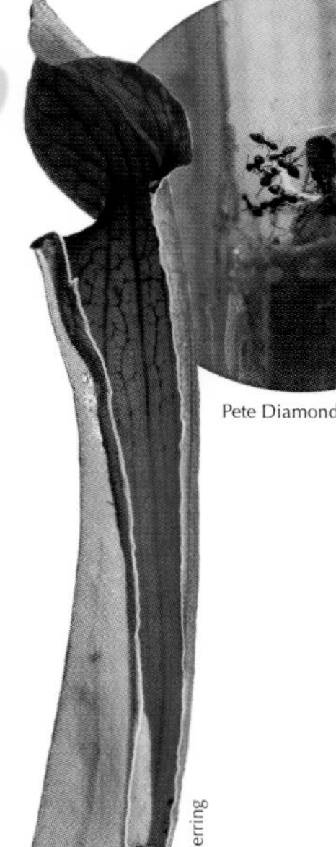

Pete Diamond

Brenda Herring

Dave Almquist

Bladderworts

The minute, sac-like traps of a bladderwort have successfully snared a young mosquito larva.

Parrot pitcherplant (*Sarracenia psittacina*)

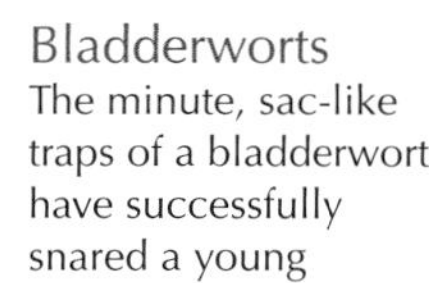

Robin Kennedy

Gulf purple pitcherplant (*Sarracenia rosea*)

Robin Kennedy

Hooded pitcherplant (*Sarracenia minor*)

Brenda Herring

Species on the Edge

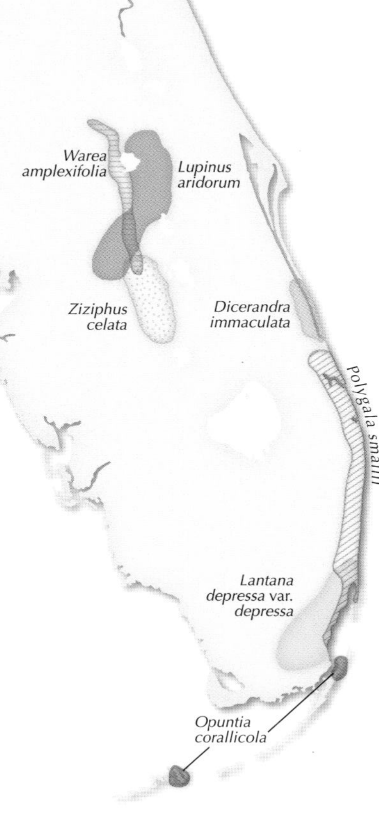

Some plant and animal species in Florida are rarer than others. Among the state's most endangered flora and fauna—those closest to extinction—are distinct species with precariously low populations, few protected sites, and specific threats that jeopardize their survival.

There are many different survival pressures, and some plants and animals are facing multiple threats. Among these are illegal collecting, hybridization with closely related non-native species, fire suppression, climate change, predation by non-native faunal species, diseases resulting from fungal infection, habitat loss, competition with invasive species, deleterious forestry practices, and changes in natural hydrologic processes.

Species living on the edge of extinction are found from tidal rock barrens in the Keys, northward to rich slope forests in the panhandle. The highlighted species represent a small number of Florida's rarest plants and the various threats they face.

Ongoing research and propagation efforts, both at botanical gardens and at protected reintroduction sites in the wild, are striving to keep these and other rare species from getting too close to the edge.

Gary Knight

Florida torreya (*Torreya taxifolia*)

Rank: G1S1
Federal Listing: Endangered
State Listing: Endangered
Habitat: slope forest
Principal Threats: decimated by fungal blight; habitat destruction; most extant individuals exist only as resprouts from dead adults

Amy M. Jenkins

Florida skullcap (*Scutellaria floridana*)

Rank: G2S2
Federal Listing: Threatened
State Listing: Endangered
Habitat: wet flatwoods; wet prairie
Principal Threats: habitat destruction (conversion to pine plantation); fire suppression

Kim Gulledge

Scrub lupine (*Lupinus aridorum*)

Rank: G1S1
Federal Listing: Endangered
State Listing: Endangered
Habitat: scrub
Principal Threats: habitat destruction; damaged by several fungal pathogens; many populations currently threatened by development; propagation difficult

© Bill Boothe

Lakela's mint (*Dicerandra immaculata*)

Rank: G1S1
Federal Listing: Endangered
State Listing: Endangered
Habitat: scrub
Principal Threats: fire suppression and habitat destruction; most populations currently threatened by development

Gary Knight

Florida semaphore cactus (*Opuntia corallicola*)

Rank: G1S1
Federal Listing: Candidate for listing
State Listing: Endangered
Habitat: Keys tidal rock barren
Principal Threats: predation by exotic cactoblastis moth

Gil Nelson

Florida lantana (*Lantana depressa* var. *depressa*)

Rank: G2T1S1
Federal Listing: Not listed
State Listing: Endangered
Habitat: pine rockland
Principal Threats: hybridization with invasive exotic *Lantana camara* leading to "genetic swamping;" exotic species invasion; habitat destruction; fire suppression

Michael Jenkins

Tiny polygala (*Polygala smallii*)

Rank: G1S1
Federal Listing: Endangered
State Listing: Endangered
Habitat: pine rockland; sandhill; mesic flatwoods
Principal Threats: fire suppression; habitat destruction

Cindy Campbell

Scrub ziziphus (*Ziziphus celata*)

Rank: G1S1
Federal Listing: Endangered
State Listing: Endangered
Habitat: scrub
Principal Threats: habitat destruction; fire suppression; exotic species invasion; trampling by cattle

Mike Heaney

Clasping warea (*Warea amplexifolia*)

Rank: G1S1
Federal Listing: Endangered
State Listing: Endangered
Habitat: sandhill
Principal Threats: habitat destruction and conversion to citrus groves; many populations currently threatened by development; invasive exotic species

Invertebrates: Overview

When most people hear the term invertebrate, they may have a vague picture of animals with no backbones and might think of a few examples, such as worms, insects, and crabs. The term actually encompasses a wide variety of organisms, including sponges, jellyfish, anemones, corals, various groups of worms, clams and their relatives, snails, octopuses, squids, horseshoe crabs, crayfish, crabs, lobsters, shrimp, spiders, mites, scorpions, millipedes, centipedes, mayflies, dragonflies, grasshoppers, crickets, katydids, earwigs, stoneflies, termites, lice, true bugs, antlions, beetles, moths, butterflies, flies, caddisflies, fleas, ants, bees, wasps, sea urchins, and starfish as well as many other, lesser-known groups. It has been estimated that more than 90% of all animal species are invertebrates (Black et al., 2001).

Invertebrates range in size from less than 1/100 inch to the giant squid, which is estimated to grow to over 40 feet and weigh over 600 pounds and has been found in Florida waters. Although most invertebrates are very small, they make up for their size in abundance, so that their total biomass is more than that of the much larger vertebrates, with estimates of arthropods alone making up 85% of the weight of all terrestrial animals (Pimentel et al., 1980).

E.O. Wilson dubbed invertebrates "The Little Things That Run the World" in 1987 and that is no less true today. While some pest species do cause millions of dollars worth of crop, structure, and other damage, only a very small percentage of invertebrate species are pests, and most are either beneficial or neutral. Some, such as pollinators or shellfish, are obviously vital to humans because of their contributions to our food supply, but many others benefit humans and the environment in less obvious ways, such as filtering water, breaking down waste, controlling pests, serving as food for other species, or simply being enjoyable to look at or listen to.

Florida Invertebrates*

Number of Invertebrate Species in Florida	ca. 15,000	
Number of Invertebrate Species in the U.S.	ca. 100,000	
Percentage of U.S. Invertebrate Species found in Florida	ca. 15%	
	Species	**Subspecies**
Number of Invertebrate Species Tracked by FNAI	474	32
Number of Federally Listed Species (Threatened or Endangered)	11	2
Number of State Listed Species (Threatened or Endangered)	1	3

*Does not include marine invertebrates.

FNAI, NatureServe, March 2010

Florida Invertebrates by Global Rarity Rank*

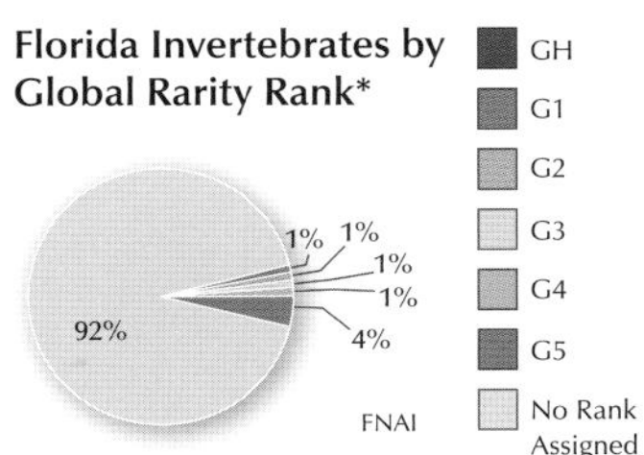

The majority of Florida's ca. 15,000 terrestrial and freshwater invertebrate species have no global rarity rank assigned, primarily due to lack of comprehensive scientific study of many invertebrates.

*full species only, does not include marine invertebrates, see page 142 for rank explanation

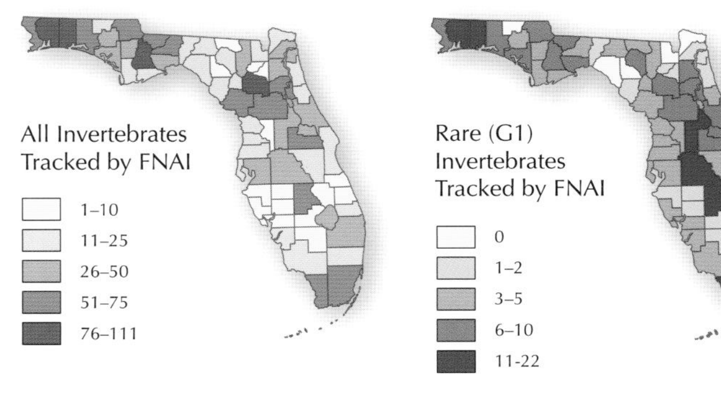

Dean Jue

Zebra heliconian (*Heliconius charithonia*)

How Florida's Biodiversity Stacks Up

Invertebrates are by far the most diverse group of organisms on the planet. This graphic compares numbers of species of insects and spiders (subset of all invertebrates) to other organisms in Florida. One cube = approximately 125 species.

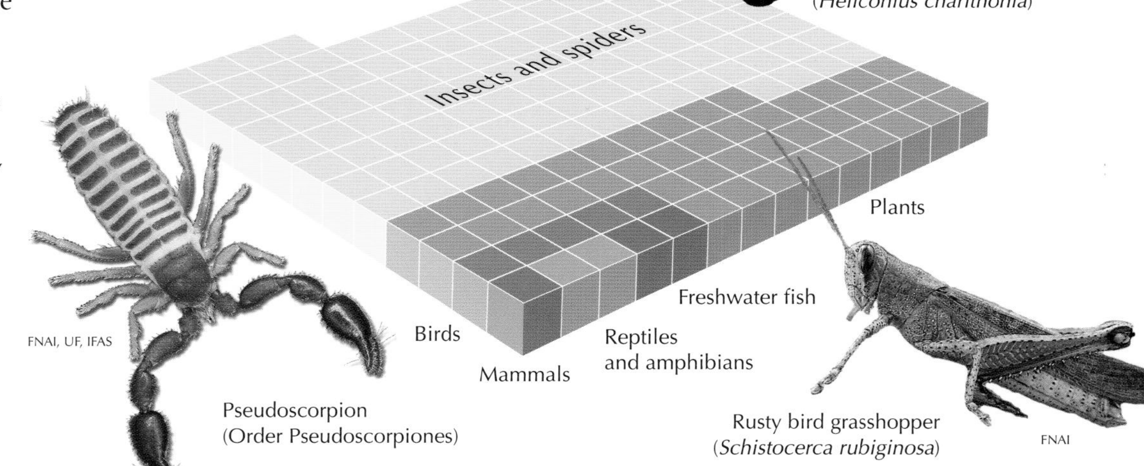

FNAI, UF, IFAS

Pseudoscorpion (Order Pseudoscorpiones)

Rusty bird grasshopper (*Schistocerca rubiginosa*)

FNAI

Important Roles of Invertebrates

Yucca moth (*Tegeticula* spp.)

Ann C. Cooper

Pollination

Native insects are responsible for pollinating approximately $3 billion worth of fruits and vegetables in the U.S. every year. Some native bees do a much better job of pollinating certain crops than the non-native honey bee, increasing fruit set up to 45% and fruit weight up to 200% in some crops. Besides their direct economic value, native pollinators, such as bees, moths, and beetles, are invaluable to the integrity of ecosystems by pollinating native plants.

Food webs

Invertebrates are a primary, and sometimes the sole, food source for many animals, including amphibians, reptiles, birds, fish, and some mammals. The economic value of native insects alone in food webs, related to fishing, hunting, and bird watching, has been estimated at almost $50 billion per year in the U.S., and this estimate does not include many other invertebrate groups, such as earthworms, snails, and shellfish, that are vital components of food webs.

Birds of North America

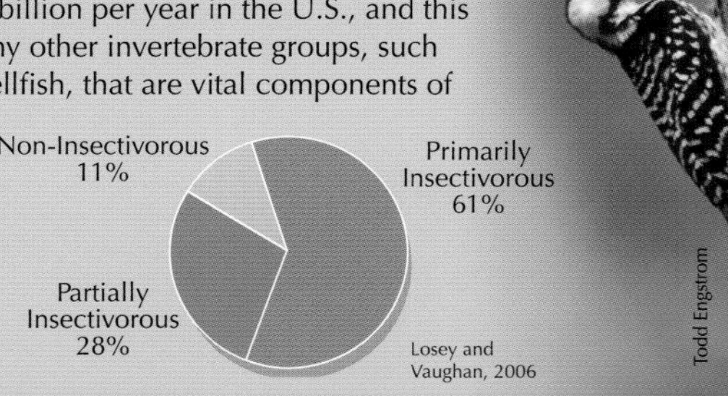

Todd Engstrom

Dave Almquist

Bees (Anthophila)

Most people are familiar with honey bees (such as *Apis mellifera*, left), which are a domesticated and exotic species, but are surprised to learn that we have more than 300 species of bees in the state, including 29 species that are endemic to Florida. Native bees are the only recorded pollinators of the rare plants eared coneflower (*Rudbeckia auriculata*), Harper's beauty (*Harperocallis flava*), white birds-in-a-nest (*Macbridea alba*), and Florida skullcap (*Scutellaria floridana*) (Diamond et al., 2006; Pitts-Singer, 2002) and have been found to be much better pollinators of other plants than honey bees.

Kenneth Catania

Earthworms (Lumbricina)

Earthworms are very important ecologically and economically. One earthworm may process as much as 10 pounds of soil per year, and there may be more than 50,000 worms in an acre of fertile soil. Many earthworm species help soil and plants by incorporating organic matter into the soil, making already-present nutrients more available to plants and making the soil more porous. "Grunting" for worms for bait is popular in the panhandle (at left, productive harvest at the Sopchoppy Worm Grunting Festival).

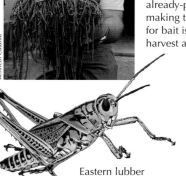

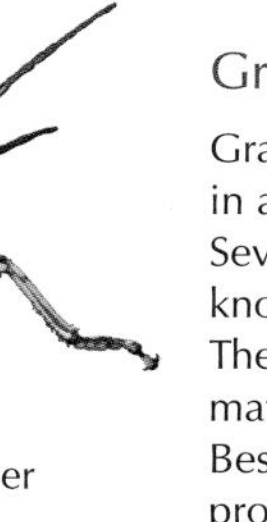
FNAI

Eastern lubber grasshopper (*Romaleo microptera*)

Grasshoppers (Orthoptera)

Grasshoppers and their relatives are found in almost all terrestrial habitats in Florida. Seventy species of acridid grasshoppers are known from Florida (including 18 endemic). They consume large amounts of plant material and are important in nutrient cycling. Besides their abundance, their size and high protein content (50-75%) make them very important in food webs to many animals.

Dave Almquist

Ants (Hymenoptera: Formicidae)

Florida has the highest ant diversity in the eastern United States with 218 species documented, including the trapjaw ant (*Odontomachus brunneus*, left). The total biomass of ants and other social insects may be more than that of all vertebrates within a given area. In the Apalachicola National Forest, ants were found to comprise 58% of the biomass eaten by red-cockaded woodpeckers, with one species responsible for 74% of the ants in their diet (Hess and James 1998).

David Moynahan

Spiders, Mites, and Scorpions (Arachnida)

Florida has a diverse arachnid fauna, with well over 1,000 (and possibly more than 2,000) mites, more than 750 spiders, and approximately 60 pseudoscorpions, with a few other species in other groups. Besides playing a key role in food webs, spiders have been shown to protect plants by consuming injurious pests. Some mites can be injurious to humans, animals, or crops. At left is the green lynx spider (*Peucetia viridians*).

Dave Almquist

Shrimp, Lobsters, and Crabs (Decapoda)

A single acre of seagrass may harbor 50 million invertebrates, and many will be decapods, such as the fiddler crab (*Uca* sp., left). A biodiversity inventory in Indian River Lagoon documented almost 200 species of decapods. Marine decapods are an important food source for wildlife, including many bird and fish species. Some species are important economically as a food source for humans as well.

Dave Almquist

Snails, Bivalves, and Relatives (Mollusca)

Molluscs (including snails, clams, oysters, squid, and octopods) are numerous, with approximately 300 species in Florida of freshwater and terrestrial snails and bivalves alone. Many are important food sources, with some animals subsisting solely or mostly on molluscs. The limpkin (*Aramus guarauna*) relies heavily on Florida apple snails (*Pomacea paludosa*). Oysters are extremely important in water filtration, as well as economically for human consumption. At left, rosy wolf snail (*Euglandina rosea*).

Invertebrates as Bioindicators

Bioindicators are species that are monitored to evaluate the ecological health of habitats, communities, or ecosystems, or to assess how a specific change has affected them. Invertebrates are often used for these purposes because many are very sensitive to seemingly minor environmental changes. Although many commonly used and well-known bioindicator species are aquatic, many terrestrial species also serve this role.

Highly Disturbed

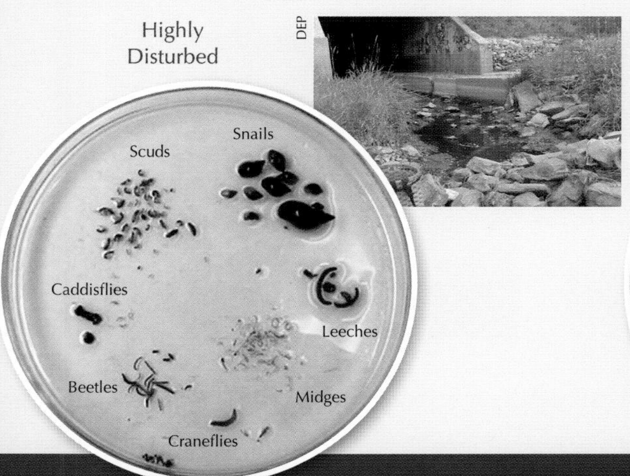

Minimally Disturbed

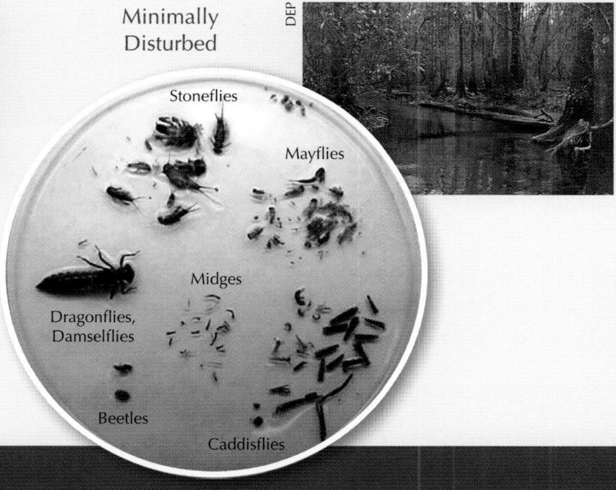

Uses of Invertebrates as Bioindicators in Monitoring Environmental Conditions

Activity/Condition Monitored	Invertebrate Group
Land Management	ants, dispersing insects
Logging	spiders, dung beetles, stream macroinvertebrates
Forest Restoration	general invertebrate community
Forest Degradation	tiger beetles, various insects, and nematodes
Grazing	several insect groups
Forest Management	mycetophilid flies, forest floor invertebrates, long-horned beetles
Habitat Fragmentation	ants, beetles, spiders, flies, other wasps or bees
Water Quality	benthic invertebrates
Coral Reef Health	foraminiferans (amoeboids)
Burning Regime in Sandhill	grasshoppers

Nutrient Cycling

Invertebrates are among the most important group of organisms involved in nutrient recycling, as many feed on dead plant or animal material, including dung, and/or incorporate this material into the soil. The incorporation of cow dung by dung beetles has been estimated to be worth a minimum of $380 million a year in the U.S. (see graph at right). Besides the direct benefit of fixing nutrients and organic matter into the soil, this also helps prevent eutrophication of waterways. Other invertebrates are involved in nutrient cycling in various situations, including aquatic environments.

Rainbow scarab dung beetle (*Phanaeus vindex*)

FNAI, UF, IFAS

Economic Losses Averted Annually as a Result of Accelerated Burial of Livestock Feces by Dung Beetles

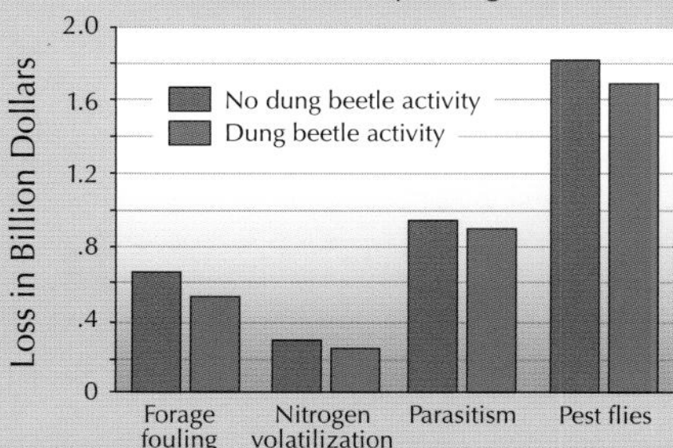

Sights and Sounds

Anyone who has enjoyed watching a butterfly flit among flowers, or listening to the songs of katydids, cicadas, and other singing insects knows that many invertebrates provide beauty in our world. Tiger beetles and dragonflies are also sought by hobbyists, and most everyone has enjoyed the beauty of seashells at the beach. Invertebrate zoos and exhibits (such as the Butterfly Rainforest at the Florida Museum of Natural History in Gainesville) are becoming more common.

FNAI

Coastal lyric cicada (*Tibicen lyricen virescens*)

Terrestrial Invertebrates

Terrestrial invertebrates include nematodes, worms, some snails, pillbugs, springtails, cockroaches, termites, mantids, earwigs, grasshoppers and their relatives, stick insects, true bugs, antlions and their relatives, beetles, fleas, flies, moths, butterflies, ants, bees, wasps, centipedes, millipedes, ticks and mites, scorpions and their relatives, spiders, and other less familiar groups. The ecological niches they fill are as diverse as their morphology, and they may be found in all terrestrial habitats in Florida. Although some may be thought of as pests, most are beneficial or neutral as far as humans and the environment are concerned.

Florida is home to hundreds of endemic and rare terrestrial invertebrates. Many endemic species only occur in upland areas that were islands long ago. There they became isolated and adapted to these dry, sandy environments. Rare tropical invertebrate species are found in the extreme southern peninsula and the Keys.

Terrestrial Invertebrate Richness

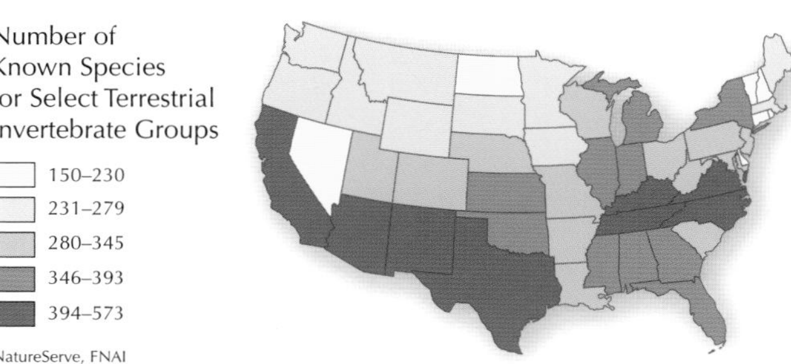

Terrestrial Invertebrates Tracked in Florida

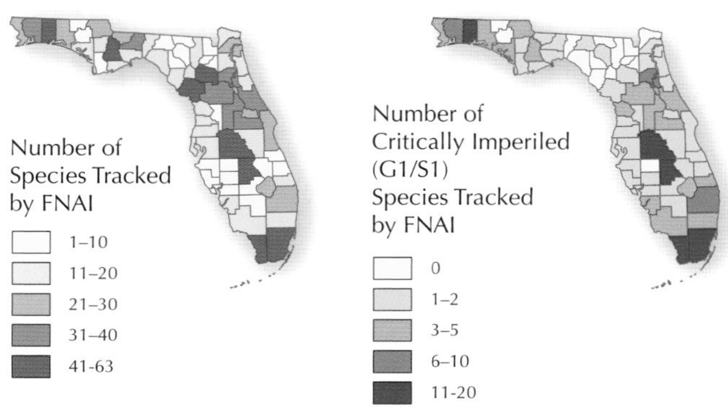

Okefenokee Zale moth caterpillar (*Zale perculta*) on climbing fetterbush (*Pieris phyllyreifolia*). Butterflies and moths are very diverse, with nearly 3,000 species in Florida. (Moths make up more than 90% of those species.)

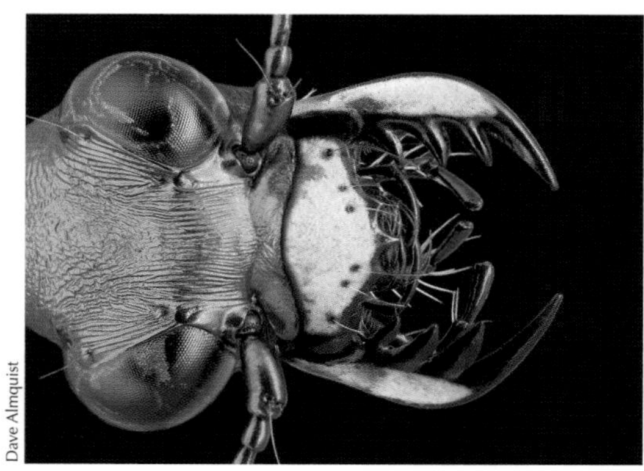

With their flying agility, large eyes, and fearsome mandibles, tiger beetles are extremely efficient predators of other arthropods. Shown here: six-spotted tiger beetle (*Cicindela sexgutttata*).

Burrow Ecosystems

This image shows a gopher tortoise (*Gopherus polyphemus*) burrow being excavated to relocate the tortoise from an area that will be developed, as well as to study invertebrate commensals. Gopher tortoise burrows are important refuges for many animals, with estimates of more than 300 species utilizing the burrows on a somewhat regular basis. But for invertebrate commensals, the tortoise burrows are an absolute necessity. There are at least 10 invertebrate species that are known only from gopher tortoise burrows, including primary decomposers and predators. Pocket gophers (*Geomys pinetis*) have similar but separate commensal fauna, with at least 30 species being dependent upon their burrows. The relatively constant temperature and humidity afforded by these burrows has led them to be termed "ephemeral caves" and some commensals, especially of pocket gophers, show adaptations similar to cave-dwelling species. Almost nothing is known about the biology of these invertebrate commensals, so excavations like the one shown here add to our knowledge of these obscure species.

Beetles

There are more than 4,675 species of beetles in Florida—approximately four times as many species as all of the freshwater fish, amphibians, reptiles, birds, and mammals in the state combined—with new species found every year. More than 550, or 12%, are endemic to Florida with about 220, or 4.7%, being non-native introductions. Beetles can be found in nearly every terrestrial habitat and microhabitat, including soil, in and under feces and carrion, in bat guano in caves, in ant nests, in tree holes, inside seeds, in between the upper and lower surfaces of leaves, inside fungal fruiting bodies, as parasites on mammals, visiting flowers, and many more. They play major ecological roles from nutrient cycling and soil conditioning to food webs and pollination, from seed dispersal to pest control/reduction and biological control of weeds.

Ground Beetles

There are nearly 400 species of ground beetles (family Carabidae) in Florida. Ground beetles are very important in food webs: they eat large numbers of other arthropods and in turn are preyed upon by robber flies, lizards, birds, spiders, scorpions, and other organisms.

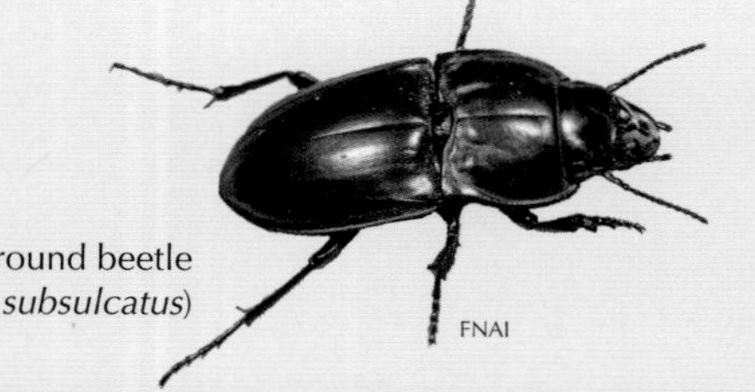

A ground beetle (*Pasimachus subsulcatus*)

Scarab Beetles

The more than 250 species of scarab beetles in Florida are very important in nutrient cycling and food webs. Some are so abundant that more than 1,000 may be caught in a single light trap in one night, while others are very rarely encountered. The Auburndale scrub scarab beetle (*Polyphylla starkae*) was only recently discovered and described in 2009, despite its being a large and conspicuous species that is attracted to lights. It is only known from one small patch of scrub habitat in Polk County. The mottled greenish males only fly for a few weeks in April, "smelling" for the females with their large antennal clubs. The reddish females appear to be flightless burrowers and have very small antennae, but otherwise little is known of their biology.

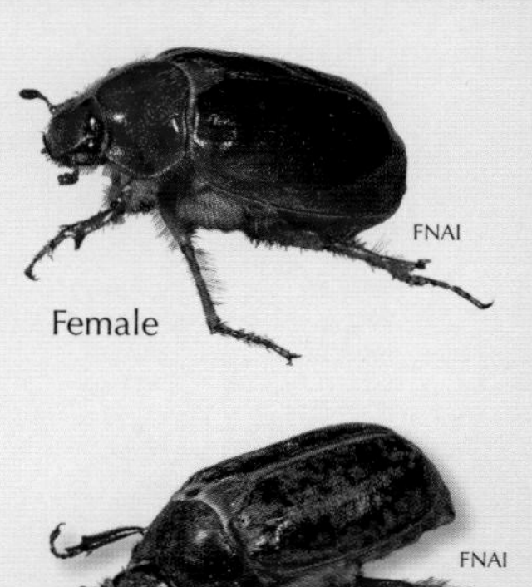

Red Hills

Apalachicola Bluffs

The Red Hills region and the nearby Apalachicola Bluffs region are centers of endemism and relictualism. Most records for the Torreya trap-door spider (*Cyclocosmia torreya*), a relative of the trap-door spider shown here, are found in the Apalachicola Bluffs region. Cartwright's mycotrupes beetle appears to be confined to the Red Hills region. Both species dig and live in burrows, although the spider covers its burrow with a camouflaged trap door.

FNAI

Cartwright's mycotrupes beetle (*Mycotrupes cartwrighti*)

Brett Tyler

Trap-door spider *Cyclocosmia* sp.

Jim Cane

Gulf Coast solitary bee (*Hesperapis oraria*)

Noah Charney

Santa Rosa wolf spider (*Arctosa sanctaerosae*)

Panhandle Coast

The barrier islands, beaches, and dunes of the panhandle are home to several endemic or near-endemic species. The Gulf Coast solitary bee is only found on a few islands and dunes from around Panama City to the far western panhandle. It appears to be dependent upon flowers of coastal plain honeycomb-head (*Balduina angustifolia*). The Santa Rosa wolf spider (*Carctosa sanctaerosae*) is very well camouflaged against the nearly white sands in this area and leaves its foot-deep burrow to hunt at night.

Dave Almquist

Florida deepdigger scarab beetle (*Peltotrupes profundus*)

Peninsular Ridges

These ancient shorelines and dunes have many rare and endemic species. Some grasshoppers of the genus *Melanoplus* are only found on one or a few localized ridges, and most are flightless. The Florida deepdigger scarab beetle (*Peltotrupes profundus*) is found on deep, well-drained sands throughout the region, while the Ocala deepdigger scarab beetle (*P. youngi*) is only known from the Ocala National Forest and vicinity. Both species dig burrows that can be up to ten feet deep.

Tequesta grasshopper (*Melanoplus tequestae*)

John Lowell Capinera

South Florida and Keys

This region features endemic and tropical species. The Keys green June beetle (*Cotinis aliena*), a relative of the green June beetle pictured here, is an undescribed species known only from Islamorada. The Stock Island tree snail (*Orthalicus reses reses*) was originally restricted to its namesake island, from which it has been extirpated, although transplanted populations survive elsewhere in Florida.

Bill Frank

Florida Keys tree snail (*Orthalicus reses*)

Jonathan Burishkin

Green June beetle (*Cotinis nitida*)

Unwanted Imports: Fire Ants

The red imported fire ant (*Solenopsis invicta*) is probably the best known of approximately 50 ant species, and more than 1,000 invertebrates, that have been introduced to Florida. Native to South America, they have been transported around the globe via human activity and were introduced to Mobile, Alabama, in the 1930s and found in Florida soon after. This species is now known from most of the southeastern U.S. west to Texas, with isolated infestations west to southern California. Fire ants are pests in agricultural as well as residential settings due to their painful sting and destructive nest-building, with annual losses for soybeans alone estimated at up to $150 million, and more than $25 million per year is spent on pesticides by private entities.

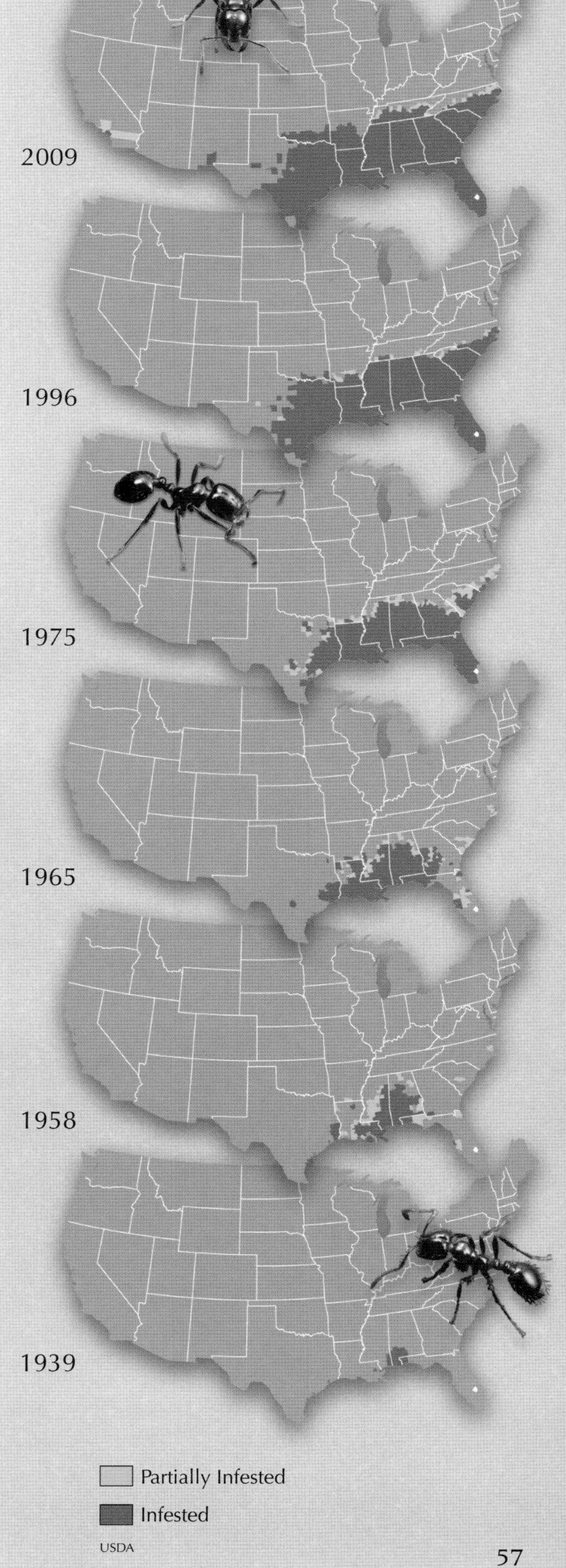

USDA

Ant images, FNAI

Beetles and Pollination

In general, some beetles play relatively minor roles in pollination, such as these yellow-marked buprestid beetles (*Acmaeodera pulchella*), but a few beetles are very important pollinators. Florida coontie is only pollinated by two beetle species: a pleasing fungus beetle (*Pharaxonotha floridana*) and a weevil (*Rhopalotria slossoni*).

Dave Almquist

Tree Borers

Most bark beetles, metallic wood boring beetles, and long-horned beetles are xylophagous (wood-eating) as larvae, breaking down dead and dying trees, which are then incorporated into the soil more quickly. Some beetles, such as the southern pine beetle, may attack live, seemingly healthy pine trees during years when they have population explosions, although this is usually during droughts or when other conditions stress trees.

FNAI, UF, IFAS

Southern pine beetle (*Dendroctonus frontalis*)

FNAI, UF, IFAS

Lined buprestis beetle (*Buprestis lineata*)

Aquatic Invertebrates

Virtually every body of water or wet habitat in Florida is home to an armada of aquatic invertebrates. Here, we use "aquatic" in its broad sense to include not only fresh waters (ponds, lakes, rivers, streams, canals, even large puddles) but also marine and estuarine habitats. While most species never leave the water, certain groups are aquatic only during specific life stages. Even normally terrestrial groups include some species that depend upon waters for feeding (e.g., fishing spiders).

Due to the higher gradient (slope) of rivers and streams in the Florida panhandle, the region's proximity to the continental landmass, and the presence of thousands of karst features such as sinkholes and caves that have developed in shallow, subsurface limestone, freshwater invertebrates reach their highest diversity in northern Florida. The vast majority of species of many groups—e.g., mussels, crayfishes, mayflies, caddisflies, and stoneflies—occur from the Suwannee River westward. Cave-dwelling amphipods, isopods, and crayfishes principally inhabit north central and panhandle Florida. In contrast, marine and estuarine invertebrates are dispersed in coastal waters statewide, with the warm waters of southern Florida and the Keys supporting especially high diversities.

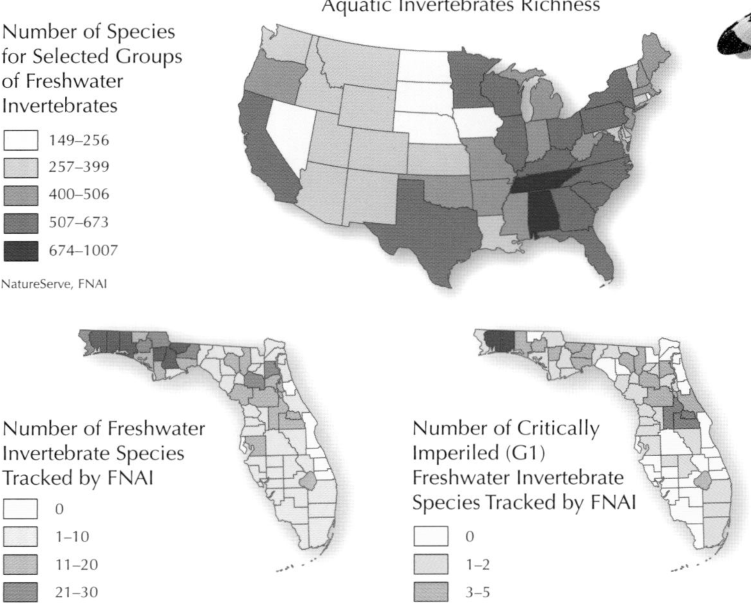

Gayle and Jeanell Strickland

Banded pennant (*Celithemis fasciata*) An eastern U.S. dragonfly that enters northern Florida.

Marine Invertebrates: An Economic Engine

Five of the top seven seafood varieties harvested in Florida are invertebrates

	2007 Dockside Value
Shrimp*	$27,261,668
Spiny lobster*	27,009,162
Stone crab*	26,488,352
Grouper	21,410,039
Blue crab (hardshell)*	10,455,317
Snapper	10,152,612
Oysters*	6,710,703

*Invertebrates

Crayfish

In contrast to their marine relatives such as crabs and lobsters, Florida's 55 species of crayfish require freshwater, either on or below the land surface. With 15 species, our cave crayfish fauna is one of the richest in the world. Crayfishes are integral components of the diets of many birds, mammals, alligators, fishes, frogs, turtles, and snakes.

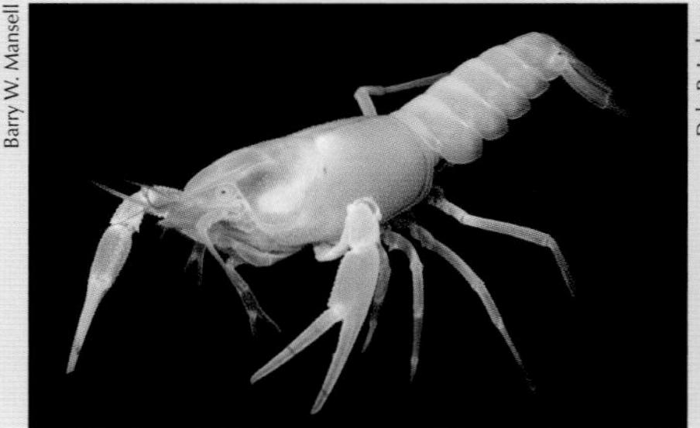

Barry W. Mansell

The coastal lowland crayfish (*Procambarus leitheuseri*) is known from fewer than 10 caves in a small region just north of Tampa Bay.

Dale R. Jackson

The strikingly colored fire-back crayfish (*Cambarus pyronotus*) builds its streamside burrows only in northern Liberty County.

Roseate skimmer (*Orthemis ferruginea*) A common dragonfly of the southern U.S.

Gayle and Jeanell Strickland

The Best of Both Worlds

Many insect groups—e.g., dragonflies, mayflies, caddisflies, and even horseflies and mosquitos—have life histories that cross the aquatic-terrestrial boundary. The flying adults usually remain near water, to which they return to lay their eggs; juvenile stages are aquatic and often have gills. Such insects can be important predators and prey in both ecosystems. As the dragonfly photographs across the page reveal, adults are often far more beautiful than the rather homely larvae. The larvae of caddisflies, however, glue debris to themselves to form exquisite protective cases, with some even resembling snail shells comprised of hundreds of tiny pebbles (facing page, upper left).

Tom Murray

Dragonfly larva (nymph)

Fighting Pollution the Natural Way

Floridians know well the economic value of the eastern oyster (*Crassostrea virginica*); the estuarine mollusk accounts for one-third of commercial dollars from seafood-rich Apalachicola Bay. But its value does not end here: a feeding oyster filters up to 50 gallons of water per day and deposits excess nitrogen, algae, and bacteria (hallmarks of pollution) in bottom sediments. Further, oyster reefs provide habitat for young fish, crabs, and myriad other creatures. Trouble is brewing, however; nearly 90% of the world's oyster reefs are already lost to harvesting and dredging, and the 2010 Gulf oil spill highlights threats to Florida's remaining reefs. While some states attempt expensive projects to reintroduce the once abundant shellfish, Florida can continue to reap the oyster's services for free, but only as long as we protect our coastal waters.

David Moynahan

Oyster bar

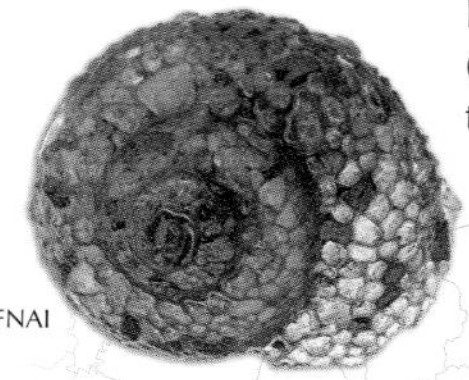

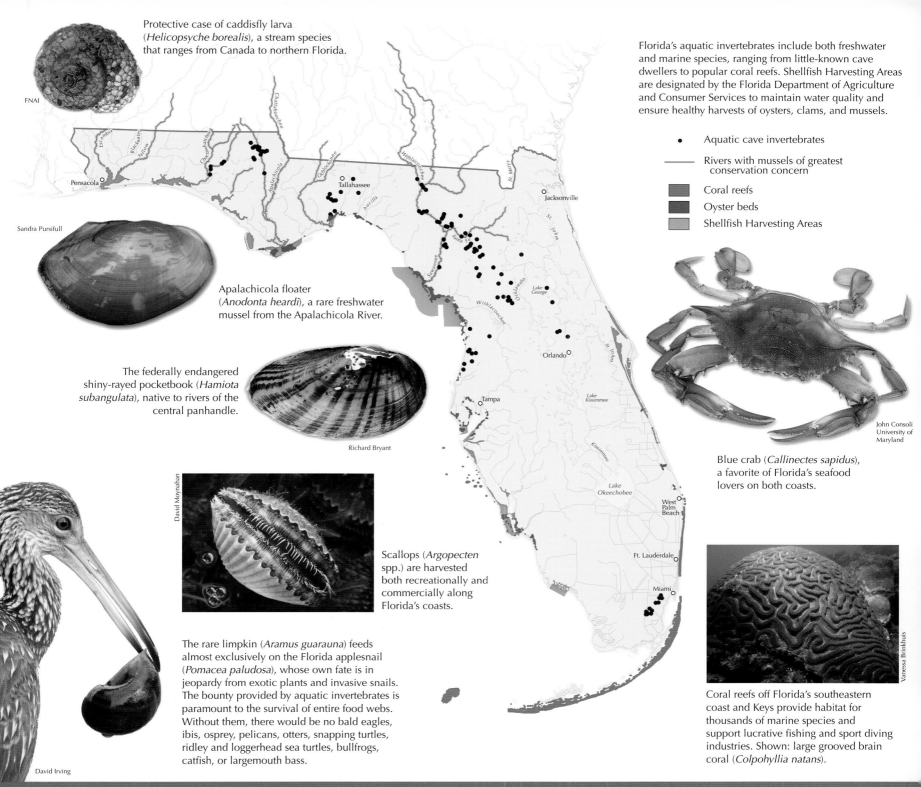

Protective case of caddisfly larva (*Helicopsyche borealis*), a stream species that ranges from Canada to northern Florida.

FNAI

Florida's aquatic invertebrates include both freshwater and marine species, ranging from little-known cave dwellers to popular coral reefs. Shellfish Harvesting Areas are designated by the Florida Department of Agriculture and Consumer Services to maintain water quality and ensure healthy harvests of oysters, clams, and mussels.

- Aquatic cave invertebrates
- Rivers with mussels of greatest conservation concern
- Coral reefs
- Oyster beds
- Shellfish Harvesting Areas

Sandra Pursifull

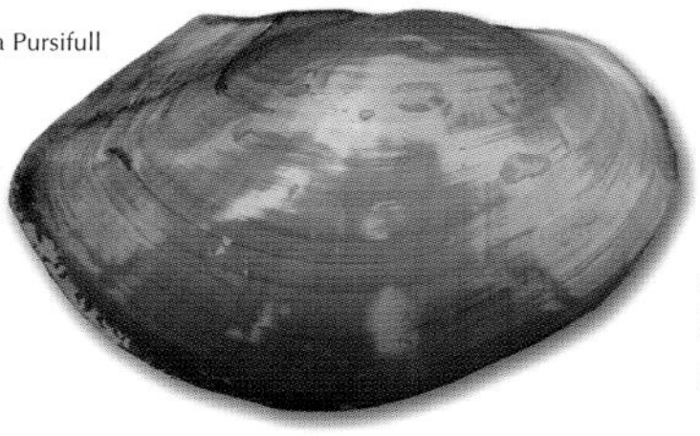

Apalachicola floater (*Anodonta heardi*), a rare freshwater mussel from the Apalachicola River.

The federally endangered shiny-rayed pocketbook (*Hamiota subangulata*), native to rivers of the central panhandle.

Richard Bryant

Blue crab (*Callinectes sapidus*), a favorite of Florida's seafood lovers on both coasts.

John Consoli University of Maryland

David Moynahan

Scallops (*Argopecten* spp.) are harvested both recreationally and commercially along Florida's coasts.

The rare limpkin (*Aramus guarauna*) feeds almost exclusively on the Florida applesnail (*Pomacea paludosa*), whose own fate is in jeopardy from exotic plants and invasive snails. The bounty provided by aquatic invertebrates is paramount to the survival of entire food webs. Without them, there would be no bald eagles, ibis, osprey, pelicans, otters, snapping turtles, ridley and loggerhead sea turtles, bullfrogs, catfish, or largemouth bass.

David Irving

Vanessa Brinkhuis

Coral reefs off Florida's southeastern coast and Keys provide habitat for thousands of marine species and support lucrative fishing and sport diving industries. Shown: large grooved brain coral (*Colpohyllia natans*).

Anatomy of An Invasion

Not all of Florida's aquatic invertebrates are well-adjusted natives. Although hailing from the Indo-Pacific region, the Asian green mussel (*Perna viridis*) probably entered Florida on the hulls of ships or in ballast water emanating from the Caribbean, where the invasive mollusk was already established. Growing to 8 cm (3 inches), these mollusks form large colonies that not only foul ships and bridges but can also block water intake at power plants and interfere with crab trapping and clam culture.

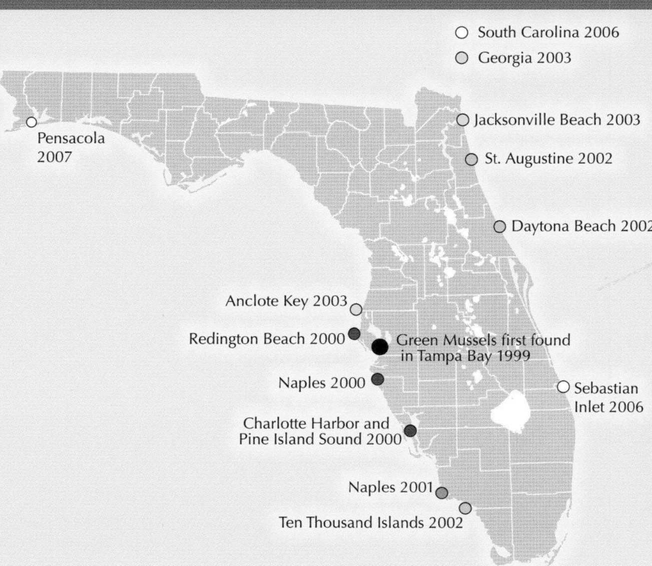

This cluster of Asian green mussels (*Perna viridis*) was found growing on a derelict crab trap pulled from Tampa Bay in January 2009.

Freshwater Fish

Nearly 800 native fish species inhabit the fresh waters of North America, making it the most diverse region in the world for temperate freshwater fish. Approximately half of these species are concentrated in the southeastern United States where Florida ranks among the top four in the number of species along with Tennessee, Alabama, and Georgia. This high diversity in Florida is best explained by its varied aquatic systems, including alluvial streams, blackwater streams, spring-run streams, upland sandhill and clastic lakes, and swamp lakes. Each of these systems may have numerous specific habitats depending on water source, flow rates, substrate, and many other factors. This myriad of physical and geological characteristics has led to Florida's fantastic fish diversity.

Anyone who is not a fish scientist would be surprised to know that Florida has more than 70 species of minnows and carp. Approximately one-third of North American fishes are in the minnow family (*Cyprinidae*). This is also true for the Southeast and Florida. Even groups that are generally familiar to the average person are surprisingly diverse; at least 19 species of the sunfish family (*Centrarchidae*), including 4 largemouth bass relatives and 13 species of sunfish, make their home in the waters of Florida. The highest numbers of fish species are found in the rivers of the panhandle, where more than 70 species of fish may be found in one watershed. This can generally be attributed to the relatively higher diversity of aquatic habitats in the panhandle and by a more complex biogeographic history.

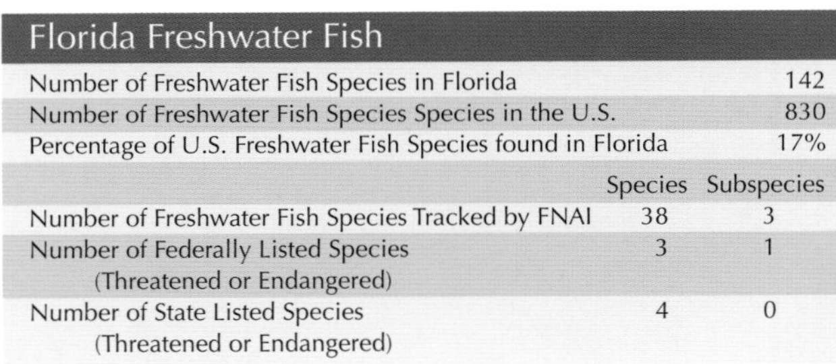

Florida Freshwater Fish		
Number of Freshwater Fish Species in Florida	142	
Number of Freshwater Fish Species Species in the U.S.	830	
Percentage of U.S. Freshwater Fish Species found in Florida	17%	
	Species	Subspecies
Number of Freshwater Fish Species Tracked by FNAI	38	3
Number of Federally Listed Species (Threatened or Endangered)	3	1
Number of State Listed Species (Threatened or Endangered)	4	0

FNAI, NatureServe, March 2010

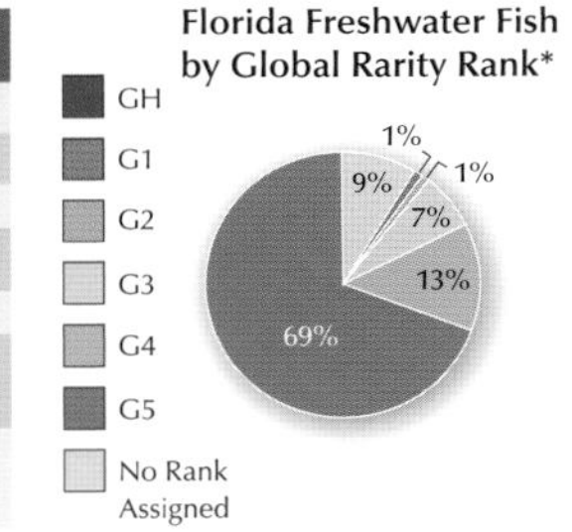

About 9% of Florida's 142 freshwater fish species (and an additional four subspecies) are considered rare (GH-G3). *full species only, see page 142 for rank explanation

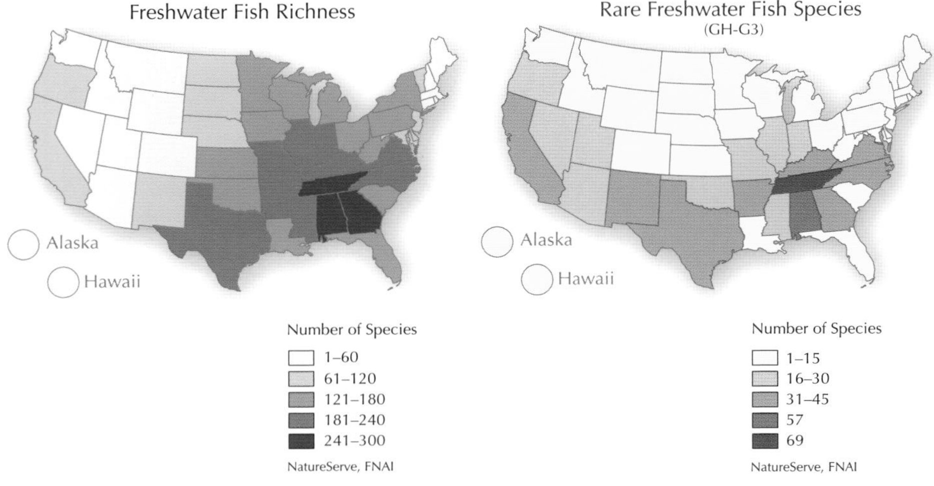

Noel Burkhead

Endemic Species

Florida has one species of fish that is found nowhere else, the Okaloosa darter (*Etheostoma okaloosae*). This species is restricted to six clear, cool, fast flowing, sand-bottom streams of the western Choctawhatchee Bay drainage. Here it inhabits the margins between sandy bottom and eddies where detritus, root mats, and vegetation are present. More than 90% of the range for the Okaloosa darter is on Eglin Air Force Base, where the natural resource managers are restoring and maintaining habitat for this tiny treasure of northwest Florida.

David Moynahan

Recreational Fishing

Based on a 2006 U.S. Census Bureau Survey, Florida again ranks number one, followed by Texas, in anglers (residents and tourists), angler expenditures, angler-supported jobs, and taxes generated by sport fishing—solid evidence for Florida's claim as the "Fishing Capital of the World." Individuals average approximately 17 days per year fishing in Florida, and about half of those days are spent freshwater fishing. Nonresident anglers spent over $1 billion in direct retail sales in Florida. The next highest state for non-resident angler spending was Wisconsin with less than $0.6 billion. Adding indirect expenditures such as food and hotel the total exceeds $7.5 billion, making recreational fishing a substantial portion of our tourism industry. An economic analysis by Southwick and Associates details the multiplier or ripple effect on the community caused by these sales and visitors.

Paul Shafland, FWC

Threats

At least 16 species of fish have become extinct in the United States since 1964. Many factors have contributed to this loss including overfishing, water pollution, and sedimentation resulting from soil erosion. The greatest threat, however, is damming. Dams block fish spawning migrations and isolate fish from upstream spawning and nursery areas, causing extirpations of populations of migratory fish. Alterations in downstream water flows and water temperatures often eliminate extensive areas of habitat for many species.

With more than 50 reproducing exotic fish species, Florida, along with California, has the largest number of introduced fishes. Exotic, introduced fish, such as the Asian swamp eel (*Monopterus albus*) shown above, have received attention for threatening native fish species through competition or predation. Although scientific evidence for such is currently lacking for natural systems, a cautious approach to the intentional introduction of an exotic fish should be taken. Care also should be taken to prevent the accidental release of non-native fish in order to prevent unanticipated effects on community structure or relationships and other potential unfortunate consequences.

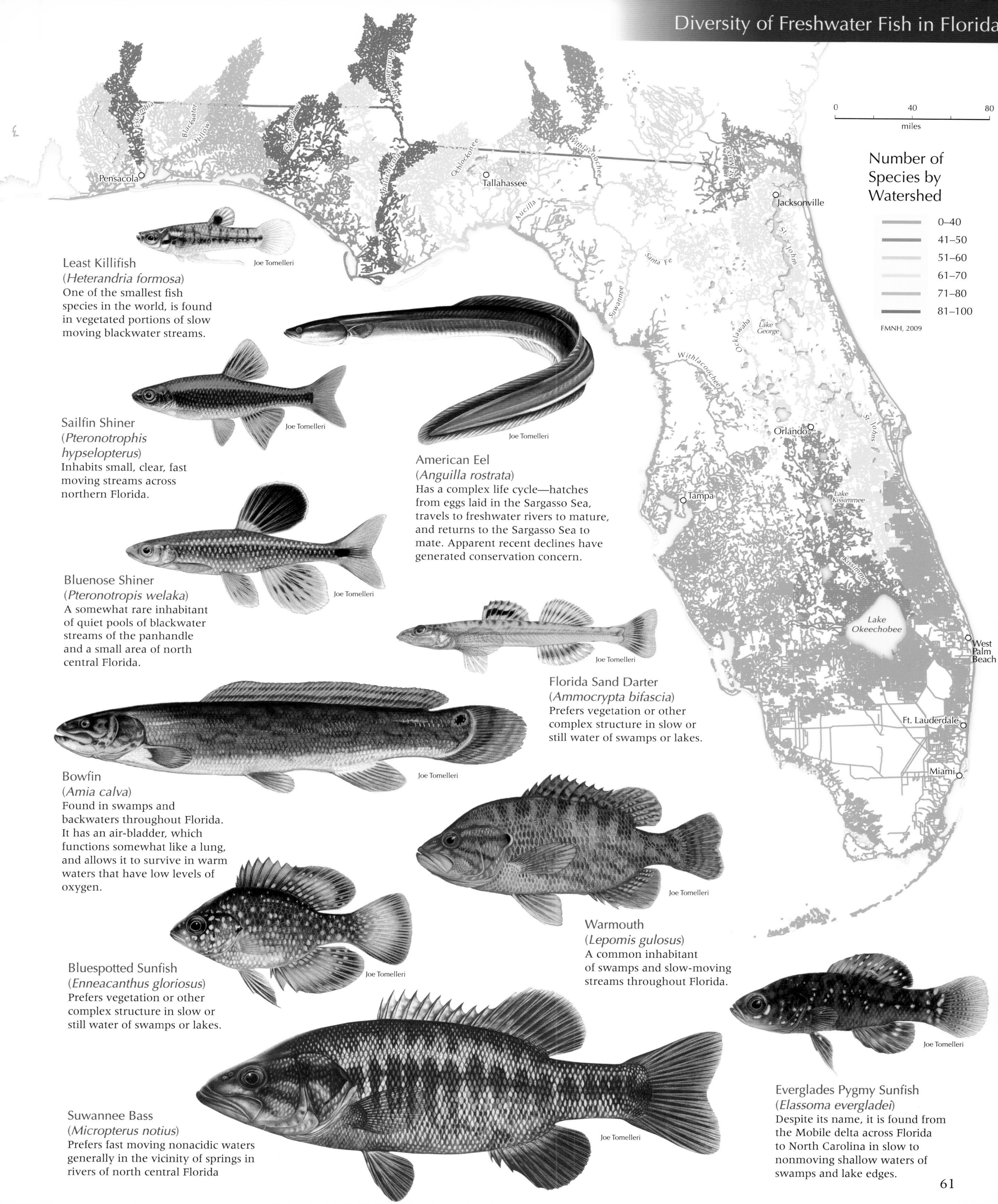

Least Killifish
(*Heterandria formosa*)
One of the smallest fish species in the world, is found in vegetated portions of slow moving blackwater streams.

Sailfin Shiner
(*Pteronotrophis hypselopterus*)
Inhabits small, clear, fast moving streams across northern Florida.

American Eel
(*Anguilla rostrata*)
Has a complex life cycle—hatches from eggs laid in the Sargasso Sea, travels to freshwater rivers to mature, and returns to the Sargasso Sea to mate. Apparent recent declines have generated conservation concern.

Bluenose Shiner
(*Pteronotropis welaka*)
A somewhat rare inhabitant of quiet pools of blackwater streams of the panhandle and a small area of north central Florida.

Florida Sand Darter
(*Ammocrypta bifascia*)
Prefers vegetation or other complex structure in slow or still water of swamps or lakes.

Bowfin
(*Amia calva*)
Found in swamps and backwaters throughout Florida. It has an air-bladder, which functions somewhat like a lung, and allows it to survive in warm waters that have low levels of oxygen.

Warmouth
(*Lepomis gulosus*)
A common inhabitant of swamps and slow-moving streams throughout Florida.

Bluespotted Sunfish
(*Enneacanthus gloriosus*)
Prefers vegetation or other complex structure in slow or still water of swamps or lakes.

Everglades Pygmy Sunfish
(*Elassoma evergladei*)
Despite its name, it is found from the Mobile delta across Florida to North Carolina in slow to nonmoving shallow waters of swamps and lake edges.

Suwannee Bass
(*Micropterus notius*)
Prefers fast moving nonacidic waters generally in the vicinity of springs in rivers of north central Florida

Amphibians

Florida's native amphibians are split almost equally between the two major sub-groups, frogs and salamanders. This number places Florida tenth among the 50 states in terms of amphibian richness. Most states with more species (Georgia, Alabama, North and South Carolina, Tennessee, Virginia, Mississippi, Texas, and California) include not only frog-rich coastal lowlands but also salamander-rich mountain ranges, especially the Appalachians, where the family of lungless salamanders has undergone extensive speciation.

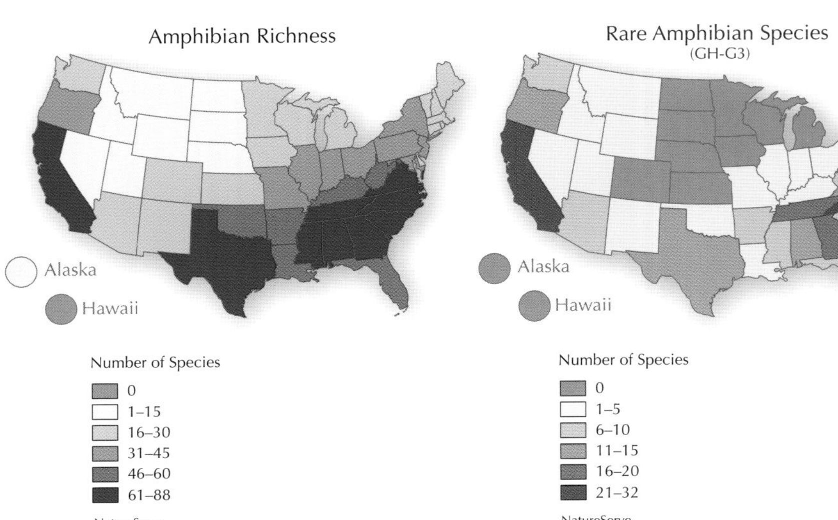

Lacking mountains, Florida owes its relatively high amphibian diversity to a conjunction of contrasting habitats. Deep, forested ravines in the panhandle provide the cool, moist conditions required by 10 species of lungless salamanders, relatives of more northern kin. Coastal wetlands, ranging from small ponds and marshes to vast floodplain swamps bordering our rivers, support a host of treefrogs, toads, ranid frogs, and salamanders of several families. The latter include not only the commonly recognized, four-legged mole salamanders, which breed in water but live as adults on land, but also three families of aquatic, eel-like species (sirens, amphiumas, and mudpuppies) whose legs are reduced in size and/or number and which even breathe via gills as adults.

In contrast to reptiles, only a few exotic species of amphibians have successfully invaded our state. Best known are the over-sized cane toad (*Rhinella marina*) and Cuban treefrog (*Osteopilus septentrionalis*), both restricted principally to the peninsula. Most widespread, however, is the diminutive and secretive greenhouse frog (*Eleutherodactylus planirostris*), which lives not only around human residences but also in natural habitats such as sandhill statewide.

Cane toad (*Rhinella marina*)

Doug Greenberg

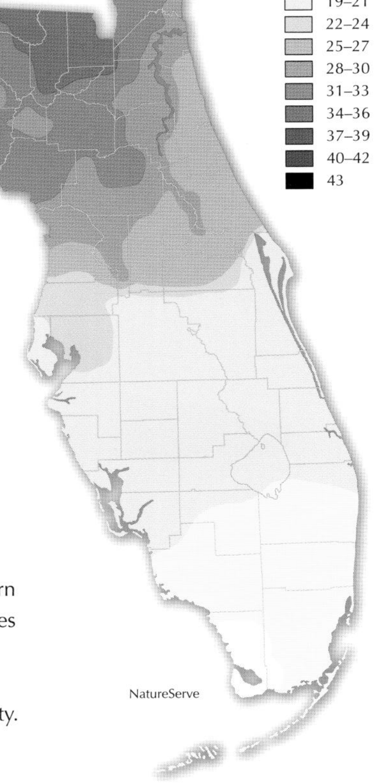

Species Richness of Native Florida Amphibians

The higher number of species in northern Florida is driven especially by the abundance of moisture-loving terrestrial salamanders whose ranges enter Florida from the north but which barely enter the peninsula. In contrast, lower numbers in central and southern Florida reflect high temperatures and sandy soils that are less hospitable to such species, as well as reduced habitat diversity.

Florida Amphibians

Number of Amphibian Species in Florida	55	
Number of Amphibian Species in the U.S.	280	
Percentage of U.S. Amphibian Species found in Florida	20%	
	Species	**Subspecies**
Number of Amphibian Species Tracked by FNAI	16	1
Number of Federally Listed Species (Threatened or Endangered)	2	0
Number of State Listed Species (Threatened or Endangered)	0	0

FNAI, NatureServe, March 2010

Florida Amphibians by Global Rarity Rank*

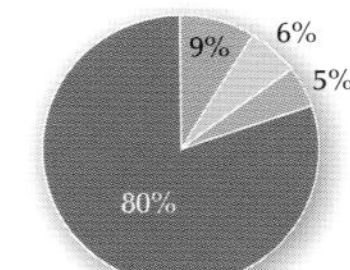

About 15% of Florida's 55 amphibian species (and an additional 5 subspecies) are considered rare (GH-G3).

*full species only, *see* page 142 for rank explanation

Global amphibian decline

Amphibians are declining globally at unprecedented rates, even beyond what can be explained by human development of their natural habitats. Scientific evidence is accumulating that disease and climatic change, both of which appear to be associated with human disturbance, may be substantial contributors. Although Florida's amphibian fauna thus far has escaped major problems, it is imperative that we remain vigilant for signs of unusual declines.

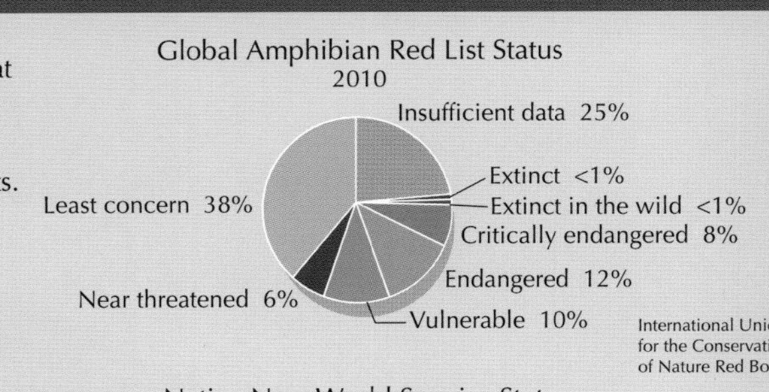

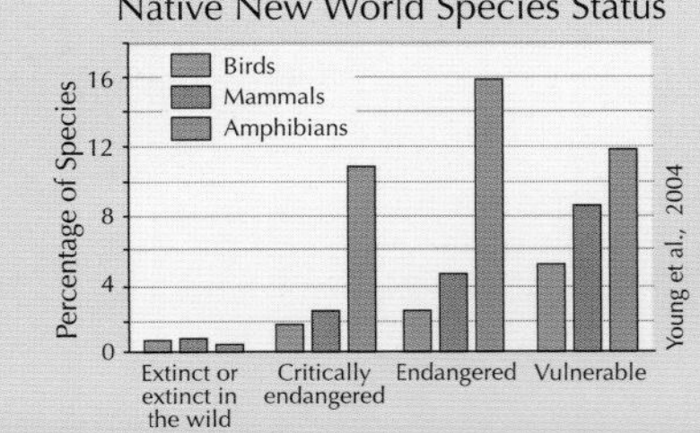

Richard D. Bartlett

Green treefrog (*Hyla cinerea)*
This common frog is one of the few amphibians to occur statewide, even reaching the Keys.

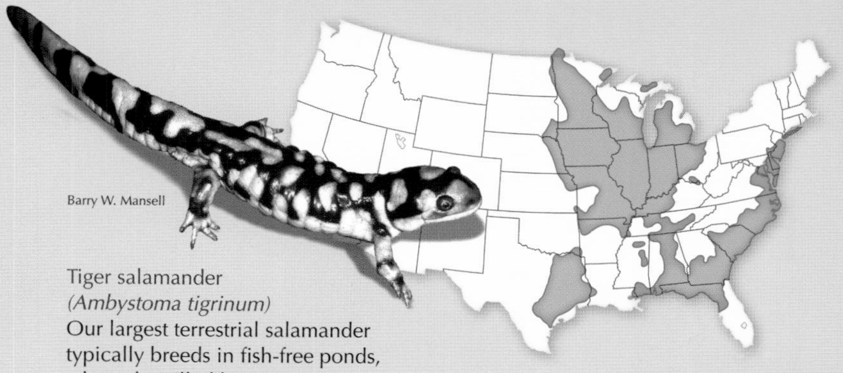

Barry W. Mansell

Tiger salamander
(Ambystoma tigrinum)
Our largest terrestrial salamander typically breeds in fish-free ponds, where the gilled larvae prey on invertebrates and tadpoles.

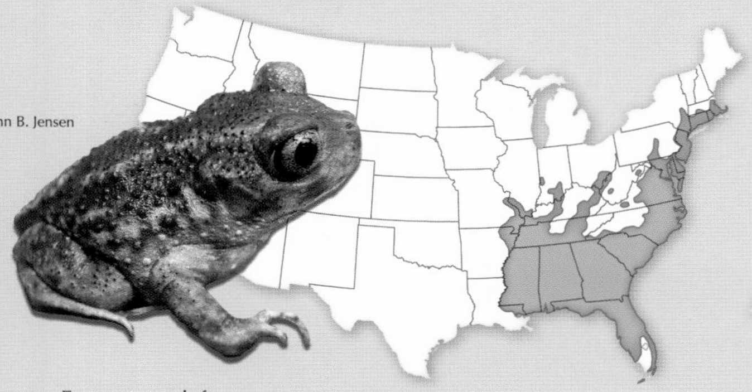

John B. Jensen

Eastern spadefoot
(Scaphiopus holbrookii)
This secretive species spends most of its life cycle burrowed into sandy soils. An exceptionally short tadpole stage (as little as 16 days) allows this toad to breed in temporary pools formed by torrential rains—sites too ephemeral for most amphibians.

Seal salamander
(Desmognathus monticola)
This Appalachian species is known in Florida from only one site in Escambia County.

Robert S. Simmons

Barry W. Mansell

Striped newt
(*Notophthalmus perstriatus)*
This rare salamander recently has been petitioned for federal protection.

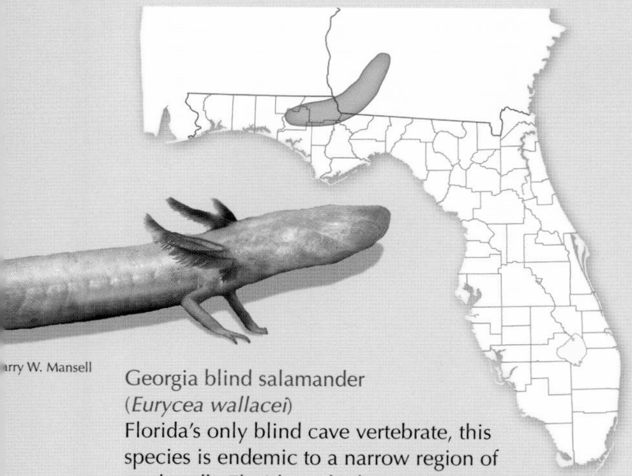

arry W. Mansell

Georgia blind salamander
(*Eurycea wallacei*)
Florida's only blind cave vertebrate, this species is endemic to a narrow region of panhandle Florida and adjacent Georgia. In Florida, it is restricted to the Chipola and Choctawhatchee river drainages.

Barry W. Mansell

Florida bog frog
(*Rana okaloosae*)
This small frog is endemic to seepage streams of western panhandle Florida; most lie within Eglin Air Force Base.

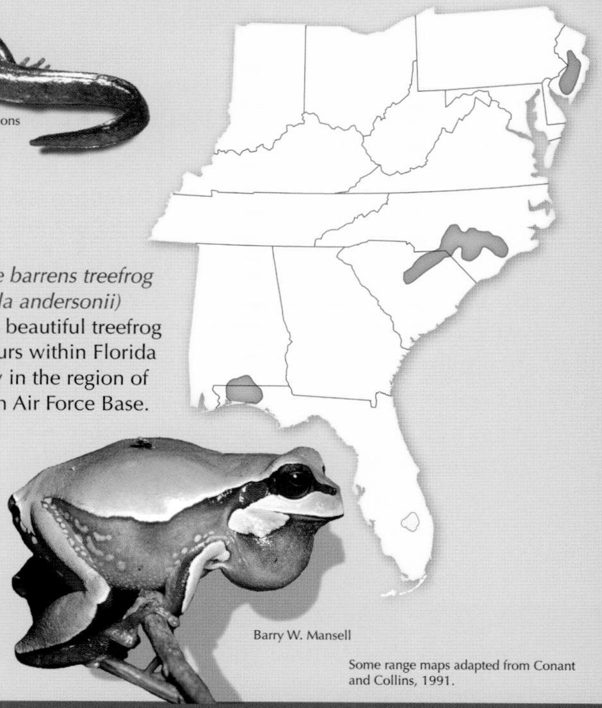

Pine barrens treefrog
(Hyla andersonii)
This beautiful treefrog occurs within Florida only in the region of Eglin Air Force Base.

Barry W. Mansell

Some range maps adapted from Conant and Collins, 1991.

Wetlands and Uplands are important

Brenda Herring

Although many species of amphibians live on land or in trees, nearly all return to water to breed. An effective conservation strategy for such amphibians is to protect large, intact landscapes that include multiple breeding wetlands within the surrounding uplands. Ephemeral or temporary ponds are especially important because they lack persistent predatory fish that can substantially reduce or prevent the survival of eggs and larvae. Periodic fires are vital to maintaining the open nature of these habitats to assure continued amphibian use.

The aerial photograph shows several small marshes or ephemeral ponds within a sandhill in the Apalachicola National Forest, Wakulla County. This site provides habitat for the striped newt (*Notophthalmus perstriatus*) and gopher frog (*Rana capito*), two amphibians of conservation concern. Like most amphibians, both species move between the wetlands and uplands during various stages of their life cycles.

Reptiles

Reptiles in the traditional sense comprise a diverse and fascinating group that includes snakes, lizards, turtles, and crocodilians. Even though recent studies suggest that the last two groups may have closer affinities with birds and mammals, we follow the broader, historical definition here. With a climatic gradient ranging from warm temperate to subtropical, Florida hosts a wonderful array of reptiles, with more native species (89) than any other state except Texas, Arizona, or New Mexico. Snakes (44 species) comprise half of our state's fauna; species range from pencil-sized to the 8-foot long threatened eastern indigo snake (*Drymarchon couperi*). Our state's combination of abundant wetlands, lakes, and rivers, coastal shorelines, and drier upland habitats supports one of the richest turtle faunas (25 species) in the world. Most species live in fresh waters, although two live on land, and six inhabit marine or coastal waters. (The gopher tortoise, *Gopherus polyphemus*, and marine turtles are described elsewhere in the atlas.) Florida also is home to the country's only two native crocodilians—the wide-ranging freshwater American alligator (*Alligator mississippiensis*) and the American crocodile (*Crocodylus acutus*) of coastal southern Florida. Lizards reach their greatest numbers in dry habitats of the American Southwest; still, Florida has 18 species, including two that occur nowhere else.

Besides being home to a rich native fauna, Florida is gaining the infamous reputation of providing a haven to a variety of non-native species, many of which have found our warm climate to their liking following their introduction via the pet trade. Although the majority of the more than two dozen established species are inconspicuous small lizards, a few pose significant ecological threats to native animals—most notorious are the Burmese python (*Python molurus bivittatus*) in the Everglades and the Nile monitor lizard (*Varanus niloticus*) along our southwestern coast.

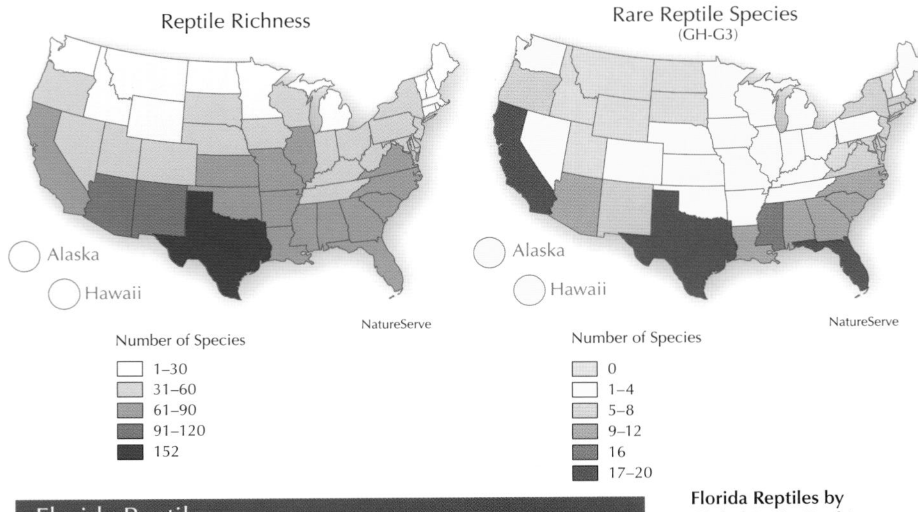

Florida Reptiles

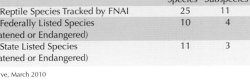

	Species	Subspecies
Number of Reptile Species in Florida	89	
Number of Reptile Species in the U.S.	311	
Percentage of U.S. Reptile Species found in Florida	29%	
Number of Reptile Species Tracked by FNAI	25	11
Number of Federally Listed Species (Threatened or Endangered)	10	4
Number of State Listed Species (Threatened or Endangered)	11	3

FNAI, NatureServe, March 2010

Florida Reptiles by Global Rarity Rank*

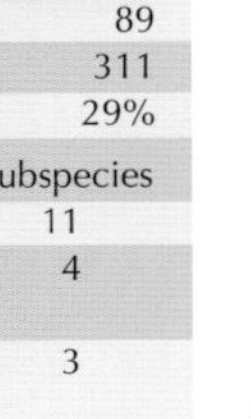

GH G1 G2 G3 G4 G5 No Rank Assigned

About one-fifth of Florida's 89 reptile species (and an additional 15 subspecies) are considered rare (GH-G3).

*full species only; see page 142 for rank explanation

Species Richness

Species richness map of native Florida reptiles, excluding marine turtles. Higher numbers of species in northern Florida, as exemplified by the Apalachicola River basin, reflect the region's greater diversity of habitats, one of the richest freshwater turtle faunas in the world, and an abundance of continental snake and lizard species that enter Florida but which do not reach its southern limits.

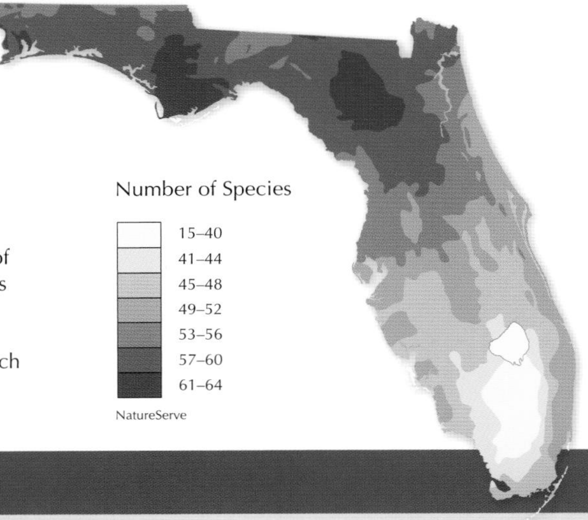

Threats to Reptiles

Skin and pet trades

Many biologists are concerned that the harvest of snakes to make belts and boots, or to be sold as pets, poses a significant threat. In 1990 alone, more than 20,000 snakes of 32 species were reported collected from the wild in Florida and sold as pets; 2,000 of these were kingsnakes, a rapidly declining species. In the same year, at least 2,500 eastern diamondback rattlesnakes (*Crotalus adamanteus*), also a species with declining populations, were killed for their skins.

Roads

The increasing fragmentation of habitats by roads puts evergrowing numbers of wildlife in the paths of automobiles. Road mortality has become a particular concern for the conservation of reptiles and may be an important factor in the declines of many populations of turtles and snakes.

Dale R. Jackson

Until recently, freshwater turtles were slaughtered by tens of thousands annually to supply Asian food markets.

D. Bruce Means

Eastern diamondback rattlesnake (*Crotalus adamanteus*)

Habitat Loss

Florida's native species are declining as native habitats disappear as a result of human alteration. Among reptiles, losses may be most severe for species restricted to dry habitats such as scrub and sandhill; examples include the sand skink (*Plestiodon reynoldsi*) and the Florida scrub lizard (*Sceloporus woodi*), two small lizards endemic to Florida.

Commercial Exploitation

Reptiles have a long history of human exploitation in Florida. Some activities such as the harvest of sea turtles and their eggs and of alligator skins are now prohibited or closely regulated, but other examples continue with inadequate oversight.

Conservation Success: Regulating Turtle Harvest

Until recently the unregulated harvest of freshwater turtles in Florida, primarily to satisfy an international appetite for turtle meat, was considered a serious threat to some species of turtles. In 2009, at the urging of conservationists, the Florida Fish and Wildlife Conservation Commission enacted stringent regulations to end this exploitation.

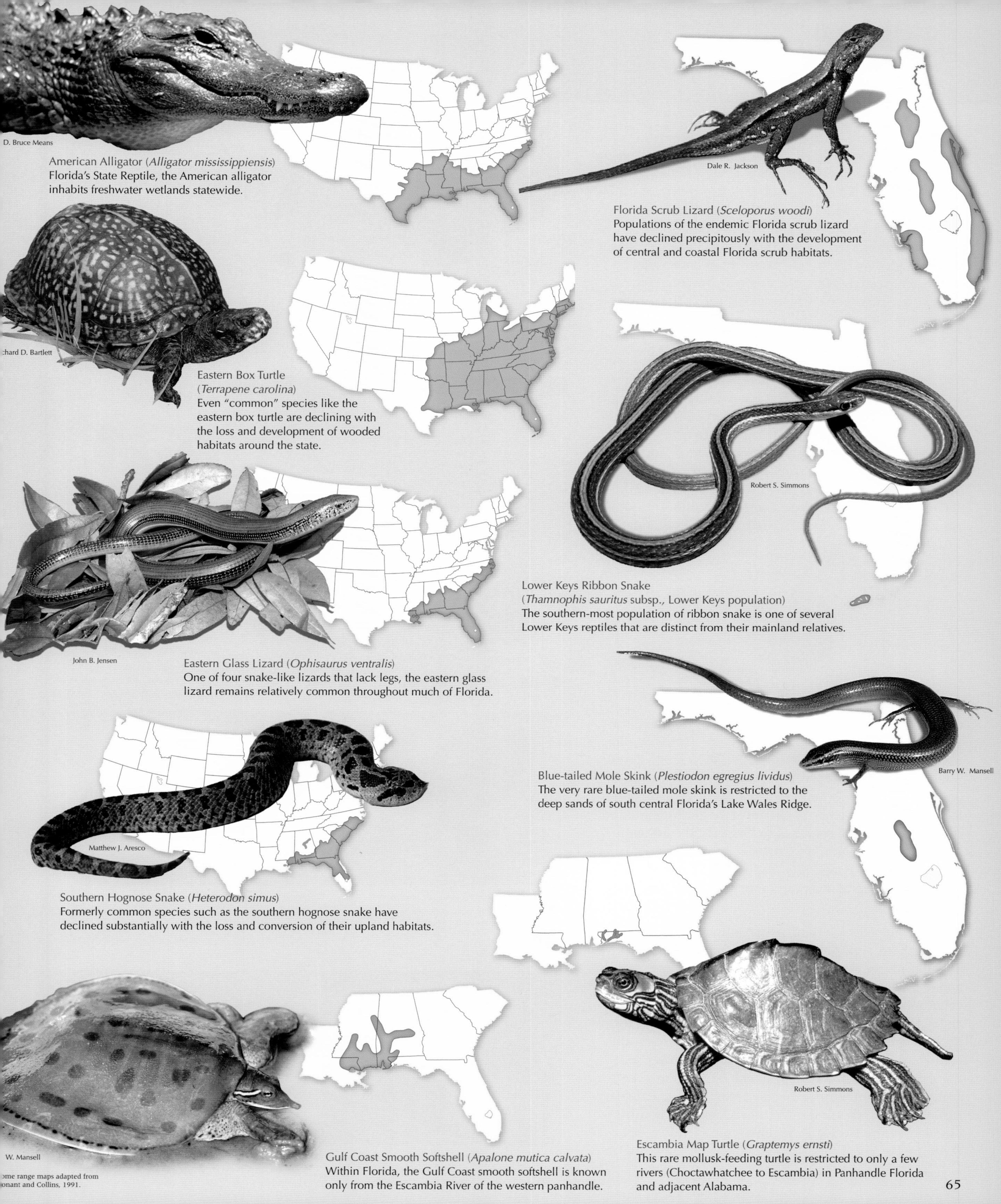

American Alligator (*Alligator mississippiensis*)
Florida's State Reptile, the American alligator inhabits freshwater wetlands statewide.

Florida Scrub Lizard (*Sceloporus woodi*)
Populations of the endemic Florida scrub lizard have declined precipitously with the development of central and coastal Florida scrub habitats.

Eastern Box Turtle (*Terrapene carolina*)
Even "common" species like the eastern box turtle are declining with the loss and development of wooded habitats around the state.

Lower Keys Ribbon Snake (*Thamnophis sauritus* subsp., Lower Keys population)
The southern-most population of ribbon snake is one of several Lower Keys reptiles that are distinct from their mainland relatives.

Eastern Glass Lizard (*Ophisaurus ventralis*)
One of four snake-like lizards that lack legs, the eastern glass lizard remains relatively common throughout much of Florida.

Blue-tailed Mole Skink (*Plestiodon egregius lividus*)
The very rare blue-tailed mole skink is restricted to the deep sands of south central Florida's Lake Wales Ridge.

Southern Hognose Snake (*Heterodon simus*)
Formerly common species such as the southern hognose snake have declined substantially with the loss and conversion of their upland habitats.

Gulf Coast Smooth Softshell (*Apalone mutica calvata*)
Within Florida, the Gulf Coast smooth softshell is known only from the Escambia River of the western panhandle.

Escambia Map Turtle (*Graptemys ernsti*)
This rare mollusk-feeding turtle is restricted to only a few rivers (Choctawhatchee to Escambia) in Panhandle Florida and adjacent Alabama.

ome range maps adapted from
onant and Collins, 1991.

Birds

Florida is a must-see port of call for people who enjoy the colorful, conspicuous, and diverse assemblage of birds that our state supports. Wildlife viewers, of which bird watchers make up more than 60%, contribute an estimated $3.2 to $5.2 billion to the Florida economy each year, and unlike many other activities, bird watching leaves a light footprint on the landscape. Birders are enthralled by the simple pleasures of observing our elegant wading birds, the ethereal swaying of a swallow-tailed kite over the treetops, the curious antics of boisterous blue jays, and even the quiet cooing of common (but declining) ground doves.

Florida's birds range from the extremely common to some that are barely hanging on. Others accidentally wander into our state while trying to reach a distant location and make an appearance only every few years. Florida officially lists the largest number of extant bird species (503) of any state east of the Mississippi River, including 490 native and 13 established exotic species. One hundred-fifty species regularly breed in the state and, like our human inhabitants, a large proportion (26%) of native species that breed elsewhere winter in Florida.

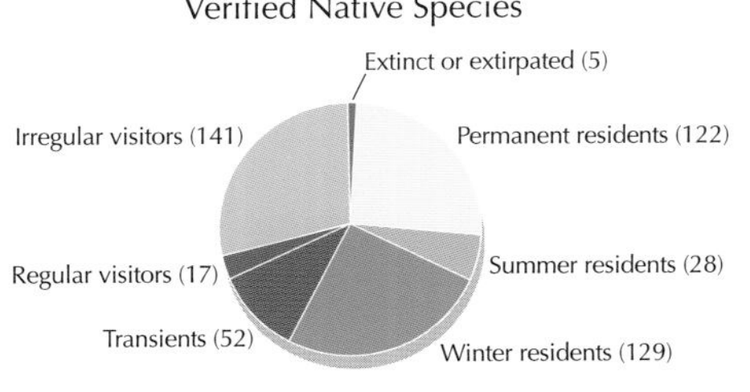

Our total species richness and rare species richness maps were created using information from the *Florida Breeding Bird Atlas* and data in the FNAI database. Overall diversity is highest in northern Florida where several species reach their southern range limits. Diversity also increases east to west as the influence of coastal areas declines and the state is closer to the center of the American continent. Similar trends are found in other vertebrates, and factors such as climate, topography, and increased habitat diversity seem to play a prominent role in shaping this diversity.

Some of our richest bird areas are found in the panhandle and northern peninsula. These are often aligned with public lands where natural habitats remain intact and common species and rare birds linked to natural conditions co-occur. Farther south, species rich areas can be found along prominent ridge systems, including the Brooksville Ridge in Citrus and Hernando counties, the Lake Wales Ridge in Polk and Highlands counties, and the Atlantic Coastal Ridge in Miami-Dade County. Less structurally complex and diverse areas, like the extensive freshwater marshes and mangrove swamps of South Florida and the Florida Keys, have consistently fewer breeding species.

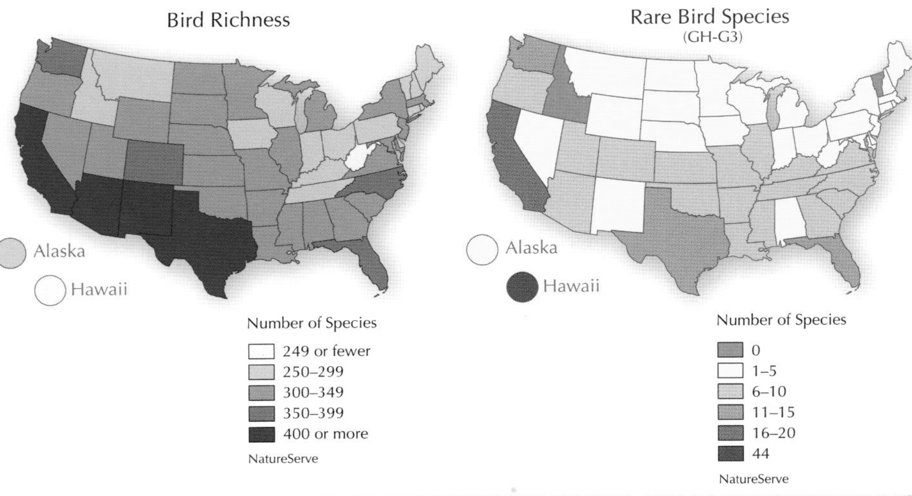

Florida Birds

		Species	Subspecies
Number of Bird Species in Florida			503
Native Species	490		
Established Exotic Species	13		
Number of Bird Species in the U.S.			ca. 888
Percentage of U.S. Bird Species found in Florida			ca. 56%
Number of Bird Species Tracked by FNAI		57	16
Number of Federally Listed Species (Threatened or Endangered)		9	3
Number of State Listed Species (Threatened or Endangered)		10	5

FNAI, NatureServe, Florida Ornithological Society Records Committee, March 2010

Florida Birds by Global Rarity Rank

Many of Florida's bird species with no rank assigned are accidental to Florida and/or are relatively common (G4-G5).

1% 1% 7% 30% 61%

*full species only, see page 142 for rank explanation

David Moynahan

Pileated woodpecker (*Dryocopus pileatus*) This large and impressive woodpecker shares its loud call (made famous in Tarzan movies) in woodlands throughout the state.

David Laliberte

Short-tailed hawk (*Buteo brachyurus*) This rare raptor occurs only in peninsular Florida in the U.S.

David Moynahan

Bald eagle (*Haliaeetus leucocephalus*) Our national symbol can be found throughout much of Florida, which boasts the 2nd largest population south of Alaska.

Larry Master www.masterimages.org

Painted bunting (*Passerina ciris*) This spectacular songbird is experiencing dramatic population decline rangewide.

David Moynahan

Northern mockingbird (*Mimus polyglottos*) This inconspicuous songster has a dazzling repertoire of around 200 songs.

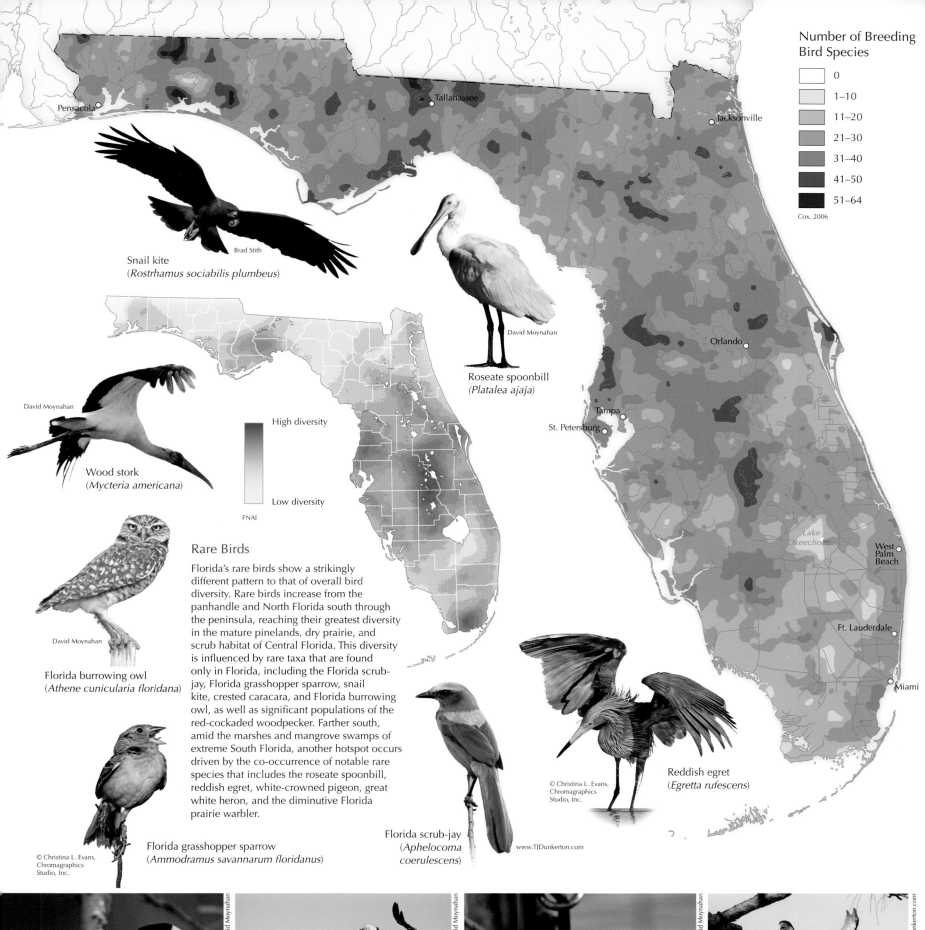

Number of Breeding Bird Species

	0
	1–10
	11–20
	21–30
	31–40
	41–50
	51–64

Cox, 2006

Pensacola · Tallahassee · Jacksonville · St. Marys · Orlando · Tampa · St. Petersburg · Lake Okeechobee · West Palm Beach · Ft. Lauderdale · Miami

Brad Stith

Snail kite
(*Rostrhamus sociabilis plumbeus*)

David Moynahan

Roseate spoonbill
(*Platalea ajaja*)

High diversity

Low diversity

FNAI

David Moynahan

Wood stork
(*Mycteria americana*)

David Moynahan

Florida burrowing owl
(*Athene cunicularia floridana*)

Rare Birds

Florida's rare birds show a strikingly different pattern to that of overall bird diversity. Rare birds increase from the panhandle and North Florida south through the peninsula, reaching their greatest diversity in the mature pinelands, dry prairie, and scrub habitat of Central Florida. This diversity is influenced by rare taxa that are found only in Florida, including the Florida scrub-jay, Florida grasshopper sparrow, snail kite, crested caracara, and Florida burrowing owl, as well as significant populations of the red-cockaded woodpecker. Farther south, amid the marshes and mangrove swamps of extreme South Florida, another hotspot occurs driven by the co-occurrence of notable rare species that includes the roseate spoonbill, reddish egret, white-crowned pigeon, great white heron, and the diminutive Florida prairie warbler.

© Christina L. Evans, Chromagraphics Studio, Inc.

Florida grasshopper sparrow
(*Ammodramus savannarum floridanus*)

Florida scrub-jay
(*Aphelocoma coerulescens*)

www.TJDunkerton.com

© Christina L. Evans, Chromagraphics Studio, Inc.

Reddish egret
(*Egretta rufescens*)

David Moynahan

Hooded warbler (*Wilsonia citrina*)
This stunning little warbler breeds in the northern part of the state and is a common migrant in spring and fall.

David Moynahan

Brown pelican (*Pelecanus occidentalis*)
This coastal icon was removed from the federal endangered species list in 2009 after a decades-long recovery effort.

David Moynahan

Green heron (*Butorides virescens*)
This small, colorful heron remains common in a variety of wetlands statewide.

www.TJDunkerton.com

Crested caracara (*Caracara cheriway*)
Florida's population is restricted to the dry prairies and ranch lands of the south central peninsula.

Challenges in Bird Conservation

Migration is one of the most exciting events in nature and one of our most unique conservation challenges. Seeing purple martins, ruby-throated hummingbirds, and swallow-tailed kites return in spring reminds us of small treasures misplaced during winter months. Hunters plan their fall and winter forays around the return of ducks to Florida's rich wetlands at the same time that bird watchers anticipate the influx of shorebirds, water birds, and confusing sparrows and warblers. April is an ideal time to see songbirds and shorebirds pass through our state. Coastal sites are primary destinations for these travelers, and huge numbers can be observed when inclement weather impedes their northward progress. Raptor migration peaks in early October and prime spectator sites include St. Joe Peninsula State Park and the barrier islands of the Atlantic coast and the Keys.

Conservation of migratory birds requires managing habitat across widely disparate geograhic areas, often across continents. Migratory birds that use Florida for extended periods (summer breeders and winter residents) make up 32% of our native species. Another 11% of Florida's native birds, including the scarlet tanager, are transient species that pass through the state on their way to warmer wintering sites or as they return to northern breeding sites. Yet others need the resources at selected spots to gorge in preparation for flights that can be hundreds of miles in a single jaunt.

David Moynahan

SUMMER RESIDENT

The graceful and acrobatic swallow-tailed kite (*Elanoides forficatus*) once nested as far north as Minnesota, but by 1940 showed a marked decline and a much contracted range. Florida may support 60-65% of U.S. population, which migrates south primarily to relatively small areas in Bolivia, eastern Paraguay, and southwestern Brazil.

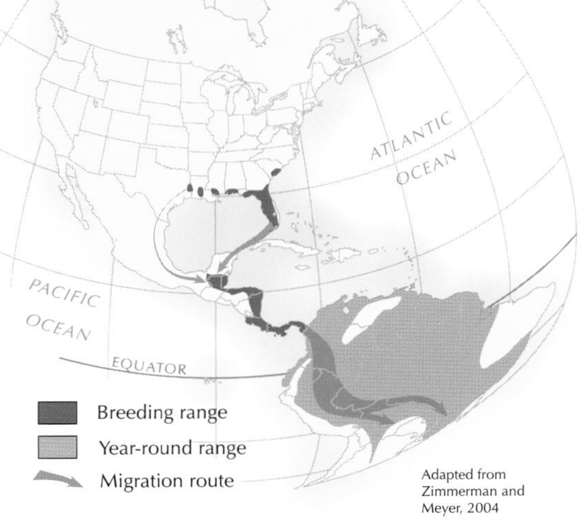

Adapted from Zimmerman and Meyer, 2004

Dean Jue

WINTER RESIDENT

Henslow's sparrow (*Ammodramus henslowii*) has a population of approximately 70,000, breeds in native prairies, agricultural hay fields, and other grasslands in the northeastern U.S. Loss of habitat has contributed to species decline, making it a high conservation priority. This secretive sparrow is a short-distance migrant that winters throughout much of Florida in open herbaceous pinelands and prairies.

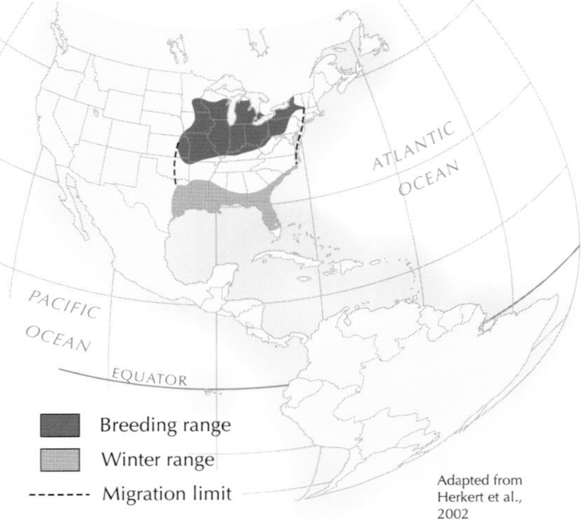

Adapted from Herkert et al., 2002

David Laliberte

TRANSIENT

The striking scarlet tanager (*Piranga olivacea*) breeds throughout the eastern U.S., outside Florida. This long-distance Neotropical migrant passes through Florida each fall on its way to northwestern South America and each spring on its way back to its breeding grounds. Its proclivity for hanging out in the forest treetops can make it challenging to observe, but stellar views can be seen on Florida's coastlines each spring.

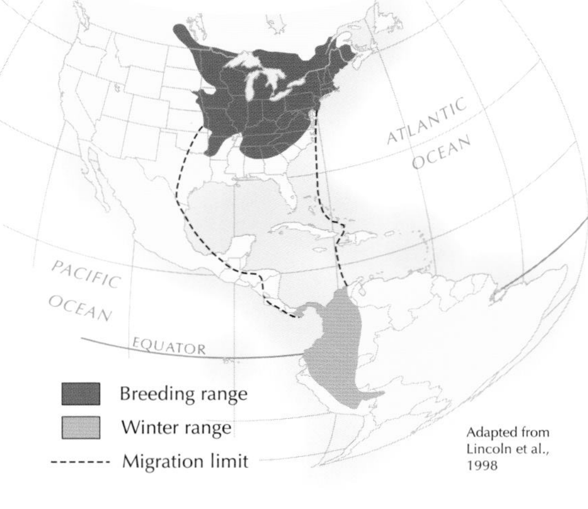

Adapted from Lincoln et al., 1998

David Moynahan

PERMANENT RESIDENT

The Florida scrub-jay (*Aphelocoma coerulescens*) is Florida's only endemic bird and is restricted to the small patches of oak scrub and scrubby flatwoods remaining in peninsular Florida. Development and lack of fire management continue to take a toll on the availability of suitable habitat for the jay despite progress acquiring lands with scrub habitat.

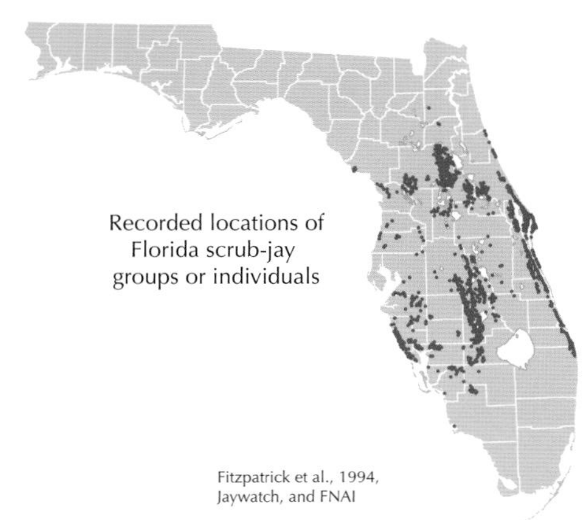

Recorded locations of Florida scrub-jay groups or individuals

Fitzpatrick et al., 1994, Jaywatch, and FNAI

Birds in Decline

In one sense, habitat conservation began out of concern for migratory birds. Many national wildlife refuges were created out of concern for migratory waterfowl, and the acreage of bird-friendly tracts has grown steadily. Yet we are losing habitat even for common migratory and resident species such as eastern kingbirds (*Tyrannus tyrannus*), eastern meadowlarks (*Sturnella magna*), and loggerhead shrikes (*Lanius rudovicianus*). Development also makes it more difficult to manage protected areas using natural tools like fire. Recreation puts a heavy burden on our shorebirds as boats and jet skis compete for nesting and resting areas. To preserve a future in Florida for migratory and resident birds, we need to continue strategic habitat protection and effective stewardship, while broadening public understanding of the unique challenges of bird conservation.

EXTINCT

Ivory-billed Woodpecker

Melynda Reid

(*Campephilus principalis*) once common in swamps and hammocks throughout Florida, now extinct or nearly so—hope remains in Louisiana, Arkansas, and in Florida's Choctawhatchee and Apalachicola river systems.

Passenger Pigeon

Melynda Reid

(*Ectopistes migratorius*) numbered in the billions, range wide, wintered in North Florida, and was perhaps the most abundant bird ever to exist.

Carolina Parakeet

Melynda Reid

(*Conuropsis carolinensis*) once ranging in large numbers over most of the state, it was shot for food and sport, and disappeared in the 1920s.

RARE

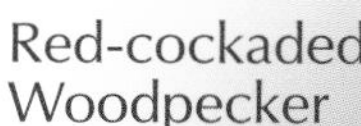

Red-cockaded Woodpecker

Diane Pierce

(*Picoides borealis*) dependent on well-managed old-growth pinelands, threatened by habitat fragmentation and lack of appropriate management.

Florida Scrub-Jay

Diane Pierce

(*Aphelocoma coerulescens*) a declining species characteristic of Florida's central and coastal scrub habitats

Diane Pierce

Snail Kite

(*Rostrhamus sociabilis plumbeus*) a declining species highly dependent on water levels in South Florida wetlands, also affected by invasion of exotic apple snails, which are difficult to eat, especially for young birds.

Diane Pierce

Florida Grasshopper Sparrow

(*Ammodramus savannarum floridanus*) rare resident dependent on threatened dry prairie habitat in south central Florida.

Diane Pierce

Snowy Plover

(*Charadrius alexandrinus*) sandy, sparsely vegetated beaches, along Gulf coast, threatened by coastal development, and human and dog recreation.

COMMON

White-breasted Nuthatch

Diane Pierce

(*Sitta carolinensis*) common throughout North America but eliminated from most of Florida; occurred south to Lake Okeechobee but now found in only two counties in North Florida.

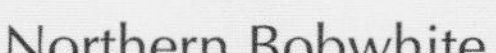

Northern Bobwhite

Diane Pierce

(*Colinus virginianus*) declining in part from conversion of pasture to more intensive agriculture and development, but receiving much attention that may help reverse the trend in this group of birds.

Diane Pierce

Eastern Meadowlark

(*Sturnella magna*) grassland and open pineland bird facing threats similar to bobwhite; move to more monocultures for biofuel may increase risk.

Diane Pierce

Loggerhead Shrike

(*Lanius ludovicianus*) prefers open prairies and pastureland with few trees; like bobwhite and meadowlark, loss of habitat to intensive agriculture and development partly responsible for declines.

Mammals

At least 57 mammal species are native to Florida. One of these species is now extinct: the Caribbean monk seal (*Monachus tropicalis*). Two others have been extirpated in Florida: the American bison (*Bos bison*) and red wolf (*Canis rufus*) are now only present as captive or experimental populations. The remaining extant species include 17 rodents, 17 bats, 12 carnivores, 6 insectivores, 2 rabbits, 1 deer, 1 manatee, and 1 opossum. The total here for Florida does not include marine mammals, or "accidental" occurrences, but does include regular migrants such as the hoary bat (*Lasiurus cinereus*). Florida is home to two mammals that are found nowhere else in the world, the Florida mouse (*Podomys floridanus*) and the Florida bonneted bat (*Eumops floridanus*). These species as well as the nearly endemic round-tailed muskrat (*Neofiber alleni*) are highlighted on the facing page.

Although Florida does not have the high diversity of mammals of several western states, its geographic and geologic history has produced many interesting and unique subspecies on isolated keys and barrier islands. Perhaps the best-known example of this is the key deer (*Odocoileus virginianus clavium*), a diminutive subspecies of the white-tailed deer, which was isolated in the Lower Keys when sea levels rose at the close of the Pleistocene epoch around 12,000 years ago. Several other subspecies also were isolated in the Lower Keys and on barrier islands along Florida's coast. Florida black bear (*Ursus americanus floridanus*), manatee (*Trichechus manatus*), and Florida panther (*Puma concolor coryi*) are individually highlighted on other pages.

Florida Mammals

Number of Mammal Species in Florida	57	
Number of Mammal Species in the U.S.	425	
Percentage of U.S. Mammal Species found in Florida	13%	
	Species	Subspecies
Number of Mammal Species Tracked by FNAI	13	24
Number of Federally Listed Species (Threatened or Endangered)	4	10
Number of State Listed Species (Threatened or Endangered)	3	12

FNAI, NatureServe, March 2010

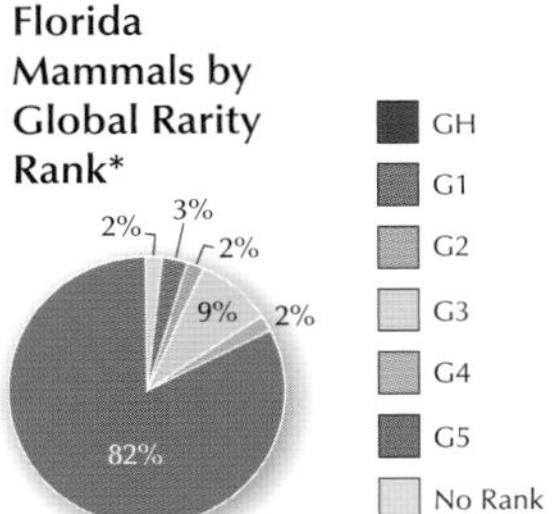

Although less than 15% of Florida's 57 mammal species are considered rare (GH-G3), an additional 20 subspecies fit that description, including several isolated coastal populations.

*full species only, *see* page 142 for rank explanation

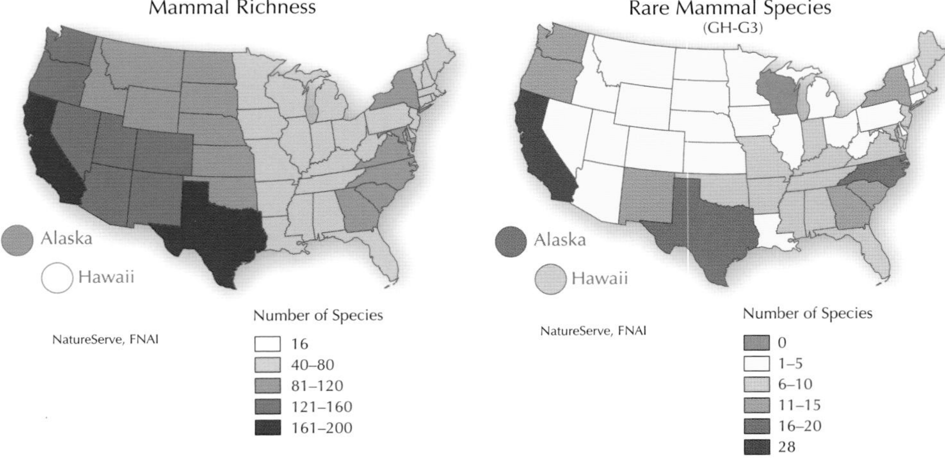

Extinct Species

The Caribbean monk seal (*Monachus tropicalis*) was the only seal native to the Gulf of Mexico and the Caribbean. It could easily be approached and killed and was driven to extinction sometime during the 19th century.

Caribbean monk seal (*Monachus tropicalis*)

Henry W. Elliot, U.S. National Museum, Courtesy of NOAA

Exotic Mammals

At least 13 species of mammals that are not native to Florida have established wild breeding populations. Some of these, like the black-tailed jackrabbit (*Lepus californicus*) in the Homestead area, are limited to small areas and appear to pose no immediate problem to humans or native wildlife. Several exotic species, however, are widespread, each with at least minor implications. The red fox (*Vulpes vulpes*) expanded its range into Florida either from introduced European stock or from native northern North American individuals, and although it may compete somewhat with the native gray fox, it is a relatively benign exotic species. The somewhat more problematic armadillo (*Dasypus novemcinctus*) was both introduced to southern Florida and expanded eastward from Texas; its digging for food has been implicated in the destruction of ground nesting birds and reptiles as well as lawn turf. Feral pigs (*Sus scrofa*) have been successful in establishing themselves throughout most of Florida and much of the Southeast and are an example of a highly detrimental exotic species. Their rooting is destructive to roads, fields, and native natural communities; they compete for food directly with many native wildlife species including squirrels, deer, ducks, and turkeys; they also indiscriminately eat amphibians, reptiles, and the eggs of ground nesting species. Efforts to reduce local populations of feral pigs through hunting and trapping have been marginally successful. Nutria (*Myocastor coypus*) is an example of a relatively recent immigrant to the state, the implications of which are yet to be seen. Nutria have been reported around the state in rural settings, but no known populations are persistent in natural areas. The well-established population in Louisiana has caused extensive damage to coastal marshes and rice crops; their burrows also have caused millions of dollars of damage in collapsed roads, something we hope to avoid here in Florida.

NASA

Feral pig (*Sus scrofa*)

USFWS

Armadillo (*Dasypus novemcinctus*)

USFWS

Red fox (*Vulpes vulpes*)

John and Karen Hollingsworth, courtesy of USFWS

Nutria (*Myocastor coypus*)

Beach Mice

During the same sea level rise that isolated the Keys, the oldfield mouse (*Peromyscus polionotus*) was isolated on barrier islands around the state. This led to the differentiation of seven different beach mouse subspecies in Florida and one restricted to Alabama, each with a series of unique features, the most obvious of which is pelage coloration. One of these species, the pallid beach mouse (*P. p. decoloratus*), is extinct. The remaining six are threatened by development, hurricanes, and feral cats and, with one exception (*P. p. leuccocephalus*), are listed as either threatened (*P. p. niveiventris*) or endangered (the remaining subspecies).

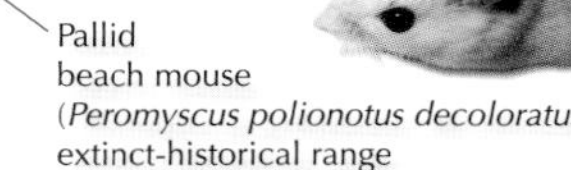

Extirpated Species

American bison (*Bos bison*) were never abundant in Florida, but apparently increased in numbers during colonial times as forests were cleared throughout the eastern U.S. They were extirpated in Florida as a result of hunting sometime late in the 18th century.

Lou Kellenberger

Dan Hipes

The red wolf (*Canis rufus*) once occurred throughout most of the southeastern U.S. They were extirpated in Florida in the 1890s. They now can be found only in captive populations and an experimental population on St. Vincent Island and a few other locations in the Southeast.

Isolated Subspecies

USFWS

The salt marsh vole (*Microtus pennsylvanicus dukecampbelli*) is a relict subspecies of the meadow vole, which is common in the mid-Atlantic. This subspecies is thought to have thrived in the vast meadows along the Florida coast prior to the same sea level rise that isolated the Florida Keys, but is now restricted to patches of salt grass meadow at a few locations along the big bend coast, and is among Florida's rarest mammals.

The Lower Keys marsh rabbit (*Sylvilagus palustris hefneri*) is one of the several mammal subspecies isolated in the Lower Keys. The subspecies name was given in honor of Hugh Hefner, whose corporation supported much of the research and protection efforts. Its cordgrass marsh habitat is extremely limited, making the Lower Keys marsh rabbit very rare.

Scott Hein, courtesy of USFWS

Endemic Species

The Florida mouse (*Podomys floridanus*) is the only member of its genus, meaning it has no living close relatives. This attractive mouse, resembling a deer mouse, lives in gopher tortoise (*Gopherus polyphemus*) burrows, generally in sandhill or scrub communities, where it digs a side chamber near the entrance, often with a separate escape tunnel to the surface.

Fiona Sunquist

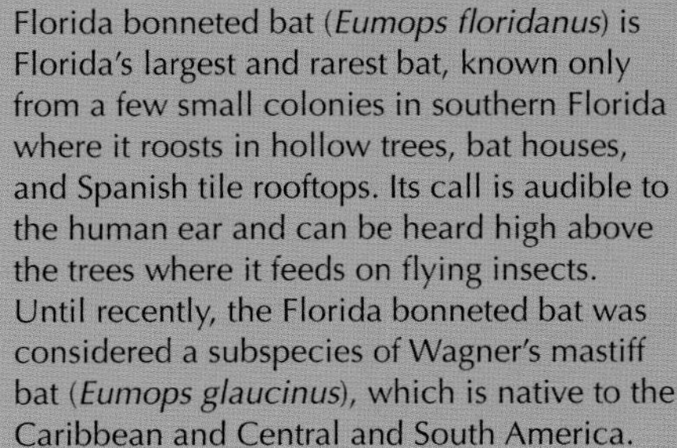

Florida bonneted bat (*Eumops floridanus*) is Florida's largest and rarest bat, known only from a few small colonies in southern Florida where it roosts in hollow trees, bat houses, and Spanish tile rooftops. Its call is audible to the human ear and can be heard high above the trees where it feeds on flying insects. Until recently, the Florida bonneted bat was considered a subspecies of Wagner's mastiff bat (*Eumops glaucinus*), which is native to the Caribbean and Central and South America.

Roger Barbour, AR Game and Fish Commission

The round-tailed muskrat (*Neofiber alleni*), also the only member of its genus, is endemic to Florida and the Okefenokee Swamp in southeastern Georgia and does not overlap with the common muskrat (*Ondatra zibethicus*), which is found throughout most of North America. The round-tailed muskrat lives in large marshes where it builds "houses" out of grasses and sedges.

Scott Cardiff

Butterflies

About 165 species of butterflies occur regularly in Florida. An additional 25 to 30 species are considered strays or irregular visitors to the state. Florida is the southernmost geographic limit for many northern butterfly species as well as the northernmost limit for some Neotropical butterfly species that just reach the United States. FNAI tracks more than one-third of the butterfly species recorded in the state.

The major threats to Florida's butterfly biodiversity are habitat loss due to human development and habitat fragmentation. Even where lands are already protected from development, many land managers focus primarily on vertebrate species rather than invertebrates when developing land management strategies. This vertebrate-centric view can sometimes adversely impact butterfly species, which face specific risks to survival (e.g., roadside mowing, timing of prescribed burns) during each stage of their life cycle.

Extreme southern Florida is the only place to see many of the rarest Florida butterfly species. This is due to the unique habitats in this region (e.g., pine rockland, subtropical hardwood hammocks). Fully one-third of the 81 butterfly species tracked by FNAI are restricted primarily or exclusively to Miami-Dade or Monroe counties.

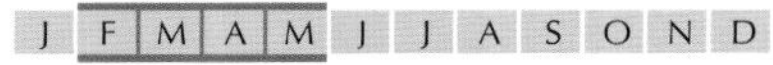

The red bar indicates the flight period for the identified species.

Dean Jue

Silvery Checkerspot (*Chlosyne nycteis*)
G5/S1
The silvery checkerspot is an Appalachian butterfly species that has a disjunct, relict population in Jackson County. It is found in Florida Caverns State Park in sunny areas within bottomland forests typical of more northern climates. Long-term survival of this species in Florida will require careful land management practices within the few hundred acres where it occurs.

J F M A M J J A S O N D

Dean Jue

Frosted Elfin (*Callophrys irus*)
G3/S1
Frosted elfins occur in fire-maintained habitats. The pupa can live beneath the soil's surface, which helps the species survive summer burns. Within Florida, this rare butterfly is known from only a few northern counties. In Florida, it uses sundial lupine (*Lupinus perennis*) as its host plant.

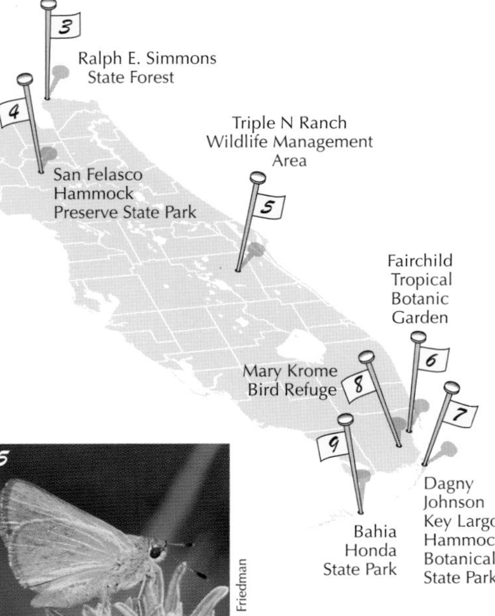

Dean Jue

Yucca Giant-Skipper
(*Megathymus yuccae*)
G5/S3S4
The adult yucca giant-skipper does not eat and, in Florida, flies for only a few weeks in late winter or early spring. The rest of the year, the caterpillars live in and feed on their host plant, yucca. The adult butterfly emerges the following spring

J F M A M J J A S O N D

Dean Jue

Monarch (*Danaus plexippus*)
G5/S5
The monarch is one of very few butterfly species that flies long distances. Each fall, monarchs from the eastern U.S. migrate south to spend the winter in Central Mexico. The St. Marks National Wildlife Refuge is a good location for seeing the fall migration of monarch butterflies, since they accumulate along the Gulf coast before flying farther south.

J F M A M J J A S O N D

MaryAnn Friedman

Arogos Skipper (*Atrytone arogos arogos*)
G3T1T2/S1
The arogos skipper is one of the rarest skippers in North America, and Florida may have the largest remaining populations of this butterfly. The long-term presence of this skipper in its preferred sandhill or prairie habitat is indicative of good land management practices.

J F M A M J J A S O N D

Dean Jue

Atala (*Eumaeus atala*)
G4/S2
The atala caterpillars feed on coontie (*Zamia pumila*). The caterpillars and adult butterflies are protected from predation by cycasin compounds in their bodies derived from the coontie host plant.

J F M A M J J A S O N D

Surveying Species

Linda Cooper

Kissimmee Prairie Preserve State Park

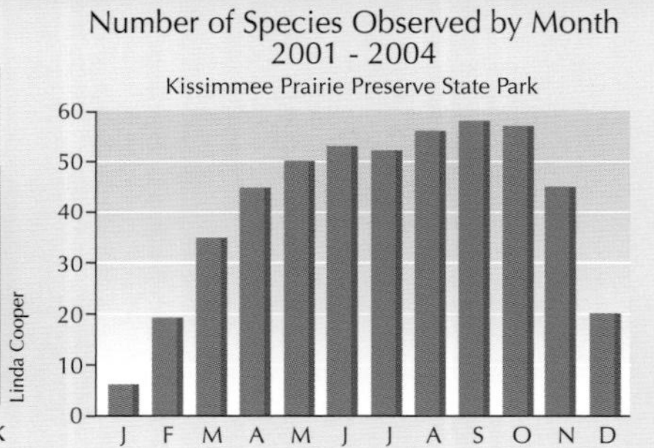

Kissimmee Prairie Preserve State Park is the first conservation land in Florida to be regularly and intensively surveyed for butterflies. Linda and Byrum "Buck" Cooper began doing monthly surveys at this 53,766-acre park in August 2001. They have recorded 87 species of butterflies in the state park through 2009 and consider this park to be one of the best places in Florida for observing a diversity of butterflies. The state park encompasses the largest remaining tracts of dry prairie in the state, which provide habitat for two S1-ranked butterflies, the berry's skipper (*Euphyes berryi*) and the Florida dusted skipper (*Atrytonopsis hianna loammi*). Other Florida sites that have had monthly butterfly surveys for at least one year include Elinor Klapp-Phipps Park, Edward Ball Wakulla Springs State Park, Colt Creek State Park, and Seminole Ranch Conservation Area.

Linda Cooper

Florida dusted skipper
(*Atrytonopsis hianna loammi*)

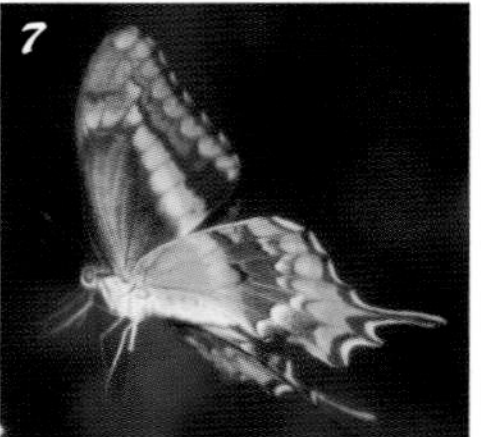

Dean Jue

Schaus' Swallowtail
(*Papilio aristodemus ponceanus*)
G3G4T1/S1
The endangered Schaus' swallowtail is one of two federally listed butterfly species in Florida. It is restricted to rockland hammock, a South Florida habitat that has almost completely disappeared due to extensive human development.

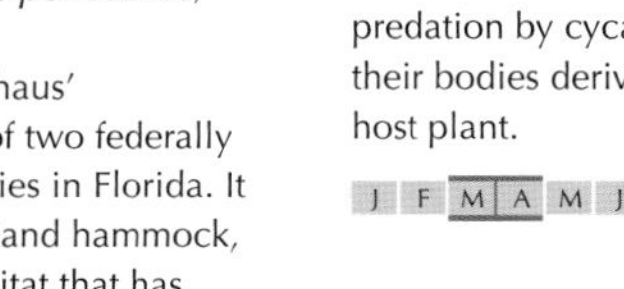

Dean Jue

Malachite
(*Siproeta stelenes*)
G5/S2
The adult malachite feeds on fallen fruits so its range in Florida expanded northward with the growth of the citrus and avocado industry. However, malachites became very rare throughout Florida following Hurricane Andrew in 1992. Its numbers are again on the rise, but northward expansion of this Neotropical species is limited by its intolerance of freezing temperatures.

J F M A M J J A S O N D

Dean Jue

Miami Blue
(*Cyclargus thomasi bethunebakeri*)
G3G4TU/S1
The Miami blue is listed as endangered by both the USFWS and the FWC in Florida. Releases of the captive-bred individuals through 2009 have not been successful in establishing new populations of this endangered butterfly.

J F M A M J J A S O N D

Flatwoods Salamander

HIGHLIGHTED SPECIES

Formerly thought to be one species, the flatwoods salamander is now considered two species divided by the Apalachicola River: the frosted flatwoods salamander (*Ambystoma cingulatum*) to the east and the reticulated flatwoods salamander (*Ambystoma bishopi*) to the west. These similarly appearing salamanders inhabit mesic and wet flatwoods with abundant grasses (often wiregrass) and low-growing shrubs. This vital vegetation structure historically was maintained by fires that naturally occurred every few years.

Dan Hipes

Dome swamp, typical breeding habitat

Flatwoods salamanders breed in isolated ephemeral ponds (dome swamps and depression marshes) that lack large predatory fish. Autumn and early winter rains prompt migration to breeding sites where females lay clusters of eggs under debris or vegetation in anticipation of rising water. Larvae hide and hunt in the submerged grasses and sedges in the ponds until early spring when they emerge and move out into the surrounding flatwoods where they live a secretive subterranean life.

Seasonality of Breeding and Habitat Use

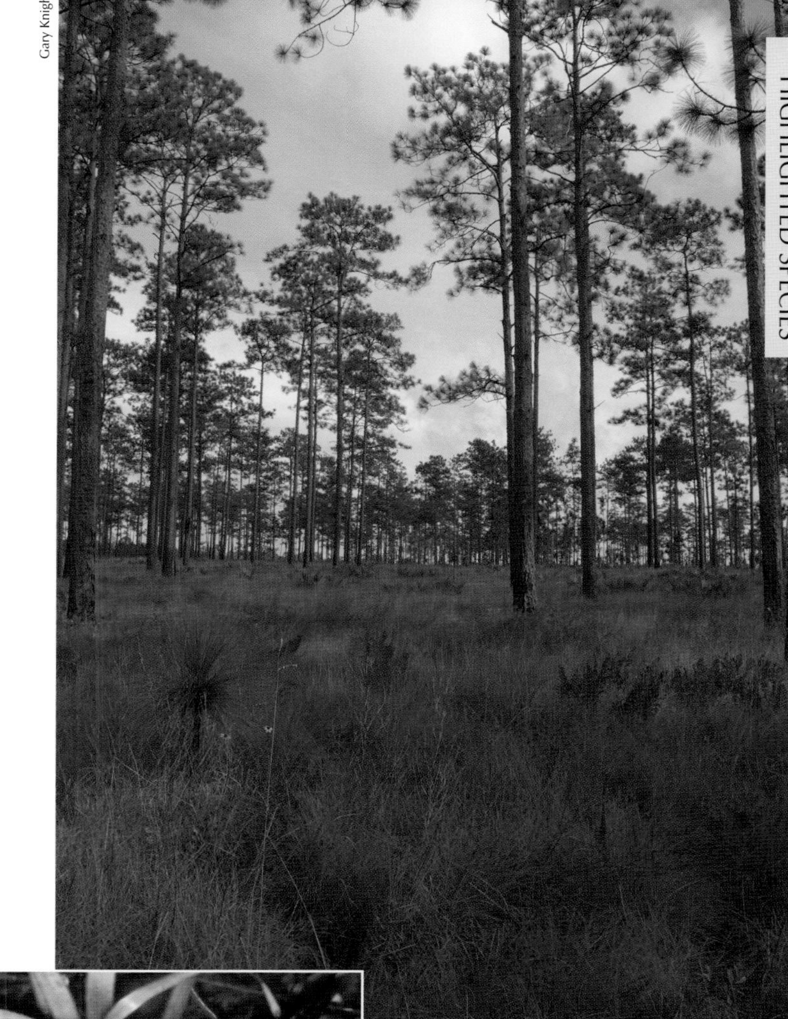
Gary Knight

Mesic flatwoods, typical uplands habitat

Habitat for flatwoods salamanders once occurred across large areas of the U.S. Southeastern Coastal Plain, but has been replaced to a large extent by agriculture, pine silviculture, and urban development. Many of the few remaining sites for both species are threatened by insufficient prescribed fire or incompatible uses that alter the native grasses either in the flatwoods or the breeding sites. The status of many populations is unknown because of the substantial effort needed to survey for individuals. A stronghold for the frosted flatwoods salamander is the Apalachicola National Forest, which supports an extensive landscape of flatwoods and swamps. The more precarious existence of the reticulated flatwoods salamander may depend on continued careful management of populations on Eglin Air Force Base.

Dan Hipes

Frosted flatwoods salamander larva (*Ambystoma cingulatum*)

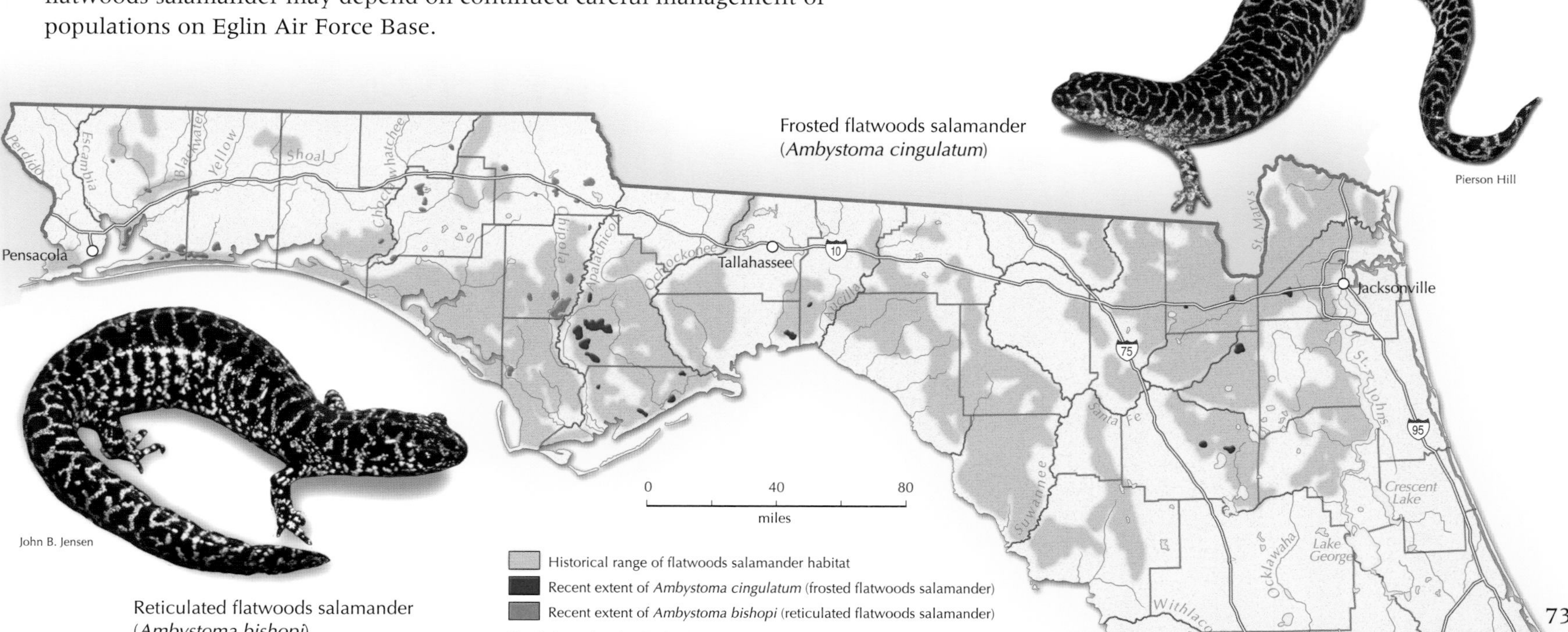

Frosted flatwoods salamander (*Ambystoma cingulatum*)

Reticulated flatwoods salamander (*Ambystoma bishopi*)

Historical range of flatwoods salamander habitat
Recent extent of *Ambystoma cingulatum* (frosted flatwoods salamander)
Recent extent of *Ambystoma bishopi* (reticulated flatwoods salamander)

Historical range based on Davis, 1967

Marine Turtles

Although ancient marine (or sea) turtles were more diverse, seven living species still ply the oceanic waters of our planet. Six of these, with hard shells, represent a single family; the seventh—the giant leatherback (*Demochelys coriacea*) with its skin-covered shell—stems from a second, distant lineage. With its position at the nexus of temperate and tropical zones, Florida is regularly home to all but two of the world's species. Our coastal waters and beaches support one of the largest concentrations of loggerhead turtles (*Caretta caretta*) on earth, and this is the species most commonly seen swimming or nesting here (as well as northward to North Carolina). Smaller populations of the globally distributed green (*Chelonia mydas*) and leatherback turtles also occur statewide, with nesting confined mostly to our Atlantic coast. The strictly tropical hawksbill turtle (*Eretmochelys imbricata*) is largely restricted to southeastern Florida and the Keys. Finally, the most endangered of all marine turtles, the relatively small Kemp's ridley (*Lepidochelys kempii*) of the Gulf of Mexico, forages in our nearshore Gulf coastal waters and bays and occasionally along our Atlantic coast.

Marine turtles are an integral component of our state's coastal waters. They are consumers of plants (green turtle) and invertebrates (all other species), and their eggs and young provide a potential banquet to a variety of mammals, fish, birds, and even crabs. Nonetheless, all species are listed as threatened or endangered because of losses to incidental capture and entanglement (often leading to drowning) in various fisheries gear, degradation of nesting beaches and nearshore foraging habitats, boat collisions, and disease. Florida has adopted many tools to counteract these and other perils. Turtle Excluder Devices (TEDs) allow many (but not all) marine turtles to escape shrimping nets. The state's network of coastal conservation lands protects many miles of nesting beaches, although whether this will be sufficient in the face of rising sea level from global warming is a concern. Many coastal counties have enacted beachfront lighting ordinances that permit only certain wavelengths and lighting angles; these have greatly reduced nest failures and deaths of countless hatchlings that previously became disoriented from improper lighting.

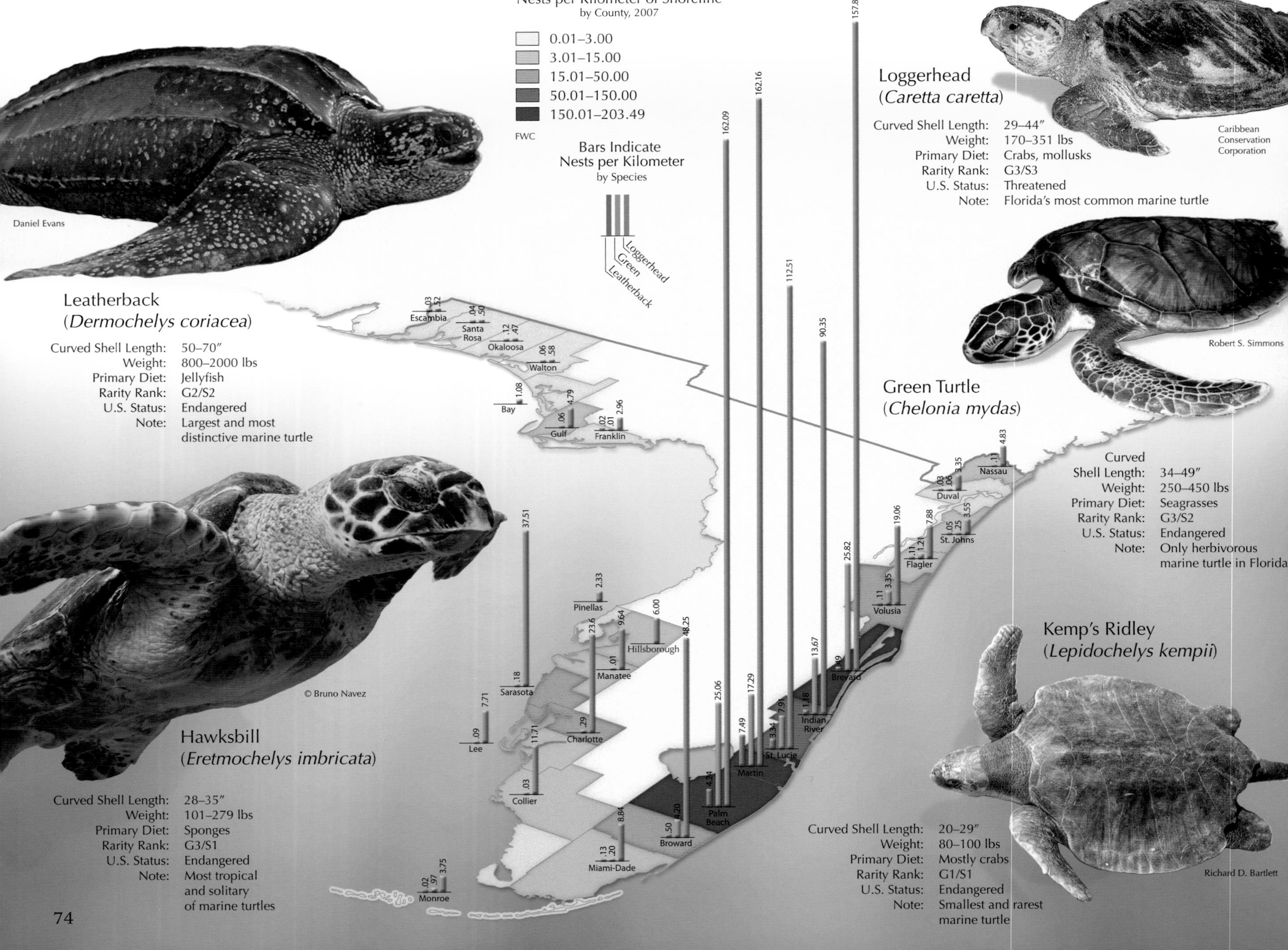

Gopher Tortoise

David Moynahan

The only true land tortoise living east of the Mississippi River, the gopher tortoise (*Gopherus polyphemus*) shares kinship with three desert-dwelling species of the western U.S. and Mexico. Florida comprises more than half of the species' remaining range, which extends from Louisiana to South Carolina and down to Cape Sable at the tip of the peninsula.

The gopher tortoise stands out among Florida wildlife for the "keystone" role it plays in the environment. Typically occupying sandy ridges and uplands, the "gopher" digs long, deep burrows for shelter from heat, cold, fire, and predators. These burrows are in turn used by more than 350 other species for similar protection. Inhabitants include frogs, snakes, mice, birds, and a host of interesting insects; the list includes more than a dozen species considered by the state to be of especially high conservation concern. Without the protective burrows of the tortoise, many of their populations would surely be lost.

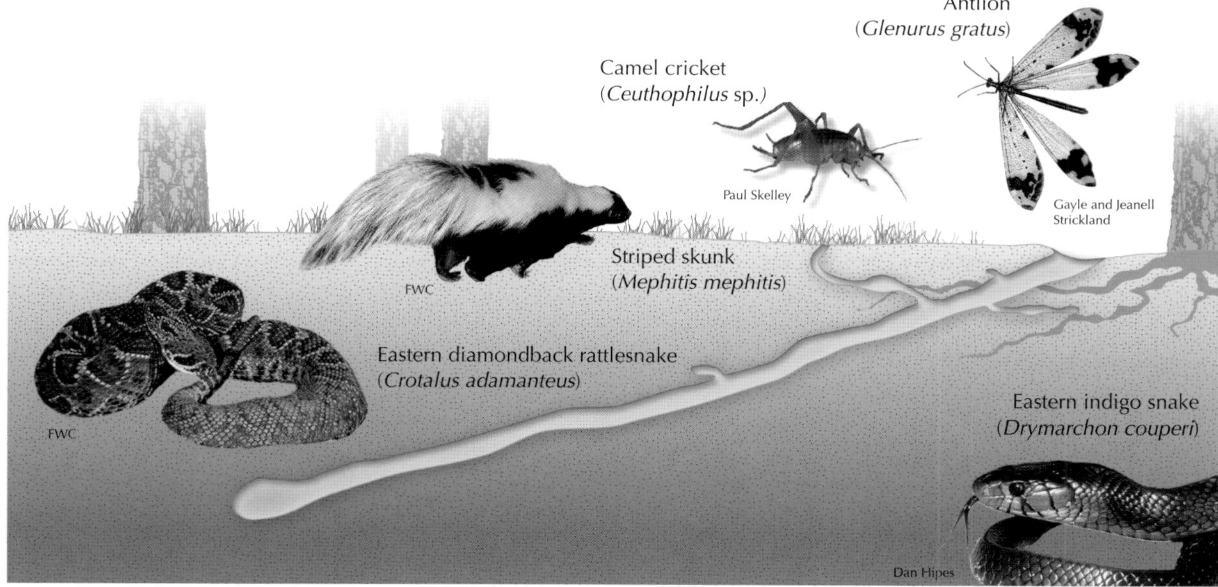

Above and Below the Surface

Burrows can be up to 15 feet deep and 40 feet long, but are only wide enough for a tortoise to turn around. These deep cool burrows provide refuge from fire, as well as from cold nights and hot summer days. Shown here are a few of the many species that use gopher tortoise burrows during some phases of their life cycles.

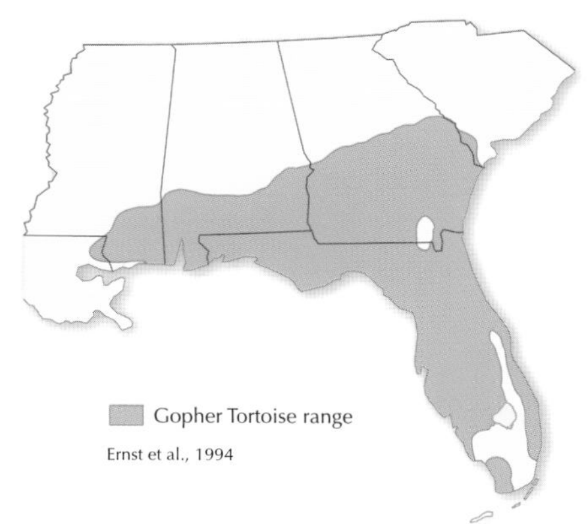

Dan Hipes

It takes a female tortoise from 16 to 21 years to reach maturity. She will lay an average of six eggs each year but may hatch only one clutch every 10 years on average due to predation. Only about 7% of tortoise hatchlings reach maturity. Juvenile shown above.

Dan Hipes

The rare gopher frog (*Rana capito*) relies on tortoise burrows and other underground refuges for shelter from desiccation (drying) and predators. Burrows maintain fairly constant temperatures and high humidity throughout the year.

Fiona Sundquist

The Florida mouse (*Podomys floridanus*) commonly digs its own tunnels off of gopher tortoise burrows. It feeds on seeds and nuts, as well as insects and other invertebrates.

Although the tortoise is still found in all 67 of Florida's counties, many populations are small and isolated, and the species is considered to be threatened here and rangewide. Florida's burgeoning development, as well as conversion of habitat for agriculture, timber production, and mineral extraction, continue to shrink remaining upland habitats. Those tracts that do remain often suffer ecologically from insufficient fire, which is essential to maintaining the herbaceous groundcover upon which the tortoise feeds.

Red-cockaded Woodpecker

RCWs drill small holes or "resin wells" around the cavity, which causes sap to flow and acts as a deterrent to tree-climbing predators.

David Laliberte

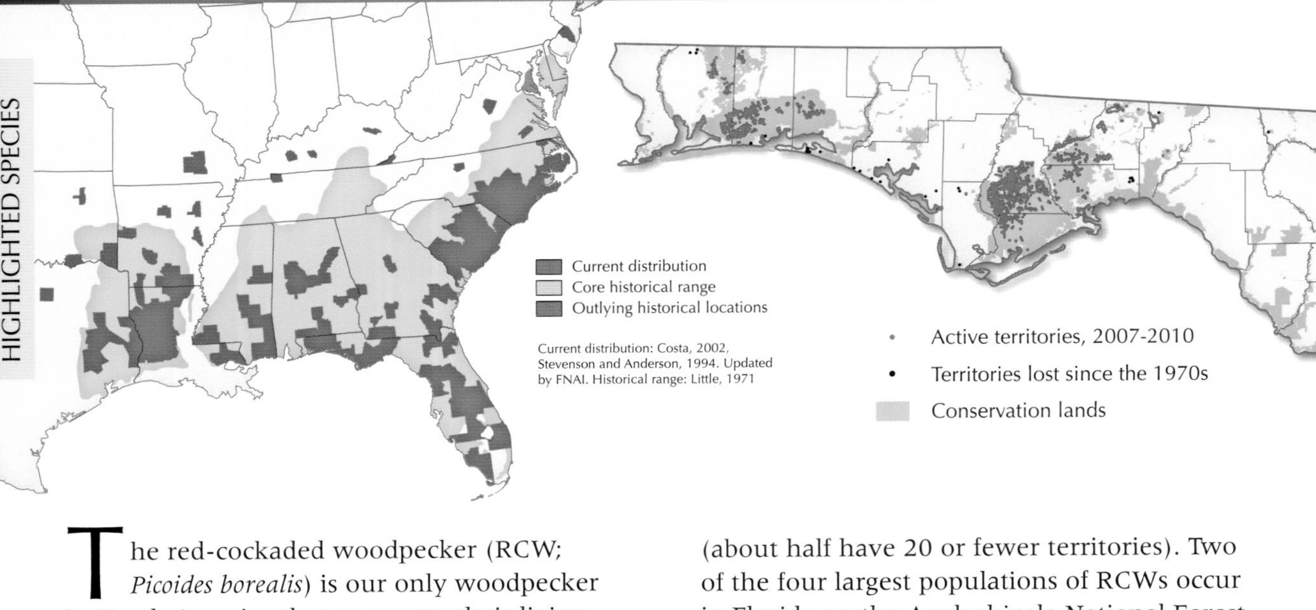

The red-cockaded woodpecker (RCW; *Picoides borealis*) is our only woodpecker in North America that excavates their living quarters in living pines. They maintain territories throughout the year, and they may require up to 200 acres or more per territory. Habitat quality depends on frequent, periodic fire to reduce brush and maintain open pinelands.

RCWs are cooperative breeders, whereby some young birds stay with their parents and help defend space and raise next year's young. Separate cavities are used by each family member so a territory often contains many completed cavities as well as a few cavities under construction. More than 25 species of wildlife are also known to use RCW cavities.

RCWs are inextricably linked to the remaining mature pine forests in the Southeast. Such pinelands once covered 90 million acres, but commercial timber harvesting, farming, urbanization, and agriculture have reduced these majestic forests by 97%. Current populations are highly fragmented and most are small (about half have 20 or fewer territories). Two of the four largest populations of RCWs occur in Florida on the Apalachicola National Forest (with the largest population in the world) and Eglin Air Force Base.

Methods for creating artificial woodpecker cavities were developed when Hurricane Hugo destroyed most of the cavity trees on South Carolina's Francis Marion National Forest in 1989. Artificial cavities represent a valuable management tool for smaller or declining populations. Special programs also have been developed to help conserve RCWs on private lands by offering financial incentives to landowners and by eliminating fears of unwanted regulation. Good habitat management, innovative strategies for bolstering and protecting populations, and maintaining endangered species as a priority concern of our federal and state agencies will help ensure the future of this unique, endangered woodpecker.

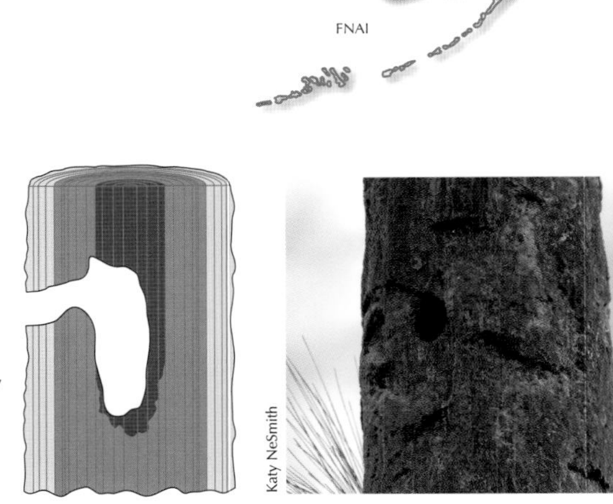

RCWs require older trees (>80 years) that are often infected with red heart fungus. The fungus softens the heartwood and allows for easier excavation in the living pine.

Extracting nestlings

Many populations of RCWs are monitored by climbing narrow 10-foot ladders stacked one on the other to reach cavities up to 50 feet high.

Mature longleaf pine forest

Prescribed fire is essential and maintains open, herbaceous, park-like conditions, preventing the development of a dense hardwood midstory.

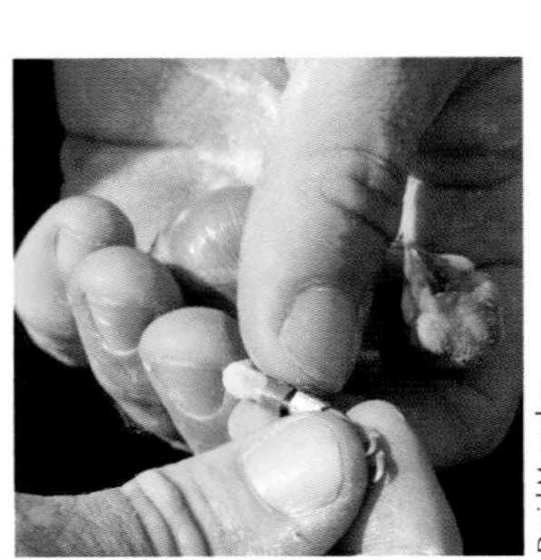

Banding nestlings

Colored bands help to identify individuals for population monitoring.

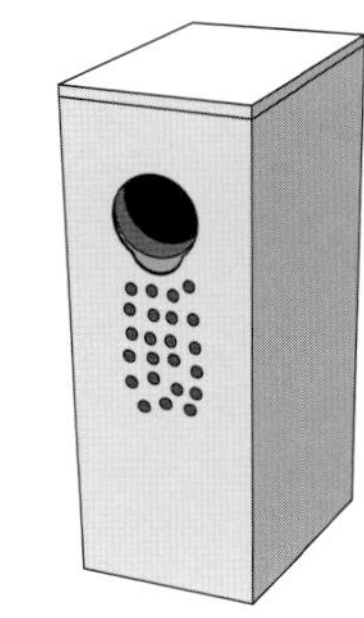

Drilling cavities or installing artificial nest boxes are important management tools.

Florida Scrub-Jay

The Florida scrub-jay (*Aphelocoma coerulescens*) is Florida's only endemic bird species. Florida scrub-jays occupy brushy scrub patches on well-drained sandy soils in the Florida peninsula. The vegetation is open and low statured as a result of periodic burning. Jays depend on a steady source of acorns and will deposit thousands of acorns under the sand to ensure a future food source.

Adolescent scrub-jays also can be every parent's dream. Scrub-jays have a cooperative breeding system where juvenile birds help parents raise additional young. Family groups may include from two to eight jays, and helpers contribute to defending the breeding territory from predators and feeding the nestlings and fledglings. Family groups with helpers generally raise more young than do lone pairs.

Jay families also have a very effective sentinel system where family members take turns watching for predators. When snakes or predatory hawks appear the sentinel gives an alarm call that sends the group diving for cover. Despite this adaptation, domestic house cats take a toll on both adults and young in suburban habitats.

Continuing loss, fragmentation, and degradation of scrub habitat has resulted in a loss of 80 to 90% of Florida scrub-jays. A greatly increased rate of decline has occurred in recent decades, dropping from a range-wide estimate of 10,700 birds in 1993 to roughly 6,930 birds in 2005. The largest remaining populations are found on federal lands (Merritt Island National Wildlife Refuge/Kennedy Space Center and Ocala National Forest) and scattered locations on the Lake Wales Ridge in Polk and Highlands counties. The Florida scrub-jay is listed as threatened by both the federal and state governments.

FWC

- Recorded locations of Florida scrub-jays since 1993 (last statewide survey)
- Sites monitored by Jay Watch in 2008 (with scrub-jays present)

Fitzpatrick et al., 1994; Jaywatch; and FNAI

Habitat Loss

Much of the scrub-jay's habitat has been lost to urban and agricultural uses. This example shows habitat degradation in Marion County west of I-75 between 1995 and 2008 (yellow outline is boundary of M.H. Carr Cross Florida Greenway).

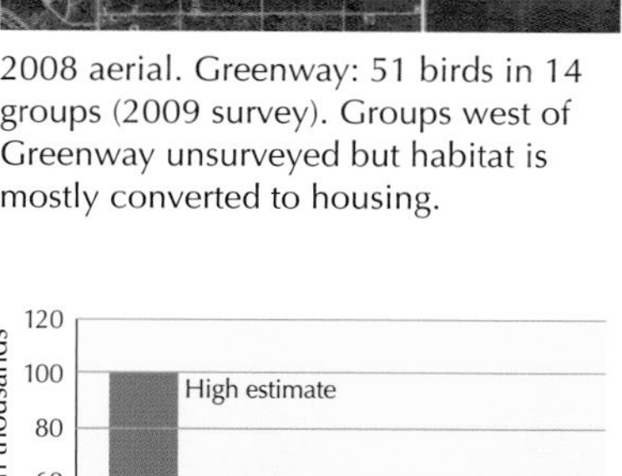

1995 infrared aerial. Greenway: 17 birds in 7 groups. West of Greenway: 21 birds in 7 groups (1992-93 survey data).

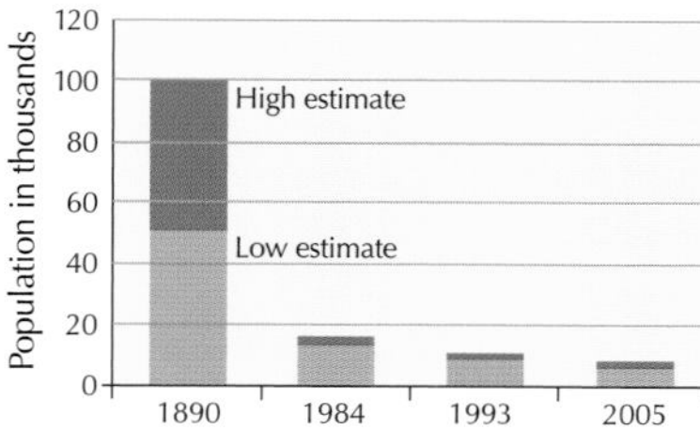

2008 aerial. Greenway: 51 birds in 14 groups (2009 survey). Groups west of Greenway unsurveyed but habitat is mostly converted to housing.

Population in thousands
High estimate
Low estimate
120, 100, 80, 60, 40, 20, 0
1890 | 1984 | 1993 | 2005

Jay Watch

Jay Watch helps everyone keep track of Florida scrub-jays. The program, developed by The Nature Conservancy in conjunction with Archbold Biological Station, tracks populations of scrub-jays across many public and some private lands. Jay Watch data also strengthen calls for increased use of fire to improve scrub-jay habitat on conservation lands. In 2009, vegetation was too dense to be suitable for jays at more than half of survey points. Jay Watch volunteers covered 63 sites in 18 counties in 2009, and the information they gather is critical to our understanding of the health of one of Florida's most unique species.

Eric Blackmore

Increase 32%
Decline 60%
No change 8%

Percentage of 62 Jay Watch sites that showed a decline, increase, or stayed the same in number of jay groups in 2009 compared with surveys in 1992-93. Twelve sites no longer had jays in 2009.

The General Relationship of Time Since Fire and Habitat Quality for Florida Scrub-Jays

Laura NeSmith, modified from figure by Liss and Huffman, 1999.

10 ft. / 5 / 0

~5 years
Excellent; acorns and open sandy areas are plentiful

~8 years
Good; still relatively open with sandy patches and low vegetation

~10 years
Good to poor; denser shrubs, fewer open sandy areas

20+ years
Not suitable; dense, tall vegetation, low acorn production, jays may persist on edge

Fire Event
In general, fire should occur every 5-10 years to maintain appropriate habitat structure and composition

~1 year
Not suitable, too early; few acorns, scarce cover

~3 years
Marginal; few acorns, few nest sites

Shorebirds, Gulls, and Terns

Shorebirds, gulls, and terns are inextricably connected to our beaches, mudflats, tidal lagoons, and sandbars. These birds depend upon Florida's sandy shores for nesting and respite, and productive estuaries provide important foods for those that pass through during long migrations. Regular beach birds include 20 species of sandpipers, 7 species of plovers, the tall and elegant oystercatcher, stilt, and avocet, in addition to numerous gulls (7 species) and terns (12 species). Most think of shorebirds as those skinny-legged sandpipers that jog amid retreating waves, but shorebirds include some of the most amazing long-distance marathoners on earth. The shorebird known as the red knot (*Calidris canutus*), for example, flies 9,300 miles between its arctic breeding grounds and southern wintering sites.

Breeding birds tend to coalesce on beaches in colonies that may include black skimmers (*Rhynchops niger*), least terns (*Sternula antillarum*), and an occasional American oystercatcher (*Haematopus palliatus*). They nest on the sandy beach above the high-water mark, while raucous colonies of laughing gulls (*Leucophaeus atricilla*) and royal terns (*Thalasseus maximus*) may nest in high dunes. Willets (*Tringa semipalmata*) prefer more cover and nest amid tufts of vegetation higher up on the beach. Resident, state-listed-as-threatened snowy plovers (*Charadrius alexandrinus*) and the federally threatened piping plover (*Charadrius melodus*)—a rare to uncommon winter resident in need of protection—can be found feeding and resting at coastal inlets and intertidal sand and mudflats.

The nesting and roosting sites used by these birds are vulnerable to hurricanes, beach renourishment projects, development, and recreation and tend to be transitory in nature. To help mitigate the impact of people crowding into the same space, management often involves establishing buffer areas around heavily used sites to protect birds with signs, fencing, and engaging volunteers who also educate the public on the importance of giving wide berth to the congregations.

Florida's beaches are one of our most sought after destinations for leisure and sport. Watching sandpipers as they race the waves or terns as they dive into the surf underscores the natural beauty of Florida's coastlines. We must be mindful of the needs of these feathered travelers that nest and roam amid the constant hum of human activity.

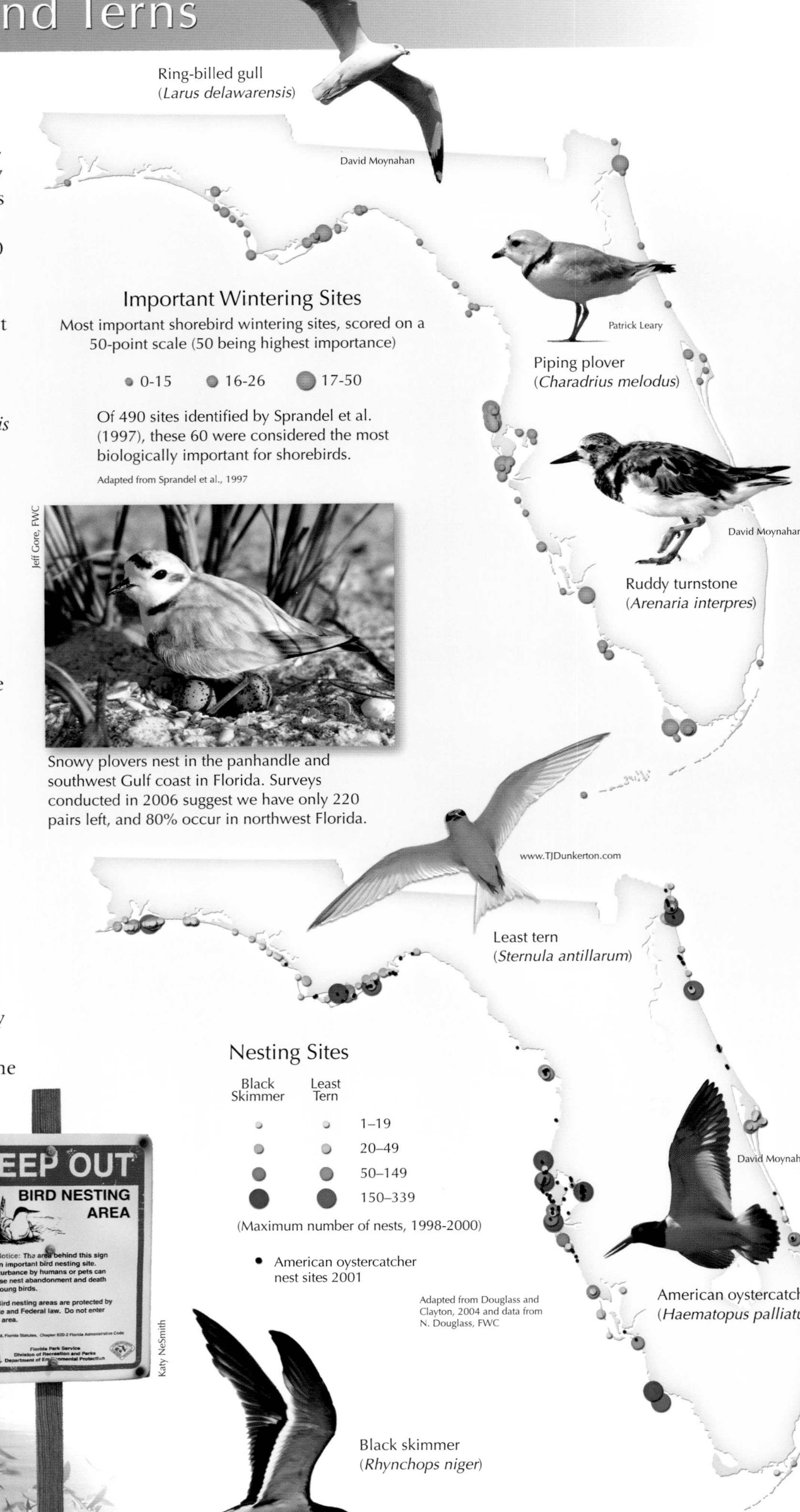

Snowy plovers nest in the panhandle and southwest Gulf coast in Florida. Surveys conducted in 2006 suggest we have only 220 pairs left, and 80% occur in northwest Florida.

Manatee

The manatee is a large, gray, nearly hairless, walrus-like aquatic mammal. The Florida manatee (*Trichechus manatus latirostris*) and Antillien manatee (*Trichechus manatus manatus*) are subspecies of the West Indian manatee. Two other species of manatees occur in northern South America and western Africa. The closely related dugong (*Dugong dugon*) is found in warm-water regions of the western Pacific Ocean.

Adult Florida manatees may reach more than 10 feet in length and weigh more than 1,200 pounds. Florida manatees are found in Florida's coastal waters, bays, rivers, and occasionally lakes, where they graze on aquatic plants, particularly seagrass. Sheltered coves are important for feeding, resting, and calving. During cold weather, they congregate at warm-water refuges offered by springs. Power-generating facilities also provide warm water regularly used by manatees, thus adding to the available wintering sites for manatees. Barring accidental death, the life expectancy of a manatee is approximately 60 years.

Primary distribution of Florida manatees

Waters occasionally used by Florida manatees

▲ Primary warm-water aggregation sites

FNAI

FWC

Counting Cows

Estimating their total population is difficult because manatees may be dispersed over a wide area of the coast. Counts are conducted from aircraft during the winter when individuals are concentrated at warm-water refuges. Several factors (including variations in water temperature, weather conditions, and water clarity) make these counts inexact for determining specific population estimates, but they nevertheless provide some sense of regional numbers and overall population.

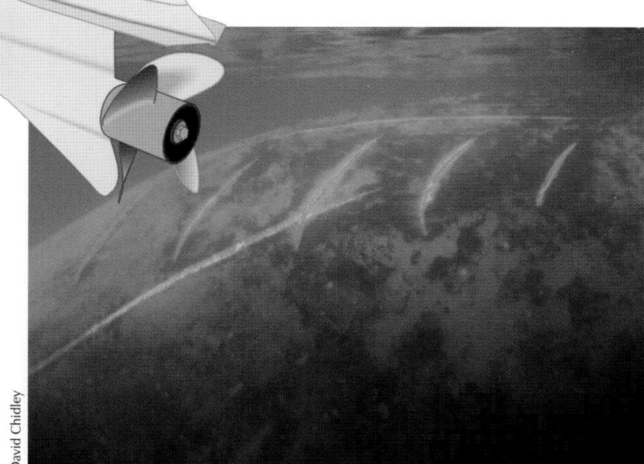

David Chidley

Probable Cause of Death (non-infant) 1987-2007

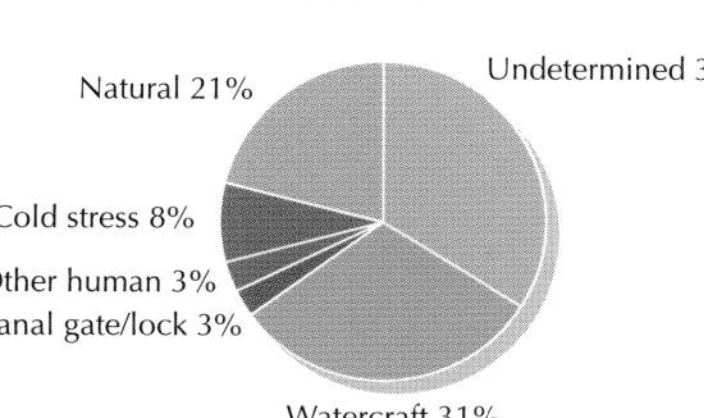

Florida Wildlife Research Institute

Threats

The primary cause of death and threat to manatee populations is collisions with watercraft, which account for approximately one-third of the annual mortality. Sanctuaries have been established to protect some wintering and calving areas. Speed zones also have been established in areas frequently inhabited by manatees to help reduce collisions. A potential long-term threat is the loss of warm-water refuges resulting from reductions in natural spring flows and the retirement of aging power plants. Other threats include marine algal blooms, such as red tide, and loss or degradation of seagrass beds.

Adult manatee and calf

Gaylen Rathburn, USFWS

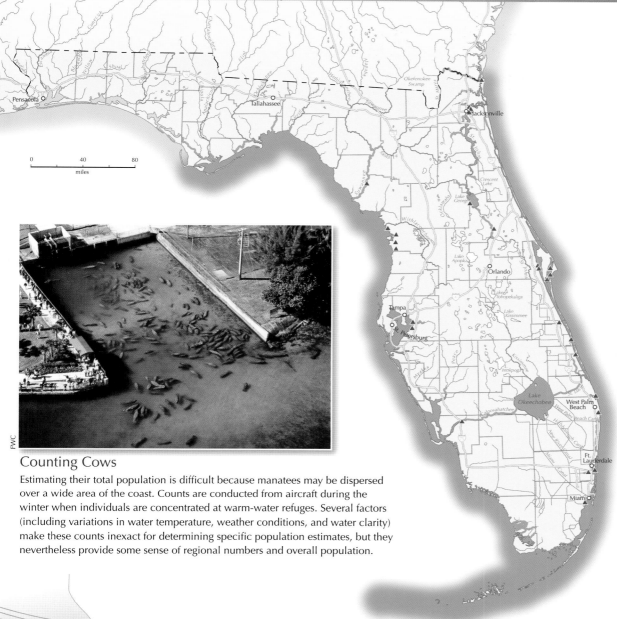

Florida Black Bear

David Godwin, FWC

Mike Orlando, FWC

Mike Orlando, FWC

Bear sign

Tree marking by scent and clawing is done primarily by male bears. Tracks or droppings (scat) can often be seen on roads throughout bear country.

The Florida black bear (*Ursus americanus floridanus*) once roamed over most of Florida and adjacent states with population estimates of over 11,000. Large-scale land clearing and unregulated harvest until the 1950s reduced their numbers to less than 1,000 by 1970. Though rebounding from this low, Florida black bears continue to face pressures of habitat loss and fragmentation, and now occur in six relatively isolated main and two small remnant populations. This large mammal requires large tracts of forest land with a variety of habitats to meet their assorted annual food needs. Preservation of the Florida black bear is dependent upon our ability to coexist while meeting the habitat needs of this wide ranging species.

Florida Black Bear Range

The Florida Fish and Wildlife Conservation Commission has identified primary and secondary bear range in Florida. Primary bear range contains core reproducing bear populations with habitat that is important for sustaining the population. Secondary bear range is important for bear movement, but has less optimal habitat and has no evidence of reproduction.

Primary
Secondary

FWC

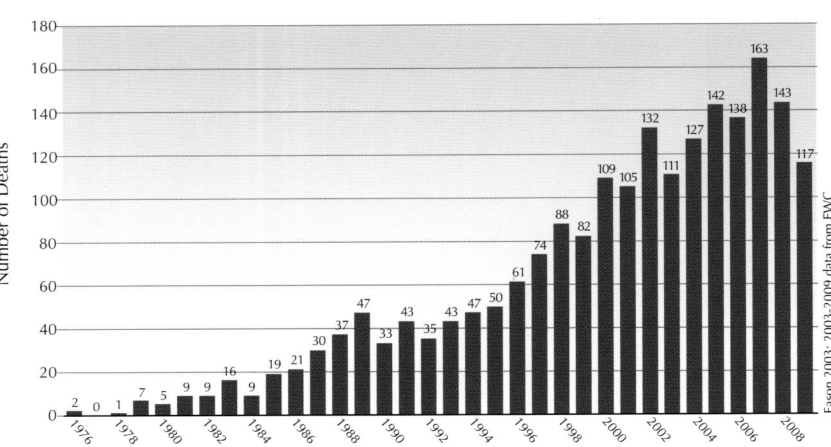

Transportation-Related Bear Deaths in Florida

Bear Mortality

As Florida's human population continues to grow and encroach upon remaining bear habitat, and as black bear populations expand from historical lows, human-bear conflicts likely will continue to grow in number. The annual number of recorded vehicle-bear collisions has steadily risen from 2 in 1976 when records were first kept to more than 160 in 2007.

Pam Anderson

Florida black bears give birth to one to four cubs every two years.

Florida Panther

The Florida panther (*Puma concolor coryi*) is the last surviving subspecies of *Puma* in the eastern U.S. It once ranged throughout the southeastern U.S. from Arkansas and Louisiana eastward across Mississippi, Alabama, Georgia, Florida, and parts of South Carolina and Tennessee. As a result of extermination efforts and habitat loss, Florida panthers were eliminated from most of their former range and now are restricted to an isolated population in southern Florida. Two other eastern subspecies, *P. c. couguar* (Northeast) and *P. c. schorgeri* (Great Plains), are considered extinct. Several western subspecies of *Puma*, commonly referred to as cougar or mountain lion, range from Canada through Central America and down the Andes Mountains to Chile.

Though protected by state and federal listing as an endangered species, the Florida panther continues to face the threats of habitat loss, road mortality, and reduced genetic health. Recovery of the Florida panther is dependent upon protection of extensive areas of habitat in South Florida with safe connections between these areas.

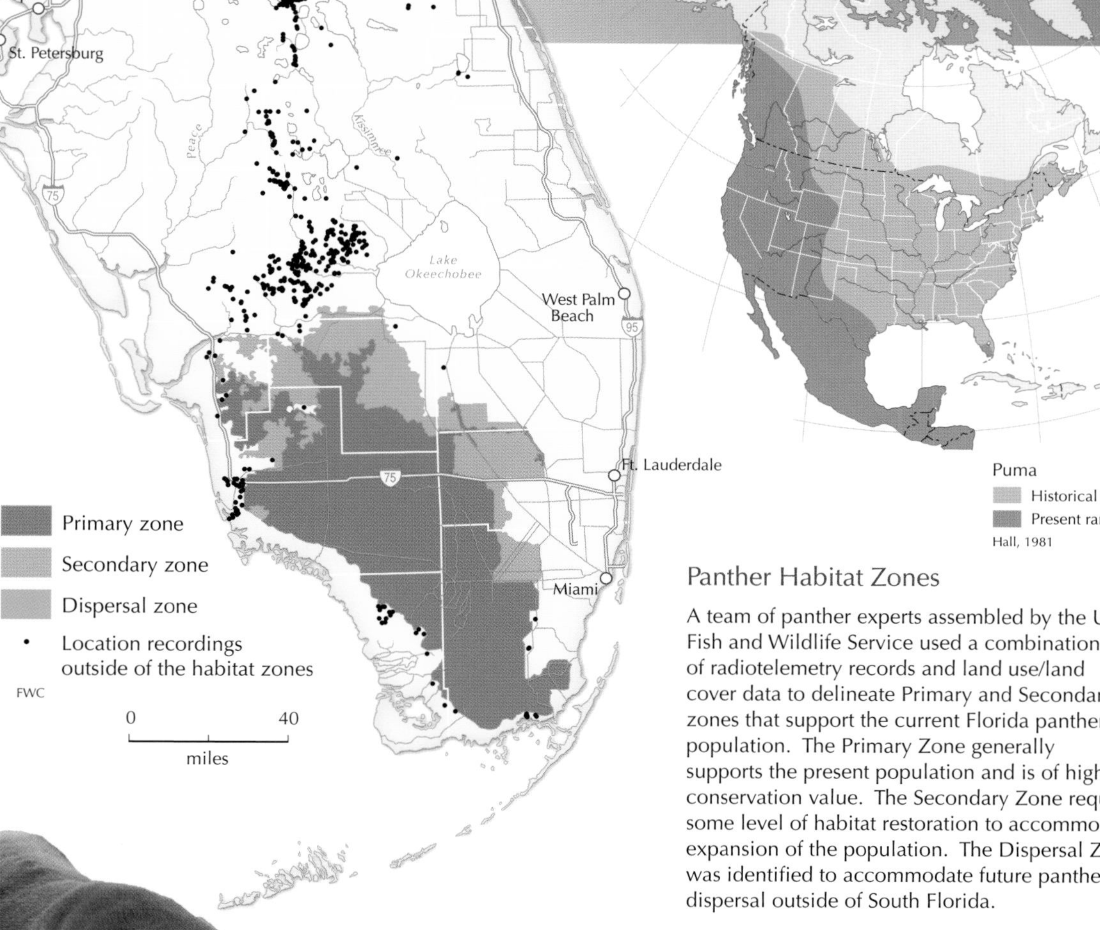

Panther Habitat Zones

A team of panther experts assembled by the U.S. Fish and Wildlife Service used a combination of radiotelemetry records and land use/land cover data to delineate Primary and Secondary zones that support the current Florida panther population. The Primary Zone generally supports the present population and is of highest conservation value. The Secondary Zone requires some level of habitat restoration to accommodate expansion of the population. The Dispersal Zone was identified to accommodate future panther dispersal outside of South Florida.

David Moynahan

Tracking Movement

Young male panthers are known to move long distances in search of new territories and mates. This is illustrated by the series of positions recorded over a three-year period of panther #130, a young male. These data also show the use of a variety of habitats for hunting and that forested areas are important for daytime resting.

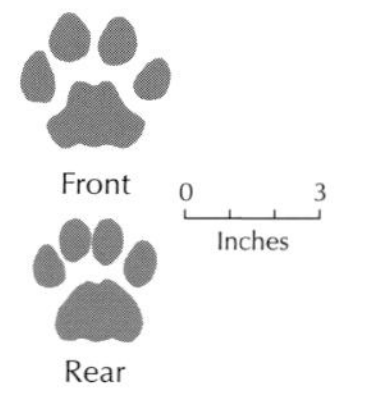

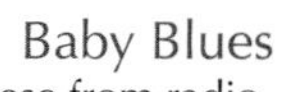

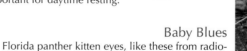

Baby Blues

Florida panther kitten eyes, like these from radio-collared panther FP158's litter, start out blue at birth and turn golden after a few months, about the same time they lose their camouflaging dark spots.

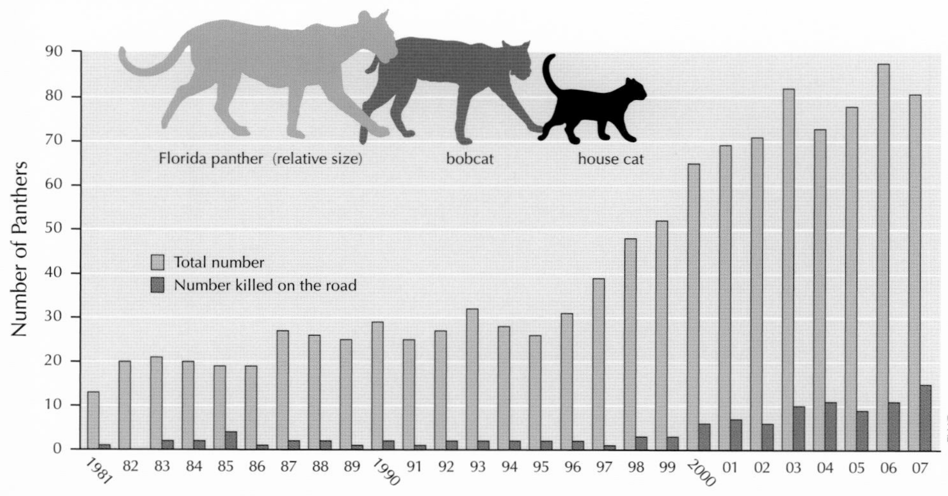

Panther Population

Because Florida panthers are secretive and wide ranging, estimating their total number is difficult. Panther biologists maintain data including approximate birth date for all individuals encountered to determine the known (minimum) number of panthers over time. These data show a notable increase in the population following the release of eight female Texas pumas (*Puma concolor stanleyana*) within South Florida during 1995, which was intended to increase the genetic health of the population.

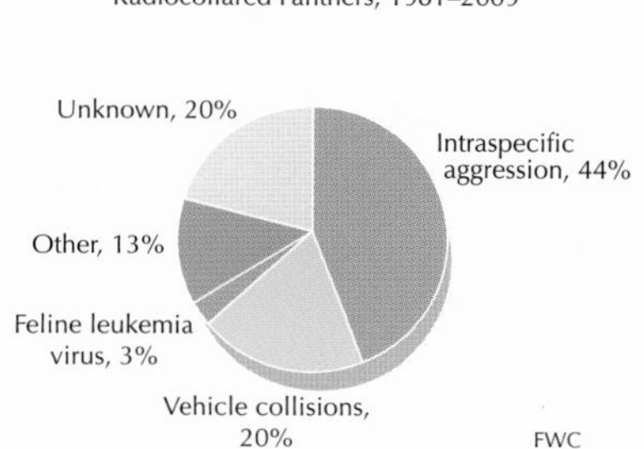

"If the biota, in the course of aeons, has built something we like but do not understand, then who but a fool would discard seemingly useless parts? To keep every cog and wheel is the first precaution of intelligent tinkering." – Aldo Leopold

III BIODIVERSITY CONSERVATION

The work of conservation is often carried out with a sense of fighting a losing battle using managed retreats. While Florida's natural heritage has retreated at an alarming rate over the last century, we can also claim many successes. A bold commitment to environmental land acquisition, together with leading edge conservation planning and land management, have set Florida apart from the rest of the U.S. over the past few decades. This section outlines major challenges facing biodiversity, innovative approaches to prioritizing places for conservation, and an overview of conservation lands, their acquisition, and management.

Mesic flatwoods, Babcock Ranch Preserve

Katy NeSmith

Habitat Loss and Fragmentation

Without question, habitat loss is the most significant challenge Florida's biodiversity has faced over the past century. Florida's economic success story is founded upon the conversion of natural lands to agricultural and urban uses. Today, just under 42% of the state remains in natural land cover. While that figure is actually quite high compared to many eastern and midwestern states (and one reason for Florida's relative wealth of remaining biodiversity), the challenge in Florida is in part due to the *rate* of loss. Unlike most states, Florida was largely undeveloped at the beginning of the 20th century, but quickly made up for lost time over the next 110 years. Urban and other intensive land uses such as mining have expanded to seven times their extent in Florida over the past 70 years.

The conversion of natural lands to human uses impacts plants and animals in a variety of ways. Beyond the direct loss of habitat area, human development patterns tend to fragment natural lands into smaller and smaller patches, isolating animal and plant populations from one another. Migration routes are lost, and with them the ability to spread genetic diversity between populations. Disturbed areas on the margins between natural and human land uses are fertile ground for invasive species. Natural fire cycles are disrupted as naturally occurring fires are unable to spread over large areas, and prescribed fires become impractical on small patches. Habitat fragmentation also tends to result in more human/wildlife interactions, often with negative consequences for both (such as roadkills, or wildlife attacks on pets or even humans). Because of those issues, a significant amount of the remaining natural lands is only marginally functional as natural systems.

If Florida's rapid rate of habitat loss and its consequences for biodiversity have a silver lining, it is the recognition by the state's residents and visitors that many precious natural places have been and are being lost at an alarming rate. This awareness has fueled the creation of landmark conservation efforts such as Florida Forever, the nation's largest environmental land acquisition program.

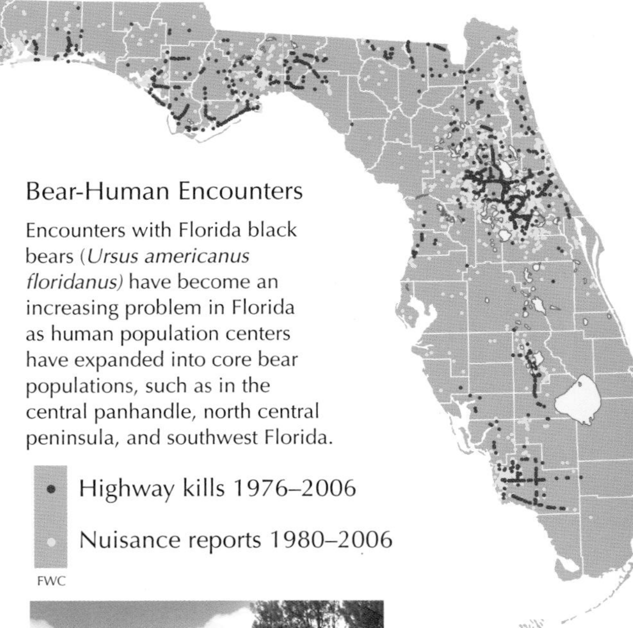

Bear-Human Encounters

Encounters with Florida black bears (*Ursus americanus floridanus*) have become an increasing problem in Florida as human population centers have expanded into core bear populations, such as in the central panhandle, north central peninsula, and southwest Florida.

- Highway kills 1976–2006
- Nuisance reports 1980–2006

FWC

FWC

Florida Park Service

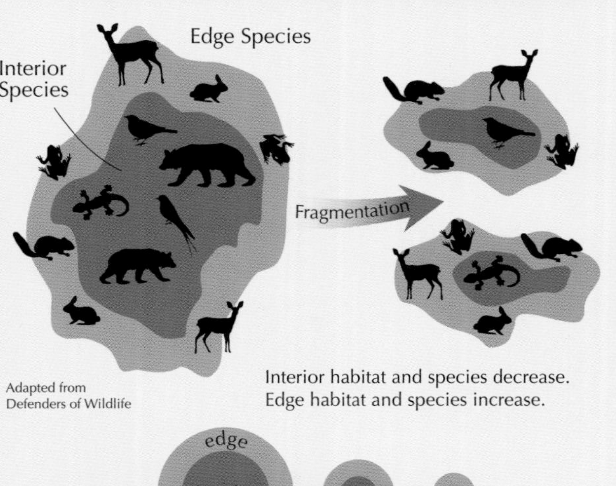

Adapted from Defenders of Wildlife

Interior habitat and species decrease. Edge habitat and species increase.

Fragmentation and Edge Effects

As natural lands are converted to human uses, remaining natural areas are increasingly fragmented into smaller isolated patches. Not only does this conversion reduce overall habitat area available for biodiversity, it also isolates populations and increases the ratio of edge to interior habitat (below left). Many species require large blocks of remote interior habitat to persist. Edge habitat is subject to human interference as well as invasion by weedy and invasive exotic species. Edge zones also present challenges for conservation land managers. For example, prescribed fire can send smoke and ash into neighboring human communities (top left), severely limiting the window of opportunity for managers to conduct burns.

An interchange on Interstate 75 has spurred development (right). While many of the wetlands have been preserved, including a linear floodplain forest, most uplands have been developed, leaving the remaining natural areas fragmented into small patches. Modern subdivisions are often developed as large units, such that hundreds of acres can be converted almost overnight. The rapid conversion of rural lands to development presents exceptional challenges for biodiversity, as plants and animals are unable to migrate away or adapt to more gradual land use change.

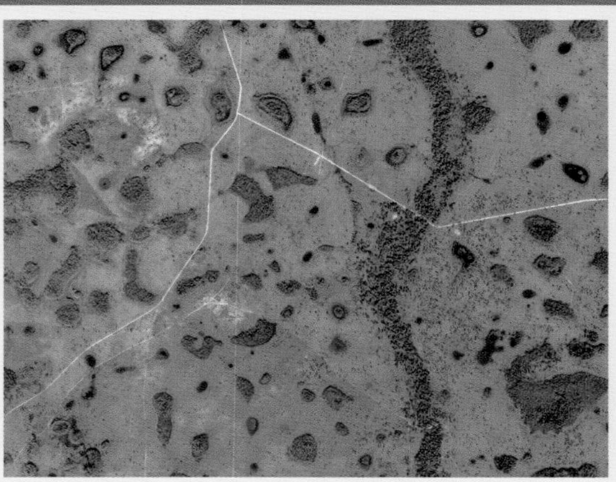

UF Map & Imagery Library

1940s

DOQQ

2004

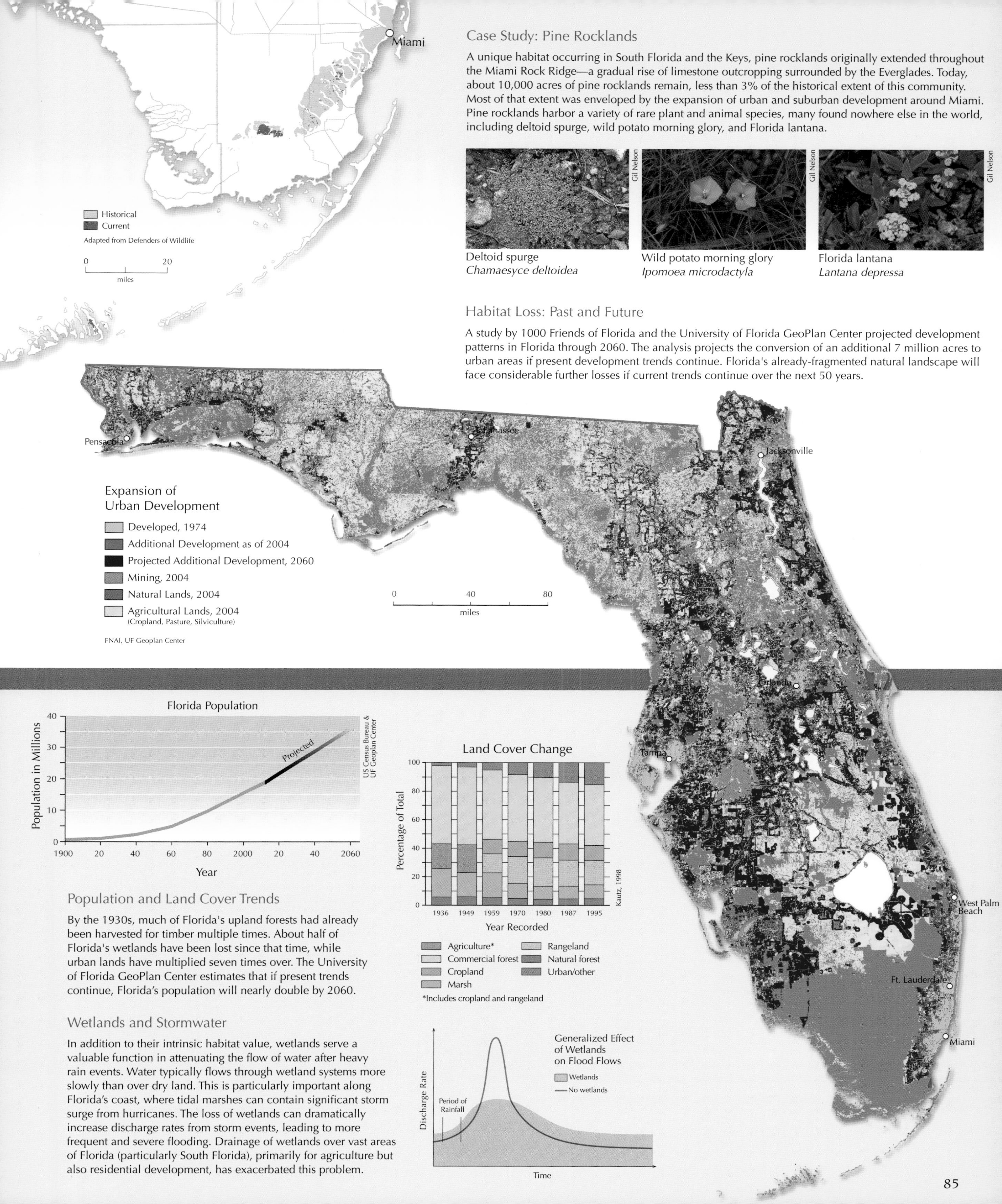

Case Study: Pine Rocklands

A unique habitat occurring in South Florida and the Keys, pine rocklands originally extended throughout the Miami Rock Ridge—a gradual rise of limestone outcropping surrounded by the Everglades. Today, about 10,000 acres of pine rocklands remain, less than 3% of the historical extent of this community. Most of that extent was enveloped by the expansion of urban and suburban development around Miami. Pine rocklands harbor a variety of rare plant and animal species, many found nowhere else in the world, including deltoid spurge, wild potato morning glory, and Florida lantana.

Gil Nelson

Deltoid spurge *Chamaesyce deltoidea*

Gil Nelson

Wild potato morning glory *Ipomoea microdactyla*

Gil Nelson

Florida lantana *Lantana depressa*

Habitat Loss: Past and Future

A study by 1000 Friends of Florida and the University of Florida GeoPlan Center projected development patterns in Florida through 2060. The analysis projects the conversion of an additional 7 million acres to urban areas if present development trends continue. Florida's already-fragmented natural landscape will face considerable further losses if current trends continue over the next 50 years.

Population and Land Cover Trends

By the 1930s, much of Florida's upland forests had already been harvested for timber multiple times. About half of Florida's wetlands have been lost since that time, while urban lands have multiplied seven times over. The University of Florida GeoPlan Center estimates that if present trends continue, Florida's population will nearly double by 2060.

Wetlands and Stormwater

In addition to their intrinsic habitat value, wetlands serve a valuable function in attenuating the flow of water after heavy rain events. Water typically flows through wetland systems more slowly than over dry land. This is particularly important along Florida's coast, where tidal marshes can contain significant storm surge from hurricanes. The loss of wetlands can dramatically increase discharge rates from storm events, leading to more frequent and severe flooding. Drainage of wetlands over vast areas of Florida (particularly South Florida), primarily for agriculture but also residential development, has exacerbated this problem.

Fire Exclusion

Fire is one of the primary natural forces that shapes Florida's terrestrial ecosystems. The plants and animals of the state's pine flatwoods, sandhills, prairies, and scrubs evolved under the influence of periodic fires, and many native species are dependent upon these fires for survival. Fire-adapted natural communities and ecosystems are referred to as "pyrogenic." Under natural conditions, Florida's vast pinelands and prairies burned on average every one to four years, creating a diverse groundcover of grasses, herbs, and low shrubs. These frequent fires were of low intensity because fuels remained low. Fires in scrub were less frequent and of higher intensity, but patchy, maintaining a mosaic of shrubs and open sand.

Lack of fire reduces the habitat value for numerous species and, with time, could result in the disappearance of many of Florida's unique fire-adapted plants and animals. Fuel accumulation resulting from lack of fire also increases the risk and hazards of wildfire in Florida's natural lands.

Historically more than 80% of Florida supported pyrogenic natural communities. Set by lightning or Native Americans, fires were once free to sweep almost unimpeded across Florida's landscape. The advance of settlers into Florida in the 1800s set in motion land altering practices that have forever changed the natural landscape. Modern developments have today created a patchwork of disconnected natural habitats that can no longer burn naturally frequently enough for ecological maintenance. Maintaining or restoring the integrity of these habitats with fire, while operating within the confines of modern-day infrastructure and burgeoning population, requires careful planning, training, and controlled burning to achieve ecological land management objectives.

William Chitty

Florida scrub-jays (*Aphelocoma coerulescens*) depend on fires to keep scrub oak habitats short and patchy, with few or no tree perches for hawk predators and plenty of open sandy places to store acorns.

Linda Cooper

The Arogos skipper (*Atrytone arogos arogos*), shown here feeding on nectar of rosy camphorweed (*Pluchea rosea*), is a rare resident of fire-maintained prairies and pinelands in Florida. Its larval host plant is lopsided indiangrass (*Sorghastrum secundum*).

William Chitty

Gopher tortoises (*Gopherus polyphemus*) depend on fire to provide a diverse diet of native grasses and herbs. Creating burrows deep in the sand, gopher tortoises provide a subterranean haven for more than 40 native Florida species.

Case Study: Prescribed Burns Can Reduce Wildfire Damage

Osceola Ranger District, National Forests of Florida

Osceola Ranger District, National Forests of Florida

Prescribed fires are used not only to enhance native plant and animal habitats, but to reduce the risks of catastrophic wildfires. In May 2007, the Bugaboo wildfire raged from Georgia into Florida and burned 108,754 acres in Baker and Columbia counties, making it the largest wildfire on record in Florida's history. Where prescribed fires had earlier taken place in the Osceola National Forest and John Bethea State Forest, the damaging effects of the wildfire on natural resources were greatly diminished.

The photo on the left shows the catastrophic effects of the wildfire in a pine flatwoods in the Osceola National Forest with no history of prescribed fire. This flatwoods was heavily overgrown with shrubs and hardwoods prior to the wildfire and tree mortality was high. The photo on the right shows effects of the wildfire in a nearby pine flatwoods with a history of prescribed fire. This flatwoods had low undergrowth, the wildfire's intensity was lower, and the trees were unharmed.

Plants and animals of Florida's pinelands have a variety of traits that make them suited to frequent, low-intensity fires. The thick bark of longleaf and slash pines insulates the trunk while scaly bark plates help dissipate heat by flaking off as they burn. Shrubby oaks, grasses, and wildflowers quickly re-sprout from underground stems or roots. Many plants have characteristics that actually promote the rapid spread of fire. The highly flammable nature of wiregrass and saw palmetto, for example, allows for the quick passage of fire that is less damaging than long-burning, smoldering fuels of heavy woody vegetation or deep organic leaf litter. Animals escape the approaching flames of low-intensity fires simply by fleeing to unburned patches or seeking underground cover. Gopher tortoise burrows and holes left by rotting tree stumps, for example, offer sanctuary for many reptiles, insects, and small mammals.

◄ **10,000 BP**
Modern weather patterns begin. Frequent, high-intensity lightning storms across Florida coincide with seasonal dry periods and set fire to the landscape.

1542
Spanish explorer Álvar Núñez Cabeza de Vaca finds a North Florida landscape with pines "riven from top to bottom by bolts of lightning which fall in that country of frequent storms and tempests."

1769
Explorers note the Creek Indians in Florida "through the whole province, continually set the grass on fire, for the convenience of hunting."

1879
Early burning regulations appear in Florida law banning fires on "any wild forests, woods, lands or marshes, except between February 15 and March 31 of each year."

1924
The U.S. Forest Service begins a campaign against woods burning.

1927
The Florida Forest Service is created to "gather and disseminate information on forests, their care and management, to prevent and extinguish forest fires, and to enforce all laws pertaining to forests and woodlands."

1931
Herbert S. Stoddard publishes chapter "The use and abuse of fire on southern quail preserves," describing the ecological benefits of prescribed fires and condemning uncontrolled burning.

1500 1600 1700 1800 1900 1910 1920 1930

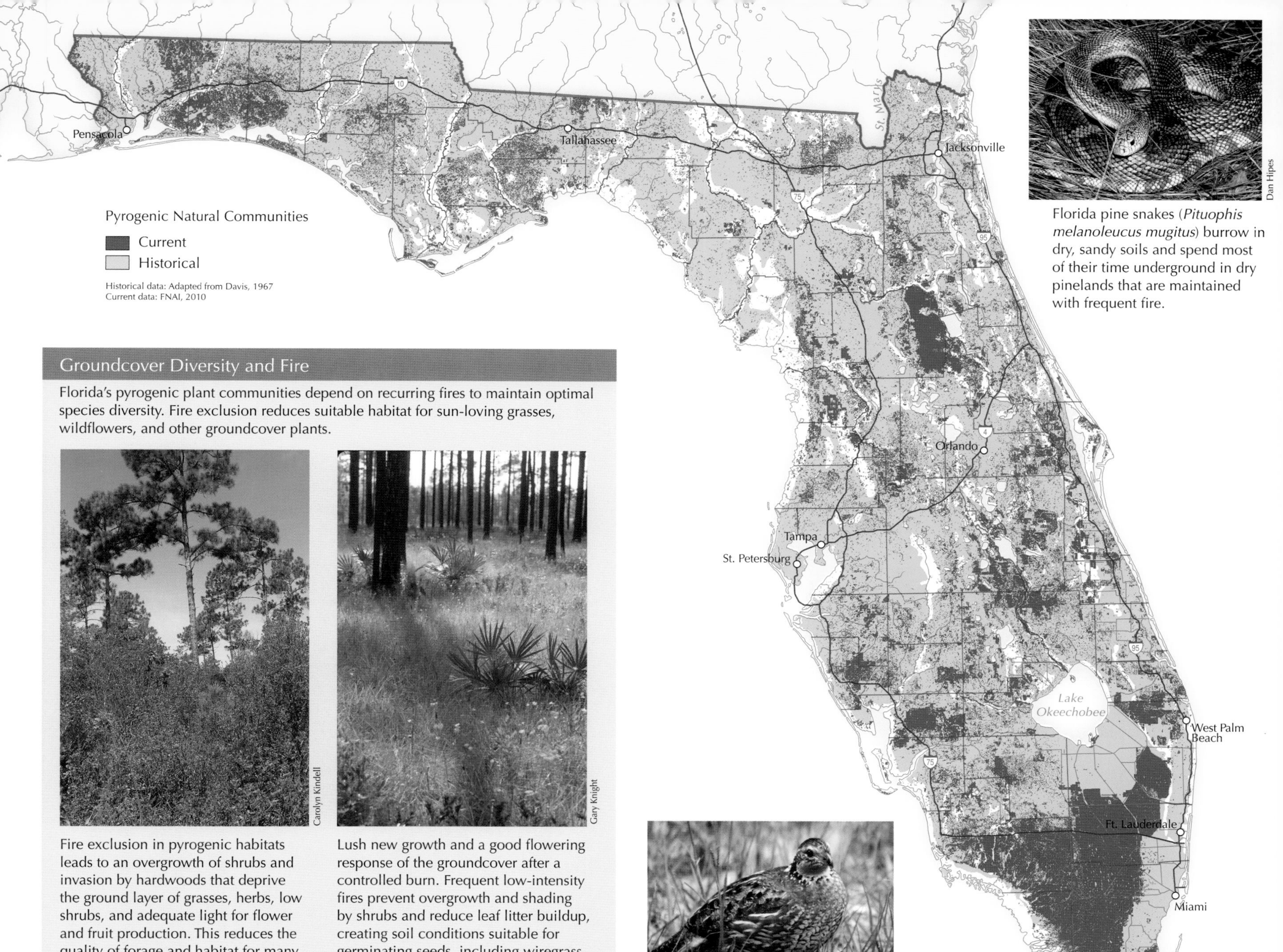

Dan Hipes

Florida pine snakes (*Pituophis melanoleucus mugitus*) burrow in dry, sandy soils and spend most of their time underground in dry pinelands that are maintained with frequent fire.

Groundcover Diversity and Fire

Florida's pyrogenic plant communities depend on recurring fires to maintain optimal species diversity. Fire exclusion reduces suitable habitat for sun-loving grasses, wildflowers, and other groundcover plants.

Carolyn Kindell

Fire exclusion in pyrogenic habitats leads to an overgrowth of shrubs and invasion by hardwoods that deprive the ground layer of grasses, herbs, low shrubs, and adequate light for flower and fruit production. This reduces the quality of forage and habitat for many wildlife species.

Heavy fuel accumulations resulting from lack of fire pose increased risks for native wildlife. Catastrophic wildfires may destroy suitable habitat, as nesting and perching sites may be turned to ash. Food sources may be killed or may require several years to recover.

Gary Knight

Lush new growth and a good flowering response of the groundcover after a controlled burn. Frequent low-intensity fires prevent overgrowth and shading by shrubs and reduce leaf litter buildup, creating soil conditions suitable for germinating seeds, including wiregrass and longleaf pines. This process is a key part of successful forest regeneration.

This allows for the coexistence of a great diversity of plants which, in turn, improves the quality of wildlife habitat. Many wildlife species, including native game such as bobwhite quail (*Colinus virginianus*), and rare species, such as the red-cockaded woodpecker (*Picoides borealis*), depend on habitats maintained by frequent, low-intensity fires.

FWC

Northern bobwhite quail (*Colinus virginianus*) have declined greatly in the southeastern U.S. due in part to decline in prescribed fire in their natural habitats. Native warm season grasses, legumes, and herbs in Florida pinelands that are maintained with frequent fires provide nesting and brood-rearing habitat for quail.

1937
Florida cattleman S. W. Greene argues "that controlled woods burning…as practiced by cattlemen and turpentine producers, to be a very great value to the production and conservation of forest and game in Florida."

1958
Southern Forest Fire Laboratory established to study fire ecology.

1962
First Annual Fire Ecology Conference at Tall Timbers Research Station near Tallahassee.

1970
Florida Park Service begins a prescribed fire management program on state parks after 35 years of fire suppression.

1977
Hawkins Bill gives Florida Division of Forestry authority to conduct prescribed burns to reduce dangerous fuel levels.

1990
Florida Prescribed Burning Act recognizes the need for prescribed fire as a "tool that benefits the safety of the public, the environment, and the economy of Florida."

1998
Droughts contribute to wildfires burning 500,000 acres in Florida, one of the worst wildfire years since the 1950s.

1999
Legislation modified to enhance the ability of prescribed burners to reduce fuel hazards in wildland/urban interface areas.

2009
Division of Forestry issues authorizations for prescribed burns on over 2 million acres. More than 2,200 prescribed burn managers in Florida.

1940 1950 1960 1970 1980 1990 2000 2010

Invasive Species

People have carried plants and animals from one place to another for thousands of years. Many of our food crops and domestic animals derive from non-native species. Most of these introductions are benign, however, in some instances the introduced species proves to be invasive, spreading into natural areas and disrupting normal ecological processes through its rampant growth. Native species have evolved in place as part of a complex ecological web with natural checks that keep populations in balance; invasive species encounter fewer of the same constraints in their new environment, and populations grow and spread rapidly. These alien invaders pose a grave threat to native species and ecosystems and annually cost the state of Florida tens of millions of dollars to control.

Many species that are invasive in Florida were brought here intentionally, with no understanding of the problem they would eventually become. The original purposes were many—new agricultural and horticultural products, exotic pets, specimens for aquarium culture, or new game species. Invasive species have also been transported to Florida by accident—"hitchhikers" in foreign shipment or in the ballast water of cargo ships. Today, with an increased awareness of the potential threat that non-native species pose, there is greater scrutiny of new introductions and inspections of foreign shipments. It is more cost-efficient to exclude potential invasive species than to manage them once established.

The challenge of controlling invasive species is difficult: managers must selectively and cost-effectively eradicate one species without adversely affecting others around it. Land managers use one or more tools for invasive plants that can be grouped into three basic methods:
1) mechanical control–physically removing the plants or animals by hand or with equipment; 2) chemical control–the use of chemical agents to kill or control growth of the invasive species; and 3) bio-control–the carefully managed introduction of living organisms intended to provide a check on a particular invasive species. Mechanical control can be very selective, targeting a single species, but it is the most expensive method and not suitable for very large areas. Chemical control can be used over very large areas, but is typically not selective and kills non-target species, as well as leaving potentially harmful chemicals in the environment. Bio-control can work over very large areas, and with appropriate research it can be very selective, but bio-control agents must be carefully screened to ensure they do not themselves become invasive, a process that takes considerable time and investment. Bio-control offers the most hope for meaningful, long-term management; however, few Florida invasive species today have approved bio-control agents. Therefore, mechanical and chemical methods must continue to be employed until appropriate bio-control agents for other invasive species are found.

Florida Invasive Species

Florida Exotic Plant List (2009)

Category I — **72 species**

Invasive exotics that are altering native plant communities by displacing native species, changing community structures or ecological functions, or hybridizing with natives. This definition does not rely on the economic severity or geographic range of the problem, but on the documented ecological damage caused.

Examples:

Australian pine	Brazilian pepper
water hyacinth	melaleuca
skunk vine	Old World climbing fern
cogon grass	

Category II — **74 species**

Invasive exotics that have increased in abundance or frequency but have not yet altered Florida plant communities to the extent shown by Category I species. These species may become ranked Category I, if ecological damage is demonstrated.

Examples:

alligator weed	Chinaberry
paper mulberry	castor bean
silverthorn	Caesar's weed

Federal Noxious Weed List (2006) — **70 species in Florida**

Any plant or plant product that can directly or indirectly injure or cause damage to crops (including nursery stock or plant products), livestock, poultry, or other interests of agriculture, irrigation, navigation, the natural resources of the United States, the public health, or the environment.

Average annual control costs for invasive plants — **$82 million**

Source: Invasive Plant Mangagement Section, FWC

Documented Invasive Animals in Florida — **>400 non-native species not all considered invasive**

Examples:
- Gambian pouch rat (mammal)
- European starling (bird)
- Burmese python (reptile)
- green iguana (reptile)
- giant toad (amphibian)
- walking catfish (fish)
- fire ant (terrestrial invertebrate)
- non-native apple snail (aquatic invertebrate)

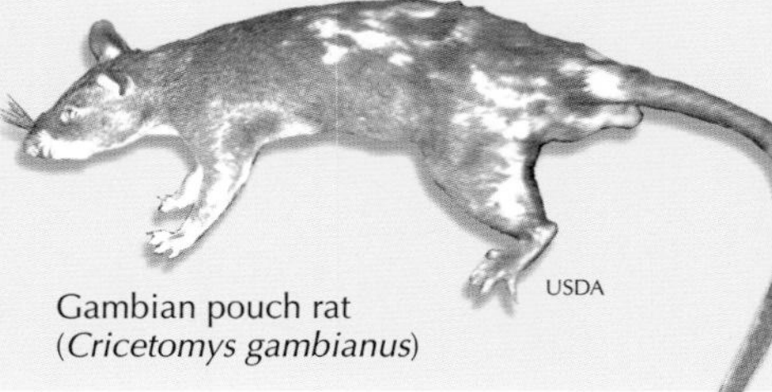

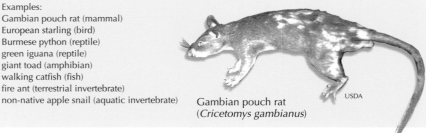

Gambian pouch rat (*Cricetomys gambianus*) USDA

Invasive Animals

FNAI

Fire ant (*Solenopsis invicta*)

Fire ants are believed to have been accidentally transported to Mobile, Alabama, along with agricultural products from South America, in the 1930s. With no natural predators, the species soon spread rapidly throughout much of Florida and the southeastern United States (see also page 57).

Gambian pouch rat (*Cricetomys gambianus*)

A cat-sized mammal imported from Africa for the pet trade, this animal first escaped and began reproducing in 2002 in the Florida Keys. The species eats and competes with native birds and mammals. It was banned from the pet trade in Florida in 2003.

Amber Ricke

Green iguana (*Iguana iguana*)

Iguanas are currently found in six South Florida counties and are spreading. This species can reach lengths of 6 feet.

Bio-control Species

Brazilian pepper stem-feeding thrips (*Pseudophilothrips ichini*)

This insect from Brazil was approved by federal and state regulators for release in Florida as a bio-control agent for Brazilian pepper.

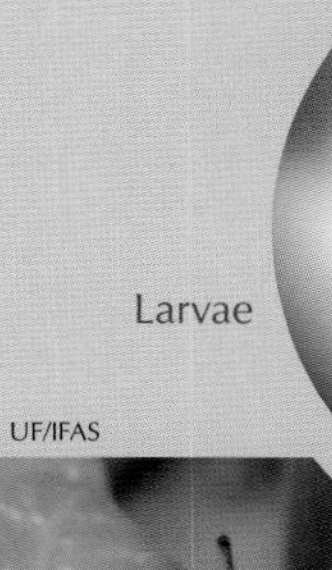

Larvae

V. Manrique, UF/IFAS

L. Buss, UF/IFAS

Stem boring weevil (*Apocnemidophorus pipitzi*)

This insect from Paraguay is being evaluated for use in Florida as a potential bio-control agent for Brazilian pepper. Scientists are currently testing to ensure no other species would be targeted by this weevil.

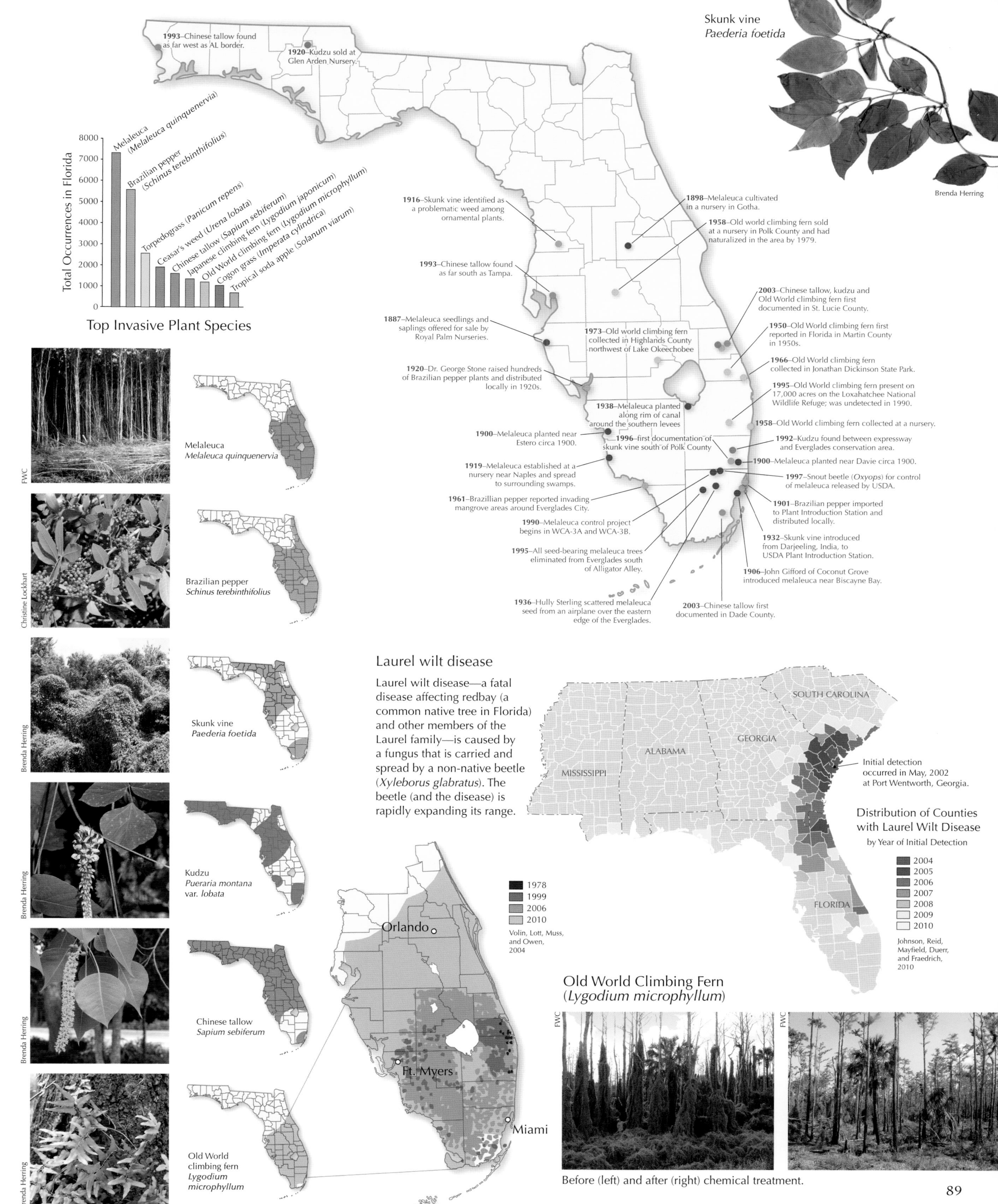
Skunk vine
Paederia foetida
Brenda Herring
1993–Chinese tallow found as far west as AL border.
1920–Kudzu sold at Glen Arden Nursery.
Total Occurrences in Florida
8000
7000
6000
5000
4000
3000
2000
1000
0
Melaleuca (Melaleuca quinquenervia)
Brazilian pepper (Schinus terebinthifolius)
Torpedograss (Panicum repens)
Ceasar's weed (Urena lobata)
Chinese tallow (Sapium sebiferum)
Japanese climbing fern (Lygodium japonicum)
Old World climbing fern (Lygodium microphyllum)
Cogon grass (Imperata cylindrica)
Tropical soda apple (Solanum viarum)
Top Invasive Plant Species
1916–Skunk vine identified as a problematic weed among ornamental plants.
1898–Melaleuca cultivated in a nursery in Gotha.
1958–Old world climbing fern sold at a nursery in Polk County and had naturalized in the area by 1979.
1993–Chinese tallow found as far south as Tampa.
2003–Chinese tallow, kudzu and Old World climbing fern first documented in St. Lucie County.
1887–Melaleuca seedlings and saplings offered for sale by Royal Palm Nurseries.
1973–Old world climbing fern collected in Highlands County northwest of Lake Okeechobee
1950–Old World climbing fern first reported in Florida in Martin County in 1950s.
1966–Old World climbing fern collected in Jonathan Dickinson State Park.
1920–Dr. George Stone raised hundreds of Brazilian pepper plants and distributed locally in 1920s.
1995–Old World climbing fern present on 17,000 acres on the Loxahatchee National Wildlife Refuge; was undetected in 1990.
1938–Melaleuca planted along rim of canal around the southern levees
1958–Old World climbing fern collected at a nursery.
1900–Melaleuca planted near Estero circa 1900.
1996–first documentation of skunk vine south of Polk County
1992–Kudzu found between expressway and Everglades conservation area.
1900–Melaleuca planted near Davie circa 1900.
1919–Melaleuca established at a nursery near Naples and spread to surrounding swamps.
1997–Snout beetle (Oxyops) for control of melaleuca released by USDA.
1961–Brazillian pepper reported invading mangrove areas around Everglades City.
1901–Brazilian pepper imported to Plant Introduction Station and distributed locally.
1990–Melaleuca control project begins in WCA-3A and WCA-3B.
1932–Skunk vine introduced from Darjeeling, India, to USDA Plant Introduction Station.
1995–All seed-bearing melaleuca trees eliminated from Everglades south of Alligator Alley.
1906–John Gifford of Coconut Grove introduced melaleuca near Biscayne Bay.
1936–Hully Sterling scattered melaleuca seed from an airplane over the eastern edge of the Everglades.
2003–Chinese tallow first documented in Dade County.
FWC
Melaleuca
Melaleuca quinquenervia
Christine Lockhart
Brazilian pepper
Schinus terebinthifolius
Brenda Herring
Skunk vine
Paederia foetida
Brenda Herring
Kudzu
Pueraria montana var. lobata
Brenda Herring
Chinese tallow
Sapium sebiferum
Brenda Herring
Old World climbing fern
Lygodium microphyllum
1978
1999
2006
2010
Volin, Lott, Muss, and Owen, 2004
Orlando
Ft. Myers
Miami
SOUTH CAROLINA
GEORGIA
ALABAMA
MISSISSIPPI
FLORIDA
Initial detection occurred in May, 2002 at Port Wentworth, Georgia.
Distribution of Counties with Laurel Wilt Disease
by Year of Initial Detection
2004
2005
2006
2007
2008
2009
2010
Johnson, Reid, Mayfield, Duerr, and Fraedrich, 2010
FWC
FWC

Laurel wilt disease

Laurel wilt disease—a fatal disease affecting redbay (a common native tree in Florida) and other members of the Laurel family—is caused by a fungus that is carried and spread by a non-native beetle (*Xyleborus glabratus*). The beetle (and the disease) is rapidly expanding its range.

Old World Climbing Fern (*Lygodium microphyllum*)

Before (left) and after (right) chemical treatment.

Competing Uses

Florida's public conservation lands—including federal, state, and local parks, forests, and preserves—form the core of biodiversity conservation in the state. However, these lands provide important public services beyond natural resource conservation, resulting in competing priorities for land management dollars. Commercial uses, recreational uses, and illegal uses all take part on Florida's conservation lands and may, or may not, be compatible with the purposes of conservation and preservation of the natural systems. Some competing commercial and recreational uses, such as timbering, livestock grazing, and public recreation, generate valuable operating revenue for land management activities. Land managers have a significant responsibility regarding what uses to allow and to what degree. Additional income from competing uses is important since natural resource management typically receives less than one quarter of total resource allowances to cover yearly operating costs.

Revenues for State Forests 2007–2008

Timber revenue	$5,840,175
Miscellaneous forest products	$416,820
Grazing and Apiary	$100,328
Recreational revenue	$1,350,852
Total Revenue	**$7,708,175**
Refund back to counties (15%)	$1,156,226

Data from Florida Division of Forestry

This example of revenues generated on state forests demonstrates the value of a variety of nonconservation uses on conservation lands and the challenges faced by land managers in balancing these uses with conservation.

Expenditures for State Lands in Florida, 2007-2008

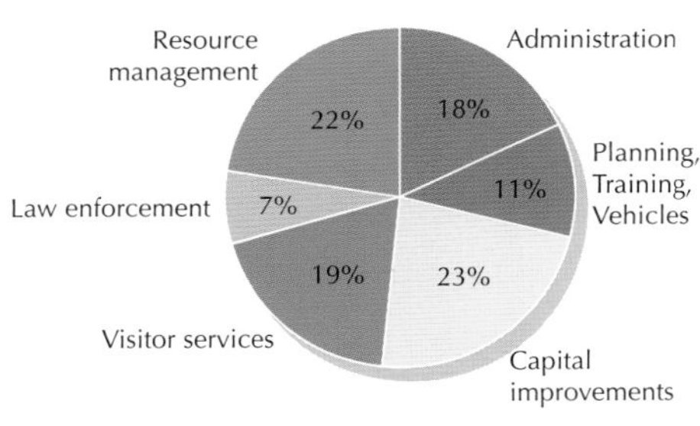

Public Land to Population Ratio

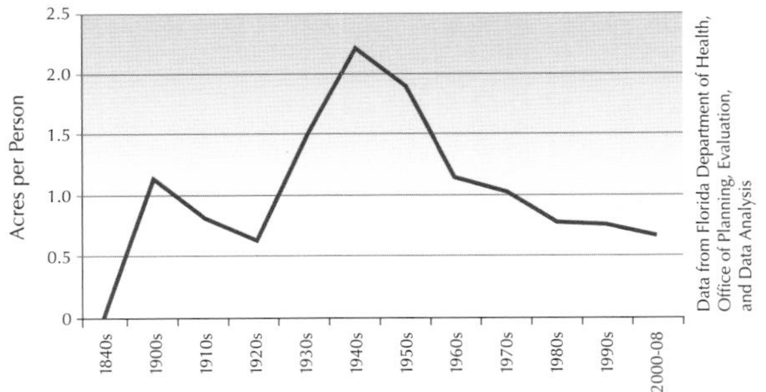

Since the 1940s, Florida's population has increased at a rate faster than the state's purchase of conservation lands, amounting to fewer conservation acres per person for citizens to enjoy. This can lead to overcrowding in the most popular parks and preserves.

Competing Uses on Conservation Lands

Hunting and fishing enthusiasts are among the strongest conservation advocates and bring much-needed revenue for conservation lands. However, management for game species (e.g. food plots and altered groundcover) can conflict with habitat preferences of many other native species.

FWC

In high-traffic areas such as multi-use trails, competition between different recreational activities can also pose a challenge to land managers.

Robin Kennedy

Many forest activities, such as beekeeping, also occur on conservation lands and supply land managers with needed revenue.

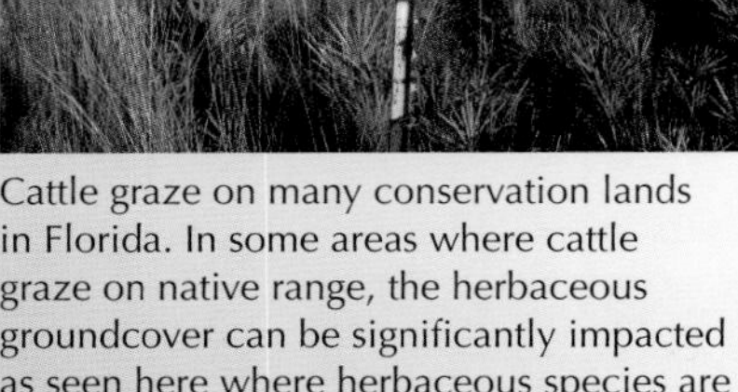
Dan Hipes

Cattle graze on many conservation lands in Florida. In some areas where cattle graze on native range, the herbaceous groundcover can be significantly impacted as seen here where herbaceous species are much more prolific (on left) in a fenced area where cattle have been excluded.

Dave Kandz

Nesting shorebirds are highly sensitive to disturbance from people and pets.

Recreational Uses

- off-highway vehicles (OHV)
- beach recreation
- buildings & facilities
- horses
- mountain bikes
- fishing
- hunting
- springs recreation

Commercial Uses

- forestry
- cattle grazing
- groundwater withdrawal
- utility rights-of-way
- pine straw and palmetto harvesting
- stumping
- biomass harvesting

Illegal Uses

- collection of restricted/rare plants & animals
- collection of restricted archaeological/historic artifacts
- off-highway vehicles outside designated areas
- trash dumping
- exotic animal dumping

FWC

Mountain biking and motorized OHV use are increasingly popular on conservation lands, but can cause erosion and damage to sensitive areas along trails.

FWC

Blue Spring

Gary Knight

Transportation and utility corridors, such as this gas pipeline at Blackwater River State Forest, cut through even the most pristine of Florida's conservation lands.

Robin Kennedy

Activities such as trash dumping on public lands cause managers to spend precious time and resources to clean-up the mess.

FWC

Burmese pythons (*Python molurus bivittatus*), released or escaped from the pet trade, are an increasing concern in the Everglades and Florida Keys.

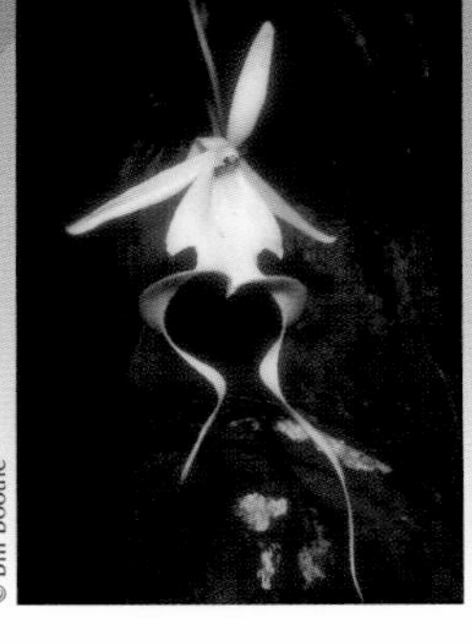
© Bill Boothe

Many species of plants and animals such as the ghost orchid (*Polyrrhiza lindenii*) are under pressure from illegal collecting. Orchids, air plants, tropical trees, snakes, turtles, tiger beetles, and tree snails among others suffer from this illegal threat.

Case Study: Competing Uses in Apalachicola National Forest

The Apalachicola National Forest in northwest Florida presents a useful case study illustrating that Florida's conservtion lands are more than simply natural areas. Recreational uses, commercial timber harvest, public wells, roads, and gas or power line rights-of-way are found throughout the forest. About 7% of the forest is set aside as wilderness areas.

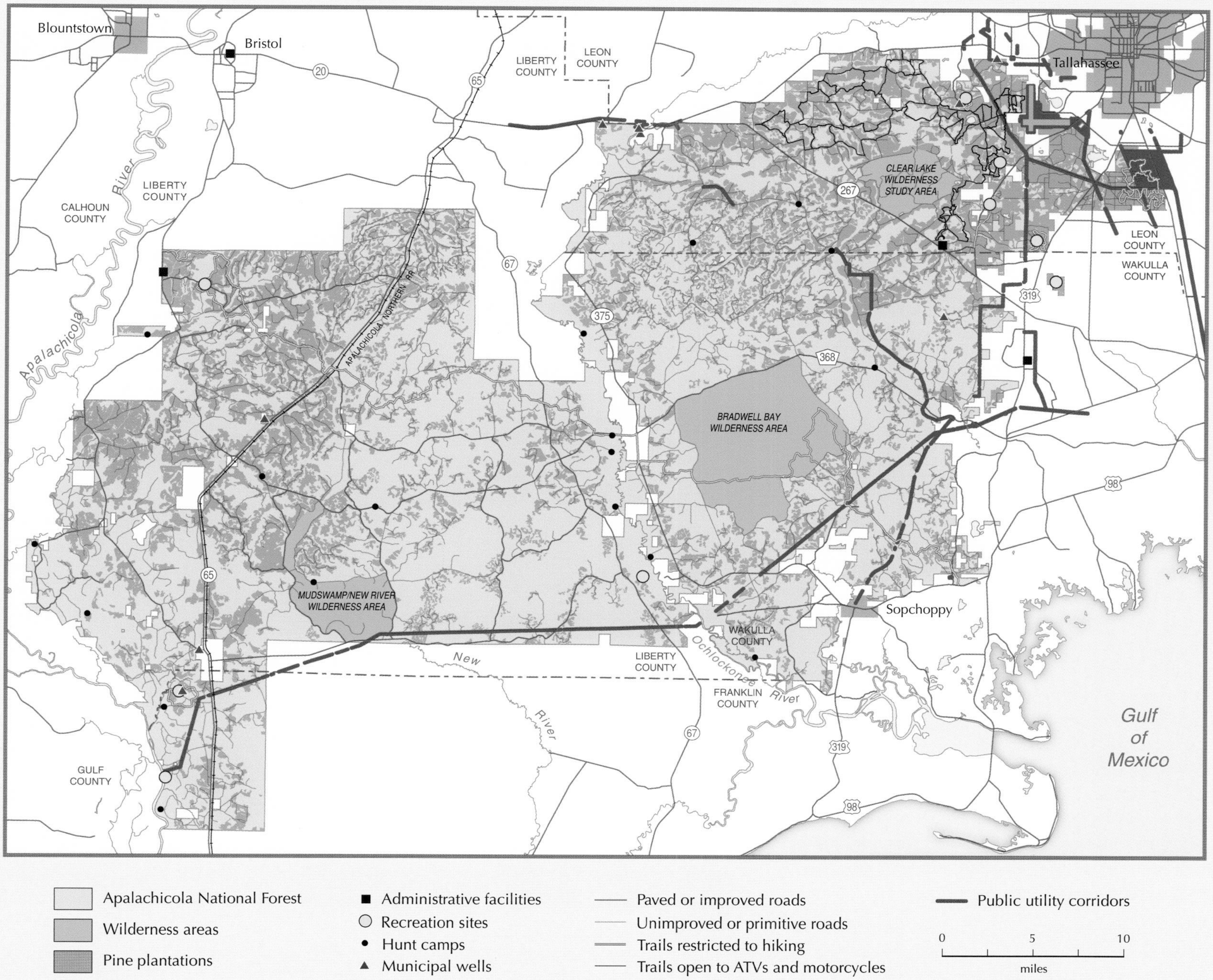

Blountstown
Bristol
LIBERTY COUNTY
LEON COUNTY
Tallahassee
CLEAR LAKE WILDERNESS STUDY AREA
CALHOUN COUNTY
LIBERTY COUNTY
Apalachicola River
APALACHICOLA NORTHERN RR
LEON COUNTY
WAKULLA COUNTY
BRADWELL BAY WILDERNESS AREA
MUDSWAMP/NEW RIVER WILDERNESS AREA
Sopchoppy
WAKULLA COUNTY
LIBERTY COUNTY
FRANKLIN COUNTY
New River
Ochlockonee River
GULF COUNTY
Gulf of Mexico

- Apalachicola National Forest
- Wilderness areas
- Pine plantations

- ■ Administrative facilities
- ○ Recreation sites
- • Hunt camps
- ▲ Municipal wells

- Paved or improved roads
- Unimproved or primitive roads
- Trails restricted to hiking
- Trails open to ATVs and motorcycles

- Public utility corridors

0 5 10 miles

Off-Highway Vehicles and Conservation Lands

In designated areas across Florida's conservation lands off-highway vehicle (OHV) use can be compatible with stated management goals. Unregulated and illegal riding may degrade habitats, erode soils, spread exotic plants, and create barriers to natural fires and hydrologic processes.

In 2008, the U.S. Forest Service restricted OHV use to an established trail system in the Ocala and Apalachicola national forests. Riders must first acquire a permit to ride on these trails. In the Osceola National Forest, OHV use is restricted to mixed-use roads. These policy changes were adopted to minimize damage to natural habitats while continuing to allow this type of recreation.

On state conservation lands, the Florida legislature in 2002 approved creation of a fund that provides financial assistance for projects that help create or improve off-highway vehicle recreation areas or trails for public use. Withlacoochee (Croom Tract) and Tate's Hell state forests allow recreational OHV use in designated areas with purchase of a required permit.

National Park Service

Aerial photos taken within Big Cypress National Preserve show damage to natural areas resulting from unregulated OHV use.

National Park Service

Consequently, the National Park Service is implementing an off-road vehicle trail system that would limit OHV use to designated trails.

Water and Biodiversity

Changes in the amount and the quality of both surface water and groundwater may have profound effects on biodiversity. Biota from the smallest invertebrates to centuries-old cypress trees are adapted to particular hydrologic regimes. As the winter rains begin, flatwoods salamanders migrate to depressional wetlands to lay their eggs; frogs breed in ephemeral ponds where tadpoles are safe from predatory fish; and cypress seedlings germinate when standing water is absent but grow best if there is enough water to kill competing species. The duration of standing water (hydroperiod) plays a strong role in determining the location of various wetland communities: forested wetlands along rivers are usually inundated for 1 to 6 months each year, whereas freshwater marshes typically have shallow standing water from 7 to 12 months each year.

Because large portions of the state are covered with well-drained sandy soil overlying limestone, groundwater as well as surface water is vulnerable to contamination from human activities. Excess nutrients from fertilizers and leachate from septic tanks can result in algae blooms and increases in non-native invasive plants. Resulting increases in turbidity may suffocate some aquatic plants and animals and impair the development of eggs and larvae. Decreased dissolved oxygen as a consequence of increased plant growth will negatively affect fish, most of which thrive when dissolved oxygen levels are 5 parts per million or greater. Other measures of water quality include pH, conductivity (a measure of concentration of minerals and salts), and temperature.

The case studies on these pages illustrate some of the ways biodiversity may be affected by changes in the timing, amount, and quality of water reaching natural communities. They also demonstrate some of the ways Florida is recognizing, documenting, and meeting these challenges.

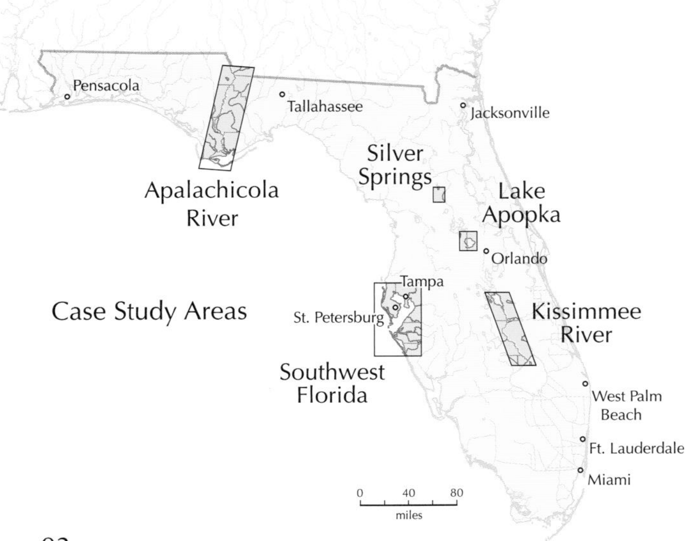

Apalachicola River

Since 1975, the majority of the Apalachicola River and floodplain forest has experienced less flow in the spring-summer of dry years as a result of upstream flow and land-use changes. The advent of center pivot irrigation in the 1970s, the doubling of the population of Atlanta since 1980, and the construction of over 23,000 ponds and reservoirs in the watershed all contributed to this reduction in flow.

Since the completion of Jim Woodruff Dam at the Georgia-Florida line in 1957, erosion has deepened the river channel downstream, reducing flooding of swamps and bottomlands. The combination of channelization and less water from upstream has dramatically reduced water levels in river swamps, especially during dry years.

A long-term study of forest trees by the U.S. Geological Survey has shown a dramatic loss of trees in the river floodplain from 1976 to 2006. Overall there are 4.3 million (17%) fewer trees—most of which are swamp species—floodplain-wide. The losses are most dramatic in the deepest swamps where the dominant species, water tupelo (*Nyssa aquatica*), bald cypress (*Taxodium distichum*), Ogeechee tupelo (*Nyssa ogeche*), and Carolina ash (*Fraxinus caroliniana*), have declined by 37%. Ogeechee tupelos, the source of tupelo honey, alone have declined by 44%. Based on subcanopy species as an indicator of the future forest, USGS predicts a 74% decline in the numbers of canopy trees in the swamps by 2085.

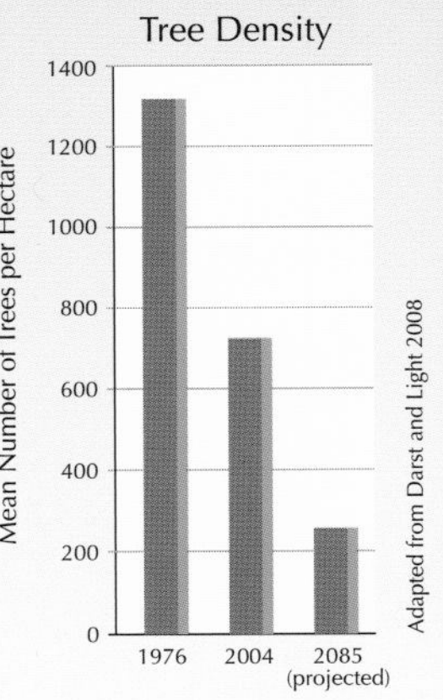

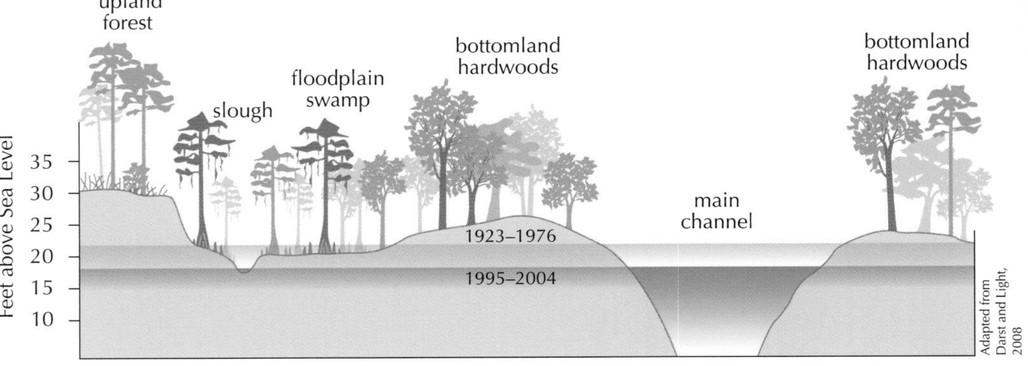

This cross section shows the decline in typical summer water levels since the 1970s that has led to a severe seasonal lack of water in the river swamps.

Silver Springs

One of the major threats to Florida's springs is pollution of groundwater from nitrates in fertilizers, human sewage, and livestock manure. These nutrients feed fast-growing algae and non-native invasives and ultimately threaten native vascular plants. In 2006, St. Johns River Water Management District restudied the ecology of Silver Springs, comparing their findings to those of ecologist Howard T. Odum from the 1950s. They found nitrates in the water had increased by 176%, water clarity had decreased, and dissolved oxygen, critical for a healthy fish community, had decreased as well. Although the total number of species of plants, birds, fish, and reptiles at the springs had not changed, the total plant and algae biomass had increased by 88%, while insect productivity had declined by 72%, and fish biomass had declined by 96%.

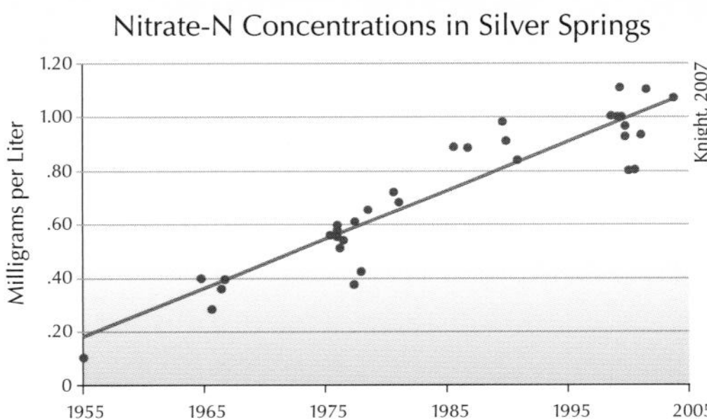

State Archives of Florida

Historical photo showing water clarity

Florida Department of Environmental Protection

Algae, September 2007

Lake Apopka

Florida's most polluted large lake in the 1980s, Lake Apopka suffered from a century of wetland losses and pollution. In the 1890s, a navigation canal lowered lake levels. In the 1940s, construction of a levee on the north shore allowed conversion of 20,000 acres of wetlands to farms. Agricultural discharges laden with phosphorus entered the lake, leading to chronic algal blooms, cloudy water, and decline of native plant and fish populations. In 2003, the St. Johns River Water Management District (SJRWMD) began operating a marsh flow-way to remove nutrients from the water and to improve water quality. The district also harvested millions of pounds of gizzard shad from the lake.

SJRWMD and the U.S. Department of Agriculture purchased farms to reduce nutrient runoff and restore wetlands. In 1998-1999, 676 birds, mostly American white pelicans (*Pelecanus erythrorhynchos*), died on newly flooded fields. Their deaths were attributed to toxicosis from pesticide residues entering the food chain in fish. SJRWMD worked with federal partners to restore the area. Soil was extensively tested, contaminated fields were remediated, and re-flooding was phased so fish and wildlife health could be monitored. In 2002, the first 683 acres were successfully flooded. By 2009, nearly 8,000 acres of the former farms provided wetland habitat for wildlife.

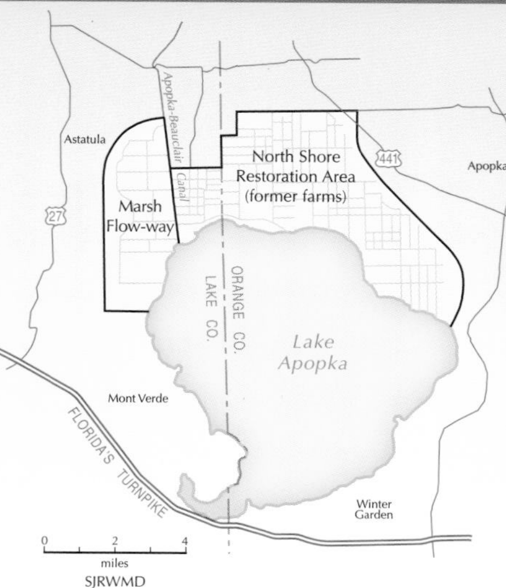

Duda Farm fields prior to its purchase and inclusion in the Lake Apopka North Shore Restoration Area in 1997.

Duda Farm fields, 2004. Before flooding, the district applied alum residual to the soil to bind phosphorus and reduce its release into the water. In 2002, a monthly average of 15 ducks, wading birds, rails, and moorhens used the area. By 2005, the average had increased to 578.

The American bittern (*Botaurus lentiginosus*), one of 353 species of birds recorded in the Lake Apopka North Shore Restoration Area. This number represents 70% of all bird species officially recorded in Florida by the Florida Ornithological Society.

Kissimmee River

The Kissimmee River meandered for 103 miles from its headwaters in Lake Kissimmee south to Lake Okeechobee. Within its vast floodplain were 43,000 acres of wetlands—wet prairies, broadleaf and sawgrass marshes, and willow, buttonbush, and cypress swamps. Upland vegetation occurred along ridges, on islands, and along the boundaries of the floodplain. These diverse habitats were home to at least 320 species of birds, fish, mammals, and other animals.

Alteration of the river began in the 1880s with dredging of the channel for navigation. In 1948, Congress authorized the U.S. Army Corps of Engineers to develop a plan for flood control in Central and South Florida. Between 1962 and 1971, the corps transformed the Kissimmee into the 56-mile long, 30-feet deep, 300-feet wide C-38 Canal and five impounded reservoirs. Six water control structures regulated inflow from the upper basin, eliminating historical water-level fluctuations, reducing flow by 90%, and destroying 30,000 acres of wetlands. Wintering waterfowl declined by 92%; bald eagle nesting dropped by 74%; wading birds were largely replaced by cattle egrets; largemouth bass were replaced by fish more tolerant of low dissolved oxygen; and invertebrates typical of large river systems were replaced by those common to ponds, lakes, and ditches.

Today, the South Florida Water Management District and the U.S. Army Corps of Engineers are restoring the river ecosystem by filling in the C-38 Canal in strategic locations and modifying water management in the Kissimmee chain of lakes to mimic natural water flow. When completed, the project will restore 27,000 acres of floodplain wetlands and water flow to 43 miles of the original meandering channel. The success of the restoration is clear: largemouth bass have increased in relative abundance by 38%; wading birds have increased dramatically in restored areas; and northern pintail, northern shoveler, American widgeon, and ring-necked duck have returned for the first time in 40 years.

Kissimmee River, Okeechobee County, using all of its many channels, 1947.

Channelized section of the Kissimmee River. The canal severed the hydrologic link between the river and floodplain, draining over two-thirds of the floodplain wetlands.

Phase I Restoration Area. In 2001, seven kilometers of the C-38 were backfilled, restoring flow to the original meanders and re-establishing a link between the river and its adjacent floodplain, 2008.

Southwest Florida

Beginning in the early 1970s, residents of Pasco and Hillsborough counties began to see the environmental consequences of decades of steadily increased pumping of groundwater from nearby regional wellfields. Freshwater was pumped from the Upper Floridan aquifer and piped as far away as St. Petersburg, which had long ago exhausted its meager freshwater supply. Water levels in both the Floridan aquifer and the overlying surficial aquifer dropped. Family wells went dry and sinkholes opened. Because groundwater and surface water are so intimately connected in much of this region, excessive withdrawals of groundwater resulted in damage to surface-water ecosystems: streamflow and spring discharge decreased, lake levels dropped, and thousands of acres of wetlands disappeared. All that was left of the 300-acre Big Fish Lake, once home to record-size largemouth bass (*Micropterus salmoides*), was a field of weeds. In 1998, Tampa Bay Water, a regional utility, was established to supply water to Hillsborough, Pasco, and Pinellas counties. An agreement with its government members requires the utility to find alternative sources of water and to minimize groundwater pumping to allow the aquifer to recharge. Alternative sources now include the Hillsborough and Alafia rivers, the Tampa Bay Bypass Canal, and the Tampa Bay Desalination Plant.

Bartle Swamp had dry soils and a die-off of trees due to an artificially lowered water table. Dry soils, dead and stressed vegetation, combined with drought in 1994, created conditions that led to the catastrophic effects of this wildfire.

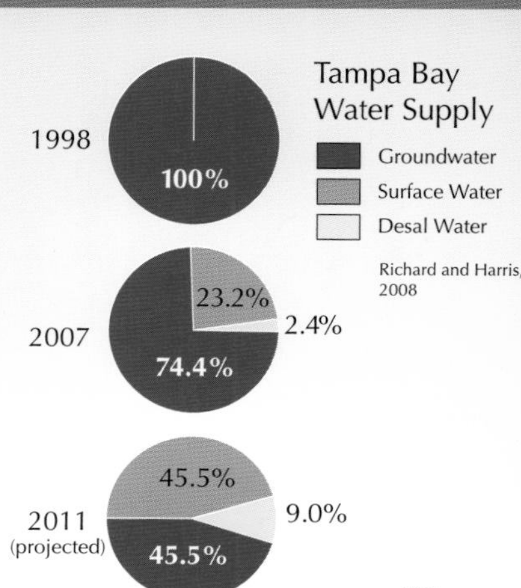

Climate Change

Of all the challenges faced today in the conservation of biodiversity, none is more difficult to assess, yet potentially more catastrophic, than climate change. Evidence has mounted to the point of clear scientific consensus that global temperature is rising, leading to rising sea level and changing weather patterns. The rate of temperature and sea level rise is also increasing, suggesting that major impacts could arrive sooner than later. These increases are linked to an increased accumulation of greenhouse gases (notably carbon dioxide) in Earth's atmosphere, primarily due to human combustion of fossil fuels including oil, coal, and natural gas. Yet, we are only beginning to understand the range of potential impacts to natural resources and the potential options available to mitigate or adapt to those impacts.

In 2007, the Fourth Assessment of the Intergovernmental Panel on Climate Change (IPCC), an international body involving thousands of climate scientists, included projections of sea level, temperature, and precipitation changes through the end of the 21st century. Current consensus indicates that the southeastern U.S. is likely to see smaller changes in temperature and precipitation than elsewhere in North America and around the planet. Florida, with the second longest coastline in the U.S., is likely to face greater impacts from sea level rise than temperature or precipitation. The IPCC projects global sea level to rise anywhere from 18-59 cm (7-23 inches) by 2100, depending on various greenhouse gas emission scenarios. The IPCC projections intentionally excluded any contribution to sea level from polar and Greenland ice melt. Current research on melting glaciers and ice caps is leading scientists to a consensus that global sea level rise of 1 meter by 2100 is realistic, with 2 meters or more suggested by some studies.

The impacts of sea level rise on Florida's coastal ecosystems and species could clearly be devastating, but precise studies are in their infancy. Some species and natural communities could potentially migrate inland if the rate of change was gradual and corridors of undeveloped land were available. Species or communities dependent on unique soils or geology, located on islands, or hemmed in by development would be much less likely to persist.

Even less understood is the range of conservation actions we should take in anticipation of climate change. Should we focus conservation efforts on coastal areas in order to create healthy, resilient natural systems better able to adapt to climate change? Or should conservation of some coastal areas be effectively abandoned in favor of focusing efforts elsewhere? Should we actively transplant coastal species to inland habitats, captive breeding populations, or greenhouses to ensure the persistence of genetic diversity? How will the migration of human populations away from the coast impact natural systems inland? These and many other challenging questions must be addressed by conservationists in the coming decades.

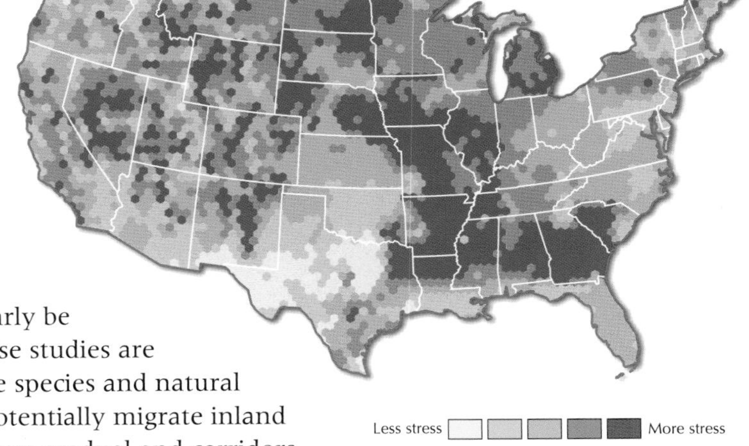

Climate Stress Index

In 2008, researchers at the U.S. Forest Service Rocky Mountain Research Station developed a climate change stress index that measures the potential impact of climate change through the 21st century on terrestrial vertebrates in the continental United States. The model considers three factors based on climate projections: changes in temperature and rainfall, changes in the area of each habitat type, and changes in habitat productivity. Based on this model, wildlife in Florida is expected to experience low to moderate climate-induced stress relative to other areas of the country. Note that this model does not consider sea level rise as a potential stress factor.

Projecting Climate Change

In 2007, the Intergovernmental Panel on Climate Change (IPCC) issued their Fourth Assessment on Climate Change. This assessment included regional projections of climate change in the 21st century. Shown here are projected changes in temperature and precipitation over North America from a starting period of 1980-1999 to 2080-2099. Temperatures are expected to rise across North America, but less so in Florida than most of the continent. Precipitation is expected to increase across the northern reaches of the continent and decrease in the southwest U.S. and Mexico. Florida is expected to see a slight (if any) decrease in precipitation. While the IPCC report expressed confidence in continent-wide trends, current projections include considerable local uncertainty and are likely to fluctuate in future assessments.

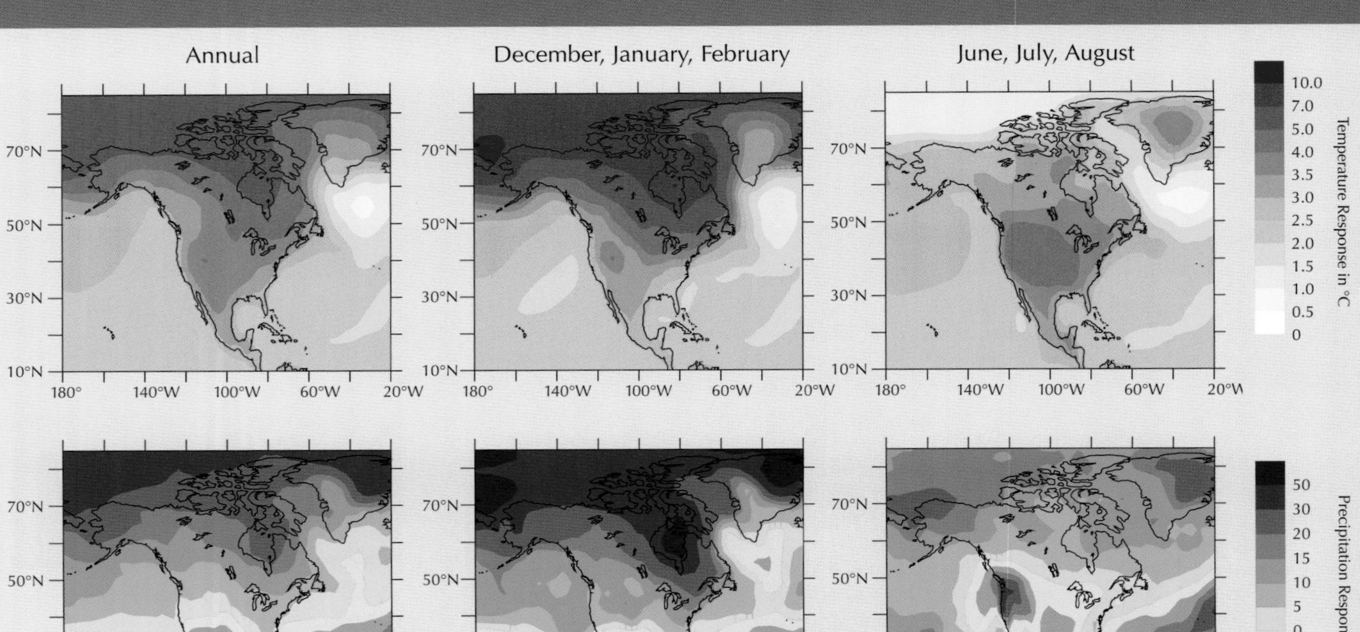

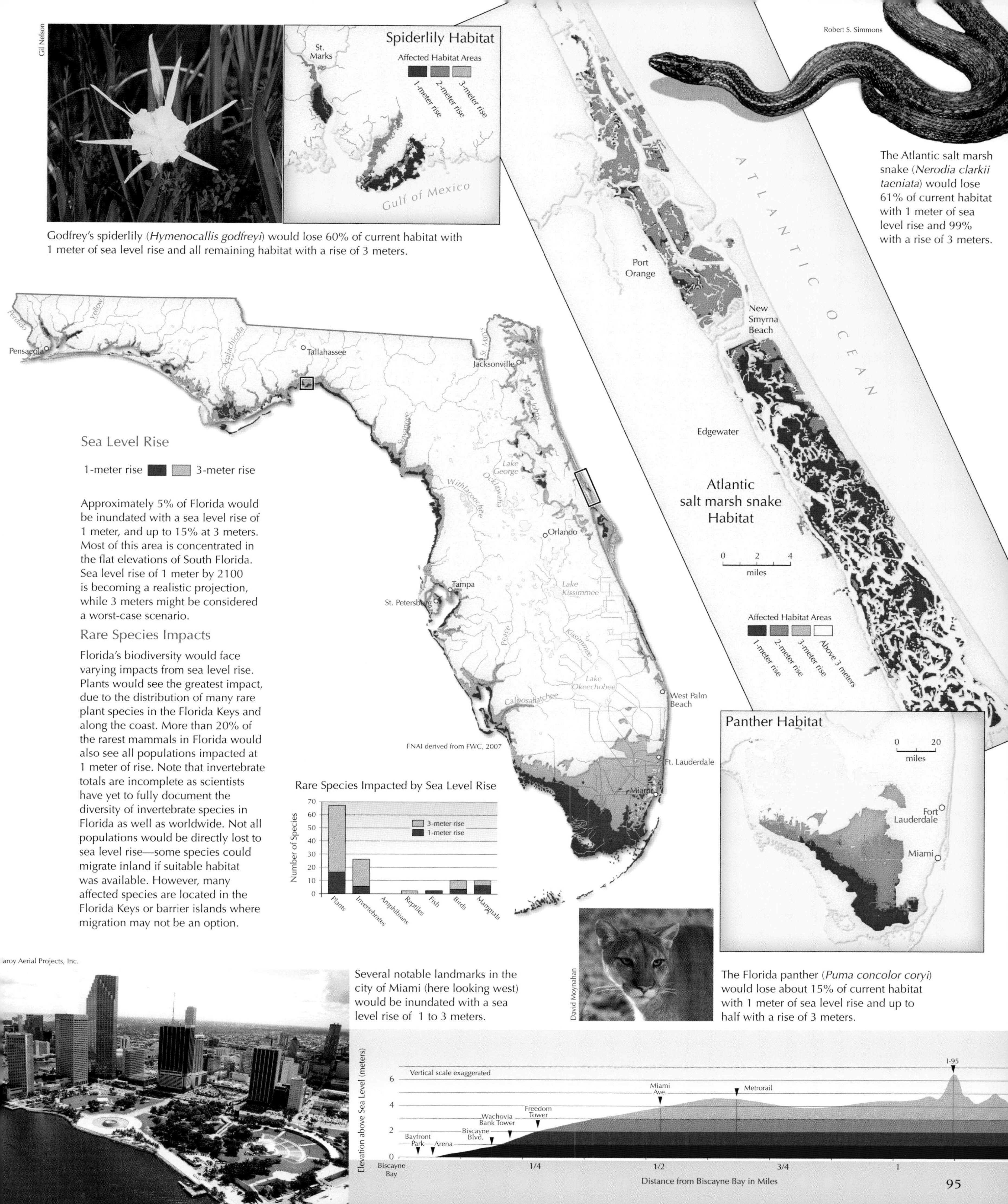

Godfrey's spiderlily (*Hymenocallis godfreyi*) would lose 60% of current habitat with 1 meter of sea level rise and all remaining habitat with a rise of 3 meters.

The Atlantic salt marsh snake (*Nerodia clarkii taeniata*) would lose 61% of current habitat with 1 meter of sea level rise and 99% with a rise of 3 meters.

Sea Level Rise

1-meter rise 3-meter rise

Approximately 5% of Florida would be inundated with a sea level rise of 1 meter, and up to 15% at 3 meters. Most of this area is concentrated in the flat elevations of South Florida. Sea level rise of 1 meter by 2100 is becoming a realistic projection, while 3 meters might be considered a worst-case scenario.

Rare Species Impacts

Florida's biodiversity would face varying impacts from sea level rise. Plants would see the greatest impact, due to the distribution of many rare plant species in the Florida Keys and along the coast. More than 20% of the rarest mammals in Florida would also see all populations impacted at 1 meter of rise. Note that invertebrate totals are incomplete as scientists have yet to fully document the diversity of invertebrate species in Florida as well as worldwide. Not all populations would be directly lost to sea level rise—some species could migrate inland if suitable habitat was available. However, many affected species are located in the Florida Keys or barrier islands where migration may not be an option.

The Florida panther (*Puma concolor coryi*) would lose about 15% of current habitat with 1 meter of sea level rise and up to half with a rise of 3 meters.

Several notable landmarks in the city of Miami (here looking west) would be inundated with a sea level rise of 1 to 3 meters.

Habitat Modeling

An important step in the conservation of rare and endangered species is knowing where those species occur on the landscape. Biologists spend thousands of hours every year surveying for rare species throughout Florida, and much of that information is compiled in the FNAI element occurrence database. Unless a species is restricted to a few accessible locations scientists are rarely able to document the full and precise extent of its habitat. Most survey work is confined to lands to which scientists have access, and many species are not easily observed without intensive search efforts. In the absence of complete information, scientists and conservation planners turn to habitat models to estimate species distributions across the landscape.

There are a variety of methods for modeling species habitat, but all rely on one or more of three basic types of information:

Known Occurrence Locations

Known locations provide information such as vegetation, soils, topography, climate, and distinctive features of the range such as "only known east of Apalachicola River." Occurrence data may also provide information on whether the species is thriving or declining in certain conditions.

Habitat Preferences

Our knowledge of a species' ecology usually involves more than simply what we know about observed locations. Years of research identify patterns in home range size, migration, population dynamics, diet, and historical range, all of which give a fuller picture of habitat preferences for a species. For most species we can then define a profile of suitable habitat types that might be included in a habitat model.

Environmental Data

Data such as land cover, soil type, temperature, rainfall, elevation, and slope are used to identify the landscape in which the species is likely to be found.

Challenges in Habitat Modeling

Every method for modeling species habitat presents limitations and challenges. The most obvious challenge is having species and land cover data that are as current and precise as possible. A common problem arises when the habitat preferences of a species do not fall neatly into the classification scheme of available land cover data. This may be the case because the land cover map lumps finer habitat types into broad categories, or because the scale of the land cover data is insufficient to identify small patches of distinct habitat types. Some species actually prefer transition zones between habitat types, or *ecotones*, which are usually not identified in land cover data and require special methods to model. Lack of documented occurrence data is also a problem for models that rely too heavily on conditions at known locations.

These pages describe and compare three habitat modeling techniques that have been used in recent Florida conservation planning analyses.

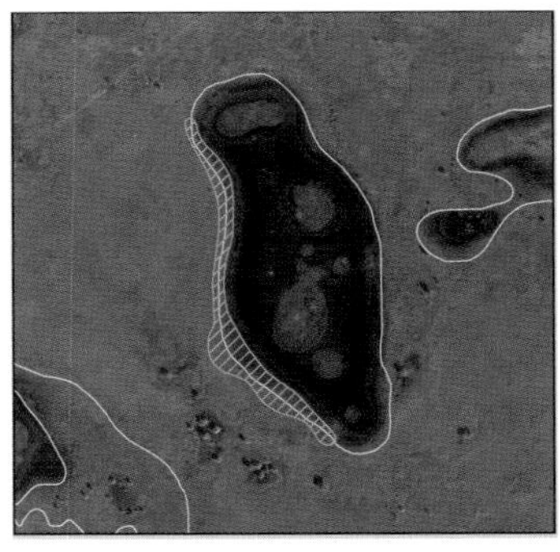

An ecotone is a transition zone between different habitat types, such as a shrubby strip between a marsh and a surrounding upland (orange hatching, above). Ecotones are preferred habitats for some species, but are missed by land cover data sets that usually focus on major vegetation types (yellow lines).

Comparison of Habitat Modeling Methods

This map shows a comparison of three habitat models for the frosted flatwoods salamander (*Ambystoma cingulatum*) based on the methods described on the facing page. The occurrence-based habitat map is restricted to areas of suitable habitat around known locations. The potential habitat model identifies suitable land cover types within the general range of the species, so it is not restricted to known locations. The predictive range model is based on more general environmental variables such as temperature and rainfall, but does not distinguish between suitable and unsuitable land cover types within the general area identified. Based on the differing methods, we would expect the predictive range model to identify the broadest area for the species, the occurrence-based habitat map to identify the least, and the potential habitat model to be intermediate. The models generally follow the expected pattern for this species, although the potential habitat model has identified some areas not found in the predictive range model.

Model uses

This comparison makes clear that different models may be suited for different purposes. FNAI's occurrence-based habitat maps were created to identify priorities for conservation land acquisition, so analysts would have high confidence that the species occupied the areas mapped. Those maps may miss areas where the species occurs but is not documented. Predictive range models are valuable for identifying overall range extents at state, regional, or national scales. Potential habitat models and predictive range models are both useful for targeting areas for future species surveys.

- Occurrence-Based Habitat Map
- Potential Habitat Model
- Predictive Range Model
- • Documented Occurrence

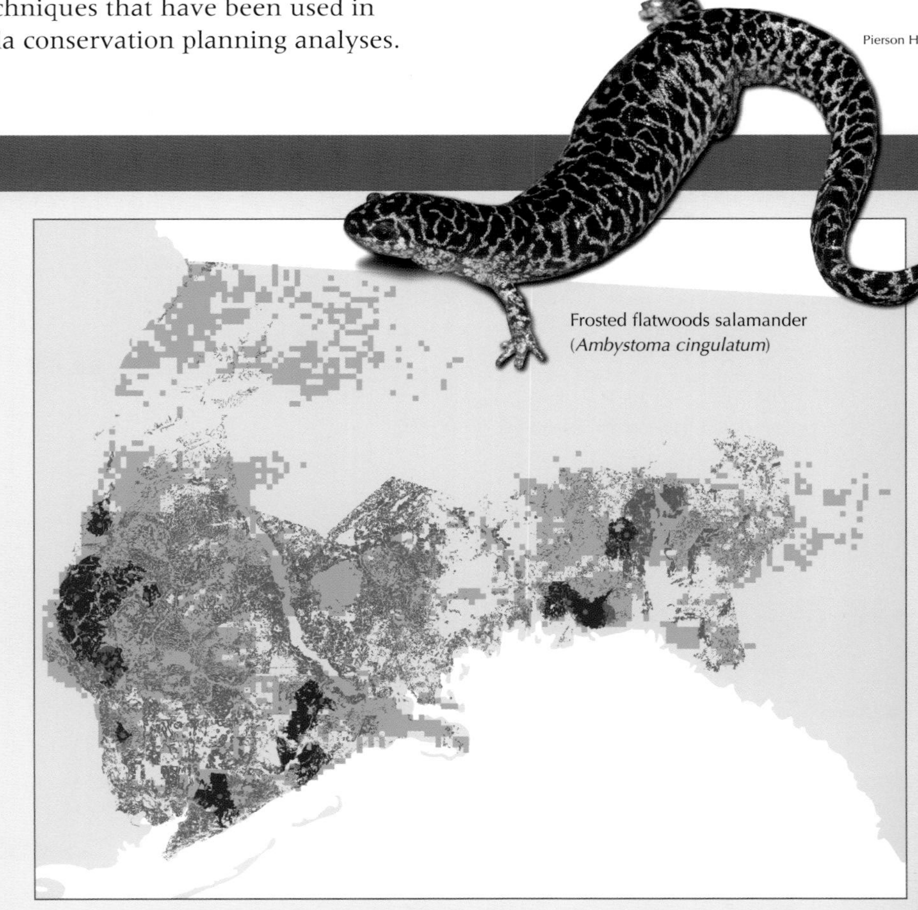

Predictive Range Modeling

There are a variety of algorithms for predictive range modeling (also known as species or element distribution modeling), but all generally involve overlaying known occurrence points on a set of environmental variables such as temperature, precipitation, elevation, slope, or soils. No prior information about the environmental conditions at each occurrence point is required—the model infers these data from the environmental layers.

In this example, known locations (red points) of the celestial lily (*Nemastylis floridana*) are overlaid on four environmental data layers. The resulting model depicts a value surface across the state that indicates the probability of occurrence of the species. In some cases, scientists may apply a cutoff value to the probability surface in order to produce a simple binary (in-or-out) map of the species' predicted range (far right).

Alfred R. Schotz

Celestial lily
(*Nemastylis floridana*)

Note that predictive range models generally do not identify specific habitat types within the species' range: the model is only predicting the general area in which the species is likely to be found.

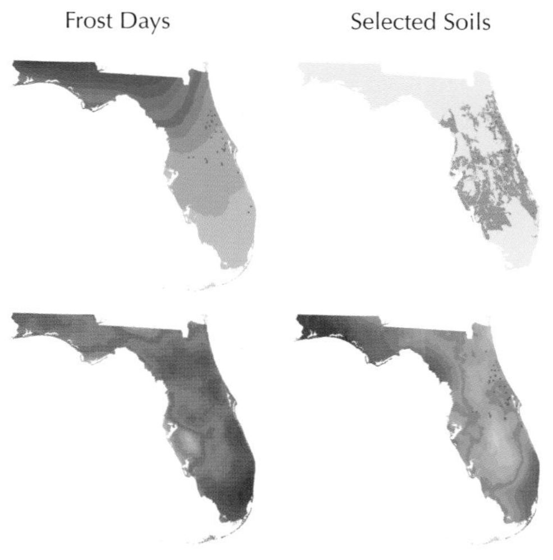
Frost Days

Selected Soils

Annual Precipitation

Precipitation Frequency

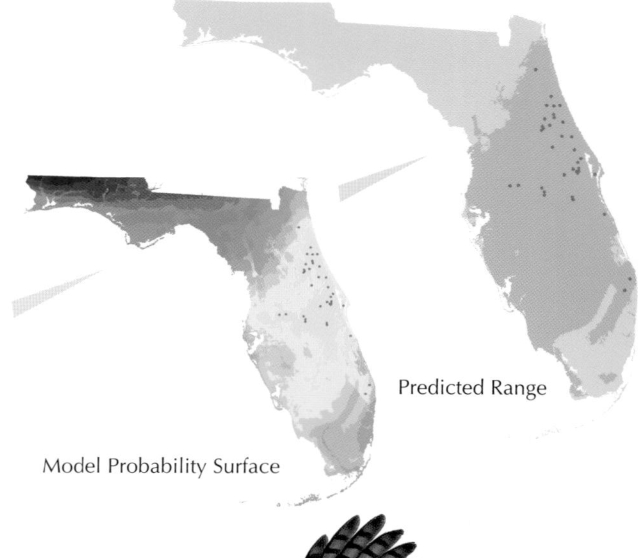
Model Probability Surface

Predicted Range

Lloyd Spitalnik

Cooper's hawk
(*Accipiter cooperii*)

Potential Habitat Modeling

Potential habitat modeling has the advantage of not requiring any known occurrence data, although these data are often used to refine the model. This method relies on general knowledge of a species' habitat preferences to identify land cover categories that will be included in the habitat model. Those categories are selected from a land cover data layer and may be modified in various ways, such as restricting the model to areas within the known range of the species, or to areas within a set distance from known locations.

This example shows a potential habitat model for Cooper's hawk (*Accipiter cooperii*) (far right), created by the Florida Fish and Wildlife Conservation Commission. Various forested land cover types were extracted from satellite imagery land cover (right). The model was restricted to range limits known from published research.

Satellite Imagery Land Cover

Suitable Land Cover Types

Occurrence-Based Habitat Mapping

This method is not a comprehensive habitat model so much as an effort to map habitat for a species around known occurrence locations. This method is used by FNAI to map species habitat in order to identify conservation priorities for the Florida Forever program. A variety of land cover data layers may be used and different land cover categories may be included based on the specific conditions of each occurrence location.

Gary Knight

Fringed campion
(*Silene polypetala*)

In the example at right, habitat for fringed campion (*Silene polypetala*) along the Apalachicola River in Gadsden and Jackson counties is mapped around known occurrences by buffering occurrence locations by 400 meters. Those buffers are overlaid on land cover data to extract suitable land cover categories, in this case hardwood forest types that intersect the buffers. FNAI also assigns a suitability value to each habitat patch based on size, land cover type, and fragmentation. In the box at the far right, red patches are high suitability, orange are medium suitability, and yellow are low suitability.

Documented Occurrences

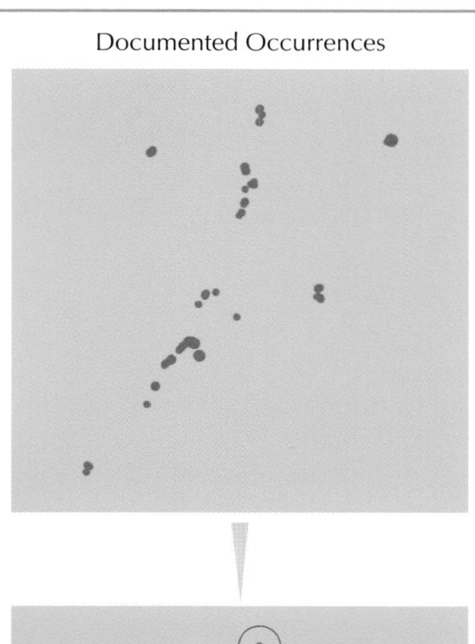

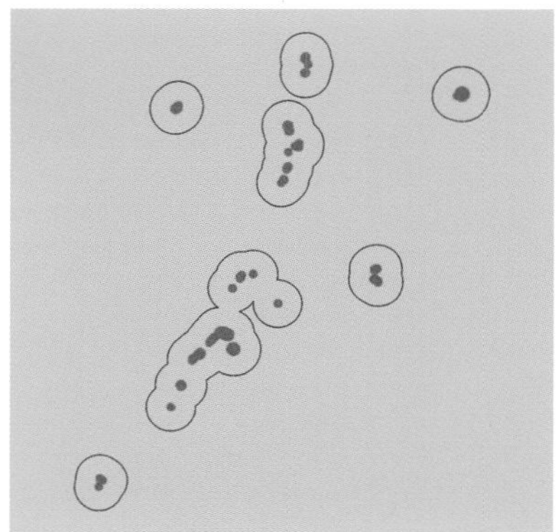
Occurrence Buffer

Selected Land Cover

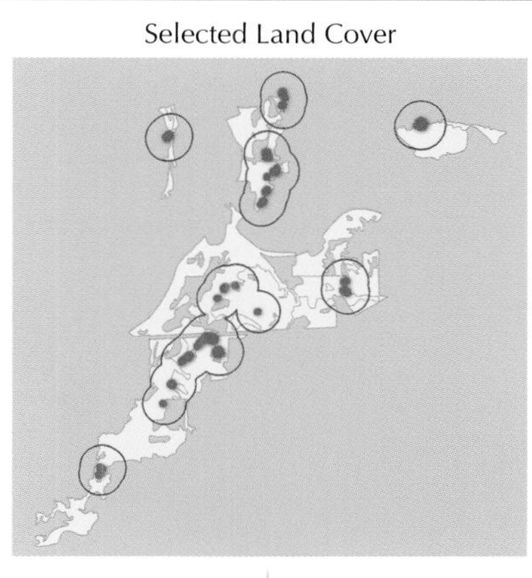

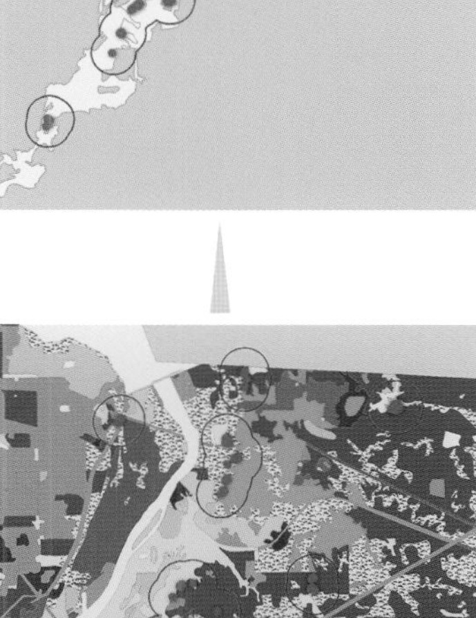

Buffers over Land Cover

Final Habitat Map

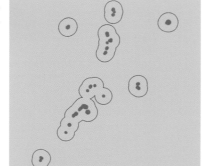

The next page illustrates how this model is used in determining conservation priority.

Habitat Conservation Priorities

The FNAI Habitat Conservation Priorities model is a biodiversity analysis that prioritizes places on the landscape that would protect both the greatest number of rare species and those species with the greatest conservation need. This model was originally developed to inform Florida Forever, the state's conservation land acquisition program. The goal was to depict a range of biodiversity values across the state, prioritized toward species that would most benefit from land acquisition. An alternate version of this model, prioritized for more general conservation planning purposes, has been developed for the CLIP analysis (*see* pp. 104-105). The map shown at right is the original Florida Forever version.

The data underlying the Habitat Conservation Priorities model is the FNAI rare species occurrence database. The model is based on occurrence-based habitat mapping, which ensures that the priorities are directly linked to known locations of species. This contrasts with other mapping efforts that rely on predictive or potential species habitat models. The Habitat Conservation Priorities model also focuses on rare species across a wide range of taxa. The analysis integrates habitat maps for about 250 rare species with a high conservation need, including plants, vertebrates and invertebrates.

In the Florida Forever version, the highest priority lands comprise about 447,000 acres with about 268,800 acres on private lands. Priority 1 lands are concentrated in several distinct regions of the state: the Apalachicola River basin in the panhandle; the Suwannee and Santa Fe river systems, Waccasassa Bay, southwestern Marion County, and springs in north-central Florida; the Lake Wales Ridge, and grasslands of the central peninsula; the Atlantic Ridge ecosystem on the east coast; Big Cypress and Everglades ecosystems in the south; and the Florida Keys.

Continual input of new species locations into the FNAI database along with new conservation land acquisitions means that conservation priorities can change. In order to capture this new information the FNAI Habitat Conservation Priorities model is updated regularly.

Distribution of Species

64 Invertebrates
142 Plants
42 Vertebrates
198 Terrestrial Species
50 Aquatic Species

The FNAI Habitat Conservation Priorities include habitat for species across a wide range of taxa. Over half of the species are plants, including 55 federally endangered or threatened species such as the globally critically imperiled (G1) beautiful pawpaw (*Deeringothamnus pulchellus*); 123 plants are state-listed endangered.

About one-quarter of the species are invertebrates. The invertebrates consist of many aquatic species, including 17 rare mussels such as the federally endangered Ochlockonee moccasinshell (*Medionidus simpsonianus*). Terrestrial invertebrates are also represented by species such as the globally critically imperiled Highlands tiger beetle (*Cicindela highlandensis*), and the globally imperiled (G2) fire-back crayfish (*Cambarus pyronotus*).

Vertebrates make up about one-fifth of the species and include wide-ranging terrestrial species such as Florida black bear (*Ursus americanus floridanus*) and crested caracara (*Caracara cheriway*) as well as habitat specialists such as the globally critically imperiled salt marsh vole (*Microtus pennsylvanicus dukecampbelli*) and Gulf Hammock dwarf siren (*Pseudobranchus striatus lustricolus*). There are also a number of aquatic vertebrates such as the federally endangered manatee (*Trichechus manatus*) and shortnose sturgeon (*Acipenser brevirostrum*). Habitat maps for aquatic species include terrestrial buffers to the water bodies in which the species occur.

Fire-back crayfish (*Cambarus pyronotus*)

Dale R. Jackson

Habitat maps were developed for 250 rare species. See previous page for mapping details.

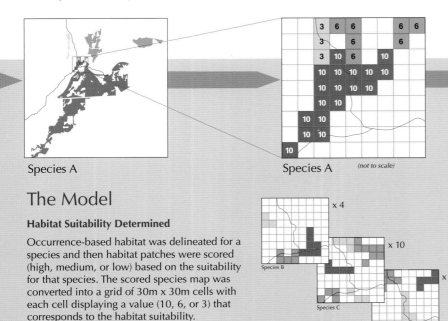

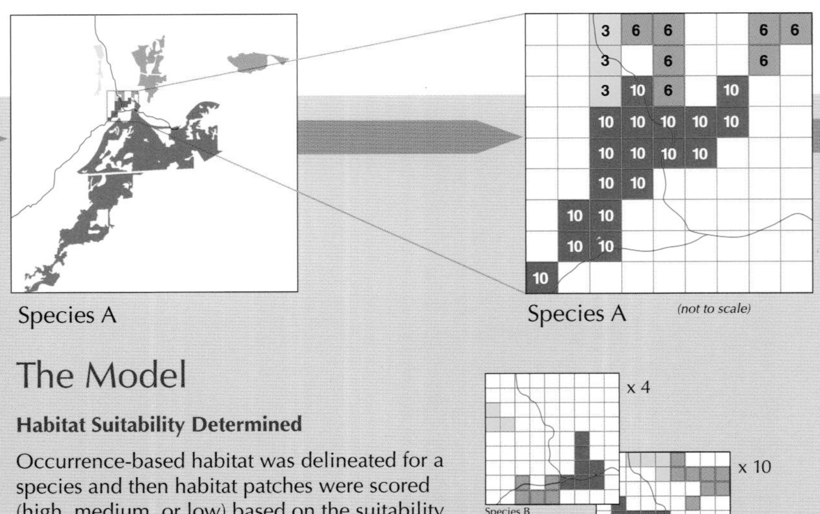

Species A

Species A

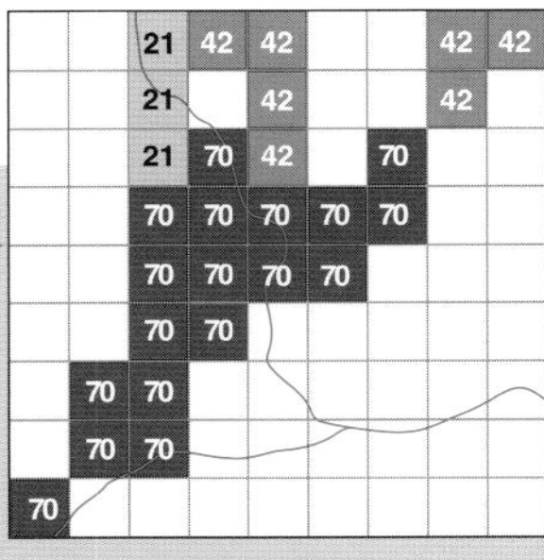

Species A

The Model

Habitat Suitability Determined

Occurrence-based habitat was delineated for a species and then habitat patches were scored (high, medium, or low) based on the suitability for that species. The scored species map was converted into a grid of 30m x 30m cells with each cell displaying a value (10, 6, or 3) that corresponds to the habitat suitability.

x 4
Species B
x 10
Species C
x Weight
Species *n*

Conservation Needs Weight Assigned

x 7

In the Florida Forever version, each species was assigned a conservation need weight of 10, 7, 4, 2, or 1 based on global rarity (G-rank), area of total habitat occupied in Florida, and percentage of habitat protected on existing conservation lands. The rarest species with the least habitat protected received the highest conservation need weight, while more common species with more habitat protected received a lower conservation need weight. The CLIP version weights species by global and state rarity (G- and S-ranks) only, and is more applicable to general conservation planning efforts.

Multiplier Applied

The assigned weights were then used as a multiplier on each species' habitat grid. In this illustration, Species A has a moderately high conservation need, so the habitat grid for Species A was multiplied by 7 before it was added into the final model. Species B has a lower conservation need, so was multiplied by 4, and so on.

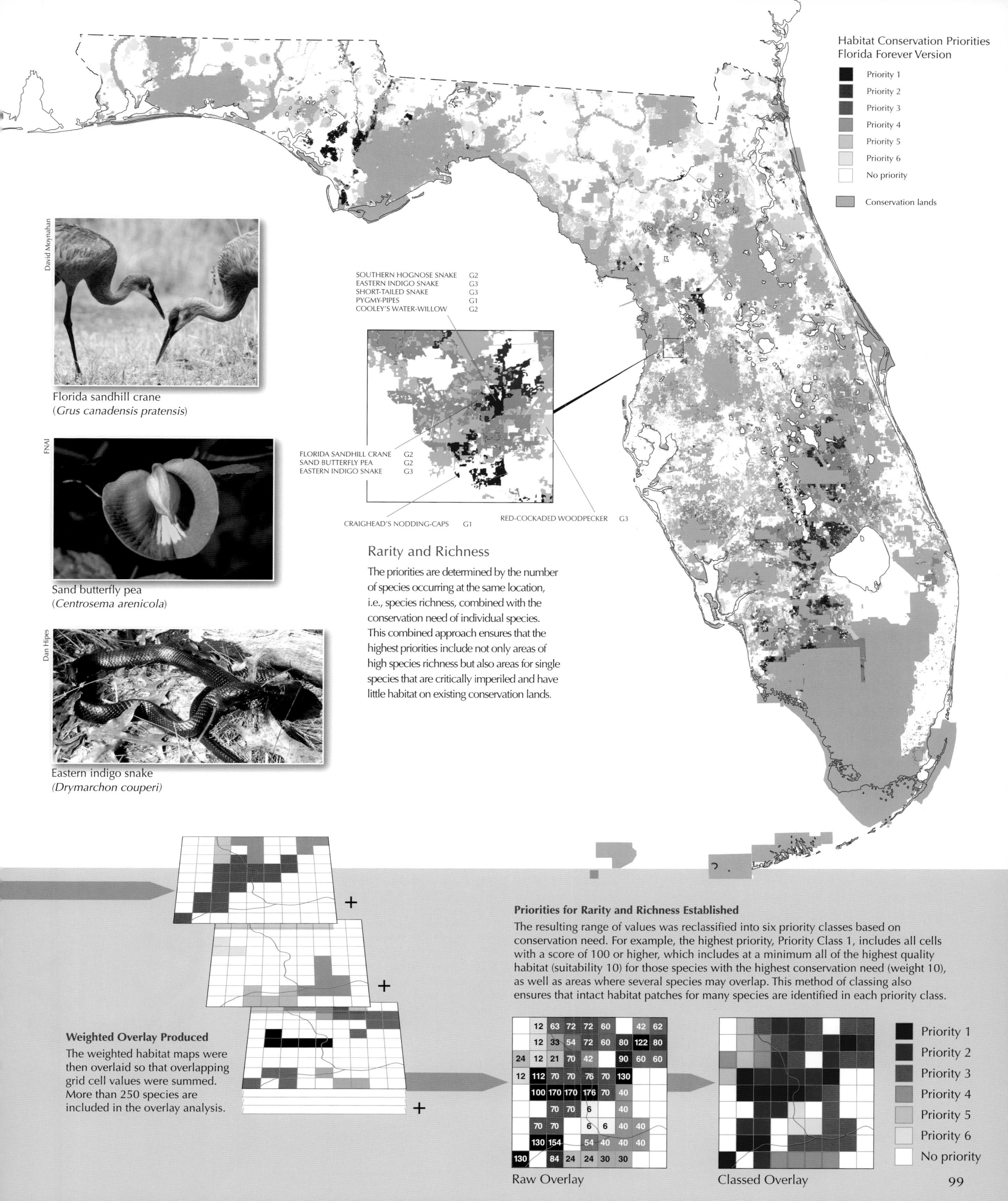
Habitat Conservation Priorities
Florida Forever Version
Priority 1
Priority 2
Priority 3
Priority 4
Priority 5
Priority 6
No priority
Conservation lands
SOUTHERN HOGNOSE SNAKE G2
EASTERN INDIGO SNAKE G3
SHORT-TAILED SNAKE G3
PYGMY-PIPES G1
COOLEY'S WATER-WILLOW G2
FLORIDA SANDHILL CRANE G2
SAND BUTTERFLY PEA G2
EASTERN INDIGO SNAKE G3
CRAIGHEAD'S NODDING-CAPS G1
RED-COCKADED WOODPECKER G3
David Moynahan
FNAI
Dan Hipes
Rarity and Richness
The priorities are determined by the number of species occurring at the same location, i.e., species richness, combined with the conservation need of individual species. This combined approach ensures that the highest priorities include not only areas of high species richness but also areas for single species that are critically imperiled and have little habitat on existing conservation lands.
Weighted Overlay Produced
The weighted habitat maps were then overlaid so that overlapping grid cell values were summed. More than 250 species are included in the overlay analysis.
Priorities for Rarity and Richness Established
The resulting range of values was reclassified into six priority classes based on conservation need. For example, the highest priority, Priority Class 1, includes all cells with a score of 100 or higher, which includes at a minimum all of the highest quality habitat (suitability 10) for those species with the highest conservation need (weight 10), as well as areas where several species may overlap. This method of classing also ensures that intact habitat patches for many species are identified in each priority class.
12 63 72 72 60 42 62
12 33 54 72 60 80 122 80
24 12 21 70 42 90 60 60
12 112 70 70 76 70 130
100 170 170 176 70 40
70 70 6 40
70 70 6 6 40 40
130 154 54 40 40 40
130 84 24 24 30 30
Raw Overlay
Classed Overlay
Priority 1
Priority 2
Priority 3
Priority 4
Priority 5
Priority 6
No priority

Florida sandhill crane
(*Grus canadensis pratensis*)

Sand butterfly pea
(*Centrosema arenicola*)

Eastern indigo snake
(*Drymarchon couperi*)

SHCAs

Strategic Habitat Conservation Areas (SHCAs) are lands required by key animal species in order to maintain viable populations of those species in Florida into the foreseeable future. The SHCA model was developed by the Florida Wildlife Conservation Commission (FWC) by modeling potential habitat for 62 focal vertebrate species and assessing the long-term viability of populations of those species on their identified habitat across the state. FWC staff assessed whether species had adequate habitat on public conservation lands in order to maintain viable populations, and for those species with inadequate protection, modeled the additional habitat on private lands that would be needed for the species' long-term persistence. Lands identified as SHCAs indicate that the area is required by one or more of those species in order for the species to persist as a viable population in Florida over the next 100 years.

The first SHCA analysis was conducted in 1994, based on habitat requirements for 30 focal vertebrate species, four natural communities (sandhill, scrub, pine rocklands, and tropical hardwood hammocks), and other important wildlife aggregation sites, including bat maternity caves, wading bird wetland habitat, and key locations for rare plants. This analysis was based on the general principle that 10 populations, each with at least 200 individuals, represented minimally viable populations for the focal species. The original SHCAs were augmented in 2000 with habitat needs for an additional 17 vertebrate species. In 2009, FWC completed an extensive revision resulting in SHCAs for 34 species (of 62 species analyzed). The 2009 SHCAs are based solely on focal vertebrates and do not include habitat for natural communities or plants.

The 2009 SHCA analysis began with potential habitat models for each candidate species, based on 2003 satellite land cover data (*see* pages 96-97). A population viability analysis (PVA) was then conducted for each species to determine if the amount of habitat on current conservation lands is sufficient to maintain the species long term. For those species for which conservation lands were determined to be insufficient, the PVA analysis and potential habitat model were used to identify a minimum amount of additional habitat on private lands that would secure the species. This additional area beyond conservation lands was designated that species' SHCA.

Strategic Habitat Conservation Areas Species List

Species		Global Rank	State Rank	Priority
Accipiter cooperii	Cooper's hawk	G5	S3	5
Ammodramus maritimus fisheri	Louisiana seaside sparrow	G4T4	S1	2
Ammodramus maritimus macgillivraii	Macgillivray's (aka Smyrna) seaside sparrow	G4T2	S2	2
Ammodramus maritimus peninsulae	Scott's seaside sparrow	G4T3	S3	3
Ammodramus savannarum floridanus	Florida grasshopper sparrow	G5T1	S1	1
Aphelocoma coerulescens	Florida scrub-jay	G2	S2	2
Athene cunicularia floridana	Florida burrowing owl	G4T3	S3	3
Buteo brachyurus	short-tailed hawk	G4	S1	2
Charadrius alexandrinus	snowy plover	G4	S1	2
Crocodylus acutus	American crocodile	G2	S2	2
Coccyzus minor	mangrove cuckoo	G5	S3	5
Desmognathus monticola	seal salamander	G5	S1	2
Elanoides forficatus	swallow-tailed kite	G5	S2	3
Hyla andersonii	pine barrens treefrog	G4	S3	4
Microtus pennsylvanicus dukecampbelli	salt marsh vole	G5T1	S1	1
Myotis grisescens	gray bat	G3	S1	1
Nerodia clarkii clarkii	Gulf salt marsh snake	G4T4	S3	4
Nerodia clarkii taeniata	Atlantic salt marsh snake	G4T1	S1	1
Notophthalmus perstriatus	striped newt	G2	S2	2
Odocoileus virginianus clavium	key deer	G5T1	S1	1
Oryzomys palustris	Sanibel Island rice rat	G5T1	S1	1
Oryzomys palustris	key rice rat	G5T2	S2	2
Patagioenas leucocephala	white-crowned pigeon	G3	S3	3
Peromyscus polionotus allophrys	Choctawhatchee beach mouse	G5T1	S1	1
Peromyscus polionotus niveiventris	southeastern beach mouse	G5T1	S1	1
Peromyscus polionotus peninsularis	St. Andrews beach mouse	G5T1	S1	1
Peromyscus polionotus phasma	Anastasia Island beach mouse	G5T1	S1	1
Plestiodon reynoldsi	sand skink	G2	S2	2
Podomys floridanus	Florida mouse	G3	S3	3
Puma concolor coryi	Florida panther	G5T1	S1	1
Rostrhamus sociabilis plumbeus	snail kite	G4T3	S2	2
Sciurus niger avicennia	mangrove (aka big cypress) fox squirrel	G5T2	S2	2
Sylvilagus palustris hefneri	Lower Keys rabbit	G5T1	S1	1
Ursus americanus floridanus	Florida black bear	G5T2	S2	2

Determining SHCAs
This example shows the relationship between potential habitat and SHCA for one focal species. A large portion of mangrove fox squirrel (*Sciurus niger avicennia*–also known as Big Cypress fox squirrel) habitat is found on existing conservation lands, but population viability analysis (PVA) indicated more habitat is required for long-term survival. In this case, not all of the fox squirrel's remaining habitat on private lands is required to meet minimum requirements for survival, so the SHCA for mangrove fox squirrel is a subset of remaining habitat.

Danielle A. Eisenburg

Mangrove fox squirrel
(*Sciurus niger avicennia*)

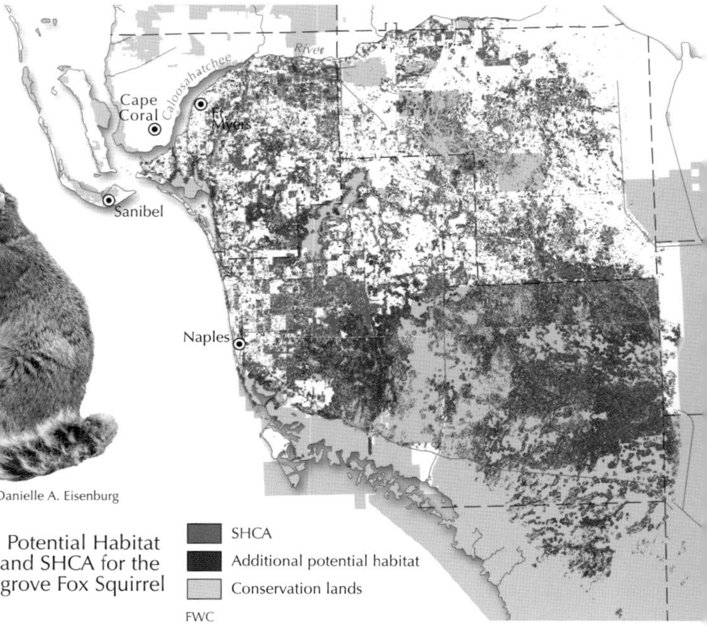

Potential Habitat and SHCA for the Mangrove Fox Squirrel

FWC

Population Viability Analysis (PVA) uses data on a species' demographic patterns, including birth, death, and migration rates, to assess the likelihood that the species will persist into the future. PVA may take the form of a simple population model, or it may incorporate species habitat modeling into a spatially explicit PVA model (as used in the SHCA analysis). This graph shows the results of a PVA for the key deer (*Odocoileus virginianus clavium*), indicating that the population is likely to decline slightly even if all remaining habitat is maintained in the future. The analysis also shows that decreased survivorship (higher mortality due to disease, predation, roadkill, or other factors) is a much greater threat to the key deer than decreased fecundity (reproductive rate). PVA results such as these were used to model SHCAs for each focal species.

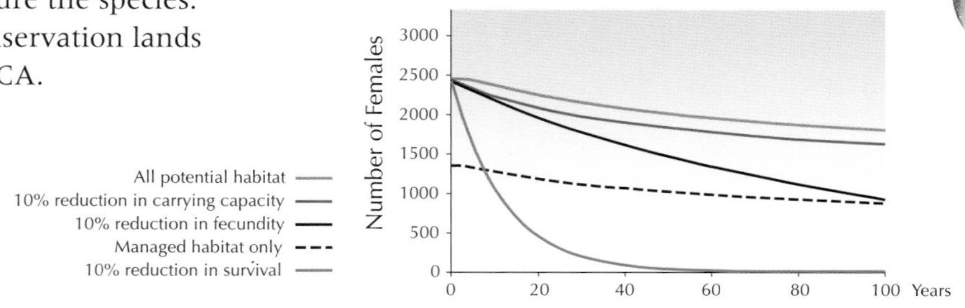

Key deer
(*Odocoileus virginianus clavium*)

Robert Wild

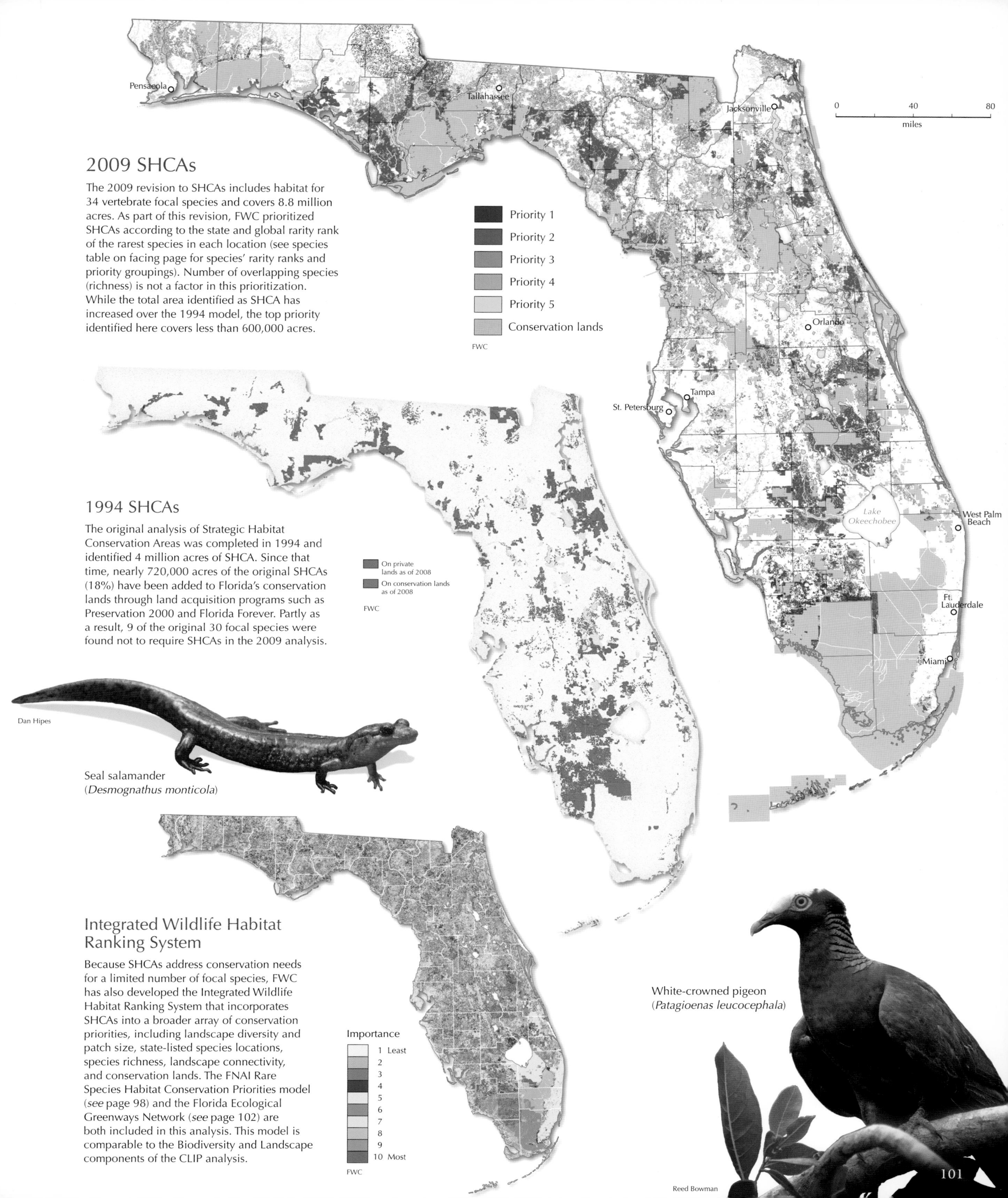

2009 SHCAs

The 2009 revision to SHCAs includes habitat for 34 vertebrate focal species and covers 8.8 million acres. As part of this revision, FWC prioritized SHCAs according to the state and global rarity rank of the rarest species in each location (see species table on facing page for species' rarity ranks and priority groupings). Number of overlapping species (richness) is not a factor in this prioritization. While the total area identified as SHCA has increased over the 1994 model, the top priority identified here covers less than 600,000 acres.

1994 SHCAs

The original analysis of Strategic Habitat Conservation Areas was completed in 1994 and identified 4 million acres of SHCA. Since that time, nearly 720,000 acres of the original SHCAs (18%) have been added to Florida's conservation lands through land acquisition programs such as Preservation 2000 and Florida Forever. Partly as a result, 9 of the original 30 focal species were found not to require SHCAs in the 2009 analysis.

Dan Hipes

Seal salamander
(*Desmognathus monticola*)

Integrated Wildlife Habitat Ranking System

Because SHCAs address conservation needs for a limited number of focal species, FWC has also developed the Integrated Wildlife Habitat Ranking System that incorporates SHCAs into a broader array of conservation priorities, including landscape diversity and patch size, state-listed species locations, species richness, landscape connectivity, and conservation lands. The FNAI Rare Species Habitat Conservation Priorities model (*see* page 98) and the Florida Ecological Greenways Network (*see* page 102) are both included in this analysis. This model is comparable to the Biodiversity and Landscape components of the CLIP analysis.

White-crowned pigeon
(*Patagioenas leucocephala*)

Reed Bowman

Ecological Greenways

In 1994, the Florida Greenways Commission recommended that Florida create a statewide system of greenways and trails to establish a network connecting existing conservation lands statewide. In response, the University of Florida GeoPlan Center and the Florida Department of Environmental Protection, Office of Greenways and Trails, developed both ecological and recreational priorities for a statewide greenways system. The Florida Ecological Greenways Network identifies areas of opportunity for maintaining a statewide network of ecological hubs and linkages designed to maintain ecological functions and ecosystem services throughout the state. It informs several conservation planning efforts in Florida, including Florida Forever land acquisition, Critical Lands and Waters Identification Project, and the Florida Wildlife Commission's (FWC's) Cooperative Conservation Blueprint.

What is a Greenway?

Greenways are generally linear corridors connecting core areas of interest. Ecological greenways serve as corridors for species habitat and migration between core areas of ecological significance, such as large intact natural landscapes that support wide-ranging species (such as black bear and panther) or feature high biological diversity. These greenways tend to follow natural features such as river corridors, ridges, shorelines, or wetlands. Ecological greenways allow interaction between dispersed populations of a species that would otherwise be cut off by conversion of natural landscapes to agricultural or urban uses, maintaining gene flow and population viability. An intact network of ecological greenways can help mitigate impacts from habitat fragmentation and will support adaptation of natural systems to climate change.

Methods

The first step in developing the ecological greenways network was to identify the core areas of ecological interest, or ecological hubs, around the state. Based on data from FNAI, FWC, and other sources, five major hubs (and many smaller hubs) were identified: Everglades/Big Cypress, Ocala National Forest, Osceola National Forest/Okefenokee National Wildlife Refuge, Apalachicola National Forest, and Eglin Air Force Base/Blackwater River State Forest. Suitable corridors were then identified to link these major hubs and minor hubs. Linkages were identified by creating suitability surfaces across the state based primarily on land cover types and potential corridor widths, and identifying optimal or least-cost paths through the suitability surface to connect one hub with another. Linkages were then optimized by identifying appropriate natural land along the corridor to achieve sufficient width and reduce edge effects. Finally, all hubs and linkages were combined into a single interconnected network.

Updates

Since the original Florida Ecological Greenways Network model was developed in 1998, the model has undergone several rounds of revisions and prioritization. In 2000, the model was prioritized into six classes, with the highest priority designated Critical Linkages. In 2007, the original top two priorities were further subdivided with Critical Linkages being identified for each, as shown on the facing page. Critical Linkages are those lands considered most important for completing a statewide ecological greenways network. The Greenways Network is currently undergoing a new revision scheduled for completion in 2012.

Riparian Corridors

The Florida Ecological Greenways Network relies to a large extent on riparian corridors—corridors that follow river courses or large, linear wetland systems—to establish linkages.

Riparian corridors often remain in a natural state while surrounding lands are developed. Often lands along rivers are wetlands that are less suitable for development, or are subject to development restrictions to protect water quality.

This aerial photo shows the confluence of the Santa Fe (right) and Suwannee (left) rivers in north central Florida. Natural lands along these two rivers clearly appear as greenways in the midst of a patchwork of crop lands.

Conceptual Greenways Network

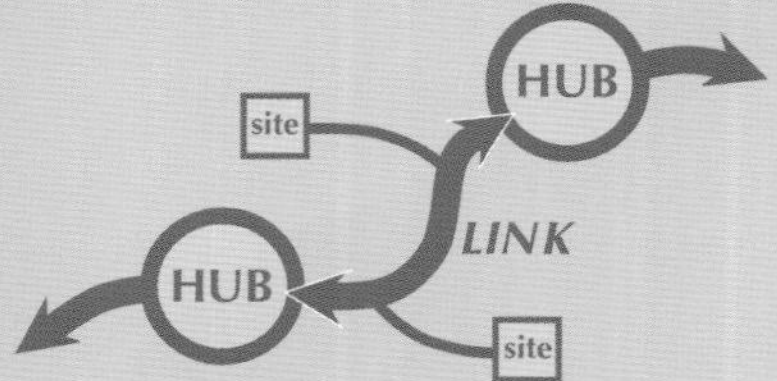

A greenways network is built around the concept of hubs and linkages. For the Florida Ecological Greenways Network, hubs represent large intact natural landscapes with high biological diversity. Linkages are linear corridors that connect hubs, allowing species migration and gene flow. Additional sites of importance can be linked into the overall network.

The Florida Greenways Commission began with a conceptual design for the greenways system. This design envisioned two complementary networks: an ecological network (green) connecting important natural landscape hubs, and a recreational/cultural network (purple) connecting population centers with important recreational open spaces and cultural and historic sites. The ecological network concept shown here ultimately led to the more refined ecological greenways network shown on the facing page.

Corridors for the Florida Ecological Greenways Network were identified by conducting a least-cost path analysis over suitability surfaces. The suitability surface, shown here in shades of blue, identifies the suitability of land uses as ecological linkages based primarily on land cover type. In this example, natural land cover types appear as darker blue and purple shades, while semi-natural lands such as tree plantations and pasture appear as lighter blue shades. Urban areas and other non-natural land uses are white. The model analyzes suitability as a "cost of travel," where darker colors represent lower costs, together with linear distance. The result is an optimal path for connecting two ecological hubs.

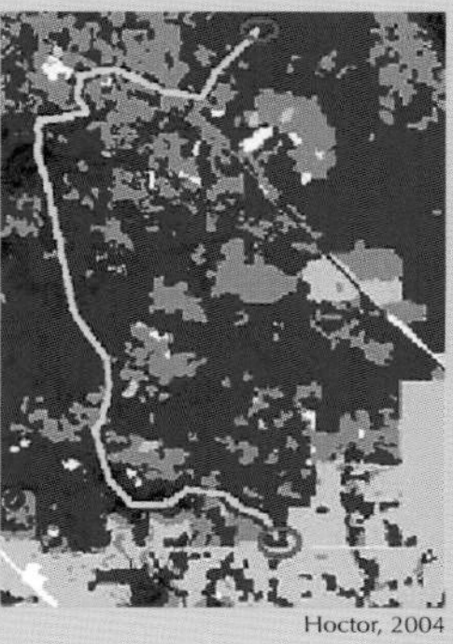

Hoctor, 2004

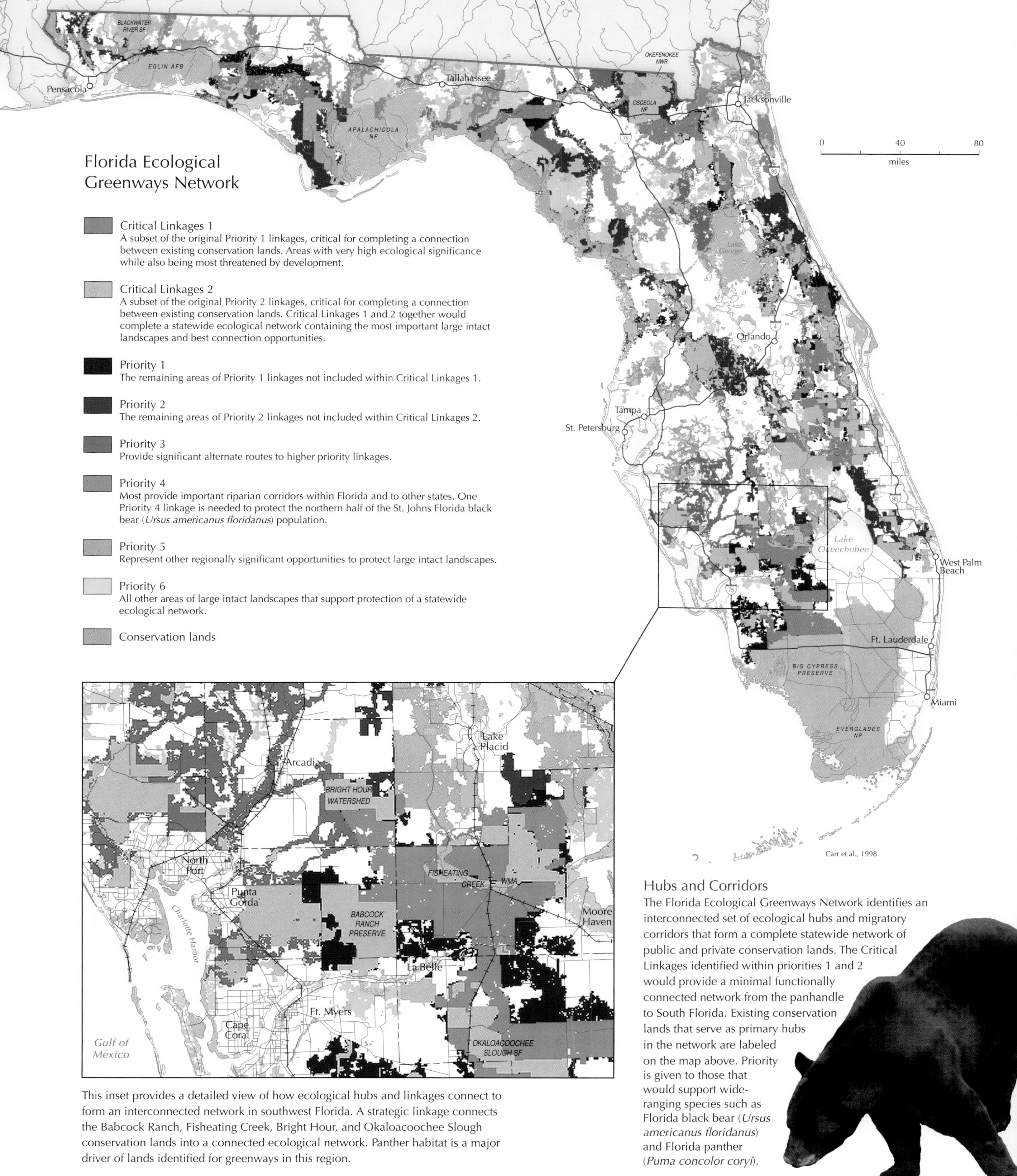
Florida Ecological Greenways Network
Critical Linkages 1
A subset of the original Priority 1 linkages, critical for completing a connection between existing conservation lands. Areas with very high ecological significance while also being most threatened by development.
Critical Linkages 2
A subset of the original Priority 2 linkages, critical for completing a connection between existing conservation lands. Critical Linkages 1 and 2 together would complete a statewide ecological network containing the most important large intact landscapes and best connection opportunities.
Priority 1
The remaining areas of Priority 1 linkages not included within Critical Linkages 1.
Priority 2
The remaining areas of Priority 2 linkages not included within Critical Linkages 2.
Priority 3
Provide significant alternate routes to higher priority linkages.
Priority 4
Most provide important riparian corridors within Florida and to other states. One Priority 4 linkage is needed to protect the northern half of the St. Johns Florida black bear (*Ursus americanus floridanus*) population.
Priority 5
Represent other regionally significant opportunities to protect large intact landscapes.
Priority 6
All other areas of large intact landscapes that support protection of a statewide ecological network.
Conservation lands
BLACKWATER RIVER SF
EGLIN AFB
Pensacola
APALACHICOLA NF
Tallahassee
OKEFENOKEE NWR
OSCEOLA NF
Jacksonville
0
40
80
miles
Lake George
Orlando
Tampa
St. Petersburg
Lake Okeechobee
West Palm Beach
Ft. Lauderdale
BIG CYPRESS PRESERVE
Miami
EVERGLADES NP
Carr et al., 1998
Arcadia
Lake Placid
BRIGHT HOUR WATERSHED
North Port
Punta Gorda
Charlotte Harbor
FISHEATING CREEK WMA
BABCOCK RANCH PRESERVE
Moore Haven
La Belle
Ft. Myers
Cape Coral
Gulf of Mexico
OKALOACOOCHEE SLOUGH SF
David Moynahan

This inset provides a detailed view of how ecological hubs and linkages connect to form an interconnected network in southwest Florida. A strategic linkage connects the Babcock Ranch, Fisheating Creek, Bright Hour, and Okaloacoochee Slough conservation lands into a connected ecological network. Panther habitat is a major driver of lands identified for greenways in this region.

Hubs and Corridors

The Florida Ecological Greenways Network identifies an interconnected set of ecological hubs and migratory corridors that form a complete statewide network of public and private conservation lands. The Critical Linkages identified within priorities 1 and 2 would provide a minimal functionally connected network from the panhandle to South Florida. Existing conservation lands that serve as primary hubs in the network are labeled on the map above. Priority is given to those that would support wide-ranging species such as Florida black bear (*Ursus americanus floridanus*) and Florida panther (*Puma concolor coryi*).

Critical Lands and Waters Identification Project

The Critical Lands and Waters Identification Project (CLIP) is a collection of spatial data that identify statewide priorities for a broad range of natural resources in Florida. CLIP was originally requested by the Century Commission for a Sustainable Florida in 2006 and has been developed through a collaborative effort between FNAI, the University of Florida GeoPlan Center and Center for Landscape and Conservation Planning, and the Florida Wildlife Commission (FWC). CLIP partners have relied upon a team of expert advisors from state and federal agencies, water management districts, NGOs, universities, and the private sector to provide consensus guidance on data compilation and model construction.

Florida is fortunate to have a variety of statewide conservation planning models already completed, including Strategic Habitat Conservation Areas, the Florida Ecological Greenways Network, and Rare Species Habitat Conservation Priorities. FNAI has also developed or compiled several statewide resource models to inform the Florida Forever program, including prioritizations for natural communities, surface waters, floodplain, wetlands, and aquifer recharge. The primary challenge for CLIP was to determine which existing models to include and how best to combine them into an overall set of priorities.

CLIP is organized into a set of core natural resource data layers, which are combined into functional resource categories and finally into an overall prioritization of natural resources. The combined CLIP priorities map (version 1.0) identifies five natural resource priority levels. The highest priority identifies approximately 8 million acres on private land. (Much of Priority 1 is found on existing conservation lands.) CLIP is an inventory of natural resource priorities; it is not a conservation plan. In particular, CLIP does not recommend that all CLIP high priorities be set aside as conservation lands. CLIP serves primarily as a decision support tool, providing a common set of data and priorities for decision makers at state and regional scales.

CLIP is informing a variety of planning efforts, including the FWC Cooperative Conservation Blueprint, as well as several regional and local plans. Future versions of CLIP will address additional resource issues, including marine and groundwater resources, water restoration priorities, and climate change.

Michael

CLIP was developed in consultation with the Technical Advisory Group (TAG) consisting of experts in Florida natural resources and/or Geographic Information Systems (GIS) data and analysis. All major decisions regarding data and analysis for CLIP were reached through TAG consensus.

Compatibility vs. Conflict

CLIP allows us to identify areas of potential conflict and opportunity around the state. Land uses compatible with natural resource priorities could be encouraged through conservation easements and landowner incentive programs. Areas of potential conflict could be the focus of proactive growth management or land acquisition efforts.

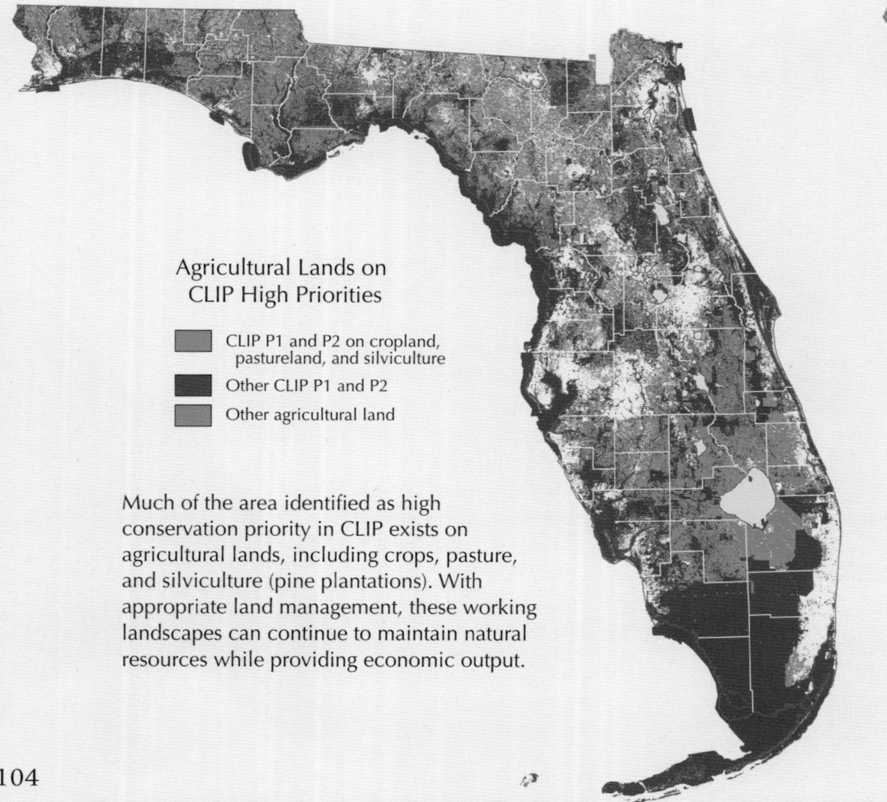

Much of the area identified as high conservation priority in CLIP exists on agricultural lands, including crops, pasture, and silviculture (pine plantations). With appropriate land management, these working landscapes can continue to maintain natural resources while providing economic output.

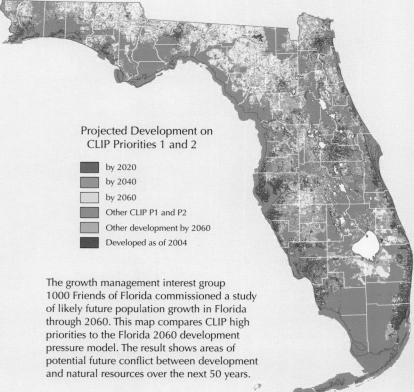

Projected Development on CLIP Priorities 1 and 2

- by 2020
- by 2040
- by 2060
- Other CLIP P1 and P2
- Other development by 2060
- Developed as of 2004

The growth management interest group 1000 Friends of Florida commissioned a study of likely future population growth in Florida through 2060. This map compares CLIP high priorities to the Florida 2060 development pressure model. The result shows areas of potential future conflict between development and natural resources over the next 50 years.

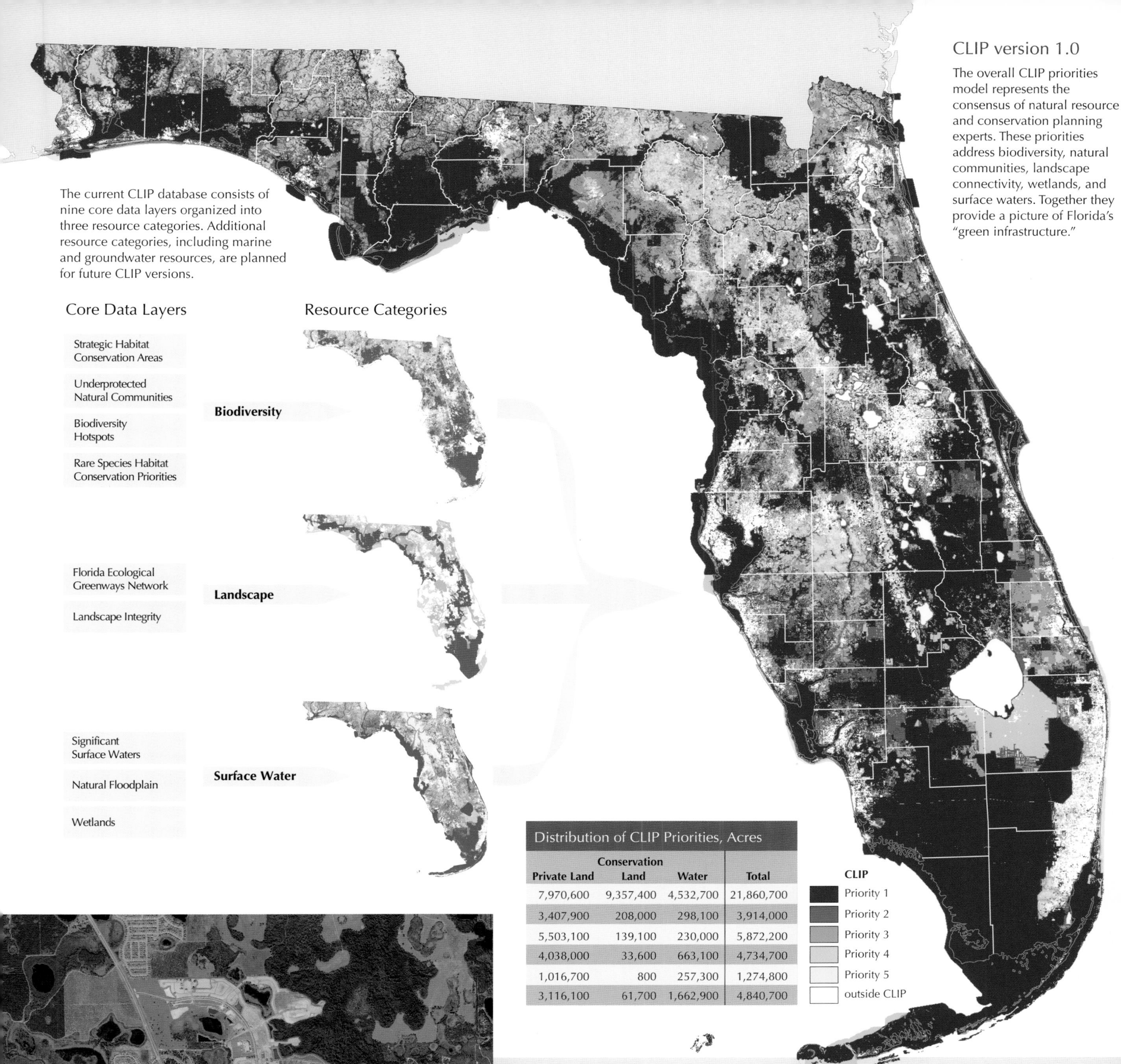

CLIP version 1.0

The overall CLIP priorities model represents the consensus of natural resource and conservation planning experts. These priorities address biodiversity, natural communities, landscape connectivity, wetlands, and surface waters. Together they provide a picture of Florida's "green infrastructure."

The current CLIP database consists of nine core data layers organized into three resource categories. Additional resource categories, including marine and groundwater resources, are planned for future CLIP versions.

Core Data Layers	Resource Categories
Strategic Habitat Conservation Areas Underprotected Natural Communities Biodiversity Hotspots Rare Species Habitat Conservation Priorities	**Biodiversity**
Florida Ecological Greenways Network Landscape Integrity	**Landscape**
Significant Surface Waters Natural Floodplain Wetlands	**Surface Water**

Distribution of CLIP Priorities, Acres

Private Land	Conservation Land	Water	Total
7,970,600	9,357,400	4,532,700	21,860,700
3,407,900	208,000	298,100	3,914,000
5,503,100	139,100	230,000	5,872,200
4,038,000	33,600	663,100	4,734,700
1,016,700	800	257,300	1,274,800
3,116,100	61,700	1,662,900	4,840,700

CLIP
- Priority 1
- Priority 2
- Priority 3
- Priority 4
- Priority 5
- outside CLIP

DOQQ

Development is increasingly encroaching on natural systems in Florida, but good design and development practices can improve compatibility between natural and built landscapes. The ultimate goal of CLIP is to help inform better land use decisions at the state, regional, and local levels.

State Archives of Florida

SFWMD

Water resource restoration is an important component of Florida's natural resource priorities that will be addressed in future versions of CLIP. One priority area would be restoration activities along the Kissimmee River.

Conservation Lands

The permanent protection of rare species and natural communities is of fundamental importance to maintaining Florida's biodiversity. To assist decision-makers in this work and to keep current the conservation status of species and communities, FNAI keeps track of lands where important aspects of biodiversity are formally protected and defines these areas as conservation lands. These managed conservation lands are the only areas where we can be assured of habitat or species protection over the long term.

Definition: For a property to be considered a conservation land by FNAI, a significant portion of the property must be undeveloped and retain most of the attributes one could expect it to have in its natural condition. In addition, the managing agency or organization must demonstrate a formal commitment to the conservation of the land in its natural condition, usually through a management plan.

FNAI maintains and continually updates its statewide database of conservation lands, which in 2010 included more than 2000 different properties formally managed for conservation. The database tracks lands managed by federal, state, and local governmental agencies, Florida's five water management districts, and private conservation organizations. FNAI relies on the cooperative efforts of all of these managing entities to keep the statewide database current. The data provided are integrated into a standardized data set available to the public on the FNAI website.

Florida's conservation lands range in size from Everglades National Park, which encompasses over 1.5 million acres, to small local preserves less than an acre. Each of these managed areas contains natural resources that contribute to protection of the state's biodiversity. Collectively, these conservation lands represent 29% of Florida's land mass.

Federal managed areas include national forests, national parks, national wildlife refuges, and military lands. Conservation lands managed by state agencies include state parks, wildlife management areas, and state forests. The water management districts are responsible for managing conservation areas and monitoring conservation easements they acquire. Counties and cities throughout the state maintain local preserves and parks used for passive recreation. Private nonprofits such as The Nature Conservancy and Audubon of Florida own and manage a variety of sanctuaries and preserves.

Florida Conservation Lands February 2011

	Area in acres[1,2,3]
Federally Managed Conservation Lands	4,044,389
State Managed Conservation Lands[4]	5,426,669
Locally Managed Conservation Lands	468,992
Total State, Federal, and Local Conservation Lands	**9,940,050**
Privately Managed Conservation Lands	183,582
Land Area of State of Florida	34,721,280[5]
Percentage of FL in Federally Managed Conservation Lands	11.6%
Percentage of FL in State Managed Conservation Lands	15.6%
Percentage of FL in Locally Managed Conservation Lands	1.3%

[1] Acreages are counted once under the primary managing agency even though there may be several owners and/or managers. For this reason, total acres for some agencies may be higher than the acres to which they hold title and others may be lower.

[2] Numbers include a total of 629,104 acres of less-than-fee properties (6.2% of total conservation lands).

[3] Acreages listed include terrestrial wetlands such as the Everglades but exclude 3,701,172 acres of submerged marine, lake, or river bottom (such as state aquatic preserves or Florida Bay) that are part of certain managed areas.

[4] This category includes lands managed by state agencies and the five water management districts in Florida.

[5] Source: *Atlas of Florida*, 1996. E.A. Fernald and E.D. Purdum, eds. University Press of Florida, Gainesville, FL.

Conservation Easements

Agencies throughout Florida are pursuing an increasing number of conservation easements on private lands. This is an innovative and flexible method of protecting biodiversity, whereby the landowner continues to manage the property but sells or donates certain development rights to the agency that holds and monitors the easement.

Conservation easements protect critical resources while maintaining local tax revenue and an economic contribution from the land, as private landowners become partners for conservation. FNAI's statewide database on conservation lands tracks permanent conservation easements acquired by governmental agencies and nonprofit conservation organizations.

In Feb. 2011, the database included 251 easements totaling 629,104 acres (6% of all conservation lands). Since its inception in 2001, the Florida Forever Program has protected 164,955 acres through conservation easements.

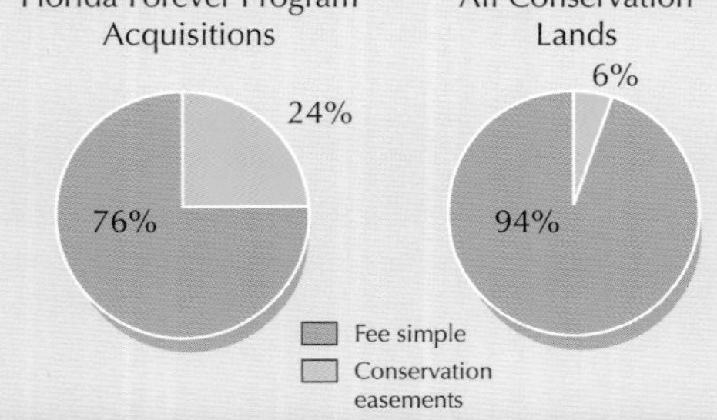

Case Study: Nokuse Plantation

Nokuse Plantation in Walton and Washington counties is a prime example of how conservation easements contribute to preservation of biodiversity. Two large tracts owned by M. C. Davis were placed under easements with the state in 2004 and 2005. The state monitors the conservation easements and supports the landowner's efforts to protect natural resources.

Matt Aresco

Nokuse Plantation serves as an important link to adjacent public lands that together provide a biological corridor and an opportunity to conduct landscape-level conservation. Biologists employed at Nokuse are conducting ecosystem restoration projects that include prescribed burns on the pine flatwoods and removal of invasive exotic species.

Matt Aresco

In a pilot project with Florida Fish and Wildlife Conservation Commission, biologists are relocating gopher tortoises (*Gopherus polyphemus*) from development sites across the state to suitable habitats on Nokuse Plantation. The goal is to determine the most efficient and successful methods of tortoise relocation and to increase the population density of this keystone species at Nokuse.

Conservation Lands by Manager

Federal
State
Local
Private

March, 2011

0 40
miles

BLACKWATER RIVER SF
EGLIN AFB
Pensacola
GULF ISLANDS NATIONAL SEASHORE
NOKUSE PLANTATION CONSERVATION EASEMENTS
APALACHICOLA BLUFFS & RAVINES PRESERVE
Tallahassee
APALACHICOLA NF
TATE'S HELL SF
ST. MARKS NWR
BIG BEND WMA
OSCEOLA NF
Jacksonville
MATANZAS SF
LOWER SUWANNEE NWR
OCALA NF
CANAVERAL NATIONAL SEASHORE
CHASSAHOWITZKA NWR
Orlando
MERRITT ISLAND NWR
STARKEY WILDERNESS PRESERVE
Tampa
St. Petersburg
LOXAHATCHEE SLOUGH NATURAL AREA
T. MABRY CARLTON, JR. MEMORIAL RESERVE
Lake Okeechobee
West Palm Beach
FISHEATING CREEK CONSERVATION EASEMENT
Ft. Lauderdale
BIG CYPRESS N PRESERVE
Miami
FAKAHATCHEE STRAND PRESERVE STATE PARK
BISCAYNE NATIONAL PARK
EVERGLADES NATIONAL PARK
GREAT WHITE HERON NWR
KEY WEST NWR

Don Herring

Eglin Air Force Base

Eglin Air Force Base, owned and managed by the U.S. Air Force, is the largest forested military reservation in North America (463,448 acres). Extending 51 miles east-west and 19 miles north-south, Eglin contains 35 natural communities and a wide diversity of rare plant and animal species. Most of the base is forested with sandhills, but there are also wetlands, flatwoods, and baygalls. Eglin has one of the four largest remaining populations of red-cockaded woodpeckers.

Pam Anderson

Apalachicola Bluffs and Ravines Preserve

The Apalachicola Bluffs and Ravines Preserve protects one of the few areas in the U.S. where steephead ravines exist. Owned and managed by The Nature Conservancy, this 6,295-acre preserve is a paleorefugium harboring plant and animal species more commonly found in the Appalachian Mountains. In addition to sheltered slopes and ravines, the preserve contains some high-quality sandhills and, since 1985, has been the site of a project to restore the uplands with historical longleaf-wiregrass vegetation.

David Moynahan

Ocala National Forest

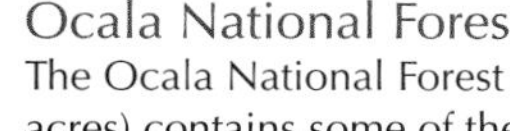

The Ocala National Forest (383,689 acres) contains some of the highest quality sandhills in Central Florida and the largest contiguous scrub in the state, home to rare species such as red-cockaded woodpecker, Florida scrub-jay, sand skink, and Florida bonamia. It also contains freshwater springs and provides important recharge for the Floridan aquifer. Owned and managed by the U.S. Forest Service, this is the oldest national forest east of the Mississippi River.

Michael Wisenbaker

Fisheating Creek/Lykes Brothers Conservation Easement

Fisheating Creek/Lykes Brothers Conservation Easement encompasses 41,596 acres in Glades County. The Florida Fish and Wildlife Conservation Commission is responsible for monitoring the easement, which was acquired by the state in 1999. Lykes Brothers, Inc., retains title to the property and has management responsibility. The easement covers extensive areas of dry prairie, wet prairie, slough, freshwater marsh, and pine flatwoods interspersed with numerous depression and basin marshes. Red-cockaded woodpecker, Florida scrub-jay, and several rare plants occur here.

©Bill Boothe

Fakahatchee Strand Preserve State Park

Fakahatchee Strand Preserve State Park, managed by Florida's Division of Recreation and Parks, protects a linear swamp forest that harbors diverse orchids and other rare plants. This 77,116-acre park is also a haven for rare animals including the Florida panther and Florida black bear. It encompasses a diversity of habitats and forest types from the wetter swamps and prairies to the drier islands of tropical hardwood hammock and pine rockland.

Dan Hipes

Starkey Wilderness Preserve

Starkey Wilderness Preserve is dominated by a complex mosaic of upland natural communities, including pine flatwoods, sandhill, and scrub. The 19,548-acre park also includes swamps and two blackwater streams, the Anclote and Pithlachascotee rivers. Southwest Florida Water Management District is the primary owner and land manager. Rare species seen here include gopher tortoise, Florida scrub-jay, and pondspice.

Jason Hedegard

Loxahatchee Slough Natural Area

Loxahatchee Slough Natural Area (12,838 acres) is the largest and most diverse of the sites acquired and managed as conservation land by Palm Beach County. The slough is a regionally significant wetland and the historical headwaters of the Loxahatchee National Wild and Scenic River. The preserve contains high-quality freshwater wetlands that provide habitat for rare birds such as snail kite, wood stork and Florida sandhill crane. Several listed plant species occur here.

History of Land Acquisition

The history of Florida's conservation lands begins with an auspicious moment for the nation's conservation history as well: in 1903, at the urging of conservationists Paul Kroegel, Frank Chapman, and William Dutcher, President Theodore Roosevelt established the United States' first national wildlife refuge at Pelican Island, near Sebastian in Indian River County. Other federal acquisitions followed resulting in national forests, national parks, national preserves, and more national wildlife refuges. By 1947, when the federal government established Everglades National Park, the majority of today's federal conservation lands in Florida were in place. Environmental land acquisition by the federal government has continued since then, primarily through the Land and Water Conservation Fund, but for the last 50 years state government has taken the leading role in Florida, with increasing contributions from local governments.

Before 1963, environmental land acquisition in Florida was somewhat opportunistic, with no primary program dedicated to the purpose. Yet, from 1926 to 1963 state agencies acquired through purchase and donation more than 500,000 acres of conservation lands comprising approximately 307,000 acres of state forests, 120,000 acres of state wildlife management areas, and 99,000 acres of state parks. The first strategic effort to acquire conservation lands began with the Outdoor Recreation and Conservation Program, enacted by the legislature in 1963. The primary focus of this program was to acquire state parks and recreation areas, based on a regularly updated statewide outdoor recreation plan.

Florida's environmental land acquisition efforts received a significant boost in funding in 1972, with the creation of the Environmentally Endangered Lands (EEL) program. The increased funding allowed the EEL program to acquire larger tracts of land with landscape-scale ecological values; most would be managed as state preserves and wildlife management areas. With the creation of the Conservation and Recreation Lands (CARL) program in 1979 came several innovations to state land acquisition that have carried over to successor programs: a competitive land acquisition list, a multiagency advisory body that selected and prioritized the acquisition list, and incentives that encouraged collaborative acquisitions, especially in partnership with local governments. Additional programs quickly came on-line with the Save Our Coasts (1980) and Save Our Rivers (1981) programs, focusing on beach access and water management and supply.

The landmark event in the history of Florida's conservation lands came in 1990 with passage of the Preservation 2000 Act, which tripled funding of the CARL program. P-2000 was the most ambitious conservation land acquisition program in the United States, and its success led to the Florida Forever program in 2000 (re-authorized in 2008). Through P-2000 and Florida Forever, the state of Florida has committed $300 million per year for 18 years toward conservation lands.

Economics of Acquisition

Florida's state-level land acquisition programs have acquired more than 3.7 million acres of conservation lands since 1963. Despite similar funding levels to Preservation 2000, Florida Forever faced steeply rising real estate values through much of the last decade, resulting in considerably fewer acres acquired.

Acres Purchased through Acquisition Program
(Million Acres)

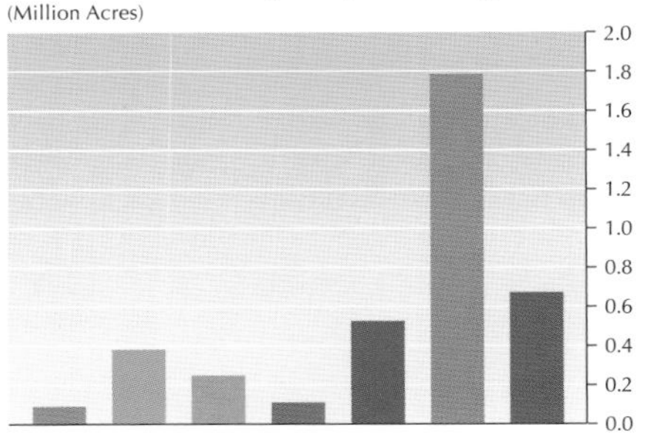

Cost per Acre by Acquisition Program
(Average Dollars per Acre)

0 $1,000 $2,000 $3,000 $4,000 $5,000

Gary Knight

Ocala National Forest

Gary Knight

Myakka River State Park

Paul Russo

Everglades National Park

1900 1910 1920 1930 1940 1950

Pelican Island National Wildlife Refuge, 1903

Ocala National Forest, 1908

Osceola National Forest, 1931

Torreya State Park, 1935
Florida Caverns State Park, 1935
Fort Clinch State Park, 1935
Highlands Hammock State Park, 1935

Apalachicola National Forest, 1936
O'leno State Park, 1936
Gold Head Branch State Park, 1936
Hillsborough River State Park, 1936
Myakka River State Park, 1936
Pine Log State Forest, 1936

Babcock-Webb Wildlife Management Area, 1941

Everglades National Park, 1947
Corbett Wildlife Management Area, 1947

Gary Knight

❶ Tarkiln Bayou Preserve State Park
Program: P2000
Superb examples of flatwoods and wet prairie.

Dan Hipes

❷ Tate's Hell State Forest
Program: P2000
Large landscape important to preserving the water quality of Apalachicola Bay.

Gary Knight

❸ Gold Head Branch State Park
Program: Outdoor Recreation and Conservation Program
Old-growth longleaf pine sandhill.

Gary Knight

❹ Wekiva Springs State Park
Program: Outdoor Recreation and Conservation Program
First-magnitude spring and spring-run stream surrounded by high-quality sandhill near Orlando.

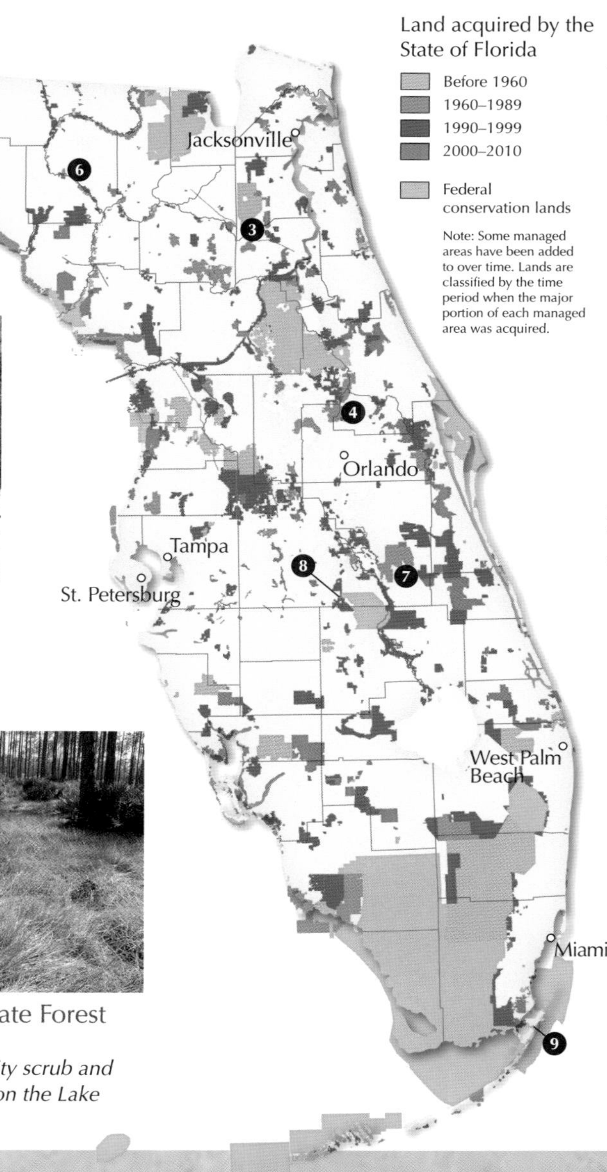

Land acquired by the State of Florida

- Before 1960
- 1960–1989
- 1990–1999
- 2000–2010
- Federal conservation lands

Note: Some managed areas have been added to over time. Lands are classified by the time period when the major portion of each managed area was acquired.

Gary Knight

❼ Three Lakes Wildlife Management Area
Program: EEL
Large, highly diverse landscape home to many rare species.

Brenda Herring

❺ St Joseph Bay State Buffer Preserve
Program: Florida Forever
Coastal flatwoods and wet prairie helping preserve the water quality of St Joseph Bay.

Edwin McCook

❻ Suwannee River Tracts
Program: SOR
Lands adjacent to the Suwannee River.

Gary Knight

❾ Key Largo Hammock Botanical State Park
Program: CARL
The largest, highest quality tropical hammock in the continental US.

Gary Knight

❽ Lake Wales Ridge State Forest
Program: CARL
Some of the highest quality scrub and associated communities on the Lake Wales Ridge.

Gary Knight

Topsail Hill Preserve State Park

Katy NeSmith

Babcock Ranch

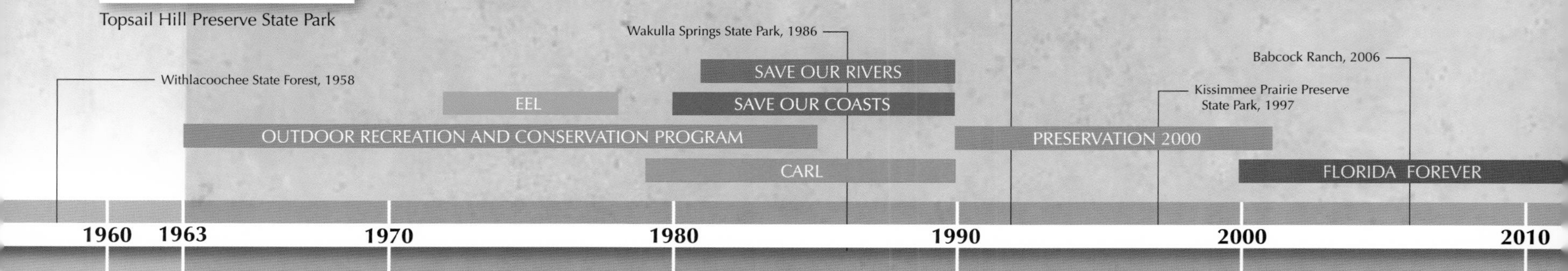

Withlacoochee State Forest, 1958
Wakulla Springs State Park, 1986
Goethe State Forest, 1992
Topsail Hill Preserve State Park, 1992
Kissimmee Prairie Preserve State Park, 1997
Babcock Ranch, 2006

EEL
OUTDOOR RECREATION AND CONSERVATION PROGRAM
SAVE OUR RIVERS
SAVE OUR COASTS
CARL
PRESERVATION 2000
FLORIDA FOREVER

1960 1963 1970 1980 1990 2000 2010

Conservation Programs

Conservation efforts by federal, state, and local governments occur on three major fronts: land acquisition, landowner incentive programs, and regulatory procedures. In Florida, the most prominent effort is the Florida Forever environmental land acquisition program. Notwithstanding recent budget cuts, Florida has led the nation in funding for land acquisition. Over the past 20 years, Florida has acquired more land for conservation than the federal government has acquired across the United States. Land acquisition includes both fee simple (outright purchase) and less-than-fee conservation easements, which allow land owners to maintain an economic return from the land and keeps the land on local tax rolls.

Many incentive programs are also operational in Florida. Both the U.S. Fish and Wildlife Service and the Florida Fish and Wildlife Conservation Commission offer technical assistance and grants to private landowners to encourage good management of natural resources on their lands. Incentives to land developers include federal Safe Harbor programs and state sector planning and Rural Lands Stewardship efforts, which are intended to encourage conservation of important natural areas as part of large-scale commercial and residential developments.

Regulation may take the form of a permitting process for water use or impacts to wetlands, mandatory local government comprehensive land use planning, and restrictions to impacts on endangered species.

Notable Conservation Programs in Florida

Name	Source	Notes
Land Acquisition		
Local government acquisition programs	Local (counties & cities)	>$2 billion since 1972 for acquisitions & easements
Land & Water Conservation Fund	Federal (National Park Service)	$125 million since 1965 for acquisitions & easements
Coastal & Estuarine Land Conservation Program	Federal (NOAA)	$217 million 2002-08 for acquisitions & easements
Incentives		
Safe Harbor Agreements	Federal (USFWS)	Avoid future regulation; technical assistance
Forest Legacy Program	Federal (USFS)	$2.7 million 2005-08 for tax incentives and easements
Wetlands Reserve Program	Federal (NRCS)	$67 million 2003-07 for easements and restoration
Mitigation Banking	Federal/State (multiple agencies)	Mitigation credits purchased to offset impacts
Regulatory		
Endangered Species Act	Federal (USFWS)	Permits required for "taking" of listed species
Comprehensive Land Use Planning	State (DCA)	Compulsory for all FL cities and counties
Wetlands Permitting	Federal (USACE) & State (DEP & WMDs)	Required for alterations of surface waters, wetlands, or stormwater runoff

Defenders of Wildlife, 2007

Acquisition Programs

A variety of acquisition, incentive, and regulatory programs contribute to conservation in Florida. As of 2010, 28 counties and 21 cities have passed local land acquisition programs that leverage state dollars to extend acquisition beyond Florida Forever. The federal Natural Resources Conservation Service and Florida's Division of Forestry both offer easement programs to maintain rural working landscapes, a benefit for agriculture and forestry as well as conservation.

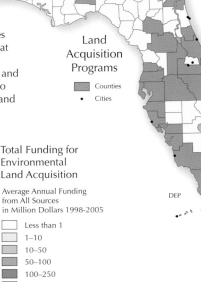

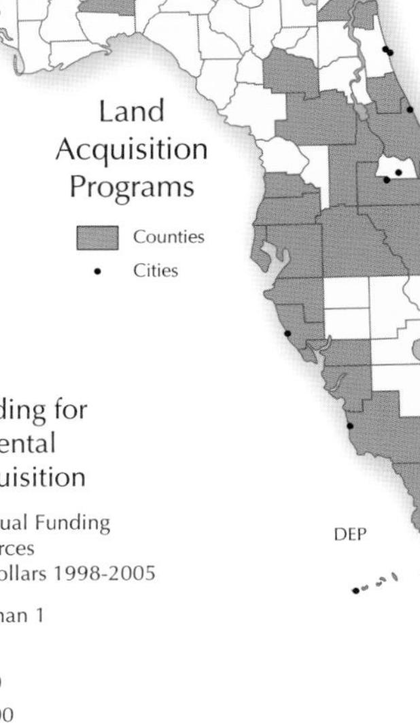

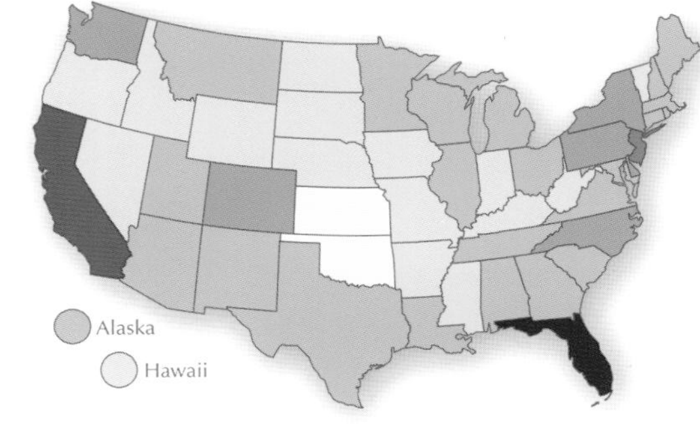

Total Funding for Environmental Land Acquisition

Average Annual Funding from All Sources in Million Dollars 1998-2005

- Less than 1
- 1–10
- 10–50
- 50–100
- 100–250
- 250–450
- More than 450

Trust for Public Land

Economic Benefits of Conservation

Conserving natural resources provides substantial economic benefits to Florida. A 2008 study by Defenders of Wildlife evaluated the conservation values provided by ten representative conservation lands and found that these sites provided, on average, more than $1.8 billion per year in economic benefits. The ten sites totaled about 379,000 acres, a little more than 4% of the state's conservation lands inventory. The Nature Conservancy issued a report in 2009 that outlines a variety of benefits of land conservation in the following categories:

Dan Hipes

Tourism and Outdoor Recreation

More than 65% of Florida's 80 million visitors in 2007 participated in nature-based activities. Outdoor recreation activities contributed more than $13 billion to Florida's economy in 2006.

Carolyn Kindell

Agriculture

The Florida Forever program has helped preserve more than 150,000 acres of working agricultural lands. Many rare species such as Florida panther, gopher tortoise, and Florida sandhill crane can co-exist with low-intensity agriculture such as ranching and timber operations.

David Moynahan

Water Resources

Maintaining natural areas in springsheds and adjacent to surface waters helps protect water supply and quality, and is typically cheaper than water treatment and restoration efforts.

David Moynahan

Coastal Communities

Florida's natural coastal resources provide more than $11 billion per year in storm protection benefits.

FDACS

Climate Change

Florida forestry and agriculture were estimated to contribute more than $340 million annually toward offsets of greenhouse gas emissions.

USGS

Green Infrastructure

Studies have shown that conservation lands improve adjacent land values, limit infrastructure-intensive urban sprawl, and improve quality of life of nearby communities.

Florida Forever: How Florida Manages the Nation's Premier Land Acquisition Program

Funding and Distribution

A conservation program as large as Florida Forever requires careful planning and rigorous evaluation to ensure that the state is achieving the best results for its investment. A willing seller program, Florida Forever attempts to balance strategic focus on priority resources with opportunities for partnerships and bargain purchases.

Florida Forever dollars are distributed across several programs. The state Board of Trustees (the governor and cabinet–BOT) makes purchases based on recommendations from the Acquisition and Restoration Council, staffed by the Florida Department of Environmental Protection. Those purchases typically become state parks, state forests, and wildlife management areas. Florida's five water management districts also purchase lands for water resource protection. The Florida Communities Trust, administered by the Florida Department of Community Affairs, awards grants to cities and counties for local parks and preserves.

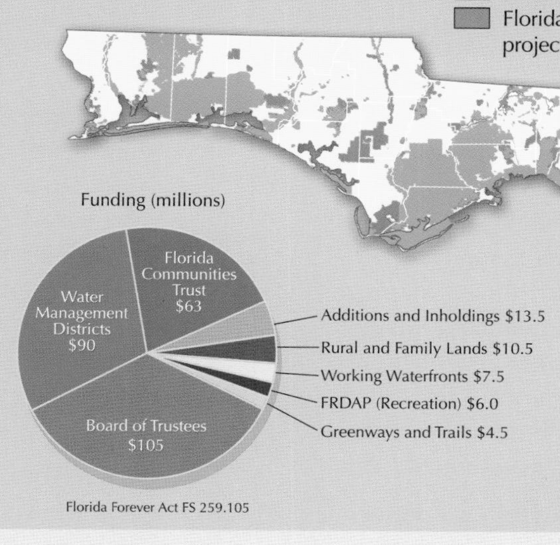

Florida Forever Act FS 259.105

Existing conservation lands
Florida Forever (Board of Trustees) projects, August 2010

Acquisition and Restoration Council (ARC)

The Acquisition and Restoration Council comprises five private citizen members and representatives from the Department of Environmental Protection, Florida Fish and Wildlife Conservation Commission, Division of Forestry, Division of Historical Resources, and the Department of Community Affairs. ARC has responsibility for the evaluation, selection, and ranking of state land acquisition projects on the Florida Forever priority list, as well as the review of management plans and land uses for all state-owned conservation lands.

The Acquisition and Restoration Council in session.

Gary Knight

Staff to ARC conduct an on-site evaluation of the Panther Glades project in Hendry County.

William Kerr

Florida Forever's Land Acquisition Process

The intricate process by which land is acquired for conservation through the Florida Forever program may be accomplished in as quickly as 13 months. (The actual time may be longer depending on the length of the negotiation process because Florida Forever is a willing seller program.) An essential part of the process to ensure the state is efficiently meeting its conservation goals is the six-month evaluation cycle, which involves review by a team of scientists, resource experts, and the Acquisition and Restoration Council. The acquisition cycle is designed to ensure the state is achieving its goals cost-effectively.

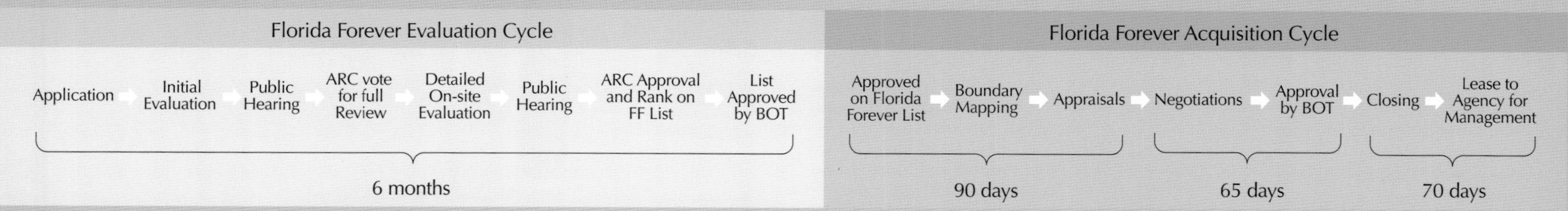

Florida Forever's Conservation Needs Assessment

FNAI has conducted a statewide analysis of natural resource conservation priorities for the Florida Forever program. The needs assessment is based in part on data shown throughout this atlas, and includes GIS data layers for rare species habitat, natural communities, ecological greenways, large landscapes, significant surface waters, natural floodplain, functional wetlands, aquifer recharge, coastal resources, cultural resources, and sustainable forestry. The needs assessment also establishes baseline protection status for each natural resource and provides a tool for tracking progress in resource acquisition. For each ARC project evaluation cycle, FNAI provides an evaluation of all Florida Forever Board of Trustees projects as well as new proposals based on the needs assessment. This evaluation aids ARC in determining how to prioritize projects for acquisition.

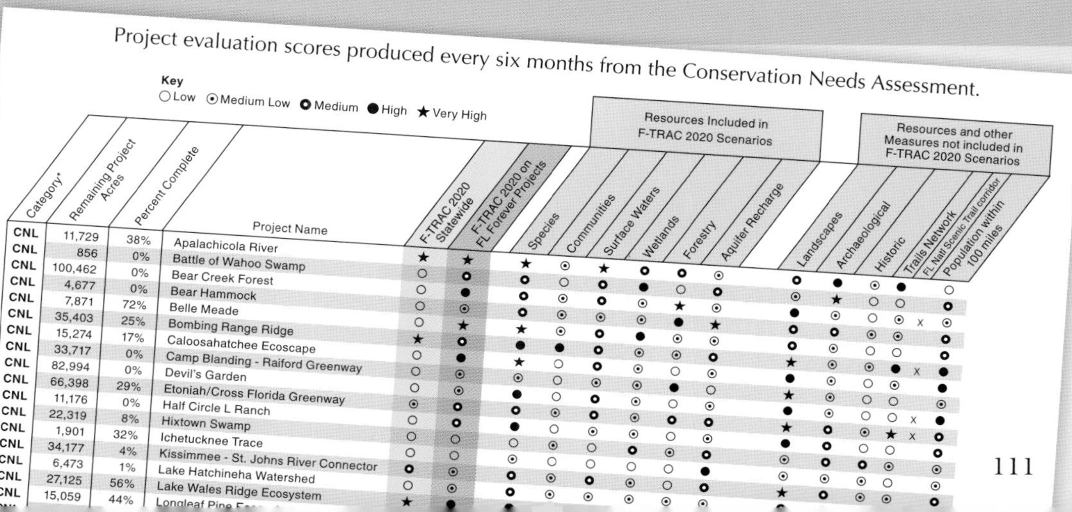

Project evaluation scores produced every six months from the Conservation Needs Assessment.

Key
○ Low ⊙ Medium Low ◉ Medium ● High ★ Very High

Category*	Remaining Project Acres	Percent Complete	Project Name	F-TRAC 2020 Statewide	F-TRAC 2020 on FL Forever Projects	Species	Communities	Surface Waters	Wetlands	Forestry	Aquifer Recharge	Landscapes	Archaeological	Historic	Trails Network	FL Nat'l Scenic Trail corridor	Population within 100 miles
						Resources Included in F-TRAC 2020 Scenarios						Resources and other Measures not included in F-TRAC 2020 Scenarios					
CNL	11,729	38%	Apalachicola River	★	★	★	⊙	★	◉	◉	⊙	◉	●	⊙	●		○
CNL	856	0%	Battle of Wahoo Swamp	○	◉	◉	○	◉	●	○	◉	⊙	★	○	○		◉
CNL	100,462	0%	Bear Creek Forest	○	●	◉	⊙	◉	⊙	★	⊙	●	⊙	○	⊙	x	⊙
CNL	4,677	0%	Bear Hammock	○	⊙	◉	⊙	⊙	⊙	●	★	◉	◉	⊙	⊙		◉
CNL	7,871	72%	Belle Meade	○	★	★	⊙	◉	●	⊙	⊙	◉	⊙	○	○		◉
CNL	35,403	25%	Bombing Range Ridge	★	◉	●	●	◉	⊙	⊙	◉	★	⊙	⊙	●	x	●
CNL	15,274	17%	Caloosahatchee Ecoscape	○	●	★	○	◉	⊙	○	⊙	●	⊙	○	⊙		●
CNL	33,717	0%	Camp Blanding - Raiford Greenway	○	⊙	⊙	○	⊙	⊙	●	○	★	⊙	○	○		⊙
CNL	82,994	0%	Devil's Garden	○	⊙	●	○	◉	⊙	○	⊙	●	⊙	○	○	x	●
CNL	66,398	29%	Etoniah/Cross Florida Greenway	⊙	◉	◉	⊙	◉	⊙	◉	◉	★	◉	⊙	★	x	◉
CNL	11,176	0%	Half Circle L Ranch	○	◉	●	○	⊙	⊙	○	⊙	●	◉	○	○		◉
CNL	22,319	8%	Hixtown Swamp	○	○	○	⊙	○	◉	⊙	◉	⊙	◉	◉	⊙		⊙
CNL	1,901	32%	Ichetucknee Trace	○	○	⊙	○	○	○	○	●	⊙	⊙	⊙	○		⊙
CNL	34,177	4%	Kissimmee - St. Johns River Connector	◉	⊙	◉	⊙	◉	⊙	○	◉	★	◉	⊙	⊙		◉
CNL	6,473	1%	Lake Hatchineha Watershed	○	⊙	◉	⊙	⊙	⊙	⊙	⊙	[illegible]					
CNL	27,125	56%	Lake Wales Ridge Ecosystem	★	●	[illegible]											
CNL	15,059	44%	Longleaf Pine E[illegible]														

Prescribed Fire

Like sunshine and rain, fire is essential to Florida's environment. Before modern land uses fragmented natural ecosystems, fires frequently swept across Florida's landscape, keeping natural pinelands, marshes, and prairies open and understory vegetation low and continually regenerating. Fire intensity was low, unlike the very damaging, high-intensity wildfires that sometimes occur today. Shaped by this history, many of Florida's plants and animals depend on habitats maintained by frequent, low-intensity fires. Today, prescribed fires—also known as controlled burns—are needed to mimic this process and keep our natural ecosystems healthy.

Prescribed burning is the application of fire "in accordance with a written prescription for vegetative fuels under specified environmental conditions while following appropriate precautionary measures that ensure that the fire is confined to a predetermined area to accomplish the planned fire or land-management objectives" (*F.S.* 590.125). Prescribed fires in Florida are regulated under the Department of Agriculture and Consumer Services' Division of Forestry (FDOF) burn authorization program.

Florida leads the nation in prescribed fire law, training, and application. *Florida Statutes* Chapter 590 and *Florida Administrative Code* Chapter 5I-2 are administered by FDOF and govern the use of prescribed fire and all open burning in Florida. On average, FDOF issues 120,000 burn authorizations a year, allowing people and agencies to treat over 2 million acres with fire. Although modern out-of-control wildfires are often highly publicized, they bear no resemblance to the well-regulated, authorized burns that take place throughout Florida every year.

FDOF data from 1981 to 2009 show that lightning was responsible for 17% of the wildfires in Florida and 34% of the total acres burned by wildfires. Humans caused the remaining 83% of the wildfires. Of the human-caused wildfires, a tiny fraction, one third of one percent, was related to authorized burns.

Prescribed fire is the most cost-effective tool used by Florida's conservation land managers to promote ecosystem health and to reduce hazardous fuel buildups, thus protecting homes and nature from damaging wildfires. Other uses of prescribed fire that help maintain Florida's native biodiversity include disease control in pines, range management, and preservation of endangered plants and animals.

A Summary of Florida's Prescribed Fire Process

PREPARATION (months to weeks before burn)

Florida Park Service

1. Training

Certified prescribed burners have a high level of training and expertise. In addition to intensive coursework, field experience with fire is required. As of 2010, there are over 1,700 certified prescribed burn managers in Florida.

Florida Park Service

2. Write a prescription

For each burn unit, the burn manager writes a detailed prescription specifying the purpose for the burn and the criteria for starting, controlling, and extinguishing the fire. It shows the fire barriers that will prevent the spread of fire outside the unit and outlines specific weather conditions, such as wind speeds and directions, soil and vegetation moisture content, that must be met to maintain safety, keep smoke away from sensitive areas, and achieve the burn's purpose. It outlines the number of persons and equipment needed, the "firing" method (drip torch, helicopter) and firing pattern (where and how to light), among many other details.

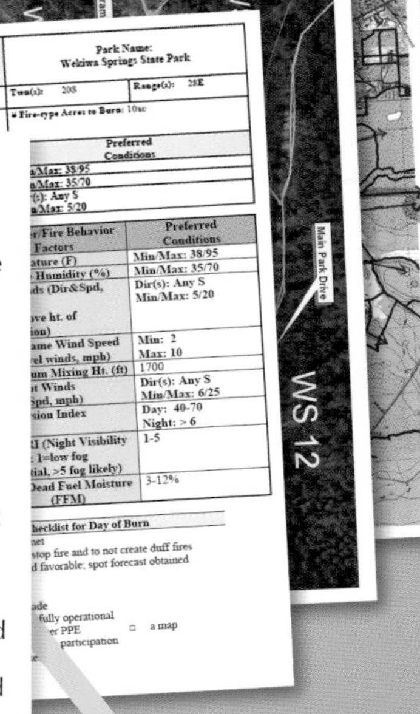

3. Prepare the burn unit

In advance of the burn, the manager ensures the unit is bounded on all sides by adequate fire barriers. These typically include roads, wetlands filled with water, or raked, disked, or plowed fire lines of exposed mineral soil lacking any fuels. These fire barriers are designed to contain the fire that is burned according to prescription.

Florida Park Service

Katy NeSmith

4. Watch the weather

Keep note of when conditions are "within prescription." Although burns may be scheduled weeks in advance, it is only during the week of a burn that weather conditions are known, and only on the day of the burn that site conditions are known; prescribed burners must be flexible.

Paul Russo

Florida Park Service

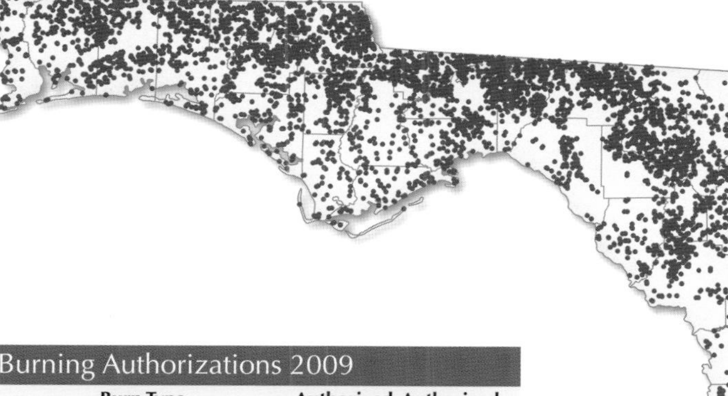

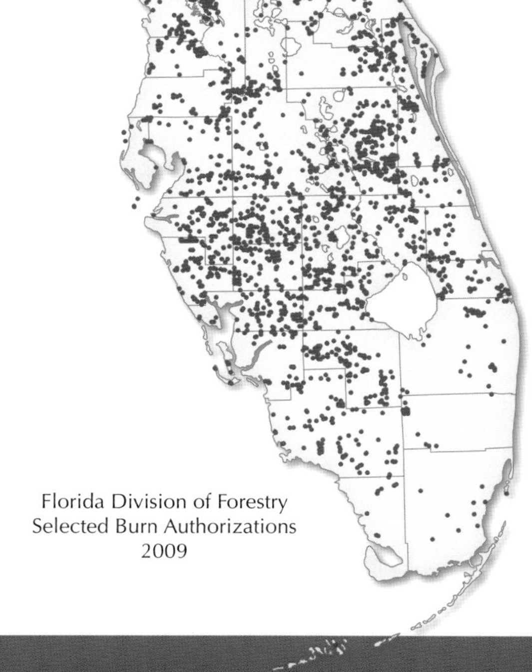

Burning Authorizations 2009

Burn Type	Authorized Fires	Authorized Acres
Agricultural–Pasture	**24,202**	**300,153**
Agricultural–Range Management	**989**	**87,258**
Agricultural–Stubble (post-harvest)	1,645	4,791
Agricultural–Sugarcane	10,089	401,827
Agricultural–Citrus	10,756	845
Land clearing–residential and non-residential	27,046	5,729
Silvicultural–Disease control	**66**	**1,095**
Silvicultural–Ecological	**1,476**	**415,816**
Silvicultural–Hazard removal	**5,254**	**927,151**
Silvicultural–Other	**0**	**0**
Silvicultural–Prior to seed	**162**	**1,610**
Silvicultural–Site preparation	**1,150**	**34,743**
Silvicultural–Wildlife	**448**	**113,656**
Total	83,283	2,294,674

Bold = burns shown in statewide map. Data exclude 128,466 pile burns.

APPLICATION (day of burn)

Florida Division of Forestry

5. Obtain authorization

The Florida Division of Forestry is responsible for issuing prescribed burning authorizations and systematically evaluates each burn request. The prescribed burn manager must contact FDOF on the morning of the burn for authorization.

Florida Park Service

6. Team Briefing

Check weather and site conditions. Whether or not a prescribed fire can occur is confirmed only the day of the burn when the site conditions are measured and the day's weather forecast for the site is evaluated. Trained prescribed burn personnel and necessary equipment are gathered for final briefing and equipment checks.

7. Burn

Test site weather and fuel conditions again. If not within prescription, cancel the burn. If within the prescription, and all requirements are met, then station crew members in designated positions with specific jobs to do during the burn. This includes weather monitors, fire monitors, ignitors, line workers, and equipment operators. Weather conditions and fire behavior are carefully monitored throughout the burn.

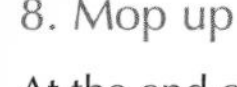

Florida Park Service

8. Mop up

At the end of the burn, the crew works to extinguish or ensure containment of any residual pockets of fire and to reduce residual smoke. Unless special authorization is given, the fire must discontinue spreading one hour after sunset.

EVALUATION (days to months after)

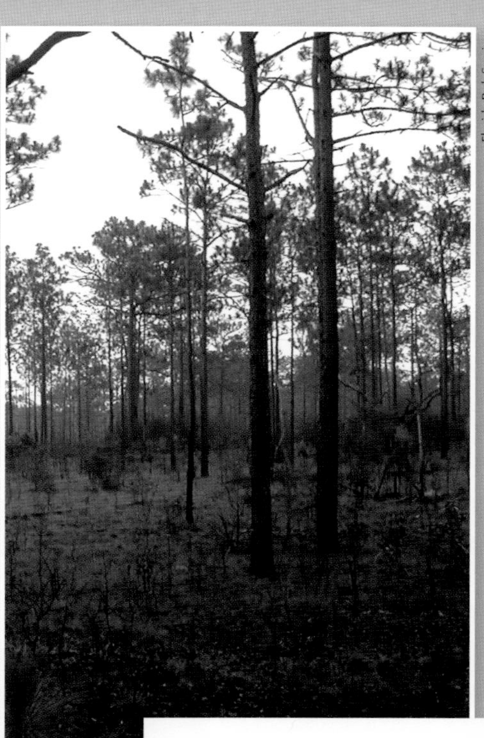

Florida Park Service

9. Evaluate the burn

Monitor fire effects to determine if prescription goals were met. This fire achieved the goals to reduce thick underbrush, promote grassy groundcover, and preserve the pine canopy.

Groundcover Restoration

Many pineland communities—sandhills and flatwoods—in Florida historically consisted of longleaf pine (*Pinus palustris*) underlain by a dominant groundcover of wiregrass (*Aristida stricta*). By the end of the Great Depression, nearly all of Florida's virgin longleaf pine forests had been logged. Since that time, many naturally forested areas across Florida have been converted to a variety of other land uses, including agricultural fields, pastures, and plantation forests. In many instances, wiregrass and the diversity of other groundcover plants usually found in these communities have been severely impacted or completely eliminated. Significant declines in species and in the densities of groundcover plants also occur in fire-excluded forests.

The presence of wiregrass, a keystone species, and other perennial groundcover plants are important elements in pinelands ecology. These fire-tolerant plants have adapted over time to periodic fires, a natural process that reduces the accumulation of fuels (fallen pine needles, dead leaves, twigs, and branches), exposes bare mineral soil necessary for longleaf pine and wiregrass regeneration, and keeps encroaching hardwood trees and other woody plants at bay.

Human activities that result in mechanical soil disturbance, such as logging and certain agricultural practices, also disrupt wiregrass and other pineland groundcover plants. Once eliminated from a site, wiregrass will not readily return on its own. Because of its dominance among groundcover herbs and its value as a high-quality natural fuel, wiregrass is often the primary aim of restoration efforts. This long-lived, bunch-type grass does not reproduce by rhizomes, and its seeds persist in the soil for only a short time. Germination rates for wiregrass are unpredictable and may fall below 10%.

Restoring flatwoods and sandhill communities, while time-consuming, challenging, and costly, offers great potential for reclaiming some of Florida's lost heritage. The best and most economical approach involves protecting intact areas of wiregrass and other groundcover plants. This may involve fencing the area from grazing livestock, thinning overstory trees, or re-introducing fire.

Undertaking a groundcover restoration project involves thorough planning and goal-setting. There are restoration challenges unique to each site, particularly in highly disturbed areas such as crop or hay fields, pastures, orange groves, and extraction mines. Thorough site preparation is essential before initiating a restoration project. Weeds generally pose greater problems on disturbed lands and on mesic and wetland sites, as opposed to xeric habitats such as sandhills. Seeds of weedy plants may remain dormant in hydric soils for many years, only to sprout and compete with emerging wiregrass and desirable groundcover species. Reintroducing fire to a restoration site is essential for enhancing and promoting wiregrass growth and flowering. Restoration projects are, invariably, complex, long-term endeavors that require commitment and determination.

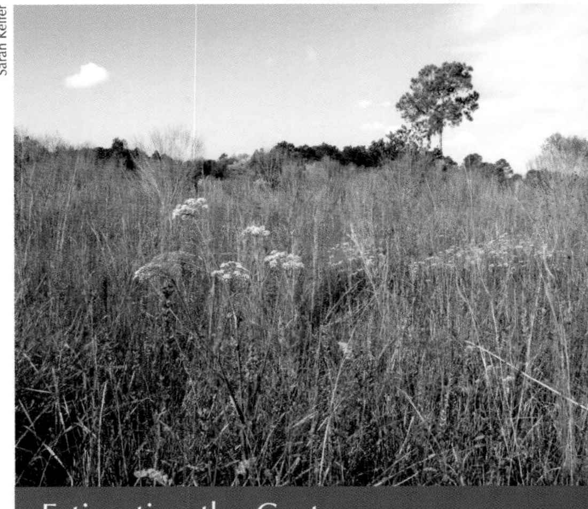
Sarah Keifer

Estimating the Cost

Cost estimates for upland groundcover restoration are variable for many reasons including restoration goals, pre-restoration site condition, site preparation costs, native seed availability, choices and availability of field equipment, prescribed fire, invasive exotic plant infestations, and others. Costs can range from $400 to $5,500 per acre for preparing a site, seeding it with a native grass mixture, and follow-up maintenance.

Example:
Three Lakes Wildlife Management Area

Costs for site preparation and restoration planting: about $42,000 over 92 acres = about $460/acre

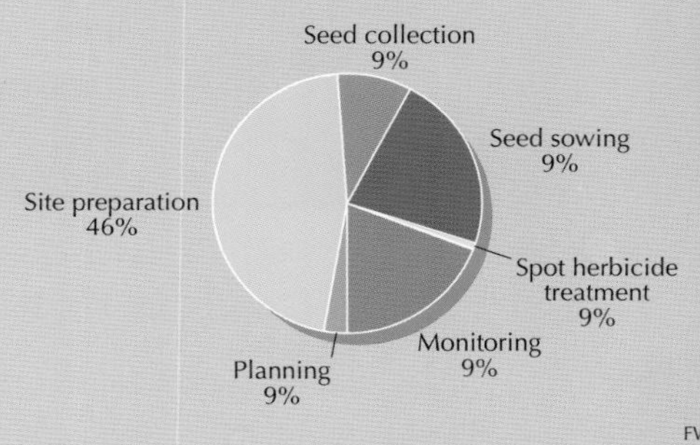

FWC

Converting Pasture to Native Groundcover: A Look at the Restoration Process

Pete Diamond

Paul Abel

Steve Glass

David Printiss, TNC

Steve Glass

Site Preparation

Site preparation of unrestored pasture (1) usually consists of multiple broadcast herbicide treatments (2) over one or two growing seasons, which may or may not be followed by soil disking (3).

Donor Site Burning & Seed Collection

Collecting native seed mix is done at a nearby donor site (4) from October to November. The donor seed site was burned during the prior growing season to promote wiregrass flowering and seed set.

Seed Planting

Planting native seed mixtures takes place anytime from December through February (5). Seeds of woody species may be sown during this time as well. Native seed mix can be sown mechanically (5) or by hand.

Fire

Burning of restoration sites usually takes place around three years after seed-sowing (6). Woody plant species, including pines, saw palmetto, and shrubs, are often planted after the first prescribed fire. Prescribed fire in established restoration sites promotes grasses and wildflowers. Restoring native groundcover is a lengthy undertaking, often requiring many years.

Highlighted Restoration Projects in Florida

David Printiss, TNC

Apalachicola Bluffs and Ravines Preserve

Recently burned wiregrass (*Aristida stricta*) three years after seeding into a sandhill restoration site at Apalachicola Bluffs and Ravines Preserve. The Nature Conservancy, an early leader in groundcover restoration, has restored around 1,100 acres of former sandhill at the preserve.

Michael Jenkins

Lake Talquin State Forest

The Florida Division of Forestry is restoring groundcover—including wiregrass and other herbs—in sandhill sites at Lake Talquin and other state forests.

Chris Matson

Disney Wilderness Preserve

The Nature Conservancy is restoring pasture to mesic flatwoods, scrubby flatwoods, and wet prairie on 512 acres at the Disney Wilderness Preserve. This photo shows native bunchgrasses re-sprouting after fire, three years after restoration activities.

Nancy Bissett

Green Swamp

The Southwest Florida Water Management District was the first state agency to undertake restoration, at a 225-acre pasture at Green Swamp.

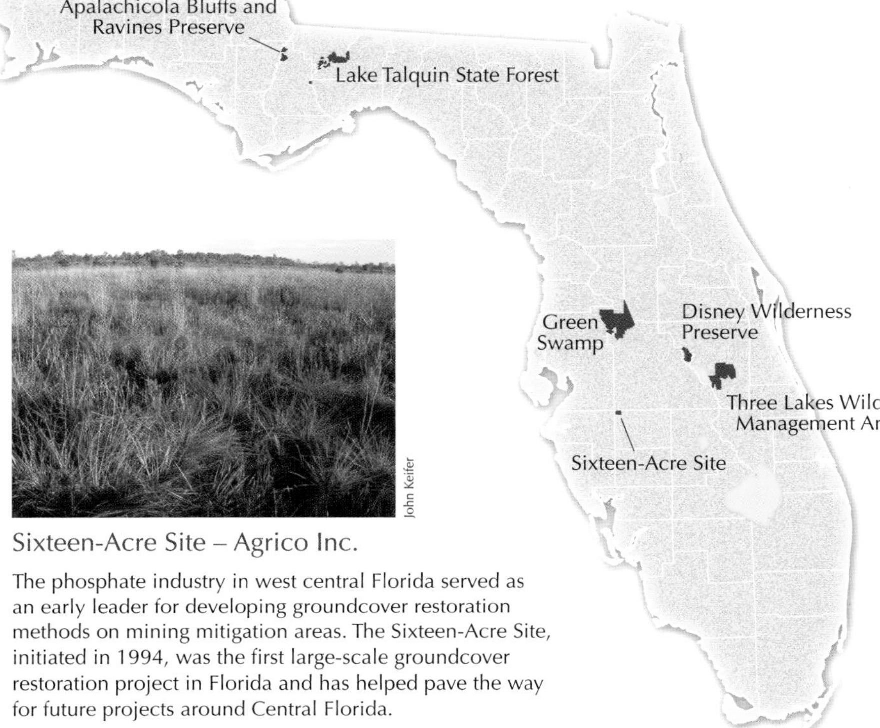

John Keifer

Sixteen-Acre Site – Agrico Inc.

The phosphate industry in west central Florida served as an early leader for developing groundcover restoration methods on mining mitigation areas. The Sixteen-Acre Site, initiated in 1994, was the first large-scale groundcover restoration project in Florida and has helped pave the way for future projects around Central Florida.

Steve Glass

Three Lakes WMA

Lopsided Indiangrass (*Sorghastrum secundum*) blooming in a 40-acre mesic flatwoods restoration site at Three Lakes WMA, approximately two years after seeding. Florida Fish and Wildlife Conservation Commission is restoring former pastures at other sites across the state including Hilochee WMA, Half Moon WMA, and Okaloacoochee Slough WMA.

Restoration of Florida's Natural Spaces

Wetlands

Much of Florida's original landscape was comprised of various wetlands (top photo at right), areas that many people historically viewed as wastelands. Thousands of acres of wetlands, including swamps and marshes, were drained for conversion to agriculture or development in the form of industry, housing, and roads. These natural wetland features are important for controlling floods, for recharging underground aquifers, for filtering pollutants, and as wildlife habitat.

Florida has long recognized the need for offsetting increases in development with the protection of wetlands and the important functions they serve. In order to maintain this balance, federal and state laws require commercial land developers, government agencies, and private landowners to mitigate or lessen impacts to wetlands. These on-site or off-site mitigation projects are intended to compensate, on an acre-for-acre basis, for the functional loss of the impacted wetland. The scope of these projects may vary but all involve enhancing, restoring, creating, and/or preserving wetland habitats. Wetland restoration in Florida has become a big business in itself, with robust demand for projects spurring a multi-million dollar industry of consultants, plant propagators, and restoration-oriented businesses.

Vicki Tauxe

David Moynahan

Beach Dunes

Protecting vegetation on Florida's coastal dunes (bottom photo at left) is important because these specialized plants help stabilize shifting sands and provide essential habitat and food for many species of wildlife. Strong tidal surges associated with tropical storms and hurricanes can damage vegetation and lead to dune erosion. Portions of dunes weakened by past storms and by foot traffic are particularly fragile and are susceptible to blowouts in future storms.

Habitat restoration efforts in coastal areas are geared toward shoring up the protective structure of these dune systems. The best line of defense is sea oats (*Uniola paniculata*), a salt- and drought-tolerant native grass that forms a network of underground stems called rhizomes. By colonizing coastal dunes, this grass traps wind-blown sands and halts erosion.

Adaptive Management

Maintaining a healthy and biologically diverse natural landscape in Florida today often requires land managers to apply deliberate management techniques such as prescribed fire and the manipulation of hydrology. These human-controlled practices are intended to replicate ecological processes that occur naturally, but today occur on a different timeline and with different frequencies and intensities than they once did because the formerly unbroken native landscape is now highly fragmented.

The diversity and complexity of Florida's ecosystems means that land managers do not have simple, consistent formulas for fire and hydrology to replicate natural ecological processes. Instead, most land managers take an iterative approach to land management working step-by-step, and adjusting along the way, as they work to achieve a desired result. This approach to land management is generally called adaptive management.

One science-based and particularly successful example of adaptive management practiced by the Florida Fish and Wildlife Conservation Commission is called Objective-Based Vegetation Management (OBVM). For each land management unit on which OBVM is implemented, several steps are required: 1) setting clear, measurable landscape-condition objectives (sometimes called Desired Future Conditions); 2) measuring and evaluating the current (baseline) landscape condition through the use of ecological sampling; 3) applying appropriate land management actions, such as prescribed fire or invasive species control, as necessary to modify the condition of the management unit and move it closer to the desired condition; 4) measure and evaluate again after treatment to determine if the management action accomplished the desired effect; and 5) repeat as necessary. Many times management units are determined to already be in desired condition, and active land management is intended to maintain that condition. Sometimes the condition of the landscape may require several treatments to eventually reach desired condition, which may take many years of intentional, steady progress.

The benefits of OBVM and other variations of adaptive management are many. The process provides the land manager with timely decision support, ensuring that land management actions are taken when needed, but only when needed which provides a cost savings. The process helps ensure accountability; there are measurable objectives against which progress can be evaluated. OBVM in particular, because it is a well-documented, science-based process, helps inform our understanding of the landscape's response to specific management actions. The knowledge gained can be applied to future land management planning making management more effective and efficient.

FNAI Baseline Natural Community Mapping and Monitoring, 2003-2010

Natural communities mapped	
Current condition	2,200,000 acres
Historical vegetation	1,500,000 acres
Natural community polygons	77,500
Ground-truth points	50,477
Minimum mapping unit	0.5 acres

Mesic Flatwoods Reference Site
Triple N Ranch Wildlife Management Area

Metric	Average Reference Value
Basal Area of Pine (sq ft per acre)	16.3
Pine Regeneration (stems within 7 m radius)	0.3
Bare Ground (%)	10.6
Herb Cover (%)	37.2
Wiry Graminoid Cover (%)	25
Exotic Plant Cover (%)	0
Weedy Species Cover (%)	0
Average Maximum *Serenoa* Height (ft)	2.2
Serenoa Cover (%)	25.7
Serenoa Petiole Density >3ft	0.8
Average Maximum Shrub Height (ft)	1
Shrub Cover (%)	18.9
Shrub Stem Density >3 ft	0.3
Maximum Shrub DBH (in)	0
Non-Pine Stem Density (stems within 7 m radius)	0
Subcanopy (stems within 7 m radius)	0

Example of reference site ecological data: Mesic flatwoods from Triple N Ranch Wildlife Management Area. Data collected and averaged from 30 sample stations.

Objective-Based Vegetation Management

Evaluating and Documenting Current Condition

Each managed area is surveyed and the natural communities (the ecological units driving most management decisions) are measured and mapped providing a well-documented baseline of landscape condition. Scientists use GPS data recorders to accurately and efficiently record data about the composition, structure, and condition of each natural community polygon.

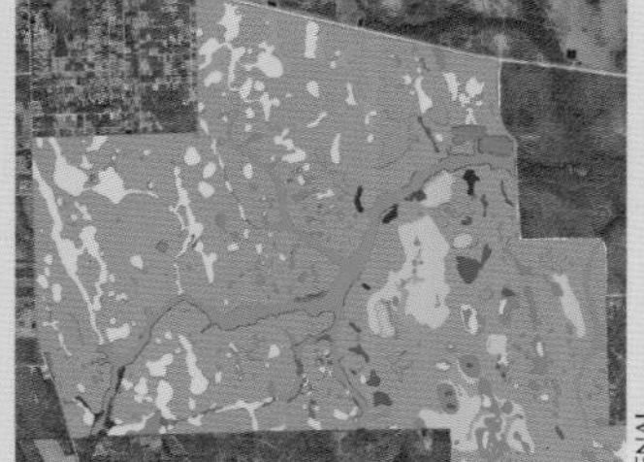

FNAI

Natural community map, Triple N Ranch Wildlife Management Area.

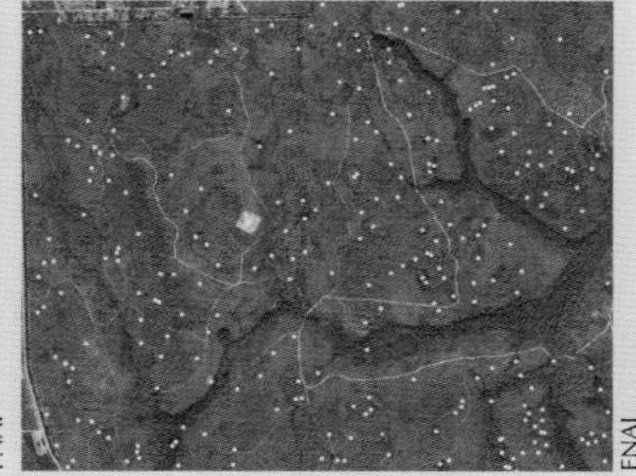

FNAI

Data collection points, Triple N Ranch Wildlife Management Area (inset).

FNAI

Scientist collecting data at ground-truth point with GPS datalogger.

Determining Desired Future Condition

A team of resource experts including the land manager meet to set the Desired Future Condition (DFC) for each natural community type. Generally, DFCs are set against established standards for each type as exemplified in reference sites across the state; however, other factors may be considered as well, such as providing optimum habitat conditions for specific rare or game species.

Dan Hipes

Assessing Desired Future Conditions to enhance habitat for red-cockaded woodpecker in a wet flatwoods at St. Marks National Wildlife Refuge.

FWC

Scientists and land managers meeting to review initial mapping data and set Desired Future Conditions.

Reference Natural Community Sites

Reference sites for natural communities have been identified for some of the most important natural community types in Florida that require active land management. These reference sites are locations in which the ecological condition of the natural community is exemplary and may be used as a model.

Seepage slope
Blackwater River State Forest

Mesic flatwoods
Apalachicola National Forest

Upland pine
Twin Rivers State Forest

Sandhill
Gold Head Branch State Park

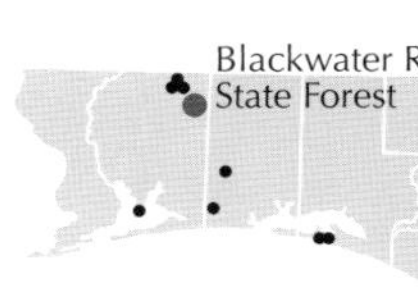

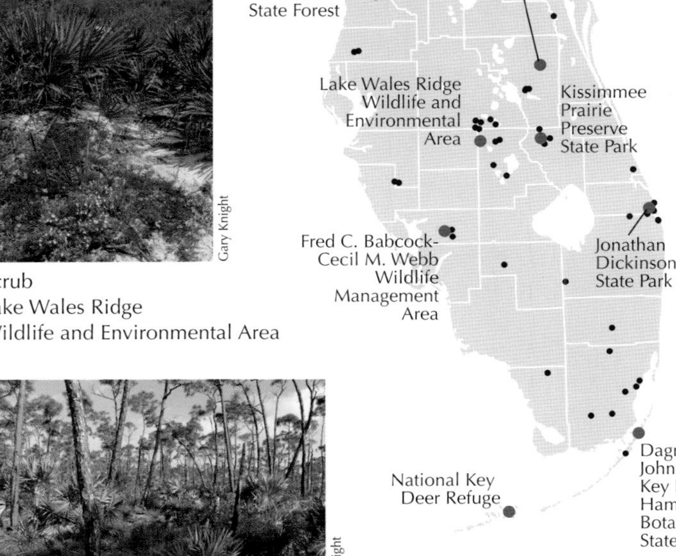

Note: All 77 sites were surveyed and are considered exemplary natural communities. Not all sites included statistical sampling. Featured sites are shown in red.

Sandhill
Withlacoochee State Forest

Scrub
Lake Wales Ridge
Wildlife and Environmental Area

Mesic flatwoods
Triple N Ranch
Wildlife Management Area

Wet prairie
Kissimmee Prairie
Preserve State Park

Dry prairie
Kissimmee Prairie Preserve State Park

Wet flatwoods
Babcock-Webb Wildlife
Management Area

Pine rockland
National Key Deer Refuge

Rockland hammock
Key Largo Hammock
Botanical State Park

Mesic flatwoods
Jonathan Dickinson
State Park

Implementing Management Actions to Accomplish Desired Condition

After establishing a Desired Future Condition for a site (e.g., sandhill with woody shrub cover between 10-20% and herbaceous ground cover >25%), land managers actively modify the ecological condition of the landscape using prescribed fire, hydrological restoration, invasive species removal, and other land management tools.

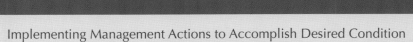

Sandhill that has grown outside of desired condition with too much woody shrub cover and too little herbaceous ground cover. Prescribed fire is used to restore desired condition.

Same location 12 months later shows highly successful results with much less woody shrub cover and greater herbaceous ground cover.

Re-evaluation and Ecological Assessment of Condition

Scientists use ecological sampling and statistical analysis to accurately assess the condition of the landscape after treatment. Statistical methods allow land managers to extrapolate the results of a relative few sample stations to characterize the overall condition of the entire site.

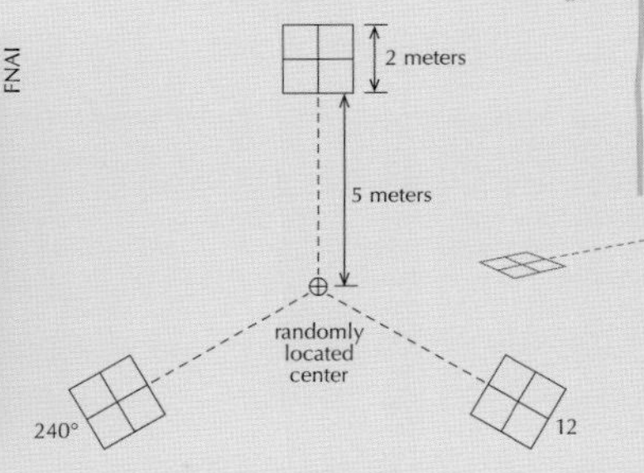

7-meter circular plot with nested 4m² and 1m² quadrats. The 7-meter circular plot is used to collect data on canopy and subcanopy components of the natural community; the 4m² quadrat is used to collect data on woody shrubs, the 1m² quadrats are used to collect data on herbaceous ground cover.

Case Study: Tate's Hell

Tate's Hell State Forest, managed by the Florida Division of Forestry (DOF), encompasses 202,437 acres in Franklin and Liberty counties. The forest represents one of the largest and most complex ecological restoration projects in the state. Historically this land—a complex mosaic of swamps, marshes, wet prairies, and pinelands—formed the backdrop for the 1870s legend of cattleman Cebe Tate, who allegedly became lost and nearly died before finding his way out and declaring he had been through "Hell."

Tate's Hell lands are vital to the maintenance of water quality in the Apalachicola Bay, one of the most productive commercial and recreational fisheries in the U.S. The property forms an important ecological link between the Apalachicola National Forest, the Apalachicola Wildlife and Environmental Area, and the Apalachicola National Estuarine Research Reserve. Tate's Hell lands also provide habitat for 42 species of rare plants and animals.

In 1994, when the Florida Conservation and Recreation Lands (CARL) program made its first purchase in Tate's Hell, the wilderness had given way to an orderly network of roads, drainage ditches, and fertilized, densely planted pine plantations. Important ecosystem functions of the historical natural landscape—such as water filtration and storage, native habitat diversity, and frequent natural fires that kept the risk of catastrophic wildfire low—had been greatly diminished. The major objectives for state ownership of Tate's Hell lands include restoration of the altered ecosystems, protection of water quality, particularly in Apalachicola Bay, conservation of native and rare species habitats, and providing for public recreational activities compatible with the natural resources.

Most of the forest's 152,000 acres of wetlands have been adversely impacted by past land uses, particularly the hundreds of miles of ditches that were designed to drain water out of the wetlands and off the property into the coastal waters, carrying with it sediments and excess nutrients from the fertilized pine plantations. DOF and the Northwest Florida Water Management District have completed twelve major hydrology restoration projects that have improved hydrology conditions over 39,000 acres of the forest. A comprehensive hydrology restoration plan for the entire forest was finalized in 2010.

Restoration of Tate's Hell also requires thinning overstocked pine plantations and controlled burning. After conversion of the property to commercial silviculture, the landscape became blanketed with dense overgrowth. Reintroducing controlled burns to Tate's Hell restores the natural habitats, improves food for wildlife, and reduces the threat of catastrophic wildfire. Tate's Hell State Forest is a showcase example of large-scale ecological restoration in progress, with tremendous benefits to Florida's environment now and into the future.

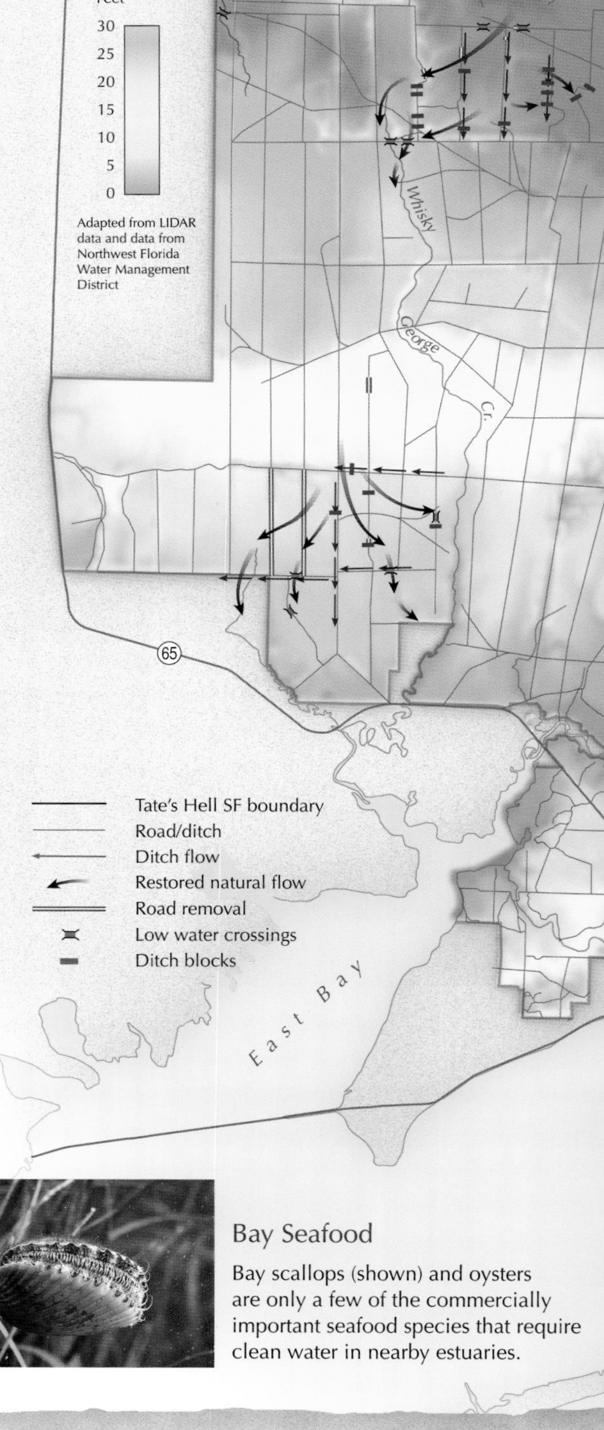

Change in Vegetation

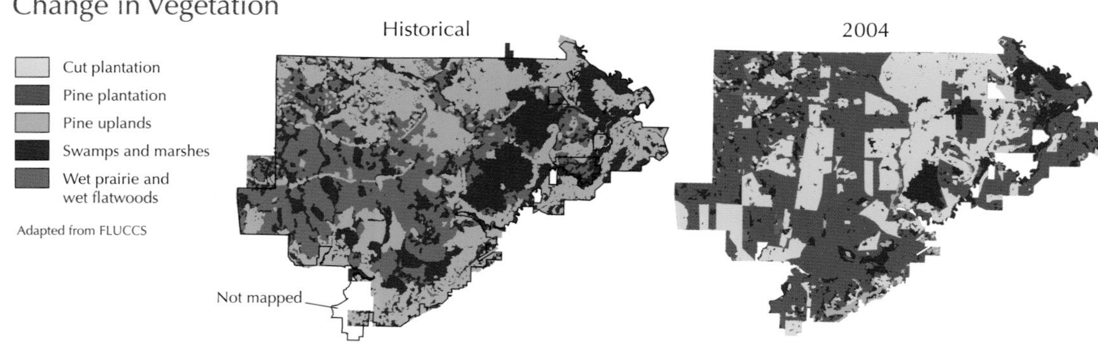

David Moynahan

Bay Seafood

Bay scallops (shown) and oysters are only a few of the commercially important seafood species that require clean water in nearby estuaries.

- **-12,000** Humans appear in the Florida fossil record.
- **-10,000** The Florida vegetation landscape begins the shift from predominantly hardwoods to pines. Charcoal records indicate frequent fires on the landscape. Modern weather patterns begin: frequent, high-intensity lightning storms coincide with seasonal dry periods, setting fire to the landscape in South Florida primarily in the winter, and in Central and North Florida in the spring.
- **1527** Pánfilo Nárvaez is the first European documented to set foot on Florida soil.
- **1769** DeBrahm (1751-1771) notes the "ancient Custom of the Indians" to use fires to "allure the Deers upon the new Grass." W. Stork notes (1769) the Creek Indians in Florida, "through the whole province, continually set the grass on fire, for the convenience of hunting."
- **1821** Florida becomes a U.S. territory.
- **1827** John Williams describes NW Florida commerce as in its "infancy," cattle important in subsistence lives of residents.
- **1873** Origination of the story of Cebe Tate, who got lost in "Hell" while rounding up his cattle. Fires are used to create forage for livestock.
- **1877** City of Carrabelle founded.
- **1890** Timber and turpentine are major exports from Carrabelle, Franklin Co. Lumber Company.
- **1893** Carrabelle, Tallahassee, and Georgia Railroad opens.

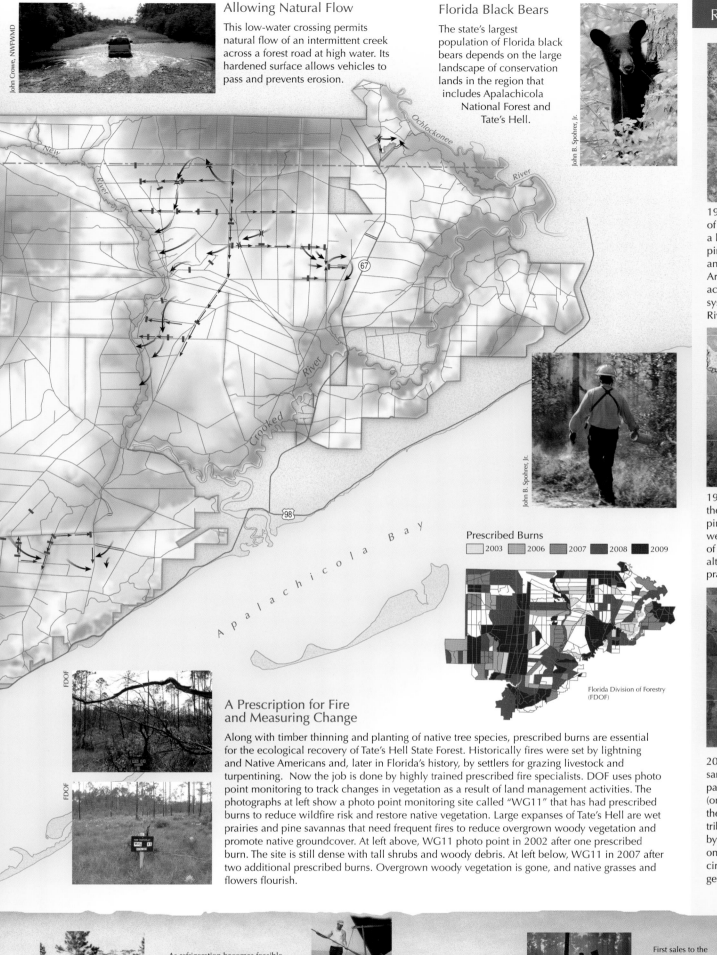

John Crowe, NWFWMD

Allowing Natural Flow

This low-water crossing permits natural flow of an intermittent creek across a forest road at high water. Its hardened surface allows vehicles to pass and prevents erosion.

Florida Black Bears

The state's largest population of Florida black bears depends on the large landscape of conservation lands in the region that includes Apalachicola National Forest and Tate's Hell.

John B. Spohrer, Jr.

Ochlockonee River

New River

Crooked River

67

98

Apalachicola Bay

John B. Spohrer, Jr.

Prescribed Burns

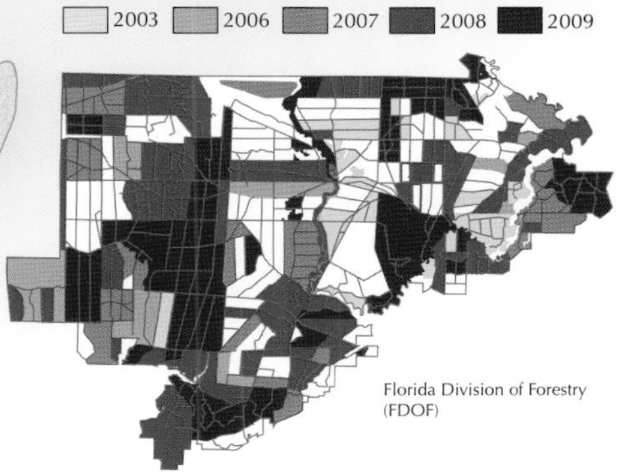

2003 2006 2007 2008 2009

Florida Division of Forestry (FDOF)

FDOF

FDOF

A Prescription for Fire and Measuring Change

Along with timber thinning and planting of native tree species, prescribed burns are essential for the ecological recovery of Tate's Hell State Forest. Historically fires were set by lightning and Native Americans and, later in Florida's history, by settlers for grazing livestock and turpentining. Now the job is done by highly trained prescribed fire specialists. DOF uses photo point monitoring to track changes in vegetation as a result of land management activities. The photographs at left show a photo point monitoring site called "WG11" that has had prescribed burns to reduce wildfire risk and restore native vegetation. Large expanses of Tate's Hell are wet prairies and pine savannas that need frequent fires to reduce overgrown woody vegetation and promote native groundcover. At left above, WG11 photo point in 2002 after one prescribed burn. The site is still dense with tall shrubs and woody debris. At left below, WG11 in 2007 after two additional prescribed burns. Overgrown woody vegetation is gone, and native grasses and flowers flourish.

Restoring the Flow

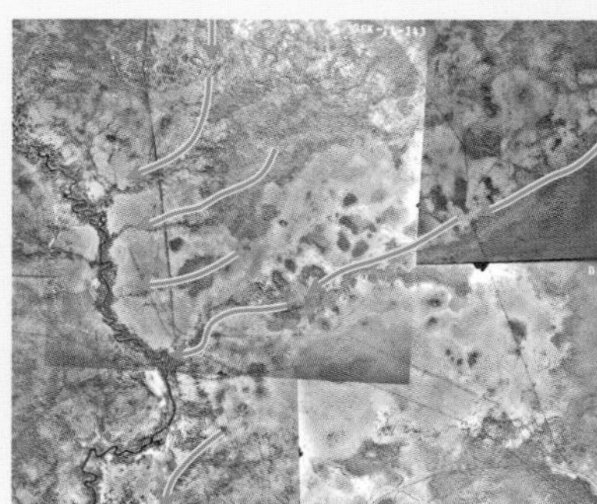

1953 black and white aerial photograph of a portion of Tate's Hell, showing a landscape mosaic of swamps and pinelands that existed prior to ditching and conversion to pine planations. Arrows denote historical flow of water across wet prairies, into small stream systems, and eventually into the New River.

1995 color infrared aerial photograph of the same area, showing ditches, roads, pine plantations, and cleared areas that were typical of the landscape at the time of state purchase. Orange arrows denote altered flow of water, by-passing the wet prairies and small tributaries.

2007 true color aerial photograph of the same area, showing restored drainage patterns. Note the locations of ditchblocks (orange diamonds) that divert water across the historical wet prairies and into small tributaries. The road remains open for use by the public and land managers. Note one of the low-water crossings (yellow circle) that allow vehicles to pass without getting mired during times of high water.

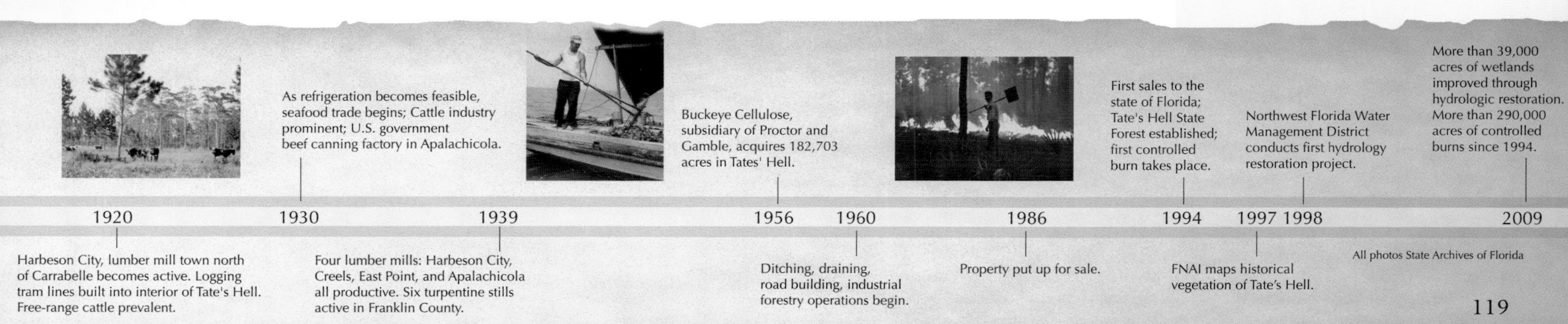

1920
Harbeson City, lumber mill town north of Carrabelle becomes active. Logging tram lines built into interior of Tate's Hell. Free-range cattle prevalent.
1930
As refrigeration becomes feasible, seafood trade begins; Cattle industry prominent; U.S. government beef canning factory in Apalachicola.
1939
Four lumber mills: Harbeson City, Creels, East Point, and Apalachicola all productive. Six turpentine stills active in Franklin County.
1956
Buckeye Cellulose, subsidiary of Proctor and Gamble, acquires 182,703 acres in Tates' Hell.
1960
Ditching, draining, road building, industrial forestry operations begin.
1986
Property put up for sale.
1994
First sales to the state of Florida; Tate's Hell State Forest established; first controlled burn takes place.
1997
FNAI maps historical vegetation of Tate's Hell.
1998
Northwest Florida Water Management District conducts first hydrology restoration project.
2009
More than 39,000 acres of wetlands improved through hydrologic restoration. More than 290,000 acres of controlled burns since 1994.
All photos State Archives of Florida

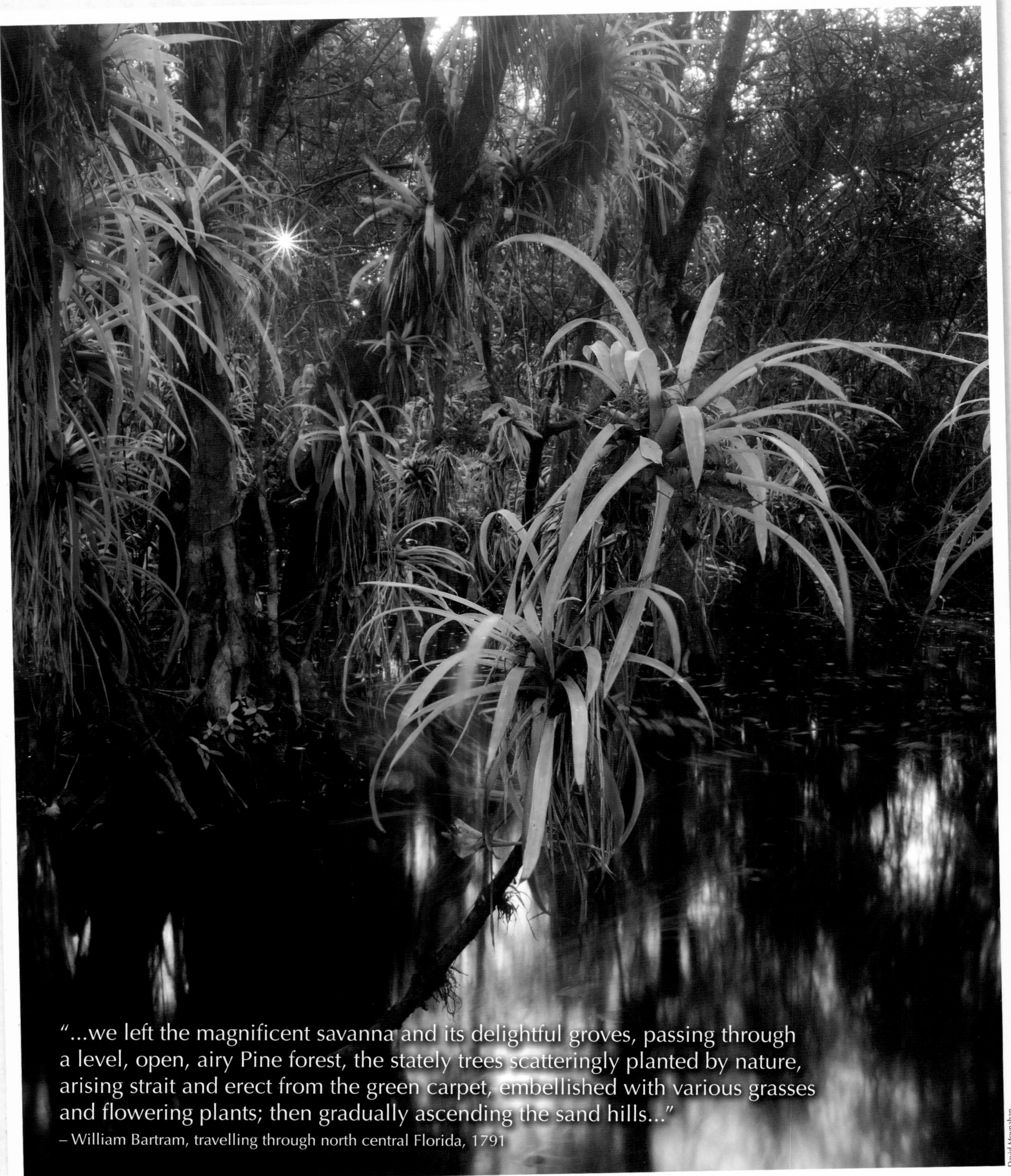

"...we left the magnificent savanna and its delightful groves, passing through a level, open, airy Pine forest, the stately trees scatteringly planted by nature, arising strait and erect from the green carpet, embellished with various grasses and flowering plants; then gradually ascending the sand hills..."
– William Bartram, travelling through north central Florida, 1791
David Moynahan

Strand swamp with bromeliads, Fakahatchee Strand Preserve State Park

IV Notable Natural Areas

A natural area is greater than the sum of its parts. From the clay hills of the Panhandle to the rocky islands of the Keys, Florida's natural landscape is made up of distinct regions, each with unique vistas, flora, and fauna. This section highlights twelve destinations in Florida that are notable for their unique—and in some places still pristine—assemblages of landscapes, flora, and fauna, viewed here as a whole through the lens of a field naturalist. (A thirteenth and unquestionably equal candidate—the Everglades—is already featured on pages 34-35.)

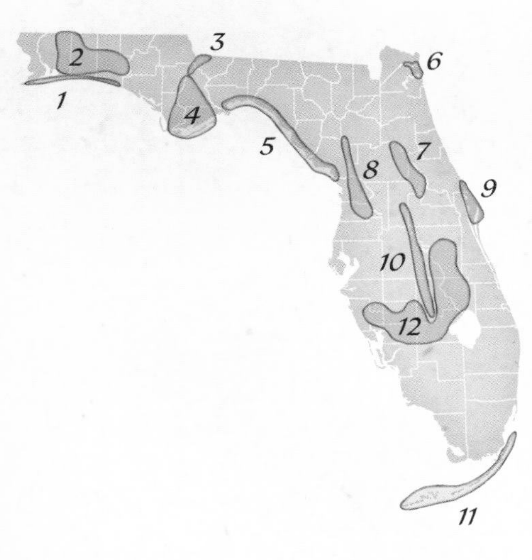

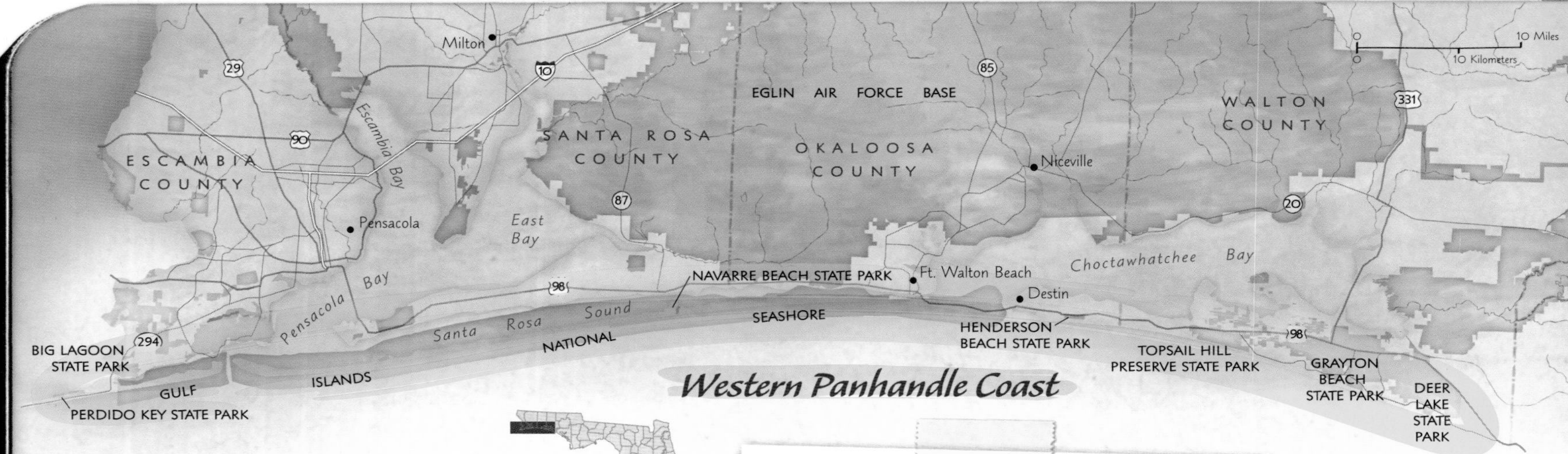

Western Panhandle Coast

The Western Panhandle Coast is famous for the exquisite beauty of its turquoise waters and its broad sugar-sand beaches. About 50 miles of its shoreline are managed as park or military land, limiting the region's development and preserving the integrity of its natural communities. A full complement of coastal natural communities, all in excellent condition, is present here: beach dunes up to 30 feet tall; an ever-changing back dune system of grassland and swale; rare freshwater coastal dune lakes restricted to this region of Florida; and maritime hammocks with closed canopied forests of hardwoods, pine, and cabbage palm. Two types of goldenaster are endemic, and the region is a stronghold for the perforate reindeer lichen (Cladonia perforata), one of only two federally listed lichens. The little-disturbed beaches and dunes are critically important habitat for three subspecies of beach mice, two of which are federally listed as endangered. Sea turtles nest along the beaches, and neotropical songbirds and monarch butterflies rest in the coastal forests just before or after their exhausting migrations across the Gulf of Mexico. The region is buffeted by winds, salt spray, and regular storms. Hurricanes strike on average about once every nine years, dramatically rearranging beaches and dunes. The beaches are never static: in the course of a human lifetime, they may move surprising distances or even become submerged. The plants, animals, and natural communities native to this dynamic environment are adapted to these natural disturbances and over the long term not only survive but thrive.

KEY ELEMENTS OF BIODIVERSITY

Natural Communities
- Beach dune
- Coastal grassland
- Maritime hammock
- Scrub

Plants

Chrysopsis godfreyi	Godfrey's goldenaster
Chrysopsis gossypina ssp. *cruiseana*	Cruise's goldenaster
Cladonia perforata	perforate reindeer lichen
Polygonella macrophylla	large-leaved jointweed

Animals

Charadrius alexandrinus	snowy plover
Charadrius melodus	piping plover
Peromyscus polionotus leucocephalus	Santa Rosa beach mouse
Peromyscus polionotus trissyllepsis	Perdido Key beach mouse

David Moynahan

Loggerhead (Caretta caretta)

Brenda Herring

Cruise's goldenaster (Chrysopsis gossypina ssp. cruiseana) →

Brenda Herring

Coastal scrub and dunes, Choctawhatchee Bay

Brenda Herring

↑ Perforate reindeer lichen (Cladonia perforata)

Seaoats (Uniola paniculata) hold sand in place and help create dunes.

Brenda Herring

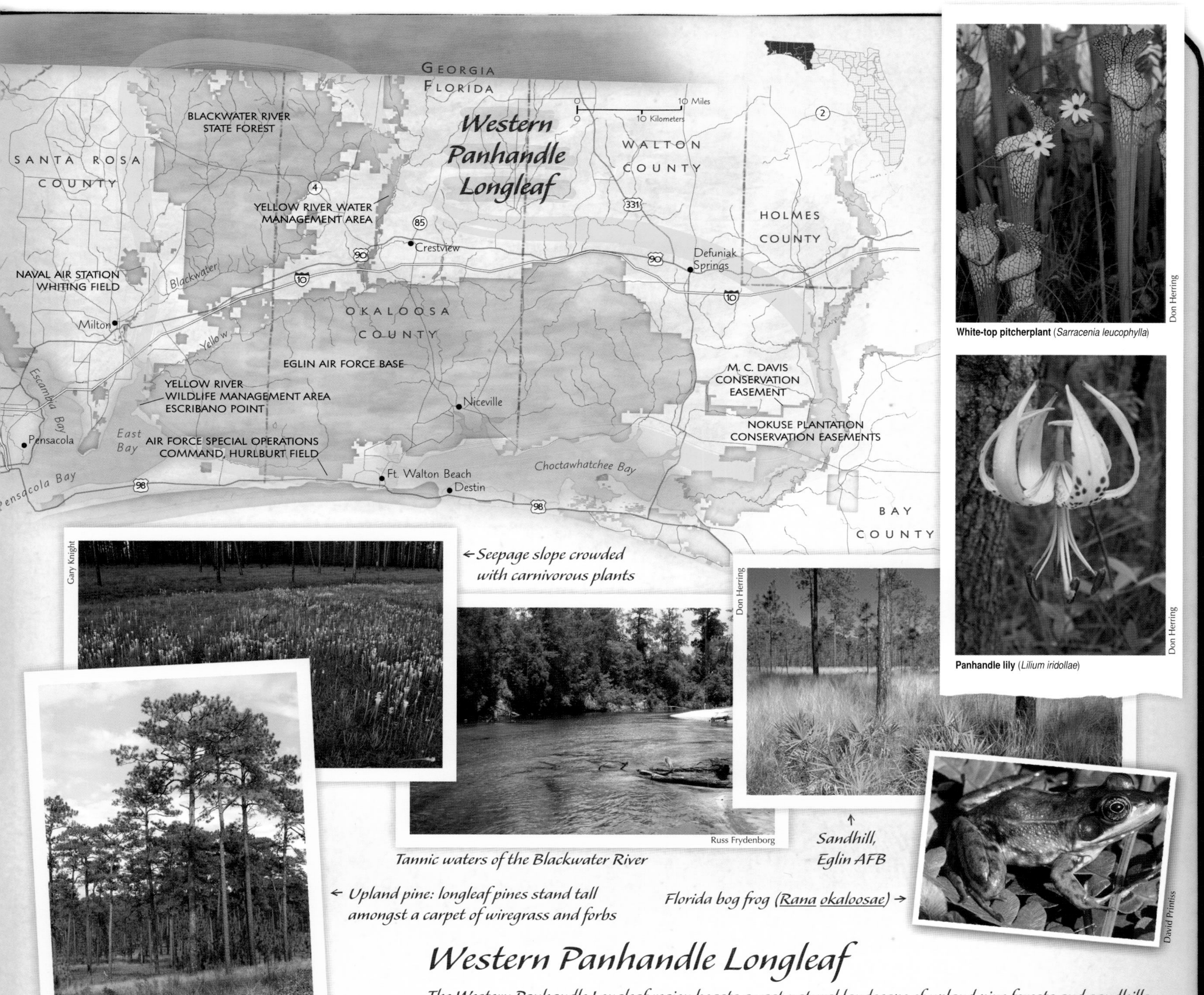

White-top pitcherplant (*Sarracenia leucophylla*)

Panhandle lily (*Lilium iridollae*)

← Seepage slope crowded with carnivorous plants

Tannic waters of the Blackwater River

↑ Sandhill, Eglin AFB

← Upland pine: longleaf pines stand tall amongst a carpet of wiregrass and forbs

Florida bog frog (Rana okaloosae) →

Western Panhandle Longleaf

The Western Panhandle Longleaf region boasts a vast natural landscape of upland pine forests and sandhills, blackwater creeks and swamps, spring-fed streams, seepage slopes and wet prairies, and is home to at least 184 rare species of plants, animals, and insects. The world's largest remaining tracts of longleaf pine are here within Florida and adjacent Alabama. The rare Bachman's sparrow (Peucaea aestivalis) nests in the knee-high grasses and shrubs of the longleaf pine forests, along with bobwhite quail and eastern wild turkey. The fourth largest population of the endangered red-cockaded woodpecker (Picoides borealis) is beginning to thrive here, with the attentive stewardship of land managers. Sparkling seepage streams emanating from deep sand ridges harbor the globally imperiled Florida bog frog (Rana okaloosae) and the Okalooosa darter (Etheostoma okaloosae), both species found nowhere else in the world. Seepage slopes—wet, open grassy patches nestled in the upland pine forest—provide spectacular displays of pitcherplants, orchids, and other sun-loving plants. This is a fire-adapted landscape. Natural fires that once were ignited by lightning and spread unrestricted across the landscape are replaced today by prescribed fire, controlled burns intentionally set by land managers to keep the landscape healthy and wildfire risk low. Eglin Air Force Base and Blackwater River State Forest are central to over 800,000 acres of land managed, in whole or in part, for conservation in this region. Eglin showcases the compatibility of conservation and its military mission, leading the Department of Defense in stewardship of its natural landscape. Nokuse Plantation, a 48,000-acre private conservation tract, helps form critical ecological linkages between public lands in the area.

KEY ELEMENTS OF BIODIVERSITY

Natural Communities

- Blackwater stream
- Sandhill
- Seepage slope
- Upland pine

Plants

Lilium iridollae	panhandle lily
Lindera subcoriacea	bog spicebush
Matelea alabamensis	Alabama spiny-pod
Sarracenia leucophylla	white-top pitcherplant

Animals

Ambysotma bishopi	reticulated flatwoods salamander
Etheostoma okaloosae	Okaloosa darter
Picoides borealis	red-cockaded woodpecker
Ursus americanus floridanus	Florida black bear

Apalachicola Bluffs & Ravines

The upper section of the Apalachicola River passes along Florida's Northern Highlands, an area of rich soils and relatively high topographic relief, ranging from 50 feet at the river's edge to more than 310 feet a few miles east. Over millions of years, the river has carved into these highlands creating high bluffs along the river's eastern shore. The highlands are further dissected by ravines and steepheads, creating distinctive dendritic topographic patterns; the land is forested with deciduous oak, beech, maple, hickory, ash, and other tree species more typical of the southern Appalachian Mountains than other parts of Florida. These forests have an enduring history, extending back into geologic time and have served as a refugium for species during the Ice Ages.

One River, Two Worlds

The Apalachicola River basin drains a watershed of approximately 20,000 square miles in Georgia, Florida, and Alabama. The river and its surrounding natural habitats in Florida are one of the top rare species biodiversity hotspots in the United States, ranking sixth in an analysis by the conservation organization NatureServe.

Habitats along the 107-mile-long river are strikingly different between the upper and lower reaches of the river. An ancient coastal shoreline, 78 miles upstream from the mouth just north of the community of Bristol, serves as a natural divide between the upper and lower reaches.

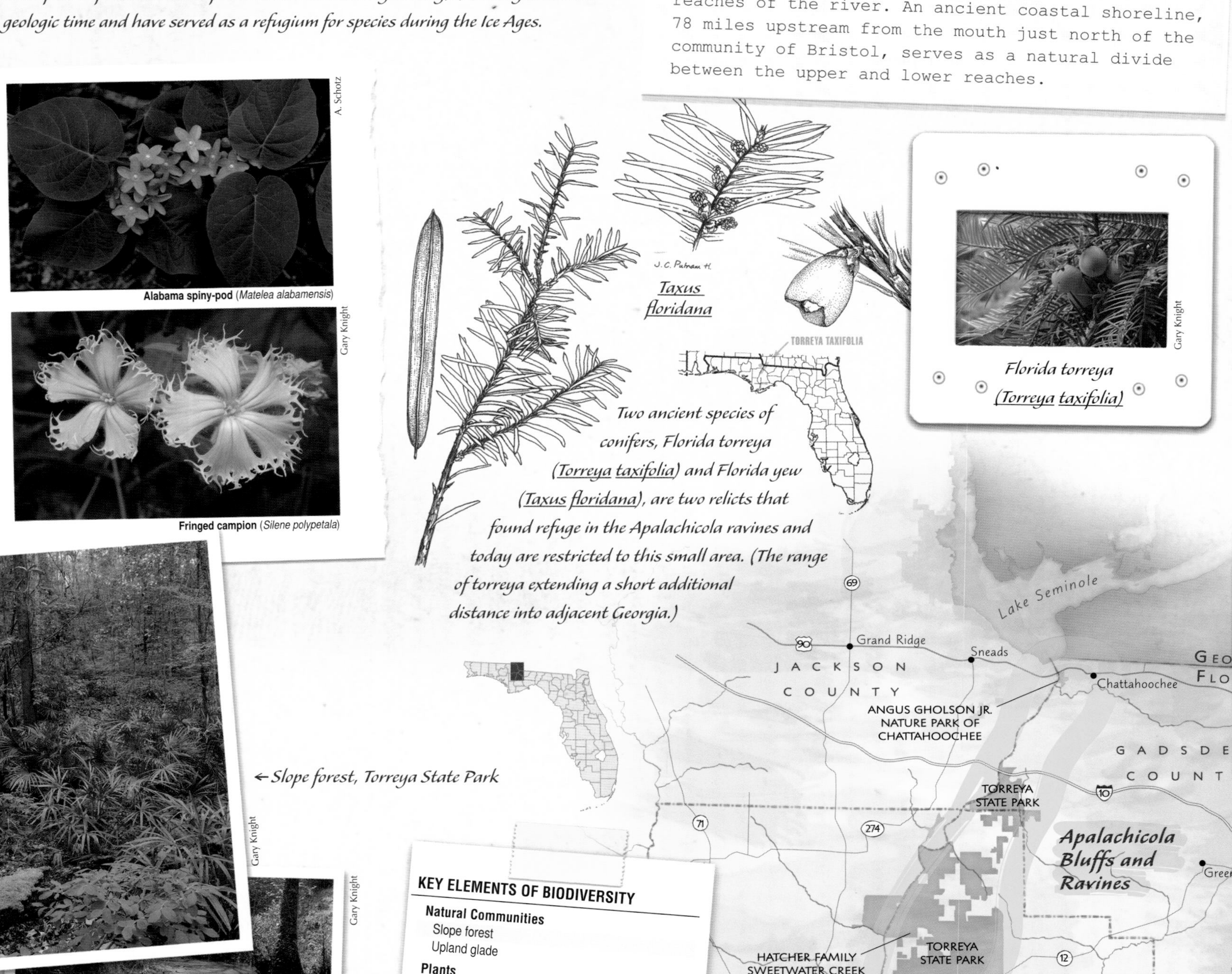

Alabama spiny-pod (*Matelea alabamensis*)

Fringed campion (*Silene polypetala*)

Florida torreya (Torreya taxifolia)

Two ancient species of conifers, Florida torreya (Torreya taxifolia) and Florida yew (Taxus floridana), are two relicts that found refuge in the Apalachicola ravines and today are restricted to this small area. (The range of torreya extending a short additional distance into adjacent Georgia.)

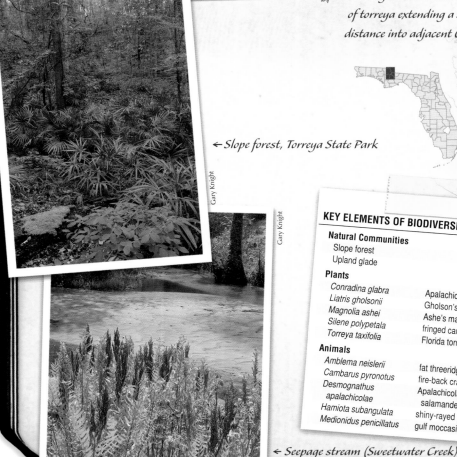

← Slope forest, Torreya State Park

Gary Knight

Gary Knight

KEY ELEMENTS OF BIODIVERSITY

Natural Communities
- Slope forest
- Upland glade

Plants

Conradina glabra	Apalachicola rosemary
Liatris gholsonii	Gholson's blazing star
Magnolia ashei	Ashe's magnolia
Silene polypetala	fringed campion
Torreya taxifolia	Florida torreya

Animals

Amblema neislerii	fat threeridge
Cambarus pyronotus	fire-back crayfish
Desmognathus apalachicolae	Apalachicola dusky salamander
Hamiota subangulata	shiny-rayed pocketbook
Medionidus penicillatus	gulf moccasinshell

← Seepage stream (Sweetwater Creek)

Apalachicola River Lower Basin

South of the bluffs and ravines, the highlands are left behind and lands in the basin range in elevation from sea level to less than 100 feet. Vast cypress/tupelo swamps line lowlands along the river, and higher elevations support an extensive mix of pine flatwoods, wet prairies, and cypress stringers. This area harbors North America's greatest concentration of carnivorous plant species and the largest stand of tupelo trees (Nyssa aquatica) in the world. Not surprisingly, the lower Apalachicola region is also a haven for wildlife. The largest known populations of federally endangered red-cockaded woodpecker (Picoides borealis) and Florida black bear (Ursus americanus floridanus), a state-threatened species, occur here. This region supports more than 150 rare plants and animals, of which 15 are listed as federally threatened or endangered. Fortunately, this remarkable landscape is well conserved. The Apalachicola National Forest, Tate's Hell State Forest, Apalachicola Wildlife and Environmental Area, and Apalachicola River Water Management Area together compose more than 850,000 acres of public lands open to all.

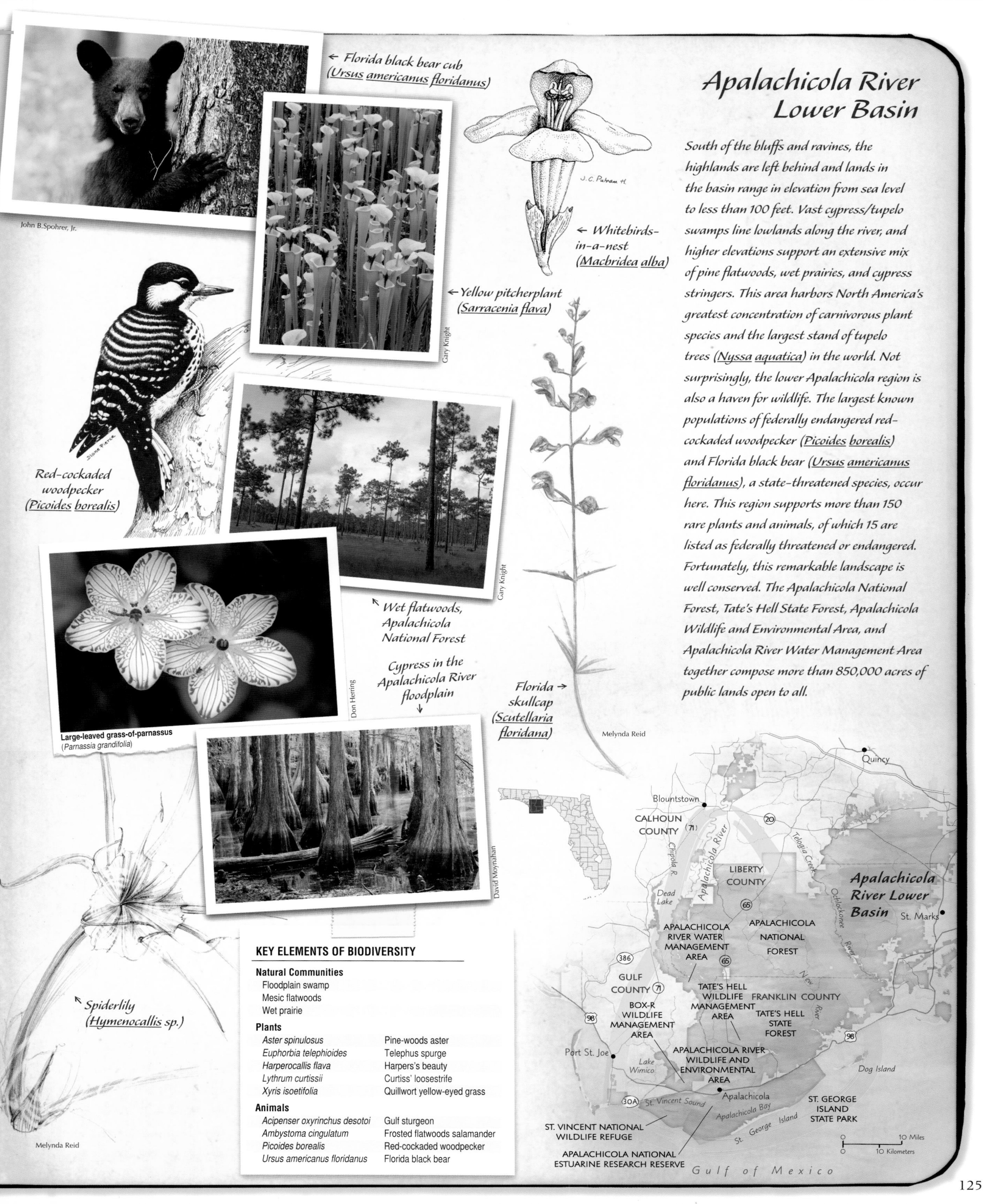

← Florida black bear cub (Ursus americanus floridanus)

John B.Spohrer, Jr.

← Yellow pitcherplant (Sarracenia flava)

Gary Knight

← Whitebirds-in-a-nest (Macbridea alba)

Red-cockaded woodpecker (Picoides borealis)

Wet flatwoods, Apalachicola National Forest

Gary Knight

Large-leaved grass-of-parnassus (Parnassia grandifolia)

Don Herring

Cypress in the Apalachicola River floodplain

David Moynahan

Florida skullcap (Scutellaria floridana)

Melynda Reid

Spiderlily (Hymenocallis sp.)

Melynda Reid

KEY ELEMENTS OF BIODIVERSITY

Natural Communities

- Floodplain swamp
- Mesic flatwoods
- Wet prairie

Plants

Aster spinulosus	Pine-woods aster
Euphorbia telephioides	Telephus spurge
Harperocallis flava	Harpers's beauty
Lythrum curtissii	Curtiss' loosestrife
Xyris isoetifolia	Quillwort yellow-eyed grass

Animals

Acipenser oxyrinchus desotoi	Gulf sturgeon
Ambystoma cingulatum	Frosted flatwoods salamander
Picoides borealis	Red-cockaded woodpecker
Ursus americanus floridanus	Florida black bear

Big Bend Coast

The Big Bend Coast today still evokes a time when Florida's ecosystems stretched uninterrupted as far as the eye could see. The expansive and unspoiled Big Bend Coast lies tucked away in the quiet northeast corner of the Gulf of Mexico. Here coastal uplands gradually grade into the Gulf, and vast seagrass beds flourish in biologically rich marine waters. This region extends mostly uninterrupted for over 150 miles from Apalachee Bay south to Central Florida. The majority of the Big Bend Coast is owned by state and federal agencies, ensuring its continuing ecological integrity. The seagrass beds, salt marshes, and hydric hammocks common to this coast are due to high sediment accumulations characteristic of low-energy coastlines. Seagrasses form extensive aquatic beds and flourish on this rich organic muck substrate. This unique natural community offers vital forage and nursery areas for commercially and recreationally important finfish and shellfish. Seagrass beds, one of the most biologically diverse ecosystems in the world, support a multitude of invertebrate species both within the water column and the underlying muck substrate. The upland natural communities of the Big Bend Coast are also biologically diverse. They support a high diversity of butterfly species, most notably the monarch butterfly (Danaus plexippus). Each spring and fall masses of monarchs gather here to feast on nectar before and after their long migrations across the Gulf of Mexico. The remote coastline also provides refuge for a wide variety of nesting and migrating birds, including breeding bald eagles (Haliaetus leucocephalus).

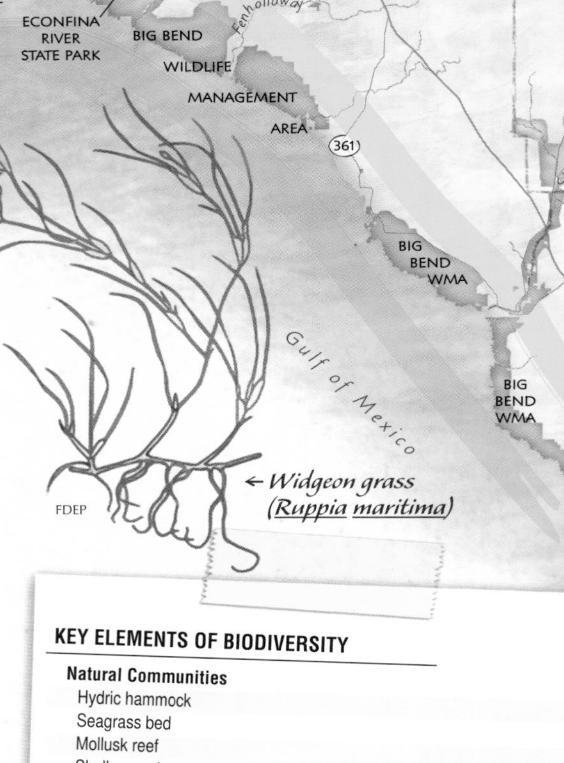

← Widgeon grass (Ruppia maritima)

KEY ELEMENTS OF BIODIVERSITY

Natural Communities
- Hydric hammock
- Seagrass bed
- Mollusk reef
- Shell mound
- Salt marsh

Plants

Hymenocallis godfreyi	Godfrey's spiderlily
Leitneria floridana	corkwood

Animals

Elanoides forficatus	swallow-tailed kite
Laterallus jamaicensis	black rail
Microtus pennslvanicus dukecampbelli	salt marsh vole
Plestiodon egregius insularis	Cedar Key mole skink

David Moynahan

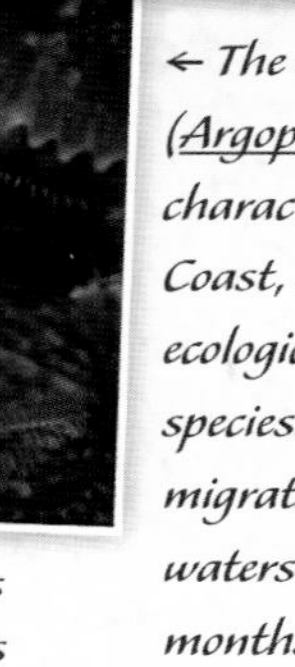

← The bay scallop (Argopecten irradians), characteristic of the Big Bend Coast, and an important ecological and commercial species. Adult bay scallops migrate to shallow inshore waters in the mid-summer months and eventually spawn in the fall.

David Moynahan

← Tidal marshes and creeks extend many miles across the Big Bend

Corkwood (*Leitneria floridana*)

Gil Nelson

Listed as threatened in Florida, corkwood is found infrequently in mucky coastal soils of the greater Big Bend region. Aptly named, the wood of this species is highly buoyant and was historically used for floats on fishing nets.

Gary Knight

← Salt marsh and flatwoods, St. Marks National Wildlife Refuge

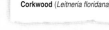

Nassau – St. Johns Marshes and Sea Islands

The sea islands stretch northward from the mouth of the St. Johns River to South Carolina, forming a series of barrier islands that protect large salt-marsh estuaries. Freshwater from the Nassau and St. Marys rivers flows into numerous creeks that pulse with the tides, moving nutrients in and out of the estuary and creating a rich environment teeming with oyster bars, fish, and wading birds. This coastline has the largest tidal range in the state, a situation that drives saltwater farther inland creating larger estuaries. Early Native Americans paddled and fished these waters for thousands of years and created numerous shell mounds from the discarded shellfish that formed much of their diet. On the Atlantic coast of the sea islands is a swath of protected coastal uplands that includes beach dunes, coastal strands, and shady hammocks, many of which became established on old shell middens and now harbor rare plant species such as terrestrial peperomia (Peperomia humilis). Visitors to the area's beaches may catch a glimpse of a rare North Atlantic right whale (Eubalaena glacialis) offshore or a black skimmer (Rynchops niger) gliding low over the water to snap up small fish. Indeed, bird watching is a popular activity in the region. On the beaches or in the marshes and tidal flats, masses of shorebirds can be found, such as red knots (Calidris canutus) that congregate each spring in the Nassau Sound to stop and refuel on their long migration from Tierra del Fuego to summer breeding grounds in the Arctic tundra.

Green ladies-tresses (Spiranthes polyantha)

Jean Putnam Hancock

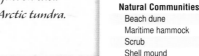

5 Miles
5 Kilometers
NASSAU COUNTY
GEORGIA
FLORIDA
Fernandina Beach
NASSAU RIVER-ST. JOHNS RIVER MARSHES AQUATIC PRESERVE
AMELIA ISLAND STATE PARK
BIG TALBOT ISLAND STATE PARK
LITTLE TALBOT ISLAND STATE PARK
PUMPKIN HILL CREEK PRESERVE STATE PARK
TIMUCUAN ECOLOGICAL AND HISTORIC PRESERVE
Nassau River
Ft. George R.
St. Johns River
Jacksonville
(DUVAL COUNTY)

Nassau- St. Johns Marshes & Sea Islands

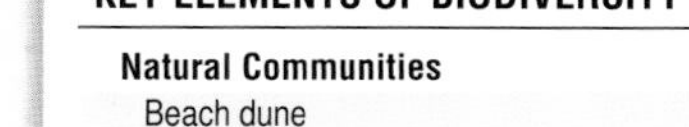

KEY ELEMENTS OF BIODIVERSITY

Natural Communities
- Beach dune
- Maritime hammock
- Scrub
- Shell mound
- Salt marsh

Plants

Forestiera godfreyi	Godfrey's swampprivet
Lantana depressa var. *floridana*	Atlantic Coast Florida lantana

Animals

Caretta caretta	loggerhead
Charadrius melodus	piping plover
Chelonia mydas	green turtle
Dermochelys coriacea	leatherback
Trichechus manatus latirostris	Florida manatee

David Moynahan

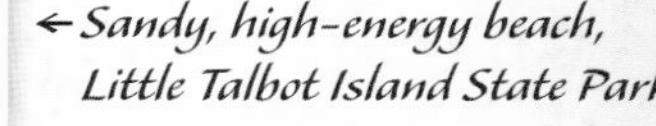

Sandy, high-energy beach, Little Talbot Island State Park

Patrick Leary

Salt marsh in Nassau County dominated by cordgrass

David Moynahan

Black skimmer (*Rynchops niger*) skimming the water with its knife-like lower beak positioned to catch fish.

David Moynahan

Marbled godwit (*Limosa fedoa*)

David Moynahan

Wood stork (*Mycteria americana*)

David Moynahan

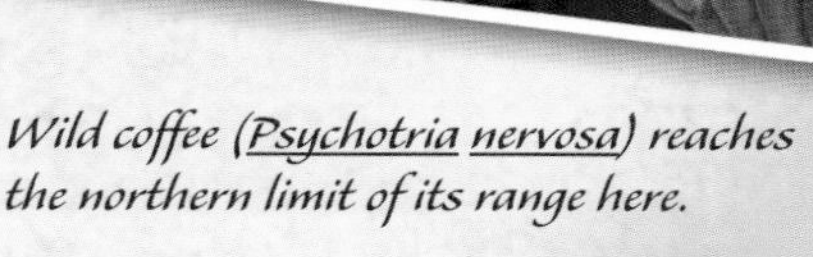

Wild coffee (Psychotria nervosa) reaches the northern limit of its range here.

Ocala Uplands

The Ocala Uplands—part of an ancient dune field—is the largest contiguous remnant of scrub in Florida. Dominated by the 384,000-acre Ocala National Forest, this region resembles a vast sea—a closed-canopy forest of sand pine scrub on low, rolling hills of white sand punctuated by islands of sandhill. Streams issue forth from crystal-clear springs, and extensive basin swamps and swamp lakes provide havens for wildlife. Today's Ocala scrub is mostly sand pine plantations. The scrub was probably formerly a patchier mix of sand pine and oak scrub more favorable to rare plants and animals, but also subject to regular catastrophic wildfires. Still critically important for biodiversity, the Ocala scrub supports the world's largest population of the federally listed Florida scrub-jay (*Aphelocoma coerulescens*) and many rare plants, including the federally listed Florida bonamia (*Bonamia grandiflora*) and Britton's beargrass (*Nolina brittoniana*). Riverside Island is an exceptional example of sandhill. An uneven-aged woodland of longleaf pine over a dense groundcover of wiregrass and associated herbs, this tract supports a healthy population of the federally endangered red-cockaded woodpecker (*Picoides borealis*). Mormon Branch, a boggy spring-fed stream and hydric hammock, is home to several rare plant species, including the large-leaved grass of parnassus (*Parnassia grandifolia*). Perhaps the southernmost location of Atlantic white cedar (*Chamaecyparis thyoides*) is found here and gives nearby Juniper Creek its name. Six first- or second-magnitude springs arise in the Ocala Uplands. In winter, the relatively warm waters of Salt and Silver Glen springs provide important refuge for Florida manatees (*Trichechus manatus latirostris*).

Crystal clear waters of an Ocala Uplands spring

Sandhill in Ocala National Forest

Florida bonamia (*Bonamia grandiflora*)

Pygmy pipes (*Monotropsis reynoldsiae*)

Sand pine scrub in Ocala National Forest

KEY ELEMENTS OF BIODIVERSITY

Natural Communities
- Sandhill
- Scrub
- Spring-run stream

Plants

Illicium parviflorum	star anise
Monotropsis reynoldsiae	pygmy pipes
Vicia ocalensis	Ocala vetch

Animals

Aphelocoma coerulescens	Florida scrub-jay
Drymarchon couperi	eastern indigo snake
Gopherus polyphemus	gopher tortoise
Picoides borealis	red-cockaded woodpecker
Plestiodon reynoldsi	sand skink
Ursus americanus floridanus	Florida black bear

Brooksville Ridge Sandhills

← Eastern indigo snake (Drymarchon couperi)

Dan Hipes

Dan Hipes

↑ Gopher tortoise (Gopherus polyphemus)

The Brooksville Ridge Sandhills occupy a prominent linear land feature in west central Florida derived from an ancient dune field. The area's rolling hills of well-drained, sandy soils support some of the largest and finest examples of sandhill—a natural community imperiled in Florida and characterized by an open canopied forest of longleaf pine, an understory of turkey oak, and ground cover of wiregrass. It is habitat for some of Florida's rarest animals, including the red-cockaded woodpecker (Picoides borealis) and Eastern indigo snake (Drymarchon couperi). Elevations on the Brooksville Ridge range from 70 to 300 feet. Higher elevation areas of deep sands serve as important recharge areas for the Floridan aquifer. The Citrus, Croom, and Two-Mile Prairie tracts of Withlacoochee State Forest are all found on the Brooksville Ridge and are characterized by extensive areas of good quality sandhill. Land managers regularly use prescribed fire to maintain the health of these forests and to reduce fuels, lessening the chance of wildfire. Outside of Withlacoochee State Forest, the area of sandhill has been much reduced by conversion to agricultural and residential uses. Other threats to sandhill include fire suppression, fragmentation, and, to a lesser extent, invasive species. Other notable natural features in the vicinity of the Brooksville Ridge Sandhills are the upland hardwood forests of Annutteliga Hammock; and in lower lying areas, a karst landscape of grottoes, sinkholes, and terrestrial caves, including Pineola Grotto and Lizzie Hart Sink, both with diverse assemblages of rare ferns.

KEY ELEMENTS OF BIODIVERSITY

Natural Communities

Mesic hammock
Sandhill
Sinkhole

Plants

Asplenium verecundum	modest spleenwort
Justicia cooleyi	Cooley's water-willow
Monotropsis reynoldsiae	pygmy pipes

Animals

Drymarchon couperi	eastern indigo snake
Gopherus polyphemus	gopher tortoise
Heterodon simus	southern hognose snake
Picoides borealis	red-cockaded woodpecker
Podomys floridanus	Florida mouse
Stilosoma extenuata	short-tailed snake

Morning glory (Ipomoea spp.)—>

Brenda Herring

Palmleaf rockcap fern (*Pecuma ptilodon*), left
Plumed rockcap fern (*Pecuma plumula*), right

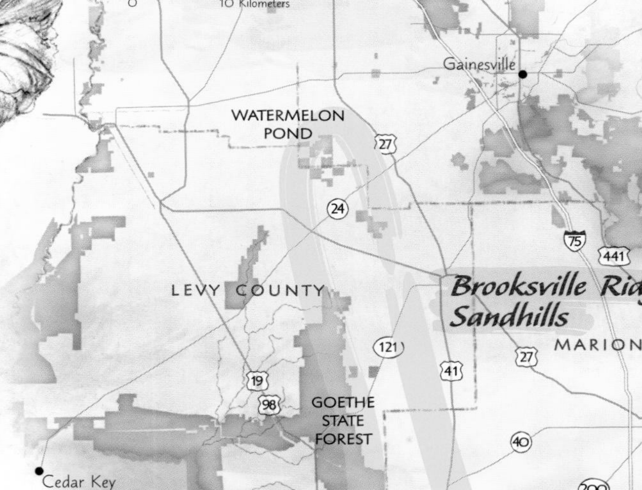

Sandhill with longleaf regeneration, → Withlacoochee State Forest

Dan Hipes

Don Herring

← Open-canopy aspect of a sandhill

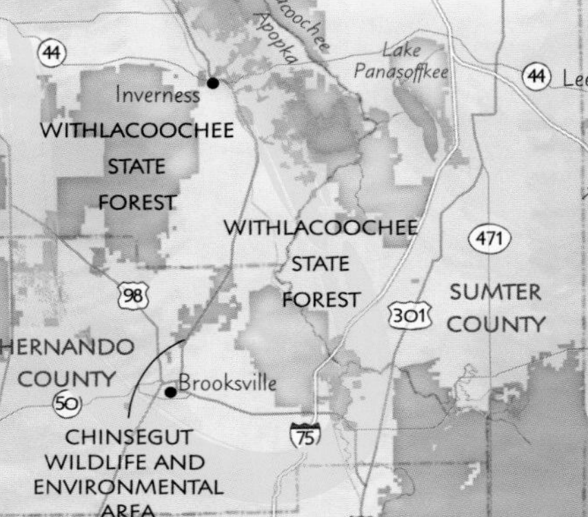

Canaveral Coast

The Canaveral Coast area is famous for its wildlife, undeveloped beaches, and space exploration launches. The area features a unique interagency partnership between Canaveral National Seashore, Merritt Island National Wildlife Refuge, National Aeronautics and Space Agency, and Cape Canaveral Air Force Station. About 40 miles of Atlantic Ocean shoreline are managed as national seashore and military base, making it the longest stretch of non-urbanized Atlantic beach in Florida. The beaches provide critical habitat for nesting sea turtles, especially loggerhead (Caretta caretta), federally listed as threatened. The wide variety of natural communities includes beach dune, coastal strand, salt marsh, scrub, scrubby flatwoods, and maritime hammock. Many tropical plants, such as sea grape and gumbo limbo, reach the northern limits of their range here. The area is a prime destination for bird watchers. Wading birds, waterfowl, shorebirds, songbirds, and raptors forage year round. During winter months, hundreds of thousands of migratory birds use the marshes and impoundments. Migrating Neotropical songbirds rely on the coastal maritime hammocks as resting areas. The endemic Florida scrub-jay (Aphelocoma coerulescens), federally listed as threatened, has one of its largest remaining populations in this region. Extensive restoration efforts are ongoing to improve scrub-jay habitat in scrub overgrown by long-term fire exclusion.

Florida scrub-jay (Aphelocoma coerulescens) →

www.TJDunkerton.com

Roseate spoonbills (Platalea ajaja) ↓

David Moynahan

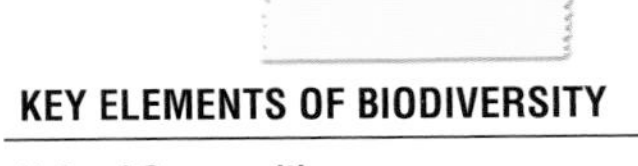

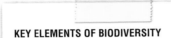

KEY ELEMENTS OF BIODIVERSITY

Natural Communities

- Coastal strand
- Salt marsh
- Maritime hammock
- Scrub

Plants

Chamaesyce cumulicola	sand-dune spurge
Harrisia simpsonii	Simpson's prickly apple
Lantana depressa var. *floridana*	Atlantic Coast Florida lantana
Tephrosia angustissima var. *curtissii*	coastal hoary-pea

Animals

Aphelocoma coerulescens	Florida scrub-jay
Caretta caretta	loggerhead
Chelonia mydas	green turtle
Dermochelys coriacea	leatherback
Drymarchon couperi	eastern indigo snake
Mycteria americana	wood stork

Melynda Reid

↖ *Purple passion-flower (Passiflora incarnata), a common vine*

↑ *Great blue herons (Ardea herodias) foraging in tidal wetlands*

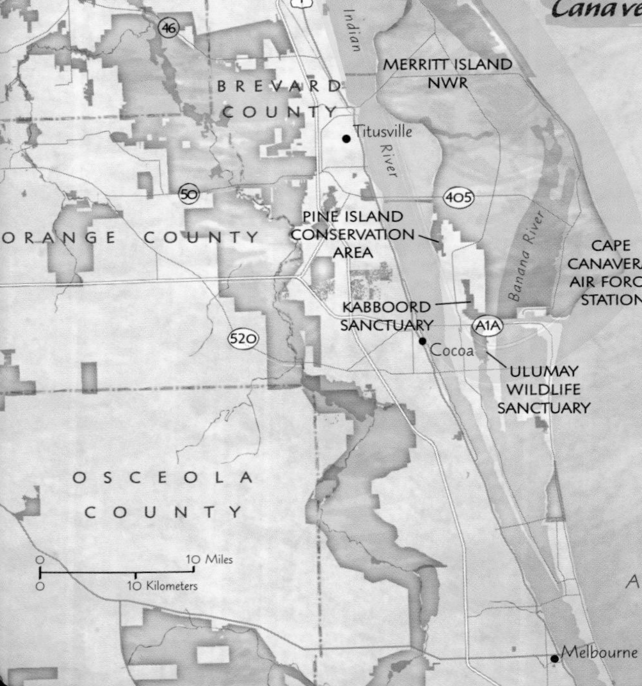

David Moynahan

↑ *Waterfowl are often abundant in winter months*

David Moynahan

Blue-winged teal (*Anas discors*), Female (left), Male (right)

Average length: Female 14 inches, Male 16 inches
Average weight: Female 0.8 lbs., Male 1.0 lbs.

Lake Wales Ridge

The Lake Wales Ridge is a series of ancient sand dunes deposited about 650,000 years ago when much of the Florida peninsula was under water. This long and narrow former chain of islands was separated from the mainland, causing its plants and animals to evolve in isolation. As a result, the ridge now contains one of the highest concentrations of rare plants and animals in the United States. The importance of the ridge to rare plant conservation in Florida—and globally—cannot be overstated. Twenty-two (39%) of Florida's 56 federally listed plants are found here. The ecological importance of the area is reflected in the creation of the Lake Wales Ridge National Wildlife Refuge, the nation's first wildlife refuge created for the recovery of endangered and threatened plants. More than 85% of the original 80,000 acres of upland habitats on the Lake Wales Ridge has been lost to development. Remnants of intact habitat are found scattered up and down the approximately 115-mile-long and up to 10-mile-wide area. Each has its own distinctive suite of species, demonstrating the need to conserve areas throughout the length of the ridge. The Carter Creek Unit of the Lake Wales Ridge Wildlife and Environmental Area, Lake Wales Ridge State Forest, and TNC's Tiger Creek Preserve are some of the best remaining examples of the original landscape. All offer exceptional opportunities to see many rare plants and animals, such as Florida scrub-jay (Aphelocoma coerulescens), dependent on these unique habitats.

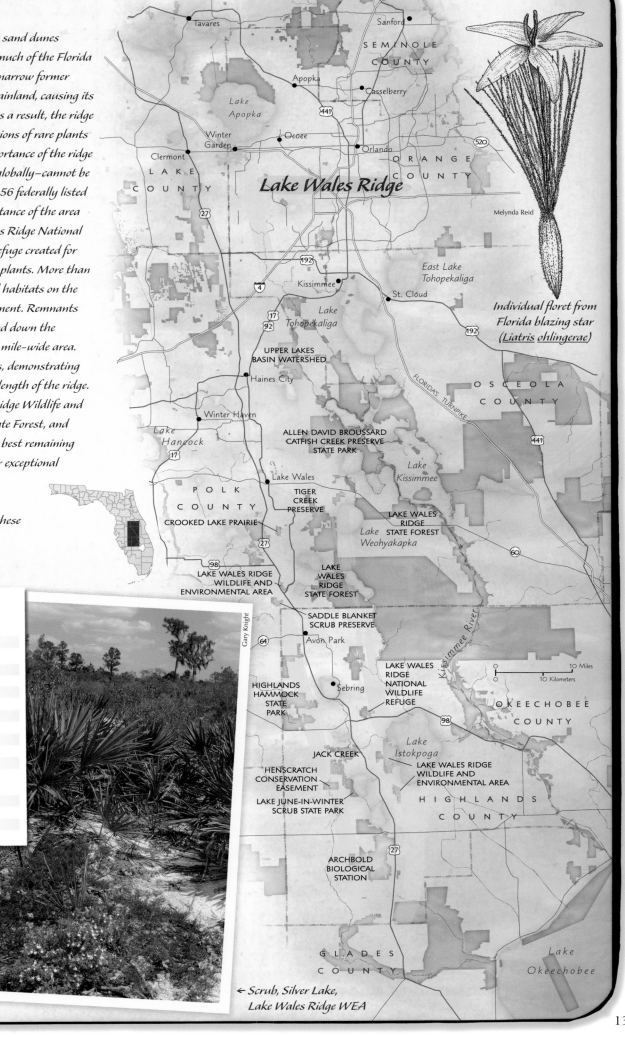

Individual floret from Florida blazing star (Liatris ohlingerae)

KEY ELEMENTS OF BIODIVERSITY

Natural Communities	
Scrub	
Plants	
Cladonia perforata	perforate reindeer lichen
Crotalaria avonensis	Avon Park rabbit-bells
Dicerandra christmanii	Garrett's scrub balm
Dicerandra frutescens	scrub mint
Eryngium cuneifolium	wedge-leaved button-snakeroot
Euphorbia rosescens	scrub spurge
Lupinus aridorum	scrub lupine
Schizachyrium niveum	scrub bluestem
Warea amplexifolia	clasping warea
Ziziphus celata	scrub ziziphus
Animals	
Aphelocoma coerulescens	Florida scrub-jay
Cicindela highlandensis	Highlands tiger beetle
Plestiodon egregius lividus	blue-tailed mole skink
Plestiodon reynoldsi	sand skink

The sandy, well-drained soils of the Lake Wales Ridge proved highly suitable for citrus cultivation. Rows of citrus trees are clearly seen in this aerial photo.

Gary Knight

← Scrub, Silver Lake, Lake Wales Ridge WEA

Florida Keys

Of Florida's thousands of miles of coastline, none are more exotic or special in terms of biodiversity than those of the Florida Keys—an archipelago of more than 1,500 limestone islands (at least 230 named) that begins near the southeastern tip of the Florida peninsula and extends in a sweeping 200-mile arc south by southwest through the warm waters of the Florida Straits to the Dry Tortugas. Although the Keys occupy latitudes north of the Tropic of Cancer, their climate and vegetation are tropical due to the moderating effect the surrounding marine waters have on air temperature. This tropical environment supports plants, animals, and natural communities found nowhere else in the state and some found nowhere else in the world, including Key deer (Odocoileus virginianus clavium) and Florida semaphore cactus (Opuntia corallicola). Altogether the area of the Florida Keys totals about 90,000 acres, much of that being mangrove wetlands although it also includes imperiled tropical communities such as rockland hammock and pine rockland. Offshore, large coral reefs add significantly to the remarkable biodiversity of this area. About 20% of the Keys has been altered by residential and commercial development, with most of the conversion affecting uplands. Parts of the Keys are managed for conservation, including federal wildlife refuges and state parks and preserves. The state continues to purchase and protect additional lands: 1,105 acres in 681 parcels have been acquired through the Florida Forever program since it began in 2000; while other important sites remain on the Florida Forever priority list for future acquisition.

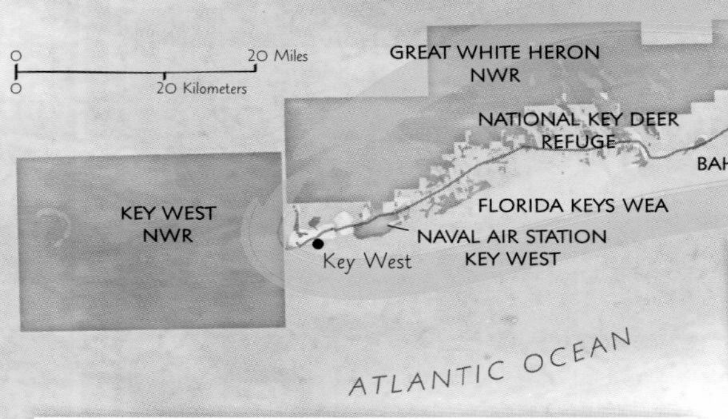

KEY ELEMENTS OF BIODIVERSITY

Natural Communities
- Keys cactus barren
- Pine rockland
- Rockland hammock

Plants

Chamaesyce deltoidea ssp. *serpyllum*	wedge spurge
Chamaesyce garberi	Garber's spurge
Guapira floridana	Rock Key devil's-claws
Linum arenicola	sand flax
Opuntia corallicola	Florida semaphore cactus
Pilosocereus robinii	tree cactus

Animals

Chelonia mydas	green turtle
Crocodylus acutus	American crocodile
Neotoma floridana smalli	Key Largo woodrat
Odocoileus virginianus clavium	key deer
Orthalicus reses reses	Stock Island tree snail
Papilio aristodemus ponceanus	Schaus' swallowtail

Gary Knight

← Pine rockland, National Key Deer Refuge

Gary Knight

The critically → imperiled semaphore cactus is threatened, in part, by herbivory from the caterpillar of a non-native moth.

J. C. Putnam H.

Lignum vitae (Guaiacum sanctum)

David Moynahan

Key deer → (Odocoileus virginianus clavium)

Gary Knight

Small-flowered lilythorn
(*Catesbaea parviflora*)

Amy M. Jenkins

Locustberry
(*Byrsonima lucida*)

Gary Knight

Florida semaphore cactus
(*Opuntia corallicola*)

Central Florida Dry Prairies

Dominic Sherony

Florida grasshopper sparrow
(*Ammodramus savannarum floridanus*)

David Moynahan

Florida burrowing owl
(*Athene cunicularia floridana*)

Down from the xeric hills of the Lake Wales Ridge is the flat, treeless dry prairie region of south central Florida. Unlike the grass-dominated prairies of the midwestern U.S., Florida's dry prairies are a unique assemblage of dwarf shrubs, wiregrass, and a huge diversity of herbs. This is Florida's big sky land where summer visitors have an unparalleled view of massive afternoon thunderclouds, the so-called "Florida Mountains." The serene vistas of this region are rivaled only by the enormous Everglades marshes, but with the advantage of easy foot travel through knee-high palmettos and runner oaks. Despite the conversion of much of this land to agriculture, some large portions of the historical landscape remain, particularly around the Kissimmee and Myakka rivers. Although early accounts refer to this area as "The Big Prairie," the ecosystem was actually a patchwork of treeless dry and wet prairies along with pine flatwoods, depression marshes, mesic prairie hammocks, and floodplain marshes. Pine tree seedlings had difficulty establishing in this area due to a combination of local rainfall patterns and poorly drained soils. Those that did gain a foothold faced frequent, often yearly fires that swept unimpeded across the level country. Prairies are a haven for species that require wide open spaces for foraging or nesting. The buzzing song of the Florida grasshopper sparrow (Ammodramus savannarum floridanus), a regional endemic, can be heard from spring to mid-summer. This is also the native land of the Florida burrowing owl (Athene cunicularia floridana), a species that has largely been driven into pastureland in the last century by habitat loss and degradation.

Gary Knight

Palmettos are a dominant species in the low, open vegetation of dry prairie (Kissimmee Prairie Preserve State Park)

Gary Knight

Large flower rosegentian (Sabatia grandiflora) and yellow milkwort (Polygala rugelii)

Crested caracara

(Caracara cheriway)

FWC

KEY ELEMENTS OF BIODIVERSITY

Natural Communities	
Dry prairie	
Floodplain marsh	
Wet prairie	
Plants	
Calopogon multiflorus	many-flowered grass-pink
Animals	
Ammodramus savannarum floridanus	Florida grasshopper sparrow
Athene cunicularia floridana	Florida burrowing owl
Atrytone arogos arogos	arogos skipper
Caracara cheriway	crested caracara
Grus canadensis pratensis	Florida sandhill crane

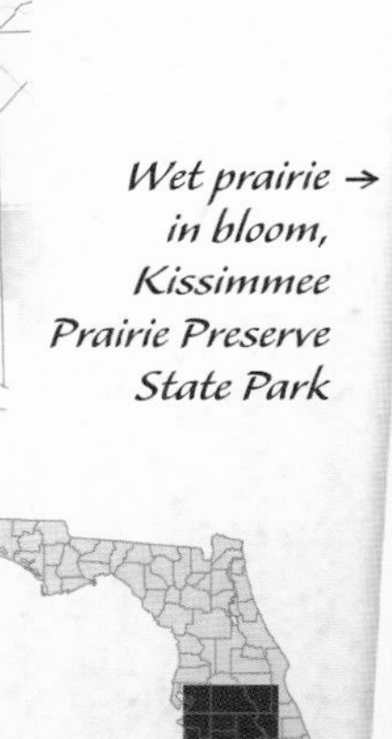

Central Florida Dry Prairies

Gary Knight

Wet prairie → in bloom, Kissimmee Prairie Preserve State Park

V APPENDICES

Dry prairie, Myakka River State Park
Gary Knight

Reference Maps and Data

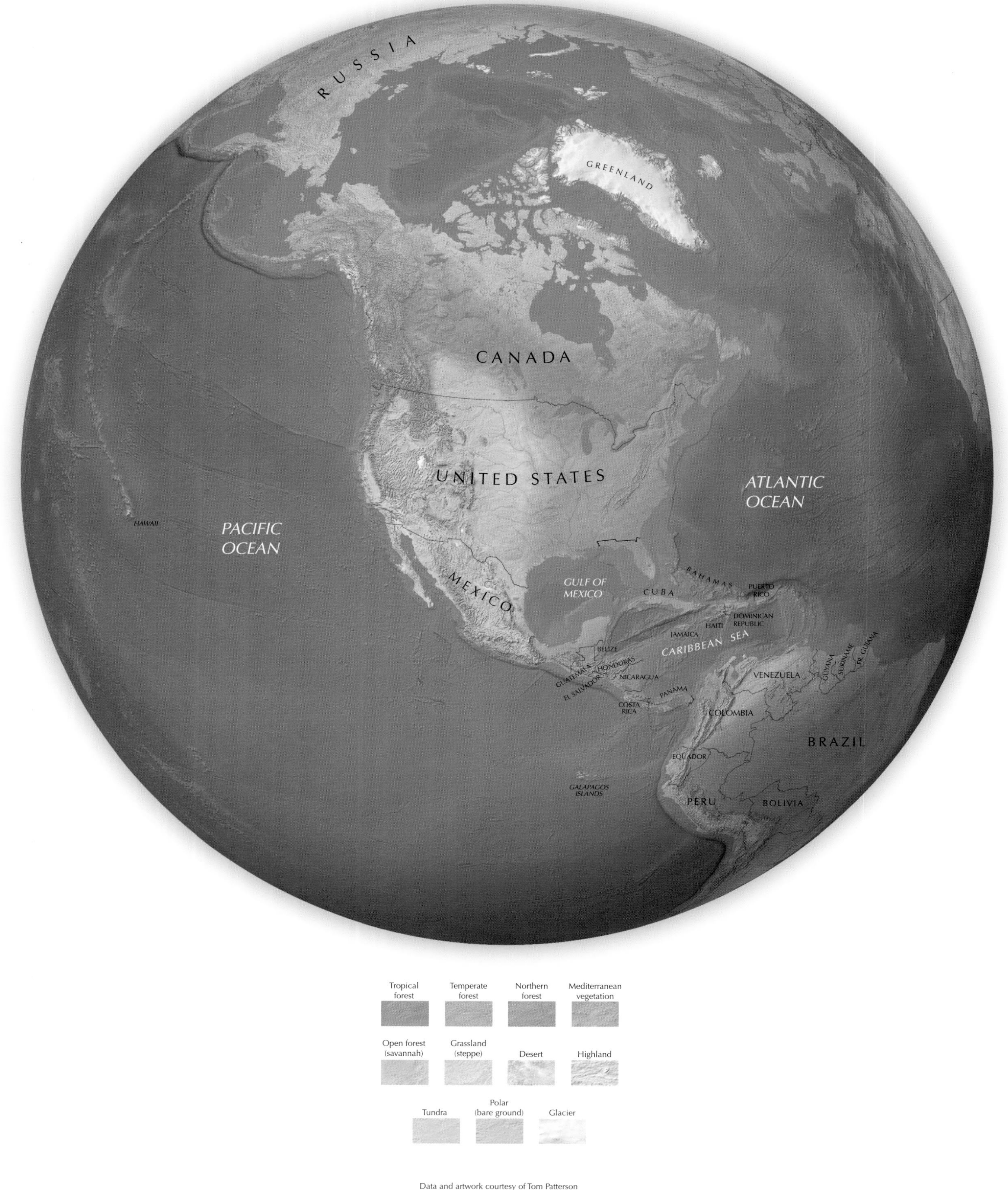

Data and artwork courtesy of Tom Patterson
naturalearthdata.com and shadedrelief.com

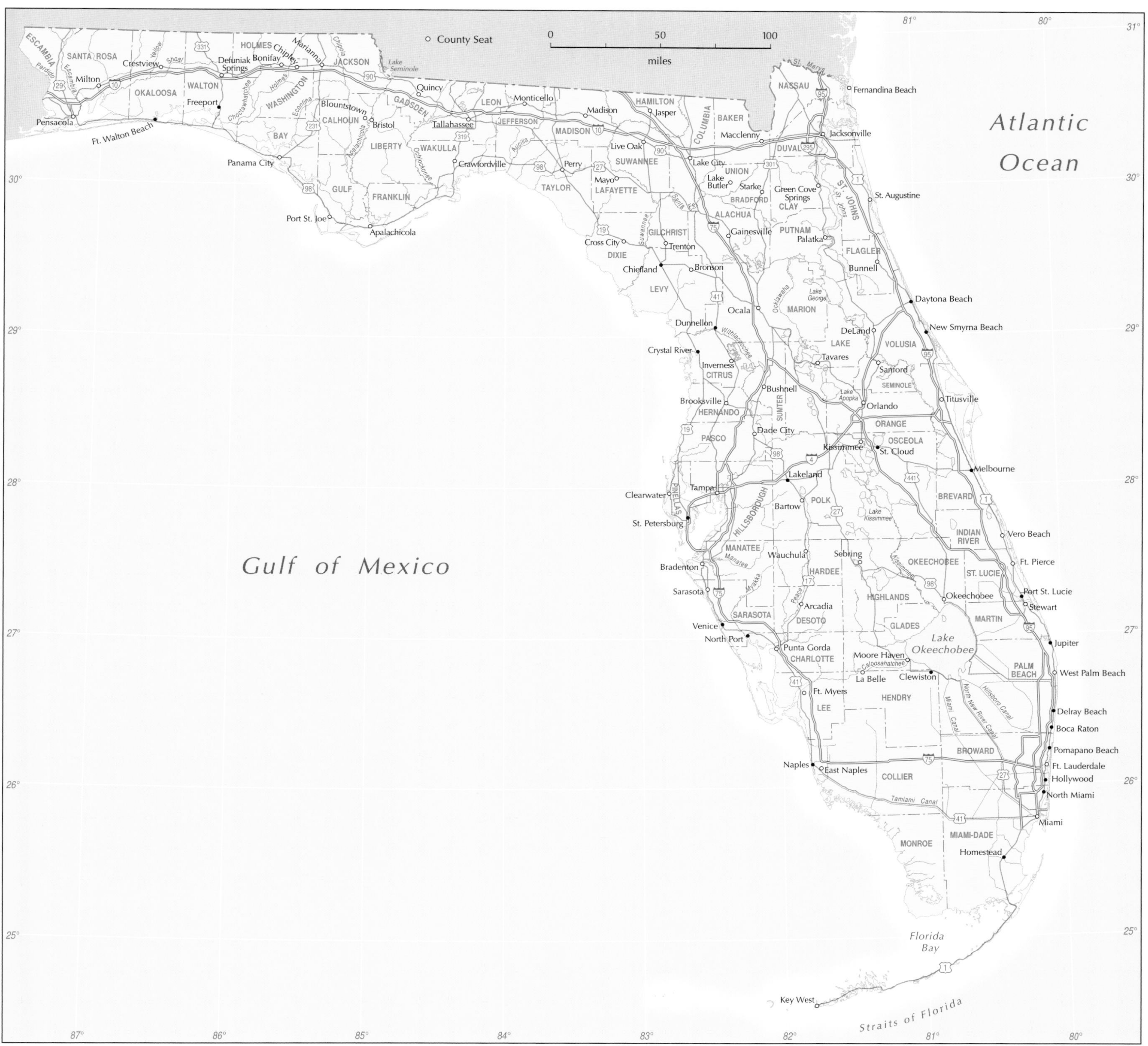

Florida Facts

Total area: 58,560 square miles
Total land area: 54,252 square miles
Total water area: 4,308 square miles
Rank among states in total area: 22nd
Length north and south (St. Marys River to Key West): 447 miles
Width east and west (Atlantic Ocean to Perdido River): 361 miles
Distance from Pensacola to Key West: 792 miles (by road)
Highest natural point: 345 feet near Lakewood in northeast Walton County
Geographic Center: 12 miles northwest of Brooksville, Hernando County
Coastline: 1,197 statute miles
Tidal shoreline (general): 2,276 statute miles
Beaches: 663 miles
Longest river: St. Johns, 273 miles
Largest lake: Lake Okeechobee, 700 square miles

Number of counties: 67
Largest county: Palm Beach, 2,578 square miles
Smallest county: Union, 245 square miles
Number of lakes (greater than 10 acres): approximately 7,700
Number of first-magnitude springs: 27
Number of islands (larger than 10 acres): approximately 4,500
First permanent European settlement: 1565, St. Augustine, by Spanish
U.S. Territory: 1821
Admitted to the union as state: March 3, 1845 (27th state)
Population 2000: 15,982,839
Population rank among states 2010: 4th
Population 2010: 18,801,310
Population growth rate 2000-2010: 17.6%
Most populous metro area (2010): Miami-Ft. Lauderdale-Pompano Beach 5,564,635

Summary of Florida Conservation Lands

Including Less-than-fee Conservation Lands Prepared by the Florida Natural Areas Inventory

February 2011

	Fee simple Acres[1,2]	Less-than-fee Acres[3,4]
FEDERAL CONSERVATION LANDS		
USDA Forest Service	1,183,108	1,696
USDI Fish and Wildlife Service	502,361	2,402
USDI National Park Service[5]	1,684,435	1,337
U.S. Dept. of Defense	664,239	0
U.S. Other	4,811	0
TOTAL FEDERALLY MANAGED non-submerged lands	**4,038,954**	**5,435**
STATE & WATER MGMT. DISTRICT CONSERVATION LANDS		
DACS Division of Forestry	1,057,234	3,200
DEP Division of Recreation and Parks	592,172	0
DEP Office of Coastal and Aquatic Managed Areas	54,117	0
DEP Office of Greenways and Trails	84,349	0
DEP Division of State Lands	0	96,150
DEP Bureau of Mine Reclamation	5,710	14,601
Fish and Wildlife Conservation Commission	1,417,506	42,888
Babcock Ranch (managed by Babcock Ranch Management, LLC)	73,239	0
Department of Corrections (managed by PRIDE)	18,200	0
Department of Military Affairs	73,076	0
State Universities	14,260	66
Water Management Districts	1,471,260	403,887
Undesignated State Lands[6]	4,754	0
TOTAL STATE & WMD MANAGED non-submerged lands	**4,865,877**	**560,792**
LOCAL (COUNTY & MUNICIPAL) CONSERVATION LANDS	**461,668**	**7,324**
TOTAL STATE, FEDERAL, AND LOCAL non-submerged lands	***9,366,499***	***573,551***
PRIVATE CONSERVATION LANDS	128,029	55,553

LAND AREA OF STATE OF FLORIDA 34,721,280 acres[7]

PERCENTAGE OF FLORIDA IN FEDERALLY MANAGED CONSERVATION LANDS	11.6%	0.02%
PERCENTAGE OF FLORIDA IN STATE-MANAGED CONSERVATION LANDS	14.0%	1.6%
PERCENTAGE OF FLORIDA IN LOCALLY MANAGED CONSERVATION LANDS	1.3%	0.02%

[1]Acreages are counted once under the primary managing agency even though there may be several owners and/or managers. For this reason, total acres for some agencies may be higher than the acres to which they hold title and others may be lower.

[2]Acreages listed include terrestrial wetlands such as the Everglades but exclude 3,720,062 acres of submerged marine, lake, or river bottom (such as state aquatic preserves or Florida Bay) that are part of certain managed areas.

[3]Numbers include a total of 606,441 acres less-than-fee properties (6.0% of total conservation lands).

[4]Represents the less-than-fee lands included in the FNAI conservation lands database as of 1 March 2010. All properties are owned by either private individuals or private foundations or corporations. Lands are classified by the agency or organization that monitors the easement on the property. The same agency or organization usually holds title to the easement, but there are a few exceptions.

[5]Acreage total includes all non-submerged acres within official federally designated boundaries of National Park Service lands.

[6]Lands owned by the State that are not currently leased to a governmental agency.

[7]Source: E.A. Fernald and E.D. Purdum, eds. 1996. Atlas of Florida, Gainesville: University of Florida Press.

FNAI 2010 Natural Community Short Descriptions

Hardwood Forested Uplands – mesic or xeric forest dominated mainly by hardwood trees

Slope Forest (G2?/S1)

Steep slope on bluff or in sheltered ravine within the Apalachicola drainage; sand/clay substrate; mesic-hydric; central Panhandle; rare or no fire; closed canopy of mainly deciduous species; American beech, Florida maple, white oak, Ashe's magnolia, southern magnolia, spruce pine, Shumard's oak.

Upland Hardwood Forest (G5/S3)

Upland with sand/clay and/or calcareous substrate; mesic; Panhandle to central peninsula; rare or no fire; closed deciduous or mixed deciduous/evergreen canopy; American beech, southern magnolia, hackberry, swamp chestnut oak, white oak, horse sugar, flowering dogwood, and mixed hardwoods.

Dry Upland Hardwood Forest
On dry slopes or along upper slopes with sand/clay substrate; mesic; temperate; rare fire; closed canopy; laurel oak and/or live oak and/or pignut hickory, southern magnolia, shortleaf pine, loblolly pine, and/or mixed hardwoods.

Mesic Hammock (G3/S3?)

Flatland with sand/organic soil; mesic; primarily central peninsula; occasional or rare fire; closed evergreen canopy; live oak, cabbage palm, southern magnolia, pignut hickory, saw palmetto.

Prairie Mesic Hammock
Isolated stands within a matrix of pyrogenic vegetation; occasional fire; live oak, cabbage palm, saw palmetto.

Rockland Hammock (G2/S2)

Flatland with limestone substrate; mesic; southern peninsula and Keys; rare or no fire; closed canopy of evergreen mixed tropical hardwoods; gumbo limbo, pigeon plum, stoppers.

Thorn Scrub
Along ecotones or within openings in rockland hammock; low-statured; dominated by spiny species; saffron plum, blackbead, hog plum, buttonwood, plus other common rockland hammock species.

Xeric Hammock (G3/S3)

Upland with deep sand substrate; xeric; primarily eastern Panhandle to central peninsula; rare or no fire; closed canopy of evergreen hardwoods; sand live oak, saw palmetto.

Hardwood Forested Uplands – hills with mesic or xeric woodlands or shrublands; canopy, if present, open and consisting of pine or a mixture of pine and deciduous hardwoods

Upland Mixed Woodland (G2/S2)

Upland with loamy soils; mesic-xeric; central Panhandle to extreme northern central peninsula; occasional fire (variable but as little as two up to 20 year interval); open to partially closed canopy over an open understory of mixed herbs and scattered shrubs; mixture of southern red oak, mockernut hickory, and longleaf or shortleaf pine with other mixed hardwoods; wiregrass infrequent.

Upland Pine (G3/S2)

Upland with sand/clay substrate; mesic-xeric; Panhandle to extreme northern central peninsula; frequent fire (1-3 years); savanna of widely spaced pines over primarily herbaceous understory; longleaf pine and/or loblolly pine and/or shortleaf pine, southern red oak, wiregrass.

Sandhill (G3/S2)

Upland with deep sand substrate; xeric; Panhandle to central peninsula; frequent fire (1-3 years); savanna of widely spaced longleaf pine and/or turkey oak with wiregrass understory.

Scrub (G2/S2)

Upland with deep sand substrate; xeric; statewide except extreme southern peninsula and Keys, mainly coastal in Panhandle; occasional or rare fire (usually 5-20 years); open or dense shrubs with or without pine canopy; sand pine and/or scrub oaks and/or Florida rosemary.

Rosemary Scrub
Along ecotones or within openings in rockland hammock; low-statured; dominated by spiny species; saffron plum, blackbead, hog plum, buttonwood, plus other common rockland hammock species.

Sand Pine Scrub
On ridges throughout the state; rare fire (20-80 years); canopy of sand pine and an understory of the three shrubby oaks, or less commonly, Florida rosemary.

Pine Flatwoods and Dry Prairie – mesic or hydric pine woodland or mesic shrubland on flat sandy or limestone substrates, may have a hardpan that impedes drainage

Wet Flatwoods (G4/S4)

Flatland with sand substrate; seasonally inundated; statewide except extreme southern peninsula and Keys; frequent fire (2-4 years for grassy wet flatwoods, 5-10 years for shrubby wet flatwoods); closed to open pine canopy with grassy or shrubby understory; slash pine, pond pine, large gallberry, fetterbush, sweetbay, cabbage palm, wiregrass, toothache grass.

Cutthroat Grass Flatwoods
On and near the Lake Wales Ridge; frequent fire (2-4 years); widely scattered pines over cutthroat grass and/or other hydrophytic herbs.

Cabbage Palm Flatwoods
On shelly sand or where limestone is near the surface; central to southern peninsula; pine canopy over cabbage palm understory.

Mesic Flatwoods (G4/S4)

Flatland with sand substrate; mesic; statewide except extreme southern peninsula and Keys; frequent fire (2-4 years); open pine canopy with a layer of low shrubs and herbs; longleaf pine and/or slash pine, saw palmetto, gallberry, dwarf live oak, wiregrass.

Scrubby Flatwoods (G2/S2?)

Flatland with sand substrate; xeric-mesic; statewide except extreme southern peninsula and Keys; occasional fire (5-15 years); widely scattered pine canopy over saw palmetto and scrub oaks; longleaf pine, sand live oak, myrtle oak, Chapman's oak, saw palmetto, wiregrass.

Pine Rockland (G1/S1)

Flatland with exposed limestone substrate; mesic-xeric; southern peninsula and Keys; frequent to occasional fire (3-7 years); open pine canopy with mixed shrubs and herbs in understory; South Florida slash pine, palms, mixed tropical and temperate shrubs, grasses, and herbs.

Dry Prairie (G2/S2)

Flatland with sand soils over an organic or clay hardpan; mesic-xeric; central peninsula; annual or frequent fire (1-2 years); treeless with a low cover of shrubs and herbs; wiregrass, dwarf live oak, stunted saw palmetto, bottlebrush threeawn, broomsedge.

Coastal Uplands – mesic or xeric communities restricted to barrier islands and near shore; woody or herbaceous vegetation; other communities may also occur in coastal environments

Beach Dune (G3/S2)

Active coastal dune with sand substrate; xeric; statewide; rare or no fire; marine influence; open herbaceous vegetation with no canopy; sea oats, railroad vine, bitter panicum, and/or mixed salt-spray tolerant grasses and herbs.

Coastal Berm (G3/S2)

Old bar or storm debris with sand/shell substrate; xeric-mesic; southern peninsula and Keys; rare or no fire; marine influence; variable vegetation structure; mixed tropical herbs, shrubs, and trees.

Coastal Grassland (G3/S2)

Coastal flatland behind dunes with stable sand substrate; mesic-hydric; statewide excluding Keys; occasional fire; marine influence; herbaceous vegetation with no canopy; salt-tolerant grasses and herbs; sea oats, bitter panicum, camphorweed, hairawn muhly, Gulf bluestem.

Coastal Strand (G3/S2)

Stabilized coastal dune with sand substrate; xeric; peninsula; rare fire; marine influence; primarily dense shrubs; saw palmetto in temperate coastal strand or seagrape and/or saw palmetto in tropical coastal strand.

Maritime Hammock (G3/S2)

Stabilized coastal dune with sand substrate; xeric-mesic; statewide but rare in Panhandle and Keys; rare or no fire; marine influence; evergreen closed canopy; live oak, cabbage palm, red bay, red cedar in temperate maritime hammock; gumbo limbo, seagrape, and white or Spanish stopper in tropical maritime hammock.

Shell Mound (G2/S2)

Small hill of shells deposited by native Americans; mesic-xeric; statewide; rare or no fire; marine influence; closed canopy of mixed hardwoods; soapberry, snowberry, white stopper.

Sinkholes and Outcrop Communities – small extent communities with karst features or on exposed limestone

Upland Glade (G1/S1)

Upland with thin clay soils over limestone outcrops; hydric-xeric; central Panhandle only; sparse mixed grasses and herbs with occasional stunted trees and shrubs that are concentrated around the edge; black bogrush, poverty dropseed, diamondflowers, hairawn muhly, Boykin's polygala, red cedar.

Sinkhole (G2/S2)

karst feature with steep walls; mesic-hydric; statewide; variable vegetation structure.

Limestone Outcrop (G2/S2)

Exposed limestone; mesic-hydric; statewide; often with mosses, liverworts, and a diversity of rare ferns.

Key Cactus Barren (G1/S1)

Small openings on flatland with exposed limestone; xeric; restricted to Keys; marine influence; open, herbaceous vegetation with some cacti, agave, and stunted trees; three-spined pricklypear, erect pricklypear, barbed wire cactus, Yucatan fly mallow, Florida Keys indigo, skyblue clustervine, dwarf bindweed.

Maritime Hammock (G3/S2)

Stabilized coastal dune with sand substrate; xeric-mesic; statewide but rare in Panhandle and Keys; rare or no fire; marine influence; evergreen closed canopy; live oak, cabbage palm, red bay, red cedar in temperate maritime hammock; gumbo limbo, seagrape, and white or Spanish stopper in tropical maritime hammock.

Shell Mound (G2/S2)

Small hill of shells deposited by native Americans; mesic-xeric; statewide; rare or no fire; marine influence; closed canopy of mixed hardwoods; soapberry, snowberry, white stopper.

Freshwater Non-Forested Wetlands – herbaceous or shrubby palustrine communities in floodplains or depressions; canopy trees, if present, very sparse and often stunted

Prairies and Bogs – short hydroperiod; dominated by grasses sedges, and/or titi

Seepage Slope (G2/S2)

On or at base of slope with loamy sand substrate; maintained by downslope seepage, usually saturated but rarely inundated; Panhandle and northern peninsula; frequent fire (1-3 years); dense herbaceous community; wiregrass, wiry beaksedges, flattened pipewort, toothache grass, pitcherplants.

Wet Prairie (G2/S2)

Flatland with sand or clayey sand substrate; usually saturated but only occasionally inundated; statewide excluding extreme southern peninsula; frequent fire (2-3 years); treeless, dense herbaceous community with few shrubs; wiregrass, blue maidencane, cutthroat grass, wiry beaksedges, flattened pipewort, toothache grass, pitcherplants, coastalplain yellow-eyed grass.

Cutthroat Seep

Eastern and western edges of the Lake Wales Ridge in central Florida; dominated by the endemic cutthroat grass.

Calcareous Wet Prairie

In central and south-central peninsula on calcareous soils; Gulf hairawn muhly typically dominant with other calcium-loving species.

Pitcherplant Prairie

In the Panhandle on wetter soils; dense stands of tall pitcherplants.

Marl Prairie (G3/S3)

Flatland with marl over limestone substrate; seasonally inundated (<4 months); southern peninsula; frequent to occasional fire (2-10 years depending on density of herbs); purple muhly, sawgrass (stunted), spreading beaksedge, black bogrush, Florida little bluestem, and/or mixed grasses, sometimes with dwarf cypress.

Shrub Bog (G4/S3)

Wetland on organic soil over sand; soil often saturated and mucky, occasionally shallowly inundated; Panhandle to north peninsula; occasional fire (10-20 years); dense stand of shrubs, trees absent or sparse, sphagnum moss common; titi, black titi, fetterbush, large gallberry, laurel greenbrier, pond pine or slash pine.

Marshes – long hydroperiod; dominated by grasses, sedges, broadleaf emergents, floating aquatics, or shrubs

Depression Marsh (G4/S4)

Small, isolated, often rounded depression in sand substrate with peat accumulating toward center; surrounded by fire-maintained community; seasonally inundated; still water; statewide excluding Keys; frequent or occasional fire; largely herbaceous; maidencane, sawgrass, pickerelweed, longleaf threeawn, sand cordgrass, peelbark St. John's wort.

Basin Marsh (G4/S3)

Basin with peat or sand substrate; seasonally inundated; statewide excluding Keys; occasional fire; largely herbaceous; maidencane, sawgrass, bulltongue arrowhead, pickerelweed, Baker's cordgrass, white water lily, coastalplain willow.

Lake Bottom

Marshes on former lake bottoms of "disappearing" lakes in northern Florida, areas that alternate between lake and marsh when the sinkholes draining them are plugged or re-opened; well-known examples are Lake Miccosukee and Paynes Prairie.

Coastal Interdunal Swale (G3/S2)

Linear wetlands between dunes on sandy barrier islands; inundated by local rainfall events; Panhandle to central peninsula; herbaceous or shrubby; sawgrass, hairawn muhly, broomsedge, seashore paspalum, Baker's cordgrass, saltmeadow cordgrass, wax myrtle, coastalplain willow.

Floodplain Marsh (G3/S3)

Floodplain with organic/sand/alluvial substrate; seasonally inundated; Panhandle to central peninsula; frequent or occasional fire (ca. 3 years, much less frequent in freshwater tidal marshes); treeless herbaceous community with few shrubs; sawgrass, maidencane, sand cordgrass, and/or mixed emergents.

Freshwater Tidal Marsh

River mouth wetland on organic/alluvial substrates; receives pulses of freshwater in response to tides; sawgrass, giant cutgrass.

Slough Marsh (G3?/S3?)

Broad, shallow channel with sand/peat substrate; seasonally inundated; intermittently flowing water; central to southern peninsula; frequent or occasional fire (3-10 years); sawgrass, maidencane, pickerelweed, and/or mixed emergents.

Glades Marsh (G3/S3)

Broad, shallow channel with peat/marl substrate directly overlying limestone; seasonally inundated; stagnant or slow flowing water; Everglades basin, Big Cypress region, and Keys; frequent to occasional fire (3-10 years); sawgrass, spikerush, maidencane, beaksedges, mixed emergents.

Keys Freshwater Marsh

Limestone depression; restricted to Florida Keys; may be saline during dry season; sawgrass.

Slough (G3/S3)

Broad, shallow channel with peat; inundated except during droughts; flowing water; statewide excluding Keys; rare fire; sparsely canopied or with emergent or floating plants; alligator flag, American white waterlily.

Pond Apple Slough

Canopied sloughs dominated by pond apple or Carolina ash, often with abundant epiphytes.

Freshwater Forested Wetlands – floodplains or depressions dominated by hydrophytic trees

Cypress/Tupelo – dominated entirely by cypress or tupelo, or these species important in the canopy; long hydroperiod

Dome Swamp (G4/S4)

Small or large and shallow isolated depression in sand/marl/limestone substrate with peat accumulating toward center; occurring within a fire-maintained community; seasonally inundated; still water; statewide excluding Keys; occasional or rare fire; forested, canopy often tallest in center; pond cypress, swamp tupelo.

Gum Pond

Underlain by a clay lens; generally occurs in upland pine; mainly Panhandle; longer hydroperiod and lower fire frequency than cypress-dominated dome swamps; dominated by swamp tupelo.

Stringer Swamp

Narrow linear swamps; occur within a pyrogenic community along intermittent streams that only flow during heavy rainfall; Panhandle; dominated by pond cypress.

Basin Swamp (G4/S3)

Typically large basin wetland with peat substrate; seasonally inundated; still water or with water output; Panhandle to central peninsula; occasional or rare fire; forest of cypress/tupelo/mixed hardwoods; pond cypress, swamp tupelo.

Strand Swamp (G2/S2)

Broad, shallow channel with peat over mineral substrate; situated in limestone troughs; seasonally inundated; slow flowing water; vicinity of Lake Okeechobee and southward; occasional or rare fire; closed canopy of cypress and mixed hardwoods; cypress, pond apple, strangler fig, willow, abundant epiphytes.

Floodplain Swamp (G4/S4)

Along or near rivers and streams with organic/alluvial substrate; usually inundated; Panhandle to central peninsula; rare or no fire; closed canopy dominated by cypress, tupelo, and/or black gum.

Freshwater Tidal Swamp

Floodplain swamp a river mouth where occasional saltwater intrusion significantly affects vegetation composition; receives pulses of freshwater in response to tides; cypress absent or infrequent; closed/open canopy of swamp tupelo, pumpkin ash, sweetbay.

Hardwood – dominated by a mix of hydrophytic hardwood trees; cypress or tupelo may be occasional or infrequent in the canopy; short hydroperiod

Baygall (G4/S4)

Slope or depression wetland with peat substrate; usually saturated and occasionally inundated; statewide excluding Keys; rare or no fire; closed canopy of evergreen trees; loblolly bay, sweetbay, swamp bay, titi, fetterbush.

Bay Swamp

Large or small peat filled depression; mainly eastern Panhandle to central peninsula; forested; dominated by bay species.

South Florida Bayhead

On tree islands in glades marsh on peat substrate; south of Lake Okeechobee in central and southern peninsula; open or closed canopy; swamp bay, sweetbay, dahoon, coastalplain willow, and/or coco plum.

Hydric Hammock (G4/S4)

Lowland with sand/clay/organic soil over limestone or with high shell content; mesic-hydric; primarily eastern Panhandle and central peninsula; occasional to rare fire; diamond-leaved oak, live oak, cabbage palm, red cedar, and mixed hardwoods.

Coastal Hydric Hammock
Occurring adjacent to coastal marshes; central Panhandle to central peninsula; species composition limited by occasional salt water intrusion; cabbage palm, red cedar, and live oak.

Prairie Hydric Hammock
Isolated stands of hydric hammock within a pyrogenic community, usually floodplain marsh; shelly sand soils; central and southern peninsula; occasional fire; cabbage palm, live oak, red cedar.

Bottomland Forest (G4/S3)

Flatland with sand/clay/organic substrate; usually connected or adjacent to a riverine community; occasionally inundated; Panhandle to central peninsula; rare or no fire; closed canopy of mixed hardwoods; deciduous or mixed deciduous/evergreen; tuliptree, sweetbay, water oak, sweetgum, diamond-leaved oak, red maple, loblolly pine, spruce pine, Atlantic white cedar.

Alluvial Forest (G4/S3)

Floodplain with alluvial substrate of sand, silt, clay or organic soil; inundated yearly during growing season; influenced by disturbance from ongoing floodplain processes (deposition of point bars, creation of "ridge and swale" topography); Panhandle to central peninsula; rare or no fire; closed canopy of mainly deciduous trees; water hickory, overcup oak, diamond-leaved oak, green ash, American elm, water locust, river birch.

Marine and Estuarine Vegetated Wetlands – intertidal or supratidal zone dominated by herbaceous or woody halophytic vascular plants; salinity >0.5 ppt.

Salt Marsh (G5/S4)

Estuarine wetland on muck/sand/or limestone substrate; inundated with saltwater by daily tides; statewide; occasional or rare fire; treeless, dense herb layer with few shrubs; saltmarsh cordgrass, needle rush, saltgrass, saltwort, perennial glasswort, seaside oxeye.

Salt Flat
Salt marsh with much exposed bare soil on slightly higher areas within marsh; high salinity and dry conditions; sparse and stunted cover of succulents and/or shoregrass.

Mangrove Swamp (G5/S4)

Estuarine wetland on muck/sand/or limestone substrate; inundated with saltwater by daily tides; central peninsula and Keys; no fire; dominated by mangrove and mangrove associate species; red mangrove, black mangrove, white mangrove, buttonwood.

Buttonwood Forest
Upper tidal area dominated by buttonwood; often transitional to rockland hammock.

Keys Tidal Rock Barren (G3/S3?)

Flatland with exposed limestone in supratidal zone; restricted to Keys; no fire; open, mainly herbaceous vegetation of upper salt marsh species and stunted shrubs and trees; buttonwood, christmasberry, perennial glasswort, saltwort, seashore dropseed, shoregrass.

Ponds and Lakes – non-flowing wetlands of natural depressions lacking persistent emergent vegetation except around the perimeter

Clastic Upland Lake (G3/S2)

Generally irregular basin in clay uplands; predominantly with inflows, frequently without surface outflow; clay or organic substrate; Panhandle to northern central peninsula; colored, acidic, soft water with low mineral content (sodium, chloride, sulfate); oligo-mesotrophic to eutrophic.

Coastal Dune Lake (G2/S2)

Basin or lagoon influenced by recent coastal processes; predominantly sand substrate with some organic matter; Panhandle; salinity variable among and within lakes, and subject to saltwater intrusion and storm surges; slightly acidic, hard water with high mineral content (sodium, chloride).

Flatwoods/Prairie Lake (G4/S3)

Generally shallow basin in flatlands with high water table; frequently with a broad littoral zone; still water or flow-through; sand or peat substrate; statewide except extreme southern peninsula and Keys; variable water chemistry, colored to clear, acidic to slightly alkaline, soft to moderately hard water with moderate mineral content (sodium, chloride, sulfate); oligo-mesotrophic to eutrophic.

Marsh Lake (G4/S4)

Generally shallow basin in flatlands with high water table; frequently with a broad littoral zone; still water or flow-through; sand or peat substrate; statewide except extreme southern peninsula and Keys; variable water chemistry, colored to clear, acidic to slightly alkaline, soft to moderately hard water with moderate mineral content (sodium, chloride, sulfate); oligo-mesotrophic to eutrophic.

River Floodplain Lake (G4/S2)

Meander scar, backwater, or larger flow-through body within major river floodplains; sand, alluvial or organic substrate; statewide except extreme southern peninsula and Keys; colored, alkaline or slightly acidic, hard or moderately hard water with high mineral content (sulfate, sodium, chloride, calcium, magnesium); mesotrophic to eutrophic.

Sandhill Upland Lake (G3/S2)

Generally rounded solution depression in deep sandy uplands; panhandle to southern peninsula; predominantly without surface inflows/outflows; typically sand substrate with organic accumulations toward middle; clear, acidic moderately soft water with varying mineral content; ultra-oligotrophic to mesotrophic.

Sinkhole Lake (G2/S2)

Typically deep, funnel-shaped depression in limestone base; statewide; predominantly without surface inflows/outflows, but frequently with connection to the aquifer; clear, alkaline, hard water with high mineral content (calcium, bicarbonate, magnesium).

Swamp Lake (G4/S3)

Generally shallow, open water area within basin swamps; still water or flow-through; peat, sand or clay substrate; statewide except Keys; variable water chemistry, but characteristically highly colored, acidic, soft water with moderate mineral content (sodium, chloride, sulfate); oligo-mesotrophic to eutrophic.

Rivers and Streams (Riverine) – natural flowing waters from their source to the downstream limits of tidal influence and bounded by channel banks

Alluvial Stream (G4/S2)

Lower perennial or intermittent/seasonal watercourse characterized by turbid water with suspended silt, clay, sand and small gravel; Panhandle; generally with a distinct, sediment-derived (alluvial) floodplain and a sandy, elevated natural levee just inland from the bank.

Blackwater Stream (G4/S3)

Perennial or intermittent/seasonal watercourse characterized by tea-colored water with a high content of particulate and dissolved organic matter derived from drainage through swamps and marshes; statewide except Keys; generally lacking an alluvial floodplain.

Seepage Stream (G3/S2)

Upper perennial or intermittent/seasonal watercourse with clear to lightly colored water derived from shallow groundwater seepage; panhandle to southern peninsula.

Spring-run Stream (G2/S2)

Perennial watercourse with deep aquifer headwaters and clear water, circumneutral pH and, frequently, a solid limestone bottom; panhandle to central peninsula.

Subterranean – twilight, middle, and deep zones of natural chambers overlain by the earth's crust and characterized by climatic stability and assemblages of trogloxenic, troglophilic, and troglobitic organisms.

Aquatic Cave (G3/S3)

Cave permanently or periodically submerged; often supporting troglobitic crustaceans and salamanders; includes high energy systems which receive large quantities of organic detritus and low energy systems; statewide.

Terrestrial Cave (G3/S2)

Cave lacking standing water; often supporting bats, such as Myotis spp., and other terrestrial vertebrates and invertebrates; includes interstitial areas above standing water such as fissures in the ceiling of caves; statewide.

Marine and Estuarine – subtidal, intertidal, and supratidal zones of the sea, landward to the point at which seawater becomes significantly diluted with freshwater inflow from the land. (The distinction between the Marine and Estuarine Natural Communities is often subtle, and the natural communities types found under these two community categories have the same descriptions. For these reasons they have been grouped together).

Mineral Based

Consolidated Substrate (G3/S3)

Expansive subtidal, intertidal, and supratidal area composed primarily of nonliving compacted or coherent and relatively hard, naturally formed mass of mineral matter (e.g., coquina limerock and relic reefs); statewide; octocorals, sponges, stony corals, nondrift macrophytic algae, blue-green mat-forming algae, and seagrasses sparse, if present.

Unconsolidated Substrate (G5/S5)

Expansive subtidal, intertidal, and supratidal area composed primarily of loose mineral matter (e.g., coralgal, gravel, marl, mud, sand and shell); statewide; octocorals, sponges, stony corals, nondrift macrophytic algae, blue-green mat-forming algae and seagrasses sparse, if present.

Faunal Based

Coral Reef (G2/S1)

Expansive subtidal area with elevational gradient or relief and occupied primarily by living sessile organisms of the Class Hydrozoa (e.g., fire corals and hydrocorals), Class Anthozoa, abd Subclass Zoantharia (e.g., stony corals and black corals); southern peninsula and Keys; includes deepwater bank reefs, fringing barrier reefs, outer bank reefs and patch reefs, some of which may contain distinct zones of assorted macrophytes, octocorals, & sponges.

Mollusk Reef (G3/S3)

Substantial subtidal or intertidal area with relief from concentrations of sessile organisms of the Phylum Mollusca, Class Bivalvia (e.g., mollusks, oysters, & worm shells); statewide; octocorals, sponges, stony corals, macrophytic algae and seagrasses sparse, if present.

Octocoral Bed (G2/S1)

Expansive subtidal area occupied primarily by living sessile organisms of the Class Anthozoa, Subclass Octocorallia (e.g., soft corals, horny corals, sea fans, sea whips, and sea pens); likely statewide; sponges, stony corals, nondrift macrophytic algae and seagrasses spares, if present.

Sponge Bed (G2/S2)

Expansive subtidal area occupied primarily by living sessile organisms of the Phylum Porifera (e.g., sheepswool sponge, Florida loggerhead sponge and branching candle sponge); statewide; octocorals, stony corals, nondrift macrophytic algae and seagrasses sparse, if present.

Worm Reef (G1/S1)

Substantial subtidal or intertidal area with relief from concentrations of sessile, tubicolous organisms of the Phylum Annelida, Class Polychaeta (e.g., chaetopterids and sabellarids); southern peninsula (east coast only); octocorals, sponges, stony corals, macrophytic algae and seagrasses sparse, if present.

Floral Based (mainly subtidal)

Algal Bed (G3/S2)

Expansive subtidal, intertidal, or supratidal area, occupied primarily by attached thallophytic or mat-forming prokaryotic algae (e.g, halimeda, blue-green algae); statewide; octocorals, sponges, stony corals and seagrasses sparse, if present.

Seagrass Bed (G3/S2)

Expansive subtidal or intertidal area, occupied primarily by rooted vascular macrophytes, (e.g., shoal grass, halophila, widgeon grass, manatee grass and turtle grass); statewide; may include various epiphytes and epifauna; octocorals, sponges, stony corals, and attached macrophytic algae sparse, if present.

Composite Substrate

Composite Substrate (G3/S3)

Expansive subtidal, intertidal, or supratidal area, occupied primarily by natural community elements from more than one natural community category (e.g., grass bed and algal bed species; octocoral and algal bed species); statewide; includes both patchy and evenly distributed occurrences.

Explanation of Ranks and Listing Status

Element and Element Occurrence

An **element** is any exemplary or rare component of the natural environment, such as a species, natural community, bird rookery, spring, sinkhole, cave, or other ecological feature. An element occurrence (EO) is a single extant habitat that sustains or otherwise contributes to the survival of a population or a distinct, self-sustaining example of a particular element.

Heritage Ranking System

Using a ranking system developed by The Nature Conservancy and the NatureServe Network, the Florida Natural Areas Inventory assigns two ranks to each element. The **global rank** is based on an element's worldwide status; the **state rank** is based on the status of the element in Florida. Element ranks are based on many factors, the most important ones being estimated number of element occurrences, estimated abundance (number of individuals for species; area for natural communities), geographic range, estimated adequately protected EOs, relative threat of destruction, and ecological fragility.

FNAI Global Rank Definitions

G1 = Critically imperiled globally because of extreme rarity (5 or fewer occurrences or less than 1000 individuals) or because of extreme vulnerability to extinction due to some natural or man-made factor.

G2 = Imperiled globally because of rarity (6 to 20 occurrences or less than 3000 individuals) or because of vulnerability to extinction due to some natural or man-made factor.

G3 = Either very rare and local throughout its range (21-100 occurrences or less than 10,000 individuals) or found locally in a restricted range or vulnerable to extinction from other factors.

G4 = Demonstrably secure globally.

G5 = Demonstrably secure globally.

GH = Of historical occurrence throughout its range, may be rediscovered (e.g., ivory-billed woodpecker).

GX = Believed to be extinct throughout range.

GXC = Extirpated from the wild but still known from captivity or cultivation.

G#G# = Range of rank; insufficient data to assign specific global rank (e.g., G2G3).

G#T# = Rank of a taxonomic subgroup such as a subspecies or variety; the G portion of the rank refers to the entire species and the T portion refers to the specific subgroup; numbers have same definition as above (e.g., G3T1).

G#Q = Rank of questionable species - ranked as species but questionable whether it is species or subspecies; numbers have same definition as above (e.g., G2Q).

G#T#Q = Same as above, but validity as subspecies or variety is questioned.

GU = Unrankable; due to a lack of information no rank or range can be assigned (e.g., GUT2).

GNA = Ranking is not applicable because the element is not a suitable target for conservation (e.g. a hybrid species).

GNR = Element not yet ranked (temporary).

GNRTNR = Neither the element nor the taxonomic subgroup has yet been ranked.

FNAI State Rank Definitions

S1 = Critically imperiled in Florida because of extreme rarity (5 or fewer occurrences or less than 1000 individuals) or because of extreme vulnerability to extinction due to some natural or man-made factor.

S2 = Imperiled in Florida because of rarity (6 to 20 occurrences or less than 3000 individuals) or because of vulnerability to extinction due to some natural or man-made factor.

S3 = Either very rare and local in Florida (21-100 occurrences or less than 10,000 individuals) or found locally in a restricted range or vulnerable to extinction from other factors.

S4 = Apparently secure in Florida (may be rare in parts of range).

S5 = Demonstrably secure in Florida.

SH = Of historical occurrence in Florida, possibly extirpated, but may be rediscovered (e.g., ivory-billed woodpecker).

SX = Believed to be extirpated throughout Florida.

SU = Unrankable; due to a lack of information no rank or range can be assigned.

SNA = State ranking is not applicable because the element is not a suitable target for conservation (e.g. a hybrid species).

SNR = Element not yet ranked (temporary).

Legal Listing Status

Federal Legal Status

These are general descriptions only. For official definitions and lists of protected species, consult the relevant federal agency.

Definitions derived from the U.S. Endangered Species Act of 1973, Sec. 3. Note that the federal status given by FNAI refers only to Florida populations and that federal status may differ elsewhere.

LE Endangered: species in danger of extinction throughout all or a significant portion of its range.

LT Threatened: species likely to become Endangered within the foreseeable future throughout all or a significant portion of its range.

LT,PDL Species currently listed threatened but has been proposed for delisting.

LT,PE Species currently listed Threatened but has been proposed for listing as Endangered.

SAT Treated as threatened due to similarity of appearance to a species which is federally listed such that enforcement personnel have difficulty in attempting to differentiate between the listed and unlisted species.

PE Proposed for listing as Endangered species.

PT Proposed for listing as Threatened species.

C Candidate species for which federal listing agencies have sufficient information on biological vulnerability and threats to support proposing to list the species as Endangered or Threatened.

XN Non-essential experimental population.

SC Not currently listed, but considered a "species of concern" to USFWS.

N Not currently listed, nor currently being considered for listing as Endangered or Threatened.

State Legal Status

These are general descriptions only. For official definitions and lists of protected species, consult the relevant state agency.

Animals: Definitions derived from "Florida's Endangered Species and Species of Special Concern, Official Lists" published by Florida Fish and Wildlife Conservation Commission, 1 August 1997, and subsequent updates.

LE Endangered: species, subspecies, or isolated population so few or depleted in number or so restricted in range that it is in imminent danger of extinction.

LT Threatened: species, subspecies, or isolated population facing a very high risk of extinction in the future.

LS Species of Special Concern is a species, subspecies, or isolated population which is facing a moderate risk of extinction in the future.

PE Proposed for listing as Endangered.

PT Proposed for listing as Threatened.

PS Proposed for listing as Species of Special Concern.

N Not currently listed, nor currently being considered for listing.

Plants: Definitions derived from Sections 581.011 and 581.185(2), Florida Statutes, and the Preservation of Native Flora of Florida Act, 5B-40.001. FNAI does not track all state-regulated plant species; for a complete list of state-regulated plant species, call Florida Division of Plant Industry, 352-372-3505 or see: http://www.doacs.state.fl.us/pi/.

LE Endangered: species of plants native to Florida that are in imminent danger of extinction within the state, the survival of which is unlikely if the causes of a decline in the number of plants continue; includes all species determined to be endangered or threatened pursuant to the U.S. Endangered Species Act.

LT Threatened: species native to the state that are in rapid decline in the number of plants within the state, but which have not so decreased in number as to cause them to be Endangered.

PE Proposed for listing as Endangered.

PT Proposed for listing as Threatened.

N Not currently listed, nor currently being considered for listing.

Special Animal Listings – State and Federal Status

Grus americana (whooping crane) – Federally listed as XN (nonessential experimental population) which refers to the Florida experimental population only; Federal listing elsewhere is LE.

Pandion haliaetus (osprey) – State listed as LS (Species of Special Concern) in Monroe County only; not listed in rest of state.

Mustela vison mink pop1 (southern mink, S. Florida population) – State listed as LT (Threatened) which refers to the Everglades population only; species formerly listed as *Mustela vison evergladensis.*

Ursus americanus floridanus (Florida black bear) – State listed as LT but not applicable in Baker and Columbia counties or the Apalachicola National Forest.

Sources

All sources unless otherwise noted are FNAI.

NATURAL HERITAGE METHODOLOGY (6–7)

Stein, B.A., and F.W. Davis. 2000. Discovering life in America: Tools and techniques of biodiversity inventory. In *Precious Heritage: The Status of Biodiversity in the United States*, eds. B.A. Stein. L.S. Kutner, and J.S. Adams, pp. 19-53. New York: Oxford University Press.

GEOLOGY AND SOILS (8–9)

Scott, T.M. 1992. A Geological Overview of Florida. Open File Report no. 50. Florida Geological Survey, Tallahassee.

Florida Department of Natural Resources, Bureau of Geology. 1975-1981. Environmental Map Series 79, 80, 84, 85, 88, 89, 90, 93, 97, 99, 100, 101. Tallahassee.

Bryan, J.R., T.M. Scott, and G.H. Means. 2008. *Roadside Geology of Florida.* Missoula, Montana: Mountain Press Publishing Company.

Scott, T.M., K.M. Campbell, F.R. Rupert, J.D. Arthur, R.C. Green, G.H. Means, T.M. Missimer, J.M. Lloyd, J.W. Yon, and J.G. Duncan. 2001. Geological Map of the State of Florida. Map Series 146. Florida Geological Survey, Tallahassee.

U.S. Geological Survey. 2005. The National Atlas of the United States of America®. Nationalatlas.gov.

TOPOGRAPHY AND PHYSIOGRAPHY (10–11)

Cooke, C.W. 1939. Scenery of Florida, Interpreted by a Geologist. Florida Geological Survey Bulletin no. 17. Florida Geological Survey, Tallahassee.

Kwit, C., M.W. Schwartz, W.J. Platt, and J.P. Geaghan. 1998. The distribution of tree species in steepheads in the Apalachicola River Bluffs, Florida. Journal of the Torrey Botanical Society 125(4): 309-318.

MacNeil, F.S. 1949. Pleistocene shore lines in Florida and Georgia. U.S. Geological Survey Professional Paper No. 221-f, pp. 95-106. U.S. Geological Survey.

Schmidt, W. 1997. Geomorphology and Physiography of Florida. In *Geology of Florida*, eds. A.F. Randazzo and D.S. Jones, pp. 1-12. Gainesville: University Press of Florida.

Scott, T.M. 1992. A Geological Overview of Florida. Open file Report no. 50. Florida Geological Survey, Tallahassee.

U.S. Geological Survey. 2004. A Tapestry of Time and Terrain: The Union of Two Maps—Geology and Topography. http://tapestry.usgs.gov .

Vernon, R.O. 1942. Geology of Holmes and Washington counties, Florida. Florida Geological Survey Bulletin 21:15-28.

Whitney, E.D., B. Means, and A. Rudloe, 2004. *Priceless Florida.* Sarasota: Pineapple Press Inc.

WATER RESOURCES (12–13)

Fernald, E.D., and E.D. Purdum, eds. 1998. *Water Resources Atlas of Florida.* Tallahassee: Florida State University, Institute of Science and Public Affairs.

Purdum, E.D. 2002. Florida Waters: A Water Resources Manual from Florida's Water Management Districts. Published jointly by Florida's water management districts, Brooksville.

Berndt, M.P., E.T. Oaksford, and G.L. Mahon. 1998. Groundwater in *Water Resources Atlas of Florida*, eds. E.A. Fernald and E.D. Purdum, pp. 38-63. Tallahassee: Florida State University, Institute of Science and Public Affairs.

CLIMATE (14–15)

Alper, J. 1992. Everglades rebound from Andrew. Science 257: 1,852-1,854

Sunquist, F., M. Sunquist, and L. Beletsky. 2002. *Florida: The Ecotravellers' Wildlife Guide.* New York: Academic Press.

Whitney, E., D.B. Means, and A. Rudloe. 2004. *Priceless Florida.* Sarasota: Pineapple Press Inc.

Winsberg, M.D. 2003. *Florida Weather,* 2nd ed. Gainesville: University Press of Florida.

LAND COVER (16–17)

Davis, J.H. 1967. General Map of Natural Vegetation of Florida. Circular S-178. Agricultural Experiment Station, Institute of Food and Agricultural Science, University of Florida, Gainesville.

Stys, B., R. Kautz, D. Reed, M. Kertis, R. Kawula, C. Keller, and A. Davis. 2004. Florida vegetation and land cover data derived from 2003 Landsat ETM+ imagery. Florida Fish and Wildlife Conservation Commission, Tallahassee.

BIOGEOGRAPHY (18–19)

Adams, J.M., and H. Faure, eds. 1997. Review and Atlas of Palaeovegetation: Preliminary land ecosystem maps of the world since the Last Glacial Maximum. Oak Ridge National Laboratory, Oakridge, Tennessee. http://www.esd.ornl.gov/projects/qen/adams1.html.

Schweitzer, P.N., and R.S. Thompson. 1996. Global Gridded Pliocene and Late Quaternary Sea Level. U.S. Geological Survey Open-File Report 96-000.

NATURAL COMMUNITIES (22–23)

Huck, R.B. 1987. Plant communities along an edaphic continuum in a Central Florida watershed. Florida Scientist 50: 111-128.

Major, J.A. 1951. A functional factorial approach to plant ecology. Ecology 32: 392-412.

Myers, R.L. 1985. Fire and the dynamic relationship between Florida sandhill and sand pine scrub vegetation. Bulletin of the Torrey Botanical Club 112: 241-252.

LARGE EXTENT UPLANDS (26–27)

Davis, J.H. 1967. General Map of Natural Vegetation of Florida. Circular S-178. Agricultural Experiment Station, Institute of Food and Agricultural Science, University of Florida, Gainesville.

LARGE EXTENT LOWLANDS (28–29)

Dahl, T.E. 1990. Wetlands Losses in the United States 1780's to 1980's. U.S. Department of the Interior, Fish and Wildlife Service, Washington, D.C.

___. 2005. Florida's Wetlands: An Update on Status and Trends 1985 to 1996. U.S . Department of the Interior, Fish and Wildlife Service, Washington, D.C.

___. 2006. Status and Trends of Wetlands in the Conterminous United States 1998 to 2004. U.S. Department of the Interior, Fish and Wildlife Service, Washington, D.C.

SCRUB (30–31)

Turner, W.R., D.S. Wilcove, and H.M. Swain. 2006. State of the Scrub: Conservation Progress, Management Responsibilities, and Land Acquisition Priorities for Imperiled Species of Florida's Lake Wales Ridge. Archbold Biological Station, Lake Placid, Florida.

IMPORTANT SMALL EXTENT COMMUNITIES (38–39)

Baskin, J.M., and C.C. Baskin. 1999. Cedar glades of the southeastern United States. In *Savannas, Barrens, and Rock Outcrop Plant Communities of North America*, eds. R.C. Anderson, J.S. Fralish, and J.M. Baskin, pp. 206-219. Cambridge: Cambridge University Press.

Schotz, A. 2005. A checklist of vascular flora in the Black Belt Prairies of Alabama. Alabama Natural Heritage Program, Montgomery, Alabama.

Bridges, E.L., S.L. Orzell, and L.C. Anderson. 1989. *Carex microdonta* Torr. & Hook. (Cyperaceae) new to Florida. Sida 13:379-381.

Quarterman, E. 1950. Major plant communities of Tennessee Cedar Glades. Ecology 31: 234-254.

Mize, R., R.E. Evans, B.R. MacRoberts, M.H. MacRoberts, and D.C. Rudolph. 2005. Restoration of pitcher plant bogs in eastern Texas, U.S.A. Natural Areas Journal 25: 197-201.

PLANTS: OVERVIEW (40–41)

Austin, D. 2004. *Florida Ethnobotany.* Boca Raton: CRC Press.

Brown, P.M. 2002. *Wild Orchids of Florida.* Gainesville: University Press of Florida.

Falk, D.A., and K.E. Holsinger. 1991. *Genetics and Conservation of Rare Plants.* New York: Oxford University Press U.S.A.

Flora of North America Editorial Committee, eds. 1993+. *Flora of North America North of Mexico.* 16+ vols. Publisher? New York and Oxford.

Goering M., T. Cook, Z. Ferdana, J. Ferdana, J. Floberg, T. Horsman, M. Summers, C. Rumsey, and P. Iachetti. 2003. An Ecological Assessment of the Georgia-Basin Trough-Willamette Valley Ecoregion: An Analysis to Identify, Integrate and Prioritize Areas of Freshwater, Terrestrial and Marine Biodiversity Significance. Georgia Basin/Puget Sound Research Conference.

Greller, A.M. 1980. Correlation of some climate statistics with distribution of broadleaved forest zones in Florida, U.S.A. Bulletin of the Torrey Botanical Club 107(2): 189-219.

Little, E.L., Jr. 1978. Atlas of United States Trees: Florida, vol. 5. Florida. U.S. Department of Agriculture Miscellaneous Publication no. 1361. Washington, D.C.

Nelson, G. 2000. *The Ferns of Florida*. Sarasota: Pineapple Press Inc.

Schnell, D.E. 2002. *Carnivorous Plants of the United States and Canada*. Portland, Oregon: Timber Press.

Strahler, A.N. 1960. *Physical Geography*, 2nd edition. New York, London: John Wiley & Sons, Inc.

Thorne, R.R. 1993. Phytogeography. In *Flora of North America North of Mexico*, vol. 1, ed. Flora of North America Editorial Committee, pp.132-153. New York: Oxford University Press.

PINES (44)

Godfrey, R.K., with the majority of illustrations by M. Darst. 1989. *Trees, Shrubs, and Woody Vines of Northern Florida and adjacent Georgia and Alabama*. Athens, Georgia: University of Georgia Press.

Frost, C.C. 1993. Four centuries of changing landscape patterns in the longleaf pine ecosystem. In Proceedings Tall Timbers Fire Ecology Conference, pp. 17-44.

Wunderlin, R.P., and B.F. Hansen. 2008. Atlas of Florida Vascular Plants. Institute for Systematic Botany, University of South Florida, Tampa. http://www.plantatlas.usf.edu.

GRASSES, SEDGES, AND RUSHES (46)

Terri, J.A., and L.G. Stowe. 1976. Climatic patterns and the distribution of C4 grasses in North America. Oecologia 23: 1-12.

Terri, J.A., L.G. Stowe, and D.A. Livingstone. 1980. The distribution of C4 species of the Cyperaceae in North America in relation to climate. Oecologia 47: 307-310.

WETLAND PLANTS (47)

Wunderlin, R.P., and B.F. Hansen. 2008. Atlas of Florida Vascular Plants. Institute for Systematic Botany, University of South Florida, Tampa. http://www.plantatlas.usf.edu.

PALMS (48)

FLEPPC. 2007. Florida Exotic Pest Plant Council. http://www.fleppc.org/.

Lewis, C.E., and S. Zona. 2008. *Leucothrinax morrisii*, a new name for a familiar Caribbean palm. Palms 52: 84-88.

Little, E.L., Jr. 1999. Atlas of United States Trees. U.S. Geological Survey. http://esp.cr.usgs.gov/info/veg-clim/.

Wunderlin, R.P., and B.F. Hansen. 2008. Atlas of Florida Vascular Plants, Institute for Systematic Botany, University of South Florida, Tampa. http://www.plantatlas.usf.edu.

Zona, S. 2000. Arecaceae. In *Flora of North America*, vol. 22. Magnoliophyta: Alismatidae, Arecidae, Commelinidae (in part), and Zingiberidae, ed. Flora of North America Editorial Committee. New York: Oxford University Press.

EPIPHYTES (50)

Daymet, University of Montana Numerical Terradynamic Simulation Group (NTGS). http://www.daymet.org

CARNIVOROUS PLANTS (52)

Wunderlin, R.P., and B.F. Hansen. 2008. Atlas of Florida Vascular Plants. Institute for Systematic Botany, University of South Florida, Tampa. http://www.plantatlas.usf.edu.

INVERTEBRATES OVERVIEW (54–55)

Losey, J.E., and M. Vaughan. 2006. The economic value of ecological services provided by insects. BioScience 56(4): 311-323.

TERRESTRIAL INVERTEBRATES (56–57)

U.S. Department of Agriculture's Animal and Plant Inspection Service. 1939-2009. Maps of Imported Fire Ant Quarantine. Fort Collins, Colorado.

FRESHWATER FISH (60–61)

Florida Museum of Natural History. 2009. Fish species distribution data compiled by Larry Page and Rob Robbins, Ichthyology Department.

AMPHIBIANS (62–63)

International Union for Conservation of Nature (IUCN), Conservation International, and NatureServe. 2006. Global Amphibian Assessment. www.globalamphibians.org (version 1.1).

Conant, R., and J.T. Collins (1991). A Field Guide to Reptiles and Amphibians: Eastern and Central North America, 3rd ed. The Peterson Field Guide Series. Boston: Houghton Mifflin.

Young, B.E., S.N. Stuart, J.S. Chanson, N.A. Cox, and T.M. Boucher. 2004. Disappearing Jewels: The Status of New World Amphibians. NatureServe, Arlington, Virginia.

REPTILES (64–65)

Conant, R., and J.T. Collins (1991). A Field Guide to Reptiles and Amphibians: Eastern and Central North America, 3rd ed. The Peterson Field Guide Series. Boston: Houghton Mifflin.

BIRDS (66–67)

Cox, J. 2006. The Breeding Birds of Florida. Part II: Trends in breeding distributions based on Florida's breeding bird atlas project. Florida Ornithological Society Special Publication no. 7: 71-140.

Derrickson, K.C., and R. Breitwisch. 1992. Northern mockingbird. In *The Birds of North America*, no. 7, eds. A. Poole, P. Stettenheim, and F. Gill. Philadelphia: The Academy of Natural Sciences; Washington, DC: The American Ornithologists' Union.

Florida Ornithological Society Records Committee. Official State List of the Birds of Florida. Updated 12 September 2008.

Florida Ornithological Society Records Committee. Updated 31 December 2010. Official State List of the Birds of Florida.

Pranty, B. 2005. *A Birder's Guide to Florida*. Colorado Springs, Colorado: American Birding Association.

Southwick Associates, Inc. 2008 (February 27). The 2006 Economic Benefits of Wildlife-Viewing Recreation in Florida. Report to Florida Fish and Wildlife Conservation Commission.

World Conservation Monitoring Centre of the United Nations Environmental Program. 2004 (September). Species Data (unpublished).

CHALLENGES IN BIRD CONSERVATION (68–69)

Fitzpatrick, J.W., B. Pranty, and B. Stith. 1994. Florida Scrub Jay Statewide Map. U.S. Fish and Wildlife Service. Cooperative Agreement #14-16-0004-91-950. Jacksonville, Florida.

Herkert, J.R., P.D. Vickery, and D.E. Kroodsma. 2002. Henslow's sparrow (*Ammodramus henslowii*). In *The Birds of North America*, no. 672, eds., A. Poole and F. Gill. Philadelphia: The Academy of Natural Sciences; Washington, D.C.: The American Ornithologists' Union

Lincoln, F.C., S.R. Peterson, and J.L. Zimmerman. 1998. Migration of Birds. Circular 16. U.S. Department of the Interior, U.S. Fish and Wildlife Service, Washington, D.C. Northern Prairie Wildlife Research Center Online. http://www.npwrc.usgs.gov/resource/birds/migratio/index.htm (version 02APR2002).

Meyer, K.D. 1995. Swallow-tailed kite (*Elanoides forficatus*). In *The Birds of North America*, no. 138, eds. A. Poole and F. Gill. Philadelphia: The Academy of Natural Sciences; Washington, DC: The American Ornithologists' Union.

Meyer, K.D. e-mail message to K. NeSmith, January 7, 2008.

Mowbray, T.B. 1999. Scarlet tanager (*Piranga olivacea*). In *The Birds of North America*, no. 479, eds. A. Poole and F. Gill. Philadelphia: The Academy of Natural Sciences; Washington, DC: The American Ornithologists' Union.

Zimmerman, G.M., and K.D Meyer. 2004. Migration Ecology of Florida's Swallow-tailed Kites in Cuba, Mexico, and Belize. Florida Fish and Wildlife Conservation Commission Project NG01-009.

GOPHER TORTOISE (75)

Ernst, C.H., J.E. Lovich, and R.W. Barbour. 1994. *Turtles of the United States and Canada*. Washington, D.C.: Smithsonian Institution.

RED-COCKADED WOODPECKER (76)

Costa, R. 2002. Red-cockaded Woodpecker. U.S. Fish and Wildlife Service, Clemson University. Clemson, South Carolina.

Jackson, J.A. 1994. Red-cockaded woodpecker (*Picoides borealis*). In *The Birds of North America*, no. 85, eds. A. Poole and F. Gill. Philadelphia: The Academy of Natural Sciences; Washington, D.C.: The American Ornithologists' Union.

Little, E.L. Jr. 1971. Atlas of United States Trees, vol. 1, Conifers and Important Hardwoods. U.S. Department of Agriculture Miscellaneous Publication 1146. http://esp.cr.usgs.gov/data/atlas/little/.

Stevenson, H.M., and B.H. Anderson. 1994. *The Birdlife of Florida.* Gainesville: University Press of Florida.

FLORIDA SCRUB-JAY (77)

Boughton, R., and R. Bowman, e-mail messages to K. NeSmith, January 22 and 23, 2009.

Bowman, R., and G.E. Woolfenden. 2001. Nest success and the timing of nest failure of Florida scrub-jays in suburban and wildland habitats. In *Avian Ecology and Conservation in an Urbanizing World*, eds. J. M. Marzluff, R. Bowman, and R. Donnelly, pp. 383-402. Norwell, Massachusetts: Kluwer Academic Publishers.

Fitzpatrick, J.W., B. Pranty, and B. Stith. 1994. Florida Scrub Jay Statewide Map. U.S. Fish and Wildlife Service. Cooperative Agreement #14-16-0004-91-950. Jacksonville, Florida.

Liss, B., and M. Huffman. 1999. Tasks prior to fire management (figure). In The Urgent Need for Fire Management to Save the Florida Scrub-Jay. The Nature Conservancy, Babson Park, Florida.

Miller, K., e-mail message to K. NeSmith, May 4, 2009.

Millett, C., e-mail message and JayWatch data file for 2008 JayWatch sites to K. NeSmith, January 5, 2009.

Millett, C., e-mail message and JayWatch data file for 2009 survey of Marjorie Harris Carr Cross Florida Greenway to K. NeSmith, February 11, 2010.

Woolfenden, G., and J. Fitzpatrick. 1996a. Florida scrub-jay (*Aphelocoma coerulescens*). In *Rare and Endangered Biota of Florida*, vol. 5, eds. J. A. Rodgers, H. T. Smith, and H. W. Kale II, pp. 267-280. Gainesville: University Press of Florida.

___. 1996b. Florida scrub-jay (*Aphelocoma coerulescens*). In *The Birds of North America*, no. 228, eds. A. Poole and F. Gill. Philadelphia: The Academy of Natural Sciences; Washington, D.C.: The American Ornithologists' Union.

SHOREBIRDS, GULLS, AND TERNS (78)

The American Ornithologists' Union. http://www.aou.org/checklist/north/full.php#Charadriiformes

Cornell Lab of Ornithology. http://www.allaboutbirds.org.

Douglass, N. Data sets for American oystercatcher, least tern, and black skimmer received November 4, 2008.

Douglass, N., and L. Clayton. 2004. Survey of Breeding American Oystercatcher (*Haematopus palliatus*) Populations in Florida. Final Report. Florida Fish and Wildlife Conservation Commission, Tallahassee.

Himes, J.G., N.J. Douglass, R.A. Pruner, A.M. Croft, and E.M. Seckinger. 2006. Status and Distribution of the Snowy Plover in Florida. 2006 study final report. Florida Fish and Wildlife Conservation Commission, Tallahassee.

Sprandel, G.L., J.A. Gore, and D.T. Cobb. 1997. Winter Shorebird Survey. Final Performance Report. Florida Game and Fresh Water Fish Commission, Tallahassee.

FIRE EXCLUSION (86–87)

Brenner, J., and D. Wade. 2003. Florida's revised prescribed fire law: Protection for responsible burners. In Proceedings of Fire Conference 2000: The First National Congress on Fire Ecology, Prevention, and Management. Miscellaneous Publication no. 13, eds. K.E.M. Galley, R.C. Klinger, and N.G. Sugihara, pp. 132-136. Tall Timbers Research Station, Tallahassee.

Cech, R., and G. Tudor. 2005. *Butterflies of the East Coast: An Observer's Guide.* Princeton: Princeton University Press.

Davis, J.H. 1967. General Map of Natural Vegetation of Florida. Circular S-178. Agricultural Experiment Station, Institute of Food and Agricultural Science, University of Florida, Gainesville.

Florida Forest Service. 1934. Bulletin No 10. Tallahassee.

Frost, C.C. 1993. Four centuries of changing landscape patterns in the longleaf pine ecosystem. In The 18th Proceedings of Tall Timbers Fire Ecology Conference, ed. S.M. Hermann, pp.17-45. Tall Timbers Research Station, Tallahassee.

Greene, S.W. 1937 (July 15). Burning the woods. The Florida Cattleman 1 (10).

Jackson, D.R., and E.G. Milstrey. 1989. The fauna of gopher tortoise burrows. In Gopher Tortoise Relocation Symposium Proceedings. Florida Game and Fresh Water Fish Commission, Nongame Wildlife Program Technical Report no. 5, eds. J.E. Diemer, D.R. Jackson, J.L. Landers, J.N. Layne, and D.A. Wood, pp. 86-98. Tallahassee.

Komarek, E.V., Sr. 1964. The Natural History of Lightning, Annual Tall Timbers Fire Ecology Conference no. 3. Tall Timbers Research Station, Tallahassee.

Myers, R.L., and J. Ewel, eds. 1990. *Ecosystems of Florida.* Orlando: University of Florida Press.

Robbins, L.E., and R.L. Meyers. 1990. Seasonal Effects of Prescribed Burning in Florida: A Review. Tall Timbers Research Station Miscellaneous Publication no. 8. Tallahassee.

Stevenson, J.A. 1998. Evolution of fire management in Florida's state parks. In Fire in Ecosystem Management: Shifting the Paradigm from Suppression to Prescription. Tall Timbers Fire Ecology Conference Proceedings no. 20, eds. T.L. Pruden and L.A. Brennan, pp. 99-101. Tall Timbers Research Station, Tallahassee, Florida.

Watts, W.A. 1992. Camel lake: A 40,000 year record of vegetational and forest history from northwest Florida. Ecology 73:1056-1066.

Whitney, E.N., D.B. Means, and A. Rudloe. *Priceless Florida.* Sarasota: Pineapple Press Inc.

Woolfenden, G., and J. Fitzpatrick. 1996. Florida scrub-jay (*Aphelocoma coerulescens*). In *The Birds of North America*, no. 228, eds. A. Poole and F. Gill. Philadelphia: The Academy of Natural Sciences; Washington: D.C.: The American Ornithologists' Union.

INVASIVE SPECIES (88–89)

Johnson, J., L. Reid, B. Mayfield, D. Duerr, and S. Fraedrich. 2010. New Disease Epidemic Threatens Redbay and Other Related Species. Joint publication of Georgia Forestry Commission, South Carolina Forestry Commission, Florida Department of Agriculture and Consumer Services, and USDA Forest Service.

Volin, J.C., M.S. Lott, J.D. Muss, and D. Owen. 2004. Predicting rapid invasion of the Florida Everglades by old world climbing fern (*Lygodium microphyllum*). Diversity and Distributions 10: 439-446.

WATER AND BIODIVERSITY (92–93)

Audubon of Florida. 2005. Lake Okeechobee: A synthesis of information and recommendations for its restoration. In Kissimmee River Restoration, eds. P.N. Gray, C.J. Farrell, M.L. Kraus, and A.H. Gromnicki, appendix A. Audubon of Florida, Miami.

Barnett, C. 2007. *Mirage: Florida and the Vanishing Water of the Eastern U.S.* Ann Arbor: University of Michigan Press.

Bousquin, S.G., D.H. Anderson, G.E. Williams, and D.J. Colangelo, eds. 2005. Establishing a Baseline: Pre-restoration Studies of the Channelized Kissimmee River. Technical Publication ERA #432. South Florida Water Management District, West Palm Beach.

Darst, M.R., and H.M. Light. 2008. Drier Forest Composition Associated with Hydrologic Change in the Apalachicola River Floodplain, Florida. U.S. Geological Survey Scientific Investigations Report 2008 5062. Tallahassee.

Purdum, E.D. 2002. Florida Waters: A Water Resources Manual from Florida's Water Management Districts. Published jointly by Florida's water management districts, Brooksville.

Richards, J.D., and J. Harris. 2008. Pasco Water Team 2008 Summary Report. Pasco County Government, Dade City, Florida.

South Florida Water Management District. 2009. Just the Facts: Kissimmee River Restoration. South Florida Water Management District, West Palm Beach.

Southwest Florida Water Management District. 2006. Southern Water Use Caution Area Recovery Strategy. Southwest Florida Water Management District, Bartow.

CLIMATE CHANGE (94–95)

Intergovernmental Panel on Climate Change. 2007. The Physical Science Basis. Contribution of Working Group I to the Fourth Assessment Report of the Intergovernmental Panel on Climate Change, eds. S. Solomon, D. Qin, M. Manning, Z. Chen, M. Marquis, K.B. Averyt, M. Tignor, and H.L. Miller. Cambridge University Press: Cambridge and New York.

Joyce, L.A., C.H. Flather, and M. Koopman. 2008. Analysis of Impacts of Climate Change on Wildlife Habitats in the U.S. U.S. Forest Service, Rocky Mountain Research Station, Fort Collins, Colorado.

Florida Fish and Wildlife Conservation Commission. 2007. Draft Digital Elevation Model. Tallahassee.

ECOLOGICAL GREENWAYS (102–103)

Carr, M. H., P. D. Zwick, T. S. Hoctor, and M. A. Benedict. 1998. Final report, phase II,
Florida Statewide Greenways Planning Project. Department of Landscape Architecture,
University of Florida.

Hoctor, T. 2004 (June 24). Update of the Florida Ecological Greenways Network. Report for the Office of Greenways and Trails, Florida Department of Environmental Protection, Tallahassee.

CONSERVATION PROGRAMS (110–111)

Defenders of Wildlife. 2008 (July 21). Conservation Incentives Toolkit: Current Conservation and Incentive Mechanisms for Biodiversity Conservation, Federal and State of Florida. Report prepared for the Florida Fish and Wildlife Conservation Commission, Cooperative Conservation Blueprint Project.

The Nature Conservancy. 2009 (March). Economic Benefits of Land Conservation: A Case for Florida Forever. The Nature Conservancy Field Office, Tallahassee.

PRESCRIBED FIRE (112–113)

Brenner, J., and D. Wade. 2003. Florida's revised prescribed fire law: protection for responsible burners. In Proceedings of Fire Conference 2000: The First National Congress on Fire Ecology, Prevention, and Management. Miscellaneous Publication no. 13, eds. K.E.M. Galley, R.C. Klinger, N.G. Sugihara, pp. 132-136. Tall Timbers Research Station, Tallahassee.

Florida Division of Forestry. 2009. Burn Authorization Data. Florida Department of Agriculture and Consumer Services, Tallahassee.

Florida Division of Forestry. 2010 (September 27). Bronson Announces Record-Breaking Prescribed Burning Season. Press Release. Florida Department of Agriculture and Consumer Services, Tallahassee.

Mulholland, R., P.E. Small, and B. Blihovde. 2003. Prescribed burning by the Florida Park Service. Paper presented at the 2nd International Wildland Fire Ecology and Fire Management Congress. Orlando.

1000 Friends of Florida. 2008. Wildlife Habitat Planning Strategies, Design Features, and Best Management Practices for Florida Communities and Landowners. Tallahassee.

TATE'S HELL (118–119)

Florida Department of Environmental Protection. 1994. Conservation and Recreation Lands Annual Report. Tallahassee.

Florida Division of Forestry. 2008. Tate's Hell State Forest Hydrological Restoration Project Summary. Tallahassee.

Florida Division of Forestry. 2007. Ten-Year Resource Management Plan for the Tate's Hell State Forest, Franklin and Liberty Counties. Tallahassee.

Kindell, C., J. Wojcik, and V. Birdsong. 2000. Historic Vegetation of Tate's Hell State Forest. Final Report for the U.S. Fish and Wildlife Service (Agreement #1448-00-96-9102). Florida Natural Areas Inventory, Tallahassee.

Memory, M., C. Newman, and J. Lammers. 1998. An Inventory and Assessment of Cultural Resources within Tate's Hell State Forest, Franklin and Liberty Counties, Florida. CARL Archaeological Survey. Bureau of Archaeological Research, Florida Department of State, Tallahassee.

Northwest Florida Water Management District. 2010. Tate's Hell State Forest Hydrologic Restoration Plan, vols. 1 and 2. Published in cooperation with Florida Division of Forestry and Northwest Florida Water Management District.

Rogers, W.W., and L. Willis, III. 1997. *At the Water's Edge: Pictorial and Narrative History of Apalachicola and Franklin County*. Virginia Beach: The Donning Company Publishers.

Watts, W.A. 1992. Camel Lake: A 40,000 year record of vegetational and forest history from northwest Florida. Ecology 73:1056-1066

Williams, J.L. 1827. A view of west Florida. In 1976 Bicentennial Floridiana facsimile 72 series, a photo reprint of edition printed for Tanner, Philadelphia 1827. Gainesville: University Press of Florida.

Index of Species by Scientific Name

Black = text
Red = photo
Blue = drawing
Green = map

Q

R

S

T

Index of Species by Common Name

Black = text
Red = photo
Blue = drawing
Green = map

Y

Z

Index

Black = text
Red = photo
Blue = drawing
Green = map

F

G

H

I

J

K

L

T

U

V

W